The Seafront

The Seafront

Allan Brodie

Published by Historic England, The Engine House, Fire Fly Avenue, Swindon SN2 2EH
www.HistoricEngland.org.uk

Historic England is a Government service championing England's heritage and giving expert, constructive advice.

© Historic England 2018

Images (except as otherwise shown) © Historic England Archive, Historic England Archive (Aerofilms Collection),
© Crown Copyright. Historic England Archive, or Source: Historic England Archive.

First published 2018

ISBN 978-1-84802-382-6

British Library Cataloguing in Publication data
A CIP catalogue record for this book is available from the British Library.

Historic England holds an unparalleled archive of 12 million photographs, drawings, reports and publications
on England's places. It is one of the largest archives in the UK, the biggest dedicated to the historic environment,
and a priceless resource for anyone interested in England's buildings, archaeology, landscape and social history.
Viewed collectively, its photographic collections document the changing face of England from the 1850s to the
present day. It is a treasure trove that helps us understand and interpret the past, informs the present and assists
with future management and appreciation of the historic environment.

For more information about images from the Archive, contact Archives Services Team, Historic England,
The Engine House, Fire Fly Avenue, Swindon SN2 2EH; telephone (01793) 414600.

Brought to publication by Jess Ward, Publishing, Historic England and Karen Rigden Editorial Limited.

Typeset in Georgia Pro 9.5/11.75

Edited by Stephanie Rebello
Indexed by Osprey Indexing
Proofread by Kim Bishop
Page layout by Ledgard Jepson

Printed in Czech Republic via Accent Media Limited.

*Front cover: This view out to sea from the 1935 De La Warr Pavilion at Bexhill-on-Sea also shows the Edwardian shelter and
seafront promenade. [DP217886]*

*Frontispiece: A girl looks on at the fun in the surf below at Newquay. Is she waiting for a visit to the aquarium on the seafront
or a chance to run into the sea? [DP196919]*

*Back cover: The seafront at Bridlington between the wars, as captured in this photograph by Walter Scott, was crowded with
holidaymakers on the beach and on the various levels of sea defence and promenade. [WSA01/01/G0606]*

Contents

Acknowledgements

I would like to begin by thanking Lucy Jessop for accompanying me on the fieldwork for this book. Apart from being great company, she brought many insights to my research. She also kindly read the draft manuscript and helped greatly to improve it. I was also very fortunate to have other friends and colleagues who were prepared to suffer similarly and I am very grateful to Mark Bowden, Fred Gray, David Jarratt and Amanda Martin for the time they took and the comments they made.

A key part of this book is the quality of the images that I have been able to select. The Archive of Historic England has millions of photographs from which to choose, and I would like to thank the archive staff, particularly Ian Leith and Gary Winter, for helping me to make my selection.

The quality of a photographic archive depends on the quality of its photographers and I would like to pay tribute to photographers past and present for their support, patience and understanding when undertaking the commissions that I have requested. My thanks go to Peter Williams, Derek Kendall and Steve Cole, who have supported me in the past, and our current photographers, Steven Baker, Alun Bull, James O Davies and Pat Payne. I have also been fortunate to be able to commission high-quality aerial photographs and my thanks go to Damian Grady, Dave MacLeod and Matt Oakey for their work.

I would also like to thank Karen Rigden and the Publishing team of Historic England, particularly Jess Ward who took the raw manuscript through to publication.

Welcome to the seafront

From pier to pier at Southsea

Southsea Common is Portsmouth's seafront. It has hotels for holidaymakers, though perhaps they now more often serve as overnight stops on either side of a cross-Channel voyage. The seafront is also lined with blocks of modern flats and buildings that are now flats, but censuses show that these houses once provided lodgings for visitors as well as being the homes of prosperous business people, people of independent wealth, and serving and retired military officers. Looking out to sea is Southsea Pier, now reopened after a five-year closure (Fig 1.1). A long promenade runs past the former Royal Marines Barracks to the eastern end of the seafront, where there is a caravan park and the 18th-century Fort Cumberland, one of Historic England's offices.[1] Turning westwards from Southsea Pier towards Portsmouth Harbour, the complexity of the seafront becomes obvious.

This is a rich, complicated public space, where evidence survives of competing, and overlapping, layers of activity spread over many centuries (Fig 1.2).

Southsea was a place of war. A mid-16th-century fortification is at the heart of its defences, an innovative gun platform built by Henry VIII's engineers. It may have witnessed the sinking of the *Mary Rose* in 1545 and remained in military use, at least technically, until 1960.[2] The D-Day Museum and Overlord Tapestry commemorate the defining event in the western theatre of World War II and serve as a welcome indoor attraction in inclement weather.[3] Today, the seafront still bristles with tanks, cannons and anti-aircraft guns, now, thankfully, only relics of past centuries of conflict.

Southsea's seafront is also a place of memory and commemoration. Its numerous war memorials range from an understated Portland stone obelisk of 1857 marking the Crimean war to the

Fig 1.1
Southsea Pier was designed by George Rake and opened in November 1879. Closed in 2012 due to public safety concerns, it has now reopened as home to an amusement arcade, a cafe and a restaurant.
[DP196992]

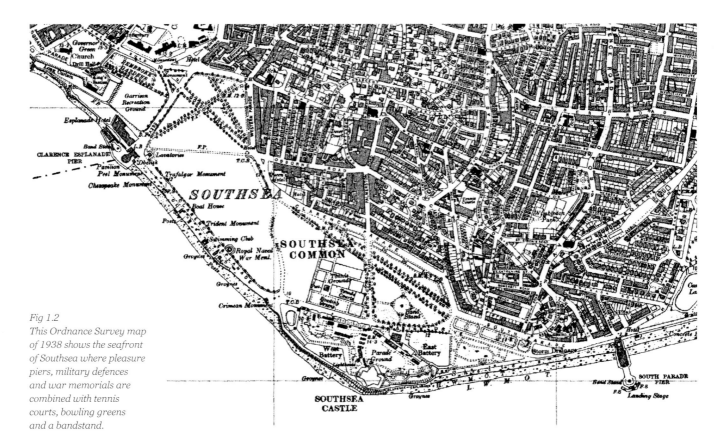

Fig 1.2
This Ordnance Survey map of 1938 shows the seafront of Southsea where pleasure piers, military defences and war memorials are combined with tennis courts, bowling greens and a bandstand.

Fig 1.3
This modest stone obelisk is one of a line of memorials on the seafront at Southsea. It commemorates the loss of 48 men who died of yellow fever on HMS Aboukir *in Jamaica in 1873–4.*
[DP196995]

gargantuan World War I memorial, tragically, but necessarily, extended after World War II (Fig 1.3, *see also* Figs 10.11 and 10.17). There are also more personal memorials along the seafront, simple plaques adorning benches donated by family and friends to celebrate the life of a loved one. Bryan Jackman (1935–2009) served in the Royal Navy from 1952 to 1975 and would have enjoyed the view from his bench of the Spithead Forts in the Solent, the Isle of Wight and passing ferries and warships.

Benches along the seafront record the lives of all sorts of people, many of whom enjoyed the same sea view as Bryan. Today's holiday-makers can sit and watch energetic morning joggers and cyclists, people on their way to work, dog walkers and evening promenaders. This dynamic, fluid community makes use of these benches and enjoys respite from the elements in welcome shelters, while various cafes and restaurants cater for a range of bodily needs.

The seafront is also a place of leisure. People swim in the sea from the shingle beach, while others fish, but most simply sit or lie down to enjoy warm summer sun. A bandstand waits for traditional and modern bands to play on sunny Sundays, but the seafront also caters for the many cold and wet days that hardy holiday-makers endure. An aquarium allows visitors to walk along the sea floor surrounded by sharks, and the Pyramids Centre provides warm water to splash around in. These facilities are set behind the seafront's military and sea defences. Between these and the first line of buildings there is a large, open area of grass, the site of festivals, informal sporting events and picnics. It is equally a place for students to chase Frisbees and dogs to chase sticks. Towards the western end of the seafront lies Southsea's second pier, reminiscent of something plucked from a 1960s Gerry Anderson television series (Fig 1.4).

To cater for such varied activities, the seafront has to be a thoroughly practical place. It provides the sea defences for the town and is arranged to combine promenading with cycling, safely separated from the nearby road that serves as a key route for traffic. There are car parks and toilets, and the unseen or disregarded services that accompany urban life, such as street lighting, sewerage and water supply. Southsea also boasts something that only one other seafront can; a hoverport. Inevitably, the other example is at Ryde, the destination on the other side of the Solent for this futuristic, yet archaic and thoroughly practical means of transport.

Southsea's seafront is a place to live, work and play. It is familiar yet unfamiliar, predictable but exciting, natural but artificial. It can be relaxing or exciting and busy or quiet, depending on the time of day and the date in the year. It is for the young and old, men and women, boys and girls. It is a civic space for events and ceremonies; it is the front line against enemies and a bulwark against the sea. It is a place to remember past holidays, happy moments and solemn losses. It is a place to sit, look out to sea and daydream.

Welcome to the seafront!

Studying the seafront

A walk on a summer's day at Southsea illustrates the complexity of something with such a simple name, something that we can easily take for granted, something we may not think of as an entity. This book is devoted to the seafront, the space between the seaward ends of seaside piers and the first line of buildings. The many and diverse aspects of its history, geography, character, function and meaning will be explored and while this study will inevitably focus on the tangible, both natural and man-made, it will also seek to capture something of the spiritual and cultural character of the seafront, its activities, people and memories.

As well as exploring its diversity, this book will outline how the seafront has been, and continues to be, subject to rapid change. Change

Fig 1.4
Clarence Pier vies for the title of England's shortest pier and, rather than being a place to promenade, is a lively fairground with rides to amuse and thrill families. The original pier opened in 1861 and was destroyed in 1941. The current pier opened on 1 June 1961, exactly 100 years after its predecessor. [DP197000]

can be natural. Erosion by the sea may eat into cliffs, which in turn may lead to the creation of beaches. Change may also be man-made. The introduction of new technology during the 19th and 20th centuries has transformed the seaside holiday, and with it the seafront. Accompanying this has been a profound growth in national wealth and personal disposable income, meaning that where handfuls of wealthy patrons once headed to seaside resorts, now millions use the seafront each year. And today's customers have very different tastes from their forebears; a rollercoaster ride might be an inconceivably terrifying idea for one of our Georgian ancestors.

The changing character of seaside holidays and resorts over the past three centuries will be examined in Chapter 2. Since the early 18th century, people have been visiting coastal towns to bathe in the sea, to breathe fresh, clean air, and to relax. The seafront has been, and remains, central to the holidaymaking experience and the life of seaside resorts (Fig 1.5). A handful of working coastal towns were initially pressed into use by wealthy people who wished to bathe in the sea. Any stretch of coastline might have provided access to the sea, but sea bathers also needed accommodation, entertainment and company. As the number of visitors increased, historic working towns that had previously looked inwards or towards their harbour, now welcomed new buildings on the seafront. These ranged from bathhouses that necessarily required access to sea water, to new houses and entertainment venues.

At the beginning of the 19th century, a busy resort might entertain hundreds of visitors at any one time, but by the end of the century, Blackpool, Britain's busiest resort, welcomed millions. New developments necessitated the transformation of the natural profile of the beach and seafront land to create sea defences to protect the larger investments being made. The modest homes of Georgian townsfolk that had welcomed small numbers of wealthy lodgers gave way to developments of tall houses and large hotels. Small bathhouses became large swimming pools and intimate, sociable and expensive entertainment venues were replaced by large, sometimes industrial-scale, winter gardens and pavilions. New technology, in the form of railways and new building techniques and materials, contributed to transforming seaside holidays and vastly increased the number of people with access to them. By the early 20th century, it had also contributed to the entertainments on show, bringing fairgrounds and cinemas to the seafront (Fig 1.6). And the new interest in swimming, sunshine and the body beautiful brought the lido, sunbathing and the bikini to the seafront. Despite the hardships endured by many resorts during World War II, and subsequently competition from foreign resorts, the domestic seaside holiday enjoyed its numerical heyday during the mid-1970s, before entering a period of decline. Nevertheless, the seafront has proved to be adaptable for more than 200 years, and in the early 21st century they are being made ready to respond to new leisure interests, a dwindling traditional market

Fig 1.5
This detail from the version of The Long Painting *by Hubert Cornish in the Royal York Hotel shows the seafront at Sidmouth at the beginning of the 19th century before any significant intervention to reshape the beach and the seafront.*
[DP021044]

Fig 1.6 (left)
This early 21st-century photograph shows a section of the seafront at Blackpool before the recent reimagining of the public realm. The old trams were still running, separated from a wide dual carriageway by fencing. Lining the seafront is a 1970s disco, the 1930s Woolworths building and the Tower, which opened in 1894.
[AA053170]

Fig 1.7 (below)
At West Bay in Dorset, the Jurassic coastline is famous for frequent collapses in its cliffs, which for 200 years have revealed intriguing fossils.
[DP000707]

and perhaps, most significantly, the challenges posed by climate change.

Chapter 3 considers the changing use of the major geographical sections of the seafront, from the edge of the sea across the beach to coastal protection schemes. Access to the sea is the reason for the existence of a seaside resort, but the price for this access is vulnerability to storms, flooding and erosion (Fig 1.7). As more money was invested in property, and more of it was located on the vulnerable shoreline, there was a greater need for sea defences. A shift occurred from the natural form of the coastline, first to fairly insubstantial, timber defences, and by today to monumental, stone and concrete sea defences (Fig 1.8). Designed to deal with what is hoped to be the worst that the sea can throw at seaside resorts, these substantial engineering projects require huge investments by local and national government.

The space created behind increasingly substantial sea defences houses a range of features designed to make the town work, as well as providing facilities for tourists. What can be located on any seafront depends on its geography, particularly the distance from the sea to where the land is suitable for substantial buildings.

Fig 1.8
To secure West Bay from the sea, new sea walls, supplemented by large amounts of rock armour defences, were completed in March 2005.
[DP004833]

At some resorts, the first line of buildings is a considerable distance from the sea, because the intervening land was too marshy or too sandy when the resort was established. A key feature created behind sea defences is a promenade and an accompanying major road running along the coast. These provide access to the first line of buildings on the seafront, which are usually approximately at sea level; where cliffs are present, the main resort buildings may be found above the seafront.

The creation of seafront promenades and accompanying roads have been a part of sea-defence programmes since the 19th century. Built in conjunction with the sea defences, these were created for the benefit of tourists, but were also a practical means for people to travel through a seaside resort on the straightest, flattest route. The seafront has also been the site for other major transport infrastructure, particularly railway stations bringing holiday-makers straight to the beach. And by the end of the 19th century, smaller-scale railways and tramways had been established at a number of resorts, a necessity to cope with a growing residential population and an expanding town. Where cliffs were present, the need for access to the beach prompted the

construction of a range of cliff lifts and cliff railways from the late 19th century onwards.

In Chapter 4, the role of the engineered seafront in the practical life of seaside towns will be examined. As well as hosting various forms of transport, the seafront also became the location for much of the vital infrastructure of rapidly expanding seaside resorts. Although much of this is unseen, it has nevertheless had a significant role in the shaping and the adaptation of seafronts. As the 19th century progressed, all towns had to provide a growing number of services, prompting an increase in the size of local government. Beginning with the provision of gas for street lighting and subsequently home lighting, from the mid-19th century onwards local and central government also began to supply water, electricity and telephones, as well as having to deal with the substantial and complicated problem of waste disposal.

Chapter 4 also examines the seafront as the location of maritime industrial infrastructure, although evidence of this has become scarcer as holidaymaking came to dominate the economy of many coastal towns. Some resorts still have beach-launched fleets, while many others have harbours. To safeguard people working at sea, a complex infrastructure of maritime safety has evolved, including lifeboats and coastguard stations. To aid navigation at sea, lighthouses, day marks and time balls have been constructed.

The seafront has been in the front line of Britain's military defences, a beach suitable for sea bathing also being an obvious place to land enemy forces. There are prominent remains at some resorts of military defences dating back to the 16th century. In the 18th century, when visitors first arrived to bathe in the sea, gun batteries were still important features of some seafronts, influencing their layout or leaving behind evidence of their existence in names.

Chapters 3 and 4 note the role of local government in the provision of the infrastructure, but Chapter 5 will examine how local authorities became increasingly active in investing in the detailing of the seafront. Although technologically akin to the seaside pier, features such as railings, bandstands and shelters could bring no direct financial return to local authorities. It was only possible to make money from them indirectly through local taxation raised from private-sector businesses that benefited from this investment.

Making the seafront ready for tourists involved providing a range of hard and soft features designed to make the space created behind sea defences work. Among the hard elements were railings, street furniture, shelters and beach huts. Amenities provided for visitors also ranged from vital toilet facilities and rubbish bins to fountains and water troughs for the working animals taking holidaymakers along the seafront. The soft dimension of a seafront is its gardens, with suitable plants and trees carefully selected to cope with wind, sea and salt. The character of any seafront depends on the size and the profile of the space between the sea and the first line of buildings (Fig 1.9). A narrow seafront will have little opportunity for gardens, but at resorts such as Southport or Skegness, there is sufficient space for substantial gardens including major water features, as well as a range of commercial and leisure facilities.

Seafronts are now predominantly associated with entertainment and leisure, but in Chapter 6 the changing attitude towards the sea and health will be examined. By the early 18th century, the sea was recognised as England's bath, where physical and mental ills could be washed away. Therefore, the seafront, inevitably, was at the forefront of delivering treatments. Bathing machines (*see* Fig 6.3) had been developed by

the mid-18th century to take bathers out into the sea for a healthy dip in the water and remained a constant presence on seafronts until the early 20th century. Many resorts also had seafront bathhouses, providing warmed sea water for patients. Between the mid-18th and the mid-19th century these evolved from small-scale, vernacular structures into grand classical essays housing elaborate suites of treatment rooms. During the 19th century, swimming for exercise and pleasure became more important, leading to larger pools being added to existing bathhouses. New purpose-built indoor and outdoor swimming facilities also began to be constructed across the country, culminating between the

Fig 1.9
At Eastbourne there is only space for a narrow strip of garden, embellished with colourful annuals in its flowerbeds. A low railing separates them from the main seafront road and behind is the Burlington Hotel of the 1850s. [DP017989]

wars in some vast and elaborate facilities at seaside resorts. An increasing awareness of the health-giving properties of fresh air and sunshine led to the construction of lidos, few of which, alas, remain in use today. This new appreciation of the therapeutic virtue of the seaside climate also led to a growing number of hospitals and convalescent homes being established at resorts. These were not necessarily on the seafront, but if sea bathing was to be a part of their regime, a seafront location was eminently desirable. Margate's Royal Sea Bathing Hospital in the 1790s led the way; however, while this proved very influential in Europe, it only had a limited following in Britain.

Although visitors came to seaside resorts to improve their health, they also expected to be amused and entertained. Chapters 7 and 8 will examine contrasting aspects of the serious business of seaside fun and games. First, the enduring, sociable events and diversions available on the seafront and the beach will be examined, before looking in Chapter 8 at how the introduction of new technology transformed the entertainment landscape. By the 19th century, the beach was at the heart of a day at the seaside, and between forays into the sea, holidaymakers enjoyed a range of activities from donkey rides, sandcastle building and collecting seashells to being entertained by Punch and Judy, minstrels and pierrots.

As sea bathing was expected to take place during the morning for medical reasons, this meant that there was ample time during the remainder of the day for socialising in entertainment venues, initially mostly paid for through subscriptions. Circulating libraries, assembly rooms, coffee houses and theatres were at the outset in the heart of the town, where most people would be spending most of their day. However, by the end of the 18th century, new entertainment venues began to appear on seafronts and this shift of location accelerated with the arrival of piers from the mid-19th century onwards. New technology transformed the nature of the leisure experience on the seafront, creating novel forms of transport, but most importantly piers and amusement parks. In Chapter 8, their role in changing the leisure experience and the visual character of seafronts will be examined (Fig 1.10).

Chapter 9 is devoted to the first line of buildings along the seafront. Compared to streets further inland, this first line of buildings is the location for a bewildering variety of structures. It was once dominated by the house, often adapted for use as a circulating library or a bathhouse, as well as providing lodgings

Fig 1.10
The seafront at Broadstairs on a warm sunny day has something for everyone. As well as bathing in the sea, there are trampolines and rides erected on the beach. On the clifftops, there are pubs, restaurants and ice-cream parlours. [DP026942]

for visitors. However, the house was gradually replaced by larger, more elaborate and more specialised structures. The central section of the seafront may now contain accommodation such as hotels, houses and flats, as well as entertainment venues and buildings associated with the working life of coastal towns. Compared to most inland streets, there tends to be greater variety in terms of date as resorts felt the pressure constantly to meet the changing tastes and growing numbers of holidaymakers during the 19th and 20th centuries. Moving outwards from the centre, a greater uniformity can be found in terms of date and function, and sometimes there are discrete zones providing terraced housing, villas, bed-and-breakfasts, flats or hotels. Inevitably, areas further from the centre of resorts tend to be later in date and are more likely to have been developed for residents rather than to accommodate tourists. Chapter 9 will conclude by considering whether it is possible to identify a seaside style or, failing that, what might be the characteristics shared by the varied buildings lining the seafront.

This book concentrates on the tangible story of the seafront, but in Chapter 10 its life as a civic and cultural space will highlight some of its more intangible, transient aspects. As a town's only 'park' for many years, the seafront is a key civic space where public events were, and still are, held, ranging from enjoyable carnivals, shows and races to more sombre occasions, such as the annual Armistice commemoration (Fig 1.11). The seafront is also a cultural space where residents and tourists can enjoy museums, art galleries and monumental works of art aimed at enriching the life of the resort and proclaiming a town's civic identity. Coastal life and seaside history can be reflected in the range and form of memorials and public art found on seafronts. While a coastal location may provide artists with a physically challenging environment, the ever-changing backdrop of sky, sea and sun has proved stimulating for artists and their audience.

The seafront is also a spiritual place. Although churches may be largely absent, church missions and the Salvation Army have valiantly attempted to take Christianity to the hedonistic seaside. Faced with the power and beauty of the sea, and with time to stop and think, the seafront is a place for people to remember. The love of family and friends may be celebrated in a simple brass plaque on a bench, while the sacrifice of a generation is often acknowledged in the seafront's largest commemorative structure. As a 'park', the seafront is also an appropriate place for a

Fig 1.11
In August 1933, an orator keeps his audience enthralled on the seafront at Bridlington. One of many photographs taken by Walter Scott between the wars, this image also shows people carrying on with the beach holiday oblivious to events on the promenade.
[WSA01/01/g0657]

town's memorials, celebrating monarchs and local worthies or mourning the loss of life at sea.

Throughout this book, a recurrent theme is the diversity of the buildings, structures and activities that occur in a small part of seaside towns. In the final chapter, another underlying theme will be reviewed: the challenges facing the seafront today. These are broadly the same as at any time during the past 200 years. The seafront is a physically challenging location for buildings, structures and gardens alike. It has also had to adapt to meet evolving public tastes, changing economic circumstances and new technologies. The vulnerability of features created with short-term economic gain in mind will also be explored, as well as issues such as the impact of investment, and underinvestment, on the fabric and image of the seafront. There is a stark, but frequent, dichotomy between the high level of public investment in the seafront and a relative lack of private-sector investment in buildings behind, an issue, at least in part, due to a range of economic challenges specifically faced by seaside resorts.

Most of the issues facing seaside resorts today might equally apply a century ago, but the modern seafront is rapidly being adapted to combat the results of anthropogenic climate change. Natural variations in the planet's climate have always occurred, but the impact of industrialisation has accelerated natural processes, leading to more rapid rises in temperature and sea level, but perhaps more importantly increased storminess. Consequently, in recent years, many seafronts have been altered to cope with the climatic challenges they are now facing. And while improving the resilience of their sea defences, many local authorities have taken the opportunity to provide new features and facilities for residents and the holiday market, with Blackpool's innovative approach to its renewed seafront leading the way (Fig 1.12). Climate change may not be a laughing matter, but behind Blackpool's new sea defences, the Comedy Carpet has been created. This is a celebration of Britain's sense of humour, but it is also a symbol of the town's desire to both entertain its traditional visitors and attract new ones (*see* Fig 10.4).

Fig 1.12
Instead of simply building sea defences to hold the line against the sea, Blackpool boldly advanced its sea defences and embellished them with giant blades of dune grass.
[DP154540]

Perspectives

The aim of this book is to look at the seafront predominantly chronologically, geographically and architecturally. However, through using over a century of terrestrial and aerial photographs from Historic England's photographic archive, it tells a series of other stories. Photographs provide an impression of what holidaymakers and other users of the seafront may have experienced since the late 19th century. They document how different times of day, the changing states of the tide and different months of the year affect the appearance and use of the seafront. At low tide on a warm summer's day, a wide sandy beach may be covered with holidaymakers, but a few hours later when the tide has come in they will be driven back onto the land. The scene of a brisk winter walk along a deserted beach would, six months later, be replaced by swimmers and sunbathers (Fig 1.13). And, as will be seen in the chapters on leisure, what a playful, energetic child would get from a seaside holiday will inevitably be very different to that of their parents or grandparents who may simply wish to sit, relax and admire the view (Fig 1.14).

Fig 1.15
*These two young women in
their fashionable swimming
costumes, again captured
by John Gay, were relaxing
at the art deco open-air
pool at the south end
of Blackpool.
[AA047938]*

necessitating physical or temporal separation of the sexes. Although most entertainments were open to everyone, the Georgian coffee house was a rare example where women were excluded due to its politically charged atmosphere. Victorian Bournemouth unusually had a gentleman's club on the seafront next to the pier, where the Oceanarium stands today. Built in 1871, it offered a dimly lit lounge bar and billiard rooms, and at its peak it had around 300 members. Amazingly, it survived until the mid-20th century, still having around 100 members in 1959 'periodically sipping drinks and reading the papers with the noise and bustle of tens of thousands of holidaymakers, right outside their windows'.[4] By the 1950s, the seafront might be the site of a beauty pageant; Miss Great Britain began in 1945, and between 1956 and 1989 it was staged at Morecambe, including at the Super Swimming Stadium.[5] Such events are now less obvious and knobbly knees contests and glamorous granny competitions have thankfully passed into books of old photographs. In their place may be competing hen and stag parties, marauding along the seafront where once Edwardian gentlemen promenaded in their suits while nursemaids pushed mighty perambulators (*see* Fig 2.16).

As well as the experience of the seafront changing through the year, or through a lifetime, the gender of a holidaymaker may contribute to how they experience their holiday (Fig 1.15). There may now appear to be little formal gender differentiation on the modern seafront, though stereotypically mother may be expected to provide the catering, while father is buried in a sandy grave. However, in the 18th century men and women bathed separately, either at different times, or on different parts of the beach. Men bathed in the nude, while women wore linen slips that undoubtedly clung when wet,

What photographs cannot convey are the sound and smells of the seafront over 300 years. The seafront is never quiet. In summer it is pop music, laughter and the three-note sounds of amusements that fill the air. In winter, it may be a roaring sea, a biting wind and the clatter of pebbles on the shore. And the smells ... In the 19th century, the heady aroma of untreated sewage washed onto the beach may have greeted visitors. Today, thankfully, the air is fresh, save perhaps for a faint whiff of suntan lotion and fish and chips.

Welcome to the seafront!

Three centuries of seaside holidays

By the early 18th century, a small number of wealthy people were following the advice of doctors and scientists, by heading to the seaside in search of improved health. This often involved stays of several weeks in houses at small coastal towns. After a morning dip in the sea, the rest of the day was spent socialising in entertainment venues, which would be in the town rather than on the seafront. However, as the popularity of the seaside grew, greater numbers of visitors led to larger investments in purpose-built facilities that were increasingly concentrated beside the sea.

By the mid-19th century, the pier had cemented its leading role in amusing visitors and contributed to making the seafront the centre of a day at the seaside. It was also a significant contributor to the popularisation of seaside holidays through reducing the cost of travel by allowing steamers to moor alongside. These were cheaper, faster and, usually, more reliable than travelling on Britain's patchy road network and this process of broadening access gathered pace with railways, so that by the end of the 19th century, millions, rather than thousands, of people could afford a holiday. This had a profound impact on the size and character of seaside resorts.

Sea defences were constructed to protect the growing towns, projects that marked a new level of commitment by local authorities, which were now also faced with providing more utilities and services for residents and visitors. Influxes of visitors also required larger entertainment venues and more accommodation, and much of this was located on seafronts that were becoming more complex, more substantial and spread further along the coastline.

During the 20th century, buses, charabancs and cars meant that the impact of visitors was no longer only focused near where railway stations existed, resulting in suburban sprawl, as well as seafront sprawl. In the second half of the 20th century, following wartime damage and a subsequent period of significant under-investment, seaside resorts were wrongly claimed by some to be in terminal decline, the additional threat of climate change adding to their woes. However, by the early 21st century this threat was also providing opportunities for new investment and a reinvigoration of many seaside resorts.

The origins of seaside resorts

Driving the development of spas during the 16th century was a belief in the medicinal value of mineral waters and among the waters examined by scientists and doctors was sea water. In the mid-16th century, Thomas Vicary, the Sergeant Chirurgion (d 1561), recommended that a patient should stand in a cold sea-water bath for 'three or fower howers or more, and he shall be perfectly holpe' (healthy), while in 1581 Richard Mulcaster advocated swimming in the sea for medical conditions.[1] Physicians were also beginning to recognise the restorative qualities of the coastal environment. In 1619, Henry Manship mentioned doctors in Cambridge who sent patients to Great Yarmouth 'to take the air of the sea'.[2] Political upheavals during the mid-17th century interrupted the scientific appreciation and application of sea water as a medical treatment, though by the end of the century a number of medical writers were again interested in the sea. Dr Robert Wittie, promoting the spa at Scarborough in his 1660 book, warned that internal consumption of sea water could be detrimental to health, but in the 1667 edition he noted that sea-water bathing had rid him of his gout.[3] By c 1700 Sir John Floyer had emerged as the leading advocate of cold-water bathing, publishing several works on the subject and he was the first writer to explicitly realise that the sea could act as a huge bath.[4]

By the early 18th century, belief in the efficacy of sea bathing was spreading from medical texts and physicians to ordinary people. Floyer had suggested that sea bathing began as a popular activity, possibly related to customary times of the year.[5] For example, it was common in Lancashire at the August spring tide, when it was believed that the sea had special powers of purification and regeneration.[6] Any such local tradition would not necessarily have left a mark in early published sources, but the *Great Diurnal* of Nicholas Blundell (1669–1737), who lived at Crosby Hall, near Liverpool, records several seaside visits at this time of year (Fig 2.1), some for no specific reason, but on other occasions he was there to shoot game. He recorded that on 5 August 1708 'Mr Aldred & I Rode to the Sea & baithed ourselves … it was extreamly hot as were also the two preceding days, the lick hardly ever known at this time in these parts.'[7] No ailments were mentioned and it seems that he was there for pleasure during hot weather, but, a year later, his children bathed on three consecutive days to cure 'some out breaks'.[8]

During the early 18th century, a handful of references to sea bathing suggest that bathing would occur wherever someone wanted to go in the sea, the only requirement being access to the sea, the only facility required, a convenient house. The absence of any mention of sea bathing in major, early travelogues, such as those written by John Macky and Daniel Defoe, implies that it was still only an occasional practice, but by the 1730s the documentary evidence begins to become more concerted. It points to small, but significant, numbers of people beginning to visit a handful of coastal towns to bathe in the sea to improve their health.

It may seem surprising that Liverpool was at the forefront of the new fad for sea bathing.

Known primarily as a great trading port with a waterfront dominated by commercial infrastructure, the muddy Mersey seems an unlikely place for a dip in the sea. However, on 1 August 1721 Nicholas Blundell wrote in his journal that 'Pat: Acton lodged here, he came with an Intention to stay some time to Baith in the Sea, I went with him to the Sea side to shew him what Conveniency there was for him.' The entry for the following day read 'I went with Pat: Acton to Leverpoole & Procured him a Place to Lodg at & a Conveniency for baithing in the Sea'.[9] As will be discussed in Chapter 6, it is clear from these references, and a similar use of the word at Scarborough in 1735, that Blundell is referring to a primitive form of bathing machine.[10] As well as early bathing machines, Liverpool provided visitors with a small, waterfront bathhouse by the time that *The South-West Prospect of Liverpoole* was published by Samuel and Nathaniel Buck in 1728.[11] The bathhouse was demolished in 1817 to make way for the Prince's Dock as the riverfront became increasingly dominated by commercial structures, displacing sea bathing to further along the coast (*see* Fig 6.11).[12]

Other large ports share a similar forgotten or obscured sea-bathing history. In 1755, 'Mr H' recorded that 'In this reign of saltwater, great numbers of people of distinction prefer Southampton for bathing'.[13] Southampton had three bathhouses beside its two quays as the town had a muddy foreshore rather than a beach.[14] Although the dockside may not seem a salubrious or glamorous location, in 1750, Frederick Prince of Wales bathed in the sea while staying nearby.[15] Count Friedrich von Kielmansegge, who visited England in 1761–2, recorded that 'Many people come here every year, partly for sea-bathing, partly by

Fig 2.1
The Blundell family appear to have visited the stretch of coast nearest their house, possibly Crosby Beach, where Antony Gormley's atmospheric Another Place *has become a modern place of pilgrimage.* [DP034504]

order of their physicians, who consider the air of Southampton to be the healthiest in all England.'[16] Baths survived on the quayside until the 1830s, when the main bathing establishment was converted into the 'Dock-house'.[17]

'Mr H' also wrote that 'Portsmouth has been now, for many months, the rendezvous of the fashionable world; every gay young man of fortune, and woman also, in their circle of joyous amusements, took a transient view of it.'[18] The reason for this was a nascent sea-bathing culture in the town, as opposed to at nearby Southsea where resort functions developed during the 19th century. Portsmouth still retains a bathhouse near the dockyard (*see* Fig 6.12). Quebec House, built in 1754, was mentioned in the same year by Dr Richard Pococke: 'The town of late has been resorted to for batheing and drinking the sea-water, and they have made a very handsome bathing-house of wood, at a great expence, with separate baths and apartments for men and women.'[19] Archibald Maxwell in 1755 wrote that 'The open and close Baths begun and finish'd by the worthy Corporation and principal Inhabitants, at their own private Expence; which for Elegance of Structure, and Salubrity of the Water, are no where exceeded.'[20] Again the bathhouse was near the docks and while this location may seem strange, a quayside position was also used for Weymouth's first bathhouse in the 18th century, despite the town having a long beach and seafront.[21]

Other ports with a significant tourist past include Dover, which by 1810 hosted a considerable, but recent, influx of visitors who used its hot baths and bathing machines, as well as its circulating libraries, a new assembly rooms and a theatre.[22] Harwich had private baths filled by the tide and by 1810 was offering bathing machines.[23] Since 1766, Plymouth provided the county and naval scene with a colourful social life and a tepid bath on the seashore.[24] By the early 19th century, Swansea was attracting sea bathers despite the pall of copper smoke that apparently hung over the edge of the town.[25] It had hot and cold sea-water baths, libraries, an assembly room and theatre, the key pieces of infrastructure for a successful resort.

Current seaside resorts also have evidence of people visiting during the mid-18th century. Scarborough's first guidebook was published in 1734; a year later an engraving depicted people bathing in the sea, while annual miscellanies of poems described the resort's hectic social life.[26] Margate was sufficiently busy in 1730 to attract a theatre company to perform during the summer and six years later a seaside bathhouse was advertised.[27] In 1736, a visitor to Brighton described how his family were 'sunning ourselves on the beach' after their 'morning business' of 'bathing in the sea'.[28]

A distinctive sea-bathing culture was developing, with a number of settlements beginning to offer formal bathing facilities in the form of bathhouses or early versions of the bathing machine. These were inevitably on the seafront, access to the precious wonder liquid being the reason that people visited small, working coastal towns, 'fishing holes' as John Byng described them.[29] At Scarborough, the 1735 engraving by John Setterington shows people bathing in the sea from boats or from a primitive bathing machine and it was these lumbering contraptions that became the preferred means of enjoying the medicinal impact of the sea (*see* Fig 6.1). The first illustration of a fully developed bathing machine with a rear modesty hood appears in the 1750s in a drawing of Margate by James Theobald inserted into an edition of John Lewis' *History of the Isle of Thanet* (1736) donated to the Society of Antiquaries. In an accompanying description the term 'bathing machine' was used alongside 'bathing waggon', implying a well-established form with its own identity, now meriting its own name (*see* Fig 6.3).[30]

Bathing took place in the morning, leaving the rest of the day free for socialising and a range of entertainment venues, albeit initially sometimes fairly haphazard in character, were consequently established. Scarborough had attracted visitors since the 1620s due to its spa, and therefore it offered the range of facilities required by its wealthy clientele.[31] By the 1730s, it had a circulating library and an assembly room, the latter being described as 'a noble, spacious building, sixty two Foot long, thirty wide, and sixteen high' with a 'Musick-Gallery' and attached card rooms.[32] These facilities were not on the seafront, but in the town, probably in an adapted existing building or in an extension. Other ports began to add new facilities in imitation of those found in spas. This process relied on local entrepreneurs becoming confident enough to make increasingly large investments. Circulating libraries were established in any suitable building and guidebooks to early resorts show that they were initially usually contained in standard houses. The need for an assembly room was first recognised by enterprising innkeepers. In 1763, an assembly room was established in Margate at the New Inn on the seafront Parade and in 1772, Thomas Hovenden held his first assembly at the Swan Inn in Hastings in 'a suitable room, with a gallery for music'.[33]

The first theatres were positively rustic. In 1754, William Smith's theatre company was able to use a converted barn in the inland Dane at Margate, and, in 1771, a theatre was created in a stable at the rear of the Fountain Inn.[34] By the 1760s, Brighton had a makeshift theatre in a barn on the north-west corner of Castle Square and in 1788 Blackpool still offered a similarly rudimentary facility.[35] The earliest purpose-built theatres appeared at seaside resorts from the 1770s, once resorts were sufficiently popular to make the investment worthwhile, and where investors were assured that laws curbing theatrical performances would not be applied rigorously. The first performance at the future Theatre Royal on the seafront in Weymouth was in 1771 and at Brighton a purpose-built playhouse was erected in North Street in 1773 by Samuel Paine, though it was superseded by a larger one in Duke Street in 1789.[36]

Just as visitors were gradually being provided with larger, more sophisticated entertainment facilities, a similar process occurred in the provision of accommodation. The first visitors had to find long-term accommodation in the homes of the local population, predominantly small, vernacular buildings that were not usually on the seafront. Fanny Burney described the house she lodged in at Teignmouth in 1773: 'Mr Rishton's House is not in the Town, but on the Den, which is the mall here: it is a small, neat, thatched & white Washed Cottage neither more nor less. We are not a hundred yards from the sea, in which Mrs Rishton Bathes every morning.'[37] Residents began to build, or rebuild, houses to make them more appealing to the growing number of visitors. One of Weymouth's early guidebooks suggested that 'the inhabitants by such an influx of money have been encouraged to rebuild, repair, and greatly enlarge the town, which in little more than twenty years has undergone a considerable transformation'.[38] Where the 18th-century fabric of historic streets survives, this piecemeal development is obvious, such as in All Saints' Street in Hastings.

In 1769, the pace of seaside development changed dramatically with the construction of Cecil Square in Margate. It symbolically breached the limits of the historic old town much as Queen Square had marked a new phase of development at Bath during the 1720s.[39] This was the first new square built at a seaside resort, but it was constructed on a field at the top of the High Street, rather than being on the seafront. At Weymouth, the first of a series of seafront terraces was constructed to the north of the historic town during the 1780s, marking a shift away from how the town had been laid out, facing inwards and towards its harbour, with the beach being used for dumping rubbish (Fig 2.2).[40] By the early 19th century, long terraces and crescents, with houses intended to accommodate summer visitors, were being erected on seafronts around the coast of England (Fig 2.3).

The attraction of a particular coastal town depended on reputation. This could be medical, in the form of a doctor's opinion and published 'scientific' texts, but perhaps more importantly, it was derived from the status of its patrons. Aspiring resorts sought to attract the highest in society, members of the Royal family being particularly prized. Southampton had briefly attracted George II's son, Frederick Prince of Wales, in 1750, but Brighton and Weymouth enjoyed longer-term relationships with royalty.[41] By 1760, the Pelham family regularly visited Brighton, prompting the Duke of Gloucester to stay in 1765, followed in 1783 by the first of many visits by the future George IV.[42] Weymouth also benefited from royal endorsement from an early date (Fig 2.4). Its first celebrated patron was Ralph Allen from Bath, who visited annually between 1750 and his death in 1764. His presence prompted visits by growing numbers of wealthy patrons, including Prince William Henry, the Duke of Gloucester. In the early 1780s, the duke built a house on the seafront and it was this grand end-of-terrace house that hosted George III, who came to improve his health on 30 June 1789 and stayed for 10 weeks.[43] The king returned each summer from 1791 to 1802, except in 1793, and in 1801 he bought Gloucester Lodge from his brother. The presence of royalty, their entourages, aspiring aristocrats and increasing numbers of wealthy, middle-class visitors would transform many small coastal towns into large, prosperous seaside resorts.

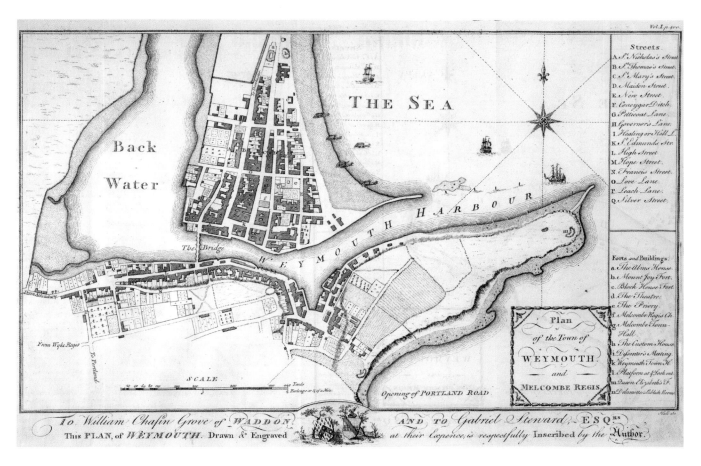

Fig 2.2 (above)
This map of Weymouth from Hutchins 1774 shows that the seafront was simply the rear of housing plots. Within a few years, the seafront would become the focus for the town and new development would reshape it and extend it northwards.
[DP022292]

Fig 2.3 (left)
Belvidere, an early 19th-century seafront terrace at Weymouth, was constructed on previously undeveloped land to the north of the historic town. These new houses were used for lodgings, with smaller houses set in the streets behind.
[DP054515]

Fig 2.4
Today, it would be surprising to find wealthy holidaymakers cramming into small houses around a harbour but at Weymouth this was originally their preferred location. Influxes of visitors led to new investment and many of the modest early houses were replaced by more elegant Georgian buildings. [DP054481]

Creating new resorts

By the mid-18th century, some sea bathers were arriving at stretches of coastline where there was little or no pre-existing settlement. But perhaps more significantly, a growing number of people were willing to invest in the provision of new facilities and accommodation in these locations, which presented a significantly greater risk than an investment in a historic town with some form of existing market and facilities.

Blackpool emerged as a resort independent of any port or harbour during the mid-18th century. The earliest reliable reference to sea-bathing visitors was by Bishop Richard Pococke in June 1754 who recorded that 'At Blackpool, near the sea, are accommodations for people who come to bathe' and William Hutton writing in 1788 and Edward Baines in 1821 also endorsed a mid-18th century origin.[44] Blackpool's coastline was largely uninhabited, though there were nearby hamlets and a small village at Poulton-le-Fylde. Its growth proves that there was sufficient interest in sea bathing to encourage people to visit stretches of coastline with limited facilities, and by the 1780s a series of large houses, predominantly along the seafront, were serving as hotels and providing the main entertainment facilities for wealthy patrons (Fig 2.5).[45]

Fig 2.5
This view of Blackpool by Edward Finden in 1840 shows the scatter of houses along the clifftop. At the far left on the cliffs is the site of the later Metropole Hotel, with small, thatched buildings in the distance behind it.
[Author's collection]

Nearby Southport also had no port on which to graft a resort function and therefore a bathing house was built in 1792 by William Sutton, followed by his hotel in 1798 and a range of other facilities accrued gradually during the early 19th century.[46] Lincolnshire faced a similar lack of ports to colonise for leisure and came up with similar solutions to Southport, though in many instances no large seaside resort subsequently resulted. This was the case with the New Inn at Saltfleet and at Freiston Shore where visitors could stay at two sea-bathing hotels or at a few lodging houses.[47] These never developed into popular destinations, but Cleethorpes, Mablethorpe, Skegness and Sutton-on-Sea also began as the sites of sea-bathing hotels.[48] In East Anglia, Old South End, a small hamlet around a farmhouse, began to develop in the mid-18th century as a resort.[49] A large house built before 1758 had become the Ship Inn by 1764 and in 1768 South-End (modern Southend-on-Sea) was first recognised as a separate administrative entity. Weston-super-Mare developed on a largely uninhabited stretch of coastline and in 1776 Herne Bay (Fig 2.6) was described as: 'Here is a public house, with good, decent accommodation for private families who came here in the summer season for the benefit of bathing in the sea.'[50]

All these new resorts began with small-scale investment and grew gradually during the 19th century. However, some people were willing to invest substantial sums in the creation immediately of new resorts, with housing, entertainment venues and bathing facilities. The earliest of these risky new developments was Hothamton, promoted by Sir Richard Hotham (1722–99), a previously successful London businessman, who invested up to £160,000 in a prestigious new development.[51] It was established near the inland village of South Bersted, now part of Bognor Regis, and first opened in 1791, leading to it being 'honoured with the company of several families of the first fashion in the kingdom'.[52] Hothamton was a dispersed settlement with some of the largest houses and terraces being constructed inland, but the hotel and accommodation for visitors' servants, as well as the subscription room, were on the seafront.[53]

In 1822–4, a bridge was built to link Hayling Island to the mainland, prompting the development of this previously inaccessible island.[54] In 1825, William Padwick the Younger bought land from the Duke of Norfolk, and a crescent was begun and a hotel was built.[55] Only half of the crescent of 10 houses was ever built, the site of the other half now being filled with modern flats. The fledgling resort also offered visitors a seafront library, a small temple-like building containing 'a spacious reading room, possessing an excellent collection of modern works, the newspapers, and periodicals of the day, many pleasing pictures, and the advantage of a separate room for chess players'.[56] It was located at the centre of

Fig 2.6
The fear of French invasion prompted an influx of soldiers and their families to Herne Bay. It also led to the erection of a number of houses and the addition of a weatherboarded assembly room on the side of Ship Inn during the 1790s.
[DP217500]

'a well-made esplanade three hundred yards in length, and which at one end is terminated by the Bath-house', which provided hot, tepid and cold baths.[57] An 1836 guidebook also features an engraving of the combined billiard room, Cosmorama and reading room, a long, single-storeyed structure with central and end pavilions.[58] Hayling Island, like Hothamton, was very ambitious, but equally unsuccessful.

Bournemouth was another speculative development on an uninhabited stretch of coastline, but it began with rather more modest investments. This slower pace of development may explain why it, like Blackpool, proved successful. Lewis Tregonwell first built a house there in 1811–12, followed by an inn and a handful of cottages to accommodate invalids in search of improved health (Fig 2.7).[59] In 1825, Bournemouth was described as a 'new-built watering-place' with excellent bathing, but it suffered at this date from limited accommodation.[60] However, an 1837 guidebook recorded that the politician and landowner Sir George William Tapps-Gervis (1795–1842) was carrying out a series of improvements: 'villas, crescents, streets and baths, in all varied styles of architecture are rearing their heads as if by magic'.[61] This development was wholly separate from the activity taking place on the other side of the River Bourne, where Tregonwell had established his 'neat marine villa', the inn and several detached houses 'in the cottage style'.[62] Development on either side of the river flanked the route through the gap in the cliffs to the seafront where the baths, reading room and later the pier were constructed (see Fig 7.22).

Grand seafront developments 1820–1850

As well as establishing new settlements, prized seafront locations flanking existing seaside resorts were also being identified as locations for huge new developments. These were designed to provide accommodation for the growing middle-class residential population and the increasing numbers of visitors. Critical to these schemes was the seafront location, the arrangement of their streets being designed to maximise the number of houses enjoying a sea view. These schemes also often contained a range of facilities for visitors and while some were clearly additions to existing settlements, others were constituted as separate towns. The pioneering schemes were erected at Brighton and Hove (Kemp Town and Brunswick Town) and at Hastings (St Leonards) and commenced during the 1820s.

In 1823, Thomas Read Kemp embarked on the construction of a large estate on his land to the east of Brighton and most of the development was completed over the next two decades. The central part of Kemp Town is the elaborate, high-status housing in Sussex Square with the quadrants of Lewes Crescent attached to its seaward ends, while along the seafront there are two flanking terraces (Fig 2.8). Just over 100 houses were eventually erected, whereas its ultimate inspiration, the Royal Crescent at Bath, only provided 30 houses. Originally Kemp Town was intended to have 250 homes, these additional houses to have been constructed behind the seafront terraces.[63]

Fig 2.7
In the centre of the Royal Exeter Hotel is Bournemouth's first villa, The Mansion, built for Lewis Tregonwell. It survives beneath the massive battlemented tower that was added c 1870; many of the other major elements were added during the late 19th century. [DP001321]

Fig 2.8
This is the western
quadrant of Lewes
Crescent, a key element of
Kemp Town in Brighton.
These elegant houses with
classical detailing provided
residents and visitors with
views out to sea and over
the gardens at the heart
of the development.
[DP054179]

Brunswick Town on the seafront at Hove to the west of Brighton began soon after Kemp Town and like its eastern rival its construction took several decades to complete (Fig 2.9). Its principal elements were the two seafront blocks of Brunswick Terrace (1824–6), each of 39 bays, with a substantial square, Brunswick Square (1825–30), between. To the west there is a later, combined crescent and square. An Act of Parliament was obtained in 1830 to appoint commissioners to be responsible for Brunswick Town.[64] They were effectively a 'town' council, with responsibility for the gardens, policing, providing a fire engine and firemen, drainage, lighting, paving and collecting rates.

The impact of Kemp Town and Brunswick Town was felt immediately. By January 1825, a prospectus had been published for a huge new development at Bognor. The Bognor New Town Company, with a proposed, eye-watering capital of £300,000, would see the architect Samuel Beazley constructing houses and facilities for visitors in a scheme inspired by what was expected to be the success of the Brighton developments. Unfortunately, the Bognor scheme did not prove popular with investors and nothing was constructed.[65]

The unrealised Bognor scheme and those erected at Hothamton and Hayling Island, where a few buildings were erected, were effectively new towns and lacked an existing settlement and transport routes to make these schemes work. However, a short distance along the Sussex coast from Brighton, the developments at Kemp Town and Brunswick Town were having a more profound impact at Hastings. Between 1824 and 1828, Thomas Pelham, Earl of Chichester, employed Joseph Kay to build a seafront crescent of houses with a large parish church at its centre and a

Fig 2.9
Like Kemp Town, the
large terraced houses of
Brunswick Town ranged in
size from three to five storeys
and were embellished with
Ionic and Corinthian
pilasters and engaged
columns. However, the use
of bow fronts in Brunswick
Square makes these houses
seem even more elaborate.
[DP054165]

large bazaar in front (*see* Figs 9.3 and 9.42).[66] A lavish bathhouse containing 11 warm baths was also erected with 'two handsome saloons, of octagonal form, and decorated with beautiful Chinese Scenery.'[67] Another scheme began on the seafront during the late 1820s with a direct link to the prestigious developments around Regent's Park in London, a clear inspiration for all these grand projects. Construction of St Leonards began in 1828 on farmland purchased by James Burton to the west of Hastings (*see* Fig 9.22).[68] As finally erected, his scheme consisted of grand terraces along the seafront flanking a hotel with an elegant, but low, composition in front containing baths, a bank and a library. The settlement included a parish church to the west (*see* Fig 9.46). Behind the seafront, there was an assembly room and a hillside park surrounded by villas. Two lower-status inland streets were constructed to meet the needs of the new settlement's inhabitants, Mercatoria to house merchants and Lavatoria for laundry services.[69] Like Brunswick Town, St Leonards was legally a separate administrative entity. An Improvement Act in 1832 appointed 75 commissioners to be responsible for its construction and management until its amalgamation with the Hastings Town Council in 1885.[70]

Elsewhere on the south coast, there were other major schemes similarly aimed at the middle-class residential and visitor trade. Some developments, such as those at Teignmouth (1825–6), Dover (1834–8) and Torquay (1845–8), were located on or near the seafront (Fig 2.10). These were large schemes, but were obviously additions to existing seaside resorts. However, at Herne Bay, one of the most ambitious schemes would have seen the creation of effectively a new town. A previous development scheme of 1816 had only led to the creation of The Terrace, its lack of success being attributed to the absence of a pier for steamers to land visitors. By 1830, a plan for the new town of St Augustine had been published and this included a much-needed pier.[71] Its construction meant that visitors could come from London for a holiday or just a day trip; in 1832 steam packets left London at 9am and returned from Herne Bay at 9pm.[72] The Herne Bay Pier Company built a sea wall and parade 50 feet (15.2m) wide, stretching for a mile (1.6km) along the shore.[73] The first building of the scheme was the Pier Hotel, with its 40 rooms, which had been built by 1832 on top of the low cliff overlooking the pier.[74] To manage the new town, a Local Act of Parliament was obtained in 1833 to establish a Board of Commissioners who would be responsible for the 'paving, cleansing, lighting, watching, repairing and improving a certain part of the Parish of Herne in the County of Kent'.[75]

Seaside holidays for all

From the 1840s onwards, the evolving railway network, combined with increased national and individual prosperity, saw the growth of a new market for seaside holidays among working people, a process with its origins in the 18th century. Margate's location on the Thames meant that from the outset it was served by sailing boats, as well as being reached by road. Hoys were single-masted trading vessels of 60 to 100 tons; gradually passengers and their luggage displaced their cargoes and dedicated sailing packets developed.[76] They were cheaper than travelling by coach; in the 1790s a single coach trip to Margate cost between 21s and 26s, while the cheapest boat

Fig 2.10
At Teignmouth, the Den Crescent, with assembly rooms at its centre, was constructed during the mid-1820s by the architect Andrew Patey of Exeter.
[BB67/08928b]

fare was only 5s.[77] Therefore, during the late 18th century, the holiday habit began to be extended from the highest in society to the growing middle classes and even the mocked London shopkeeper.[78]

Steamers revolutionised waterborne travel, allowing the faster transport of industrial goods, passengers and tourists. Steam was first applied to powering boats on the Clyde as early as 1785, but it was not perfected until 1812 with the launch of the *Comet*.[79] Steamers had a profound impact on tourism on the Thames, lowering fares and cutting journey times. In 1815, the cheapest fare on the earliest steamer was 12s, but 20 years later it had fallen to 6s, reduced fares prompting a signi-ficant growth in visitor numbers.[80] At the beginning of the 19th century, around 20,000 people arrived at Margate by sea, but by 1821, this had risen to 44,347 and in 1835–6, the number of travellers landing peaked at 108,625 (Fig 2.11).[81]

The most important legacy of steamers on the seafront was the pier, as the increased draught of ships prevented them from using existing facilities in shallower water. The pier usually awarded the accolade of being the earliest seaside pier opened on 26 July 1814

at Ryde on the Isle of Wight, although there were stone piers forming harbours at Scarborough, Lyme Regis and Weymouth, as well as the timber jetty at Great Yarmouth where commerce and promenading had been combined.[82] The new pier at Margate, the stone arm of the harbour with a raised promenade, was nearing completion in time for steamers to begin sailing along the Thames in 1815 (Fig 2.12).[83]

Fig 2.11 (above)
This late 19th-century photograph shows the paddle steamer Princess Mary *on the River Thames, a 100-ton (90.7 tonne) ship that was in service from 1878 until 1908. During the 19th century, steamers grew in size, speed and comfort, and remained a key means of visiting Margate until the early 20th century.*
[CC97/01580]

Fig 2.12 (left)
Margate Pier has a raised promenade along its seaward side. It could not cope with steamers at low tide and therefore a timber jetty was erected in 1824. It was replaced by the cast-iron jetty during the 1850s, which can be seen beside the original harbour in this 1920 Aerofilms photograph. See also Fig 8.1.
[EPW000162]

A few timber piers were constructed during the 1820s and 1830s, but by the 1830s the first iron piles were being used, though the definitive shift to iron only took place during the 1850s.

Steamers brought thousands of visitors to resorts, but the railways would bring millions more. By the end of the 1830s, a number of major companies had ambitions to link London and large towns and cities in what would merge into a national network.[84] During the 1840s, many resorts began to be connected to this rapidly growing railway network. Brighton led the way, followed by more than a dozen existing resorts including Great Yarmouth, Scarborough, Margate, Hastings, Teignmouth, Whitby and Torquay by the end of the decade.[85] Between 1851 and 1901, while the population of Britain grew by just over half, many resorts grew much faster and ticket sales reflected the growing number of working-class travellers on the network. Between 1850 and 1870, first-class ticket sales rose by 280 per cent, second-class by 193 per cent and third-class by 584 per cent.[86] Seaside resorts came to be within the reach of most working people, even if only for a day. Blackpool, a small town in 1861, entertained 135,000 visitors, but by 1879, it welcomed almost a million annually. During the 1890s, the town's two railway stations were rebuilt on a large scale, so that by 1914 around four million passengers were travelling to Blackpool each year, a mixture of regular

travellers and excursionists on trips organised by railway companies, workers' organisations and enlightened employers (Fig 2.13).[87]

The influx of millions of holidaymakers each year inevitably created tensions. In larger resorts, and those with twin settlements, like Brighton and Hove, Hastings and St Leonards, or Margate and Cliftonville, it was possible to have some level of separation between determined day trippers and genteel residents. Hove and West Brighton began to be considered as 'Belgravia-sur-Mer', but in other towns, more or less formal attempts at social zoning developed by directing arrivals away from polite residential areas or sometimes more overtly through measures such as enclosing and policing estates.[88] At Scarborough, a separate excursion station allowed trippers to be directed to the beach without having to go through the respectable centre of town.

The residential population of resorts grew quickly during the latter half of the 19th century. Higher-status estates were established on the seafront and in areas away from the town centres, while more affordable homes were created in less desirable areas, often in and around stations and along railway lines. At Whitby, West Cliff began to be developed with new housing and at Lowestoft, the arrival of the railway opened up the area to the south of the town to develop as a fashionable resort.[89] In contrast, at Blackpool, the visitors with the least money found lodgings in Bonny's Estate near the Central Station just behind the seafront, while wealthier visitors and residents enjoyed the solace of life behind the gates of the Claremont Park Estate on North Shore.

While middle-class residents and visitors could retreat into their own, sometimes gated and closed, communities, no such separation could be achieved on the seafront and the beach. A particular area of tension related to the observance of the Sabbath. For most people, Sunday was the only full day of rest or leisure and railway companies were keen to exploit this market and use rolling stock that would have otherwise been idle. An article in the *Dunfermline Sunday Press* in September 1867, entitled 'Aberdour versus the Sunday Steamers', described the author's traumatic visit to Blackpool. While some visitors were enjoying the beach and the countryside, 'for the most part the excursionists take a short course from the railway station to the neighbouring beer-houses, which on Sundays are crowded to

Fig 2.13
By the mid-20th century, Blackpool's central station had expanded so that it could handle tens of thousands of passengers on a busy day. Located just behind the seafront near Central Pier, it has been demolished, its site now providing car parking.
[EAR020518]

excess, and the "day out" means drinking in Blackpool instead of drinking in Preston'.[90] Residents of Blackpool, Lytham, Southport and Morecambe successfully petitioned railway companies to suspend Sunday excursions, but this was only a temporary victory.[91]

Seafronts, new technology and changing seaside holidays

The impact of huge numbers of visitors was felt particularly on the seafront, where local government recognised the need to invest increasing sums on visitor facilities, but also on sea defences to safeguard the growing towns. Investment at any one time might range from small amounts to provide a shelter to costly schemes creating stone and concrete sea walls running the length of the town's coastline, transforming, forever, the once natural profile of the area between the sea and the land. Local authorities also became involved, to a greater or lesser extent, in the entertainment industry. At some resorts venues including bandstands were provided, while some more interventionist authorities also provided town bands and municipal orchestras. And all this investment, which might be specific to seaside resorts, had

to be managed alongside the provision of the utilities and services that would be expected in any growing, modern town.

The presence of large numbers of visitors also prompted substantial private-sector investment in increasingly large venues, culminating in the industrial-scale entertainment complexes erected at Blackpool. The winter gardens opened in 1878, but were dramatically increased in size during the late 1880s and mid-1890s through the addition of an opera house, a vast new ballroom and a Ferris wheel. This complex was a short distance inland, but on the seafront Blackpool Tower opened in 1894, offering visitors a large circus, a ballroom, a menagerie and an aquarium among its many attractions (Fig 2.14). Adjacent to it was the Alhambra, which opened in 1899 with a theatre that could hold an audience of 3,000, a circus with a capacity of 2,000 and the 'most enchanting Ballroom in all Europe', which catered for 3,000 people or 500 couples dancing.[92] What marked out the Alhambra, apart from its size, was its lavishness, its halls having floors laid with Italian marble and Venetian mosaic, while its main stairs were built using Carrara marble. These new venues employed a different economic model compared to their Georgian predecessors. They were no longer funded by a small number of wealthy people paying a

Fig 2.14
When it opened in 1894, Blackpool Tower was Britain's tallest building. Soon after, the Alhambra opened beside it and both these buildings dwarfed existing buildings lining the seafront. The Ferris wheel shown in this c 1900 photograph was constructed at the winter gardens in 1896.
[OP00480]

large subscription, but instead relied on thousands, and hundreds of thousands, each paying a small fee. Blackpool Tower offered visitors a wide range of entertainments for 6d and for an extra fee they could ascend the Tower or enjoy a show in the 3,000-seat circus. By the end of the 19th century, Blackpool also offered three piers, swimming pools, theatres and a host of other seafront attractions including the earliest rides on the site that would become Blackpool Pleasure Beach.

By 1914, there were over 100 piers around the coast, ranging from uncluttered promenade piers such as at Clevedon (Fig 2.15) and Saltburn-by-the-Sea, both dating from 1869, to pleasure piers bristling with oriental-inspired pavilions and kiosks, such as Brighton's West Pier (opened 1866) and the town's Palace Pier constructed 30 years later. A pier was an affirmation of the success of a resort, an indicator that investors were confident of making a significant return. The same motivation

Fig 2.15
A masterpiece of elegant engineering, Clevedon Pier is the only Grade I listed pier that can still be visited, the other being the skeletal remains of Brighton's West Pier. As well as being a place to promenade, ships tie up at the pier head, including each year PS Waverley, *the last seagoing, passenger-carrying paddle steamer in the world.* [DP081827]

also drove the creation of other forms of entertainment venue. From the 1870s onwards, winter gardens, aquaria and swimming pools became key attractions at many seaside resorts (*see* Figs 9.30 and 9.32).

The same mastery of industrial materials and production techniques that created Blackpool Tower also allowed the creation of transport systems along and up from the seafront, ranging from pioneering electric railways and trams to cliff lifts and funicular railways where there were cliffs to overcome (*see* Figs 3.28 and 3.32– 3.34). As well as providing practical, but novel, features on the rapidly evolving seafront, new technologies created brilliantly lit fairgrounds and cinemas, unashamedly popular attractions designed to amuse and entertain the vast crowds flooding into seaside resorts.

Alongside the new technologically based entertainments, the character of seaside holidays was changing. Throughout the 19th century, the bathing machine remained a key feature of every popular beach, but increasingly it was being sidelined by unofficial, and later official, 'Mackintosh bathing', in which bathers arrived at the beach with their swimming costume secreted beneath their coats. By the early 20th century, the bathing machine would gradually give way to the beach hut and would finally disappear as a result of the clearance of beaches to install military defences during World War II.

At the beginning of the 19th century, the beach had been a place from which to bathe, but increasingly the seafront became a location where a family could spend the whole day. Charles Dickens in 1836 described a typical day on Ramsgate Sands:

It was a fine, bright, clear day, with a light breeze from the sea. There were the same ladies and gentlemen, the same children, the same nursemaids, the same telescopes, the same portable chairs. The ladies were employed in needlework, or watch-guard making, or knitting, or reading novels; the gentlemen were reading newspapers and magazines; the children were digging holes in the sand with wooden spades, and collecting water therein; the nursemaids, with their youngest charges in their arms, were running in after the waves, and then running back with the waves after them; and, now and then, a little sailing-boat either departed with a gay and talkative cargo of passengers, or returned with a very silent and particularly uncomfortable-looking one.[93]

Ten years later the Brown family in John Leighton's cartoon book, *London Out of Town*,[94] spent a similar day on the beach, but fast forward to the beginning of the 20th century, photography and early films record vast crowds filling piers and beaches (Fig 2.16). Rush-covered chairs

Fig 2.16
This photograph of Weymouth seafront in c 1900 shows people promenading perhaps in their Sunday best, while others sit on the beach. Weymouth's distinctive bathing saloons can be seen, and further up the beach there is a photographic studio to provide holidaymakers with souvenir portraits. [BB88/02329]

favoured by the Tuggses had become deckchairs during the 1890s, the same decade that saw the introduction of the picture postcard. Through this simple device, perhaps the ultimate ancestor of social media, it became quick, cheap and easy to share holiday news with family and friends and encourage them to visit in the future. Although there was a growing appreciation of the curative value of sea air and sunshine, photographs show Victorian men in buttoned-up suits and women with large hats and parasols, the joy of exposure to the sun having to wait to the interwar years.

The 20th-century seaside

Photographs of the interwar years reveal new attitudes to holidays. Large swimming pools set amid new man-made sea defences became a common sight, the local authorities at Blackpool and Hastings leading the way in such investments. More revealing bathing costumes allowed greater exposure to the sun to create the prized suntan, but even in the mid-20th century, determined sun bathers can still be seen alongside men wearing suits and women in dresses on the beach, in an era before leisurewear became king (*see* Fig 1.14). However, perhaps more remarkable in contemporary photographs of the seafront was the evidence of the rapid growth of car ownership. The car, and its much less lauded bigger brothers, the omnibus and the chara-banc, continued the process of democratising the seaside that had begun with steamers and railways. They would also add a line of clutter that would impair views from seafront buildings and they caused previously fairly compact settlements to expand along the

seafront during the decades between the 1930s and the 1960s. Buses and cars also allowed the creation of plotlands, such as Peacehaven, on previously undeveloped stretches of coastline, settlements with low-quality architecture that attracted fierce criticism between the wars.

Debates about the likely impact of extending the right to paid holidays, which culminated in 1938 with the Holidays with Pay Act, focused on how resorts would cope with an even larger number of holidaymakers.[95] Largely unspoilt stretches of coastline previously fairly immune from the tourist gaze began to open up to holidaymakers, leading some commentators to fear that the combination of new transport and the right to a holiday would create inappropriate development. One writer was concerned that new holiday camps would spread onto pristine clifftops.[96] However, when the challenges came to untouched coastlines, it was more often through the creation of large holiday settlements populated with caravans and chalets, such as on the Suffolk coast at Kessingland and north of Skegness on the Lincolnshire coast where thousands have accrued over recent decades near Billy Butlin's first holiday camp (Fig 2.17). On the south coast, the popularity of the seaside as a place to live led to the creation in Sussex of a long coastal area of residential development, sometimes uncharitably nick-named 'Costa Geriatrica' due to its popularity with retirees.

World War II interrupted the growth of seaside resorts and the extension of the holiday habit, and resorts such as Margate suffered considerable physical damage. Blackpool, however, far from the front line, continued to welcome visitors alongside military staff and civil servants, many of whom were evacuated from London and the South East. Seaside holidays restarted in earnest as soon as the war in Europe was over, Butlins holiday camp at Filey actually opening in June 1945 with the help of RAF personnel. The 1950s are often portrayed as the decade that saw the seaside enjoying the peak of its popularity, but statistically this seems to have taken place during the mid-1970s. However, the seeds of decline were also beginning to become evident. Prolonged austerity after 1945 led to underinvestment in seaside resorts, their seafront and sea defences, the deficiency of these leading to catastrophic damage during the 1953 storm surge, which resulted in the deaths of more than 300 people. This prompted

Fig 2.17
Behind the substantial sea defences at Lowestoft, a large caravan park has been created, with residential caravans that provide both affordable holiday homes for a week at the seaside, but also year-round places to spend a weekend away from home. [MF99/0639/20]

an immediate review of Britain's ageing sea defences and significant new investment. However, facilities on seafronts, such as piers and pavilions, continued to suffer from under-investment and storm damage, so that by the 1970s British seaside resorts seemed unfavourably shabby and old-fashioned compared to the bright, new resorts being constructed around the Mediterranean.

By the early 21st century, there was growing recognition of the need to invest in improving the environment of seaside resorts, and particularly the seafront. This was economically desirable, but also a practical necessity, due to the realisation of the pace of climate change, meaning that seafronts had to be strengthened, reconfigured and sometimes raised to deal with rising sea levels and increased storminess. The largest of these projects was at Blackpool where the whole of the central part of the seafront has been rebuilt to create convex headlands, projecting into the sea (*see* Fig 11.7). While the new arrangement is intensely practical, it has also afforded opportunities to create new services, features and attractions for the town's residents and the huge number of visitors that still come each year. Another major challenge facing seaside resorts is image. Once decried as a place where benefits tourists lurked, new investment and new ways of thinking about seaside resorts as historic towns and attractive destinations for shopping and gastronomy have contributed to a revival. Half a century ago, a stay at a seaside resort was likely to be a family's main, and probably the only, holiday of the year. Today the seaside is more likely to be used for day trips and short breaks that may be supplementary to a main holiday taken abroad.

Conclusion

Over the course of three centuries, a seaside holiday has gone from being an exclusive activity enjoyed by handfuls of people to an almost universal experience. By the end of the 18th century the numbers of tourists were sufficiently large to begin to transform a series of coastal towns into seaside resorts. Purpose-built entertainment venues and new lodging houses became the most obvious reflection of the growing holiday habit, and confidence in the longevity of seaside holidays even encouraged some entrepreneurs to invest in new settlements or huge extensions to existing resorts. This process marked a shift from small-scale investment by local landowners and businessmen to projects funded by regional companies, and today many of the major businesses are parts of national and inter-national leisure and accommodation groups.[97]

In the course of 300 years of holidaymaking, the role and the significance of the seafront has changed over time. Subsequent chapters will tell the story of the transformation of natural coastline into man-made spaces. The seafront, once ignored in favour of natural harbours, became prized for providing access to the sea. In due course, it became the focus for entertainment and leisure, an all-day playground, a place to bathe and later swim, as well as to relax and breathe in the fresh sea air. The arrival of piers from the mid-19th century onwards marked a fundamental shift of emphasis towards the seafront, and by the early 20th century, it had often become the site for huge entertainment facilities and fairgrounds catering for millions of visitors spilling out of nearby railway stations.

To protect all this investment in new facilities, sea defences became an essential feature of every seafront. The sea is a seaside resort's greatest asset, but it is also its greatest threat. Stretches of natural coastline once admired by romantic painters and writers have been transformed through increasingly large-scale human intervention, creating the infrastructure of the seafront that we now see today. In the next chapter, the story of sea defences will be described, providing seaside towns with oppor-tunities to create a seafront that would attract visitors and drive the growth of their economy.

3

The geography of the seafront

Seaside resorts exist to provide access to the sea, but the price of this access is vulnerability to storms, flooding and erosion. Therefore, increasingly substantial sea defences will have been constructed over time to separate the sea and beach from the seafront and its buildings. These engineering structures are designed to prevent flooding, but may also be created to reduce the erosion of cliffs.

The creation of sea defences establishes a space behind them for a range of features designed to make the town work for residents and tourists. They create promenades, as well as hosting one of the main vehicular routes through the town. This space may also be a location for rail services primarily aimed at depositing visitors at the seafront, and in the past, it was also a key locus for sea travel. Smaller-scale railways and tramways also appeared at a number of resorts, practical requirements for a growing residential population, but also sometimes novelties. Where cliffs are present, a range of cliff lifts and cliff railways were built from the late 19th century onwards.

What can be located on a seafront depends on its geography, particularly the distance between the sea and solid land suitable for substantial buildings. Although this intervening land may have originally been considered incapable of supporting major structures as it was too sandy or marshy, it may have been 'improved' to allow construction through drainage schemes accompanying the construction of the sea wall.

The promenade and the accompanying road usually give access to the first line of buildings on the seafront. However, where cliffs are present, the main resort buildings may have been raised above the beach and its activities. At resorts such as Bournemouth, Filey or the north part of Blackpool, the first line of buildings is on the clifftops.

This chapter will review the geography of seafronts, considering the impact of the sea and how resorts seek to prevent it from causing damage to property. In subsequent chapters, the usage of this complex, new space over the past 250 years will be examined in detail, reviewing how it has been adapted to serve residents and visitors to seaside resorts.

The beach, cliffs and access to the sea

Centuries of human settlement in England have necessitated the construction of approximately 860km of protection against coastal erosion, while a further 1,000km of coastline requires measures to prevent flooding.[1] In its natural form, the coastline would consist of stretches of more or less friable cliffs, headlands largely impervious to the sea, areas of salt marsh that regularly flood and stretches of shingle and sandy beach created, depleted and nourished by the sea.

Access to the sea was the key geographical factor behind the creation of a seaside resort. A beach was essential, not because a Georgian holidaymaker expected to spend much time there, but because bathing machines favoured a gently sloping beach. The first resorts achieved access to the sea where harbours or active beach-launched fleets already existed. When new resorts began to develop from the mid-18th century onwards, some were located on low-lying stretches of coast, but others were established in gaps in the cliffs, with much of the holiday development being on the clifftops rather than on the seafronts.

The early resorts that had harbours included Scarborough, where the town was laid out on the hill behind, and later, on the cliffs above the spa. Documents and early depictions of Margate show that sea bathing took place at the harbour, with access from the seafront Parade. At Weymouth, the historic town of Melcombe Regis on the north side of the harbour was extended northwards due to the presence of large numbers of wealthy sea bathers from the 1780s onwards, exploiting what was in effect a wide sandbank that had been further built up to link the one-time island to the mainland (*see* Fig 2.2). On the south side of the harbour was the ancient, and once legally separate, town of Weymouth, part of which was at sea level, with later expansion taking place on cliffs behind. The early resorts of Brighton and Hastings had no natural harbours, their fishing fleets being launched from the shingle beaches. Brighton's wide bay opens on to flat land, flanked by higher cliffs to the east. At Hastings, the cliffs were the site of the castle and later housing, but there was also sufficient space at sea level for substantial resort development, including later the new town of St Leonards.

Cliffs may seem an inconvenience for visitors struggling back from the beach, but from the mid-18th century onwards they could be the sites of key features of resorts, as long as there was convenient access to the sea below. The first such new development was at Blackpool and by the 1780s, a number of larger clifftop houses for sea-bathing visitors had been constructed among a scatter of earlier huts (*see* Fig 2.5).[2] At the south end of Blackpool, the land is at sea level, rising gently towards the north where there are high cliffs on which hotel development took place during the early 20th century. Interestingly, most of the early development

took place at the midway point in this sloping cliff (Fig 3.1). Bournemouth's cliffs are much less heavily disguised than at Blackpool. The reason for the resort's precise location is much more obvious than at Blackpool; the town, its pier, gardens and bathing facilities were originally grouped around a gap in the cliffs, with the first housing being developed on the slopes on either side of where the River Bourne ran into the sea.

Among the other resorts with much of their development on clifftops is Filey, which developed mostly from the 1840s onwards with the arrival of the railway and Cromer, where the Hotel De Paris stands at a high point above the pier. Folkestone's focus was originally its harbour and the area in and around the Old High Street. With the arrival of the railway in 1843, and the development of regular cross-Channel services, the town needed to grow further along the clifftops (Fig 3.2).[3] However, there was also sufficient space below the cliffs for some substantial seafront development, including a crescent, a terrace, a Victorian hotel (largely rebuilt in the 1970s) and a large amusement park, which has now been entirely cleared.[4] At Whitby, the historic town had developed behind its harbour, beneath the abbey on the clifftop to the east. When substantial amounts of new accommodation for visitors were required, the obvious location for new development was the previously undeveloped

Fig 3.1
Most visitors to central Blackpool today probably don't realise that they are walking on clifftops, but William Bartlett's view of 1840 shows the natural cliff's friable form that required sea defences from the 1840s onwards to counter erosion. [Author's collection]

Fig 3.2 (right)
*This Aerofilms photograph of 1920 shows the seafront at Folkestone including the prestigious gated development as well as large hotels and apartments on the clifftop Leas, the town's most fashionable location.
[EPW000582]*

Fig 3.3 (below)
*Brighton has a shingle beach, which did not prove to be an obstacle to bathing machines, sunbathing or swimming, but is lousy for children who want to build sandcastles.
[DP054388]*

clifftop to the west of the town.[5] Cliffs may have provided cheap land on which to erect new housing, but they also offered challenges to people wishing to bathe in the sea, though the compensation would be the stunning views and apparently sweeter air.

Resorts often market themselves on the length, quality and particulate nature of their beaches, glorious miles of sandy beach often being a key selling point. Photographs reveal that the beach at Margate was much lower a century ago and an early photograph of Weymouth, taken a few decades after the early 19th-century sea wall was constructed, reveals that the beach was a metre or two lower than today (*see* Fig 3.7).[6] During the 18th century, beach material was less important than straightforward access to the sea for bathing machines, but the existence of sand or shingle did condition the form of the seafront and therefore the experience of bathing in the sea. Sandy beaches have gently sloping profiles, while shingle and pebble beaches are steeper (Fig 3.3). Shingle beaches may afford greater protection for seafront development when the stones bank up to effectively create a berm, a feature imitated at Margate where a sand berm is artificially created during the winter. At Westward Ho! there is a rocky stretch of coast to the west and a shingle beach to the north-east of the resort, built up like a miniature version of the tombolo at Chesil Beach.

The other major difference between sandy and shingle beaches is the distance between the high and low tide marks. At shallow, sandy beaches such as Margate, Scarborough or, in the extreme case, Weston-super-Mare, the sea retreats a considerable distance at each low tide, whereas at Brighton and Hastings the steeper shingle beaches may witness comparable changes in sea level, but over a much shorter distance. Surrounded by the Atlantic Ocean and the North Sea, English coastal towns undergo huge tidal ranges every day. In the Mediterranean, it is around 1m between high and low tide, but around the British coast it is usually several metres, the highest tidal range being over 12m at Weston-super-Mare.

The distance between the high and low tide marks depends on the beach material and therefore the shape of the beach and the seabed. Over the years, materials can be deposited on the seafront, in effect moving the sea further away from where the first line of buildings would be erected. On parts of the seafront at Weston-super-Mare, a wide strip of land exists between the sea and the first line of buildings, allowing the creation of gardens, while at Southport over the past 200 years, the rate of sand build-up and a reclamation means that the beach is now around half a mile from the front of town, creating an area for gardens and less aesthetically pleasing industrial units and large entertainment facilities.

Around the coast a number of resorts are blessed with multiple beaches, while others, in contrast, have more modest, or difficult to reach, beaches. At St Ives, the crenulated form of the coast means there are a number of sandy beaches along its coastline, while the geology of the coast at Newquay has created various beaches along its north-western side, as well as the west-facing Fistral Beach. Llandudno in north-west Wales developed on a piece of land between two beaches, while Hugh Town on St Mary's in the Isles of Scilly stands on a former sandbank (Fig 3.4). In contrast, some seaside resorts face a range of geographical challenges that might inhibit tourism, though more often they simply shape the form of seafront development. Ilfracombe's Tunnel Beaches were only made practically accessible after Welsh miners cut a tunnel through the cliff in 1823. The creation of the tunnel allowed access to the beaches, but it also permitted the control of a valuable revenue stream. In Britain, access to beaches is thought to be an inalienable human right, though the legal basis for that belief may be uncertain, but in Europe public access often comes at a price during the summer season.[7] In parts of Europe, such as in Italy, Slovenia and the Cote d'Azur, privately run beachfront facilities allow businesses to monetise the beach and the sea, charging a fee for the use of sun loungers, as well as providing cafes, bars and restaurants for sunbathers.

Fig 3.4
As Hugh Town in Scilly has been constructed on a sandbank, it is prone to inundation during storms and, at high tide, water laps up against seafront buildings.
[NMR 23938/020]

Some stretches of coastline set developers other challenges or opportunities (Fig 3.5). At Hastings, Dymchurch and Swanage streams that flowed into the sea have required the creation of conduits or outflows running across the beach. Large rocks might also complicate access, though some were celebrated as landmarks. A major storm on 22 November 1824 destroyed the Chit Rock at Sidmouth, a prominent landmark for returning fishermen seeking the beach.[8] The White Rock at Hastings was seen as a barrier to expansion and the unification of Hastings with St Leonards and therefore, in 1834, it was cut away.[9] At some resorts, islands exist close to the seafront. Knightstone Island at Weston-super-Mare has been a focus for health activities since the 1820s; the first bathhouse and accommodation were created on the island when it was still only accessible at low tide.[10] Further to the north, Birnbeck Island lies a little further off the coast and in 1867, it became the ingenious destination for a pier designed by Eugenius Birch.[11]

Fig 3.5
At Newquay, a dramatic suspension bridge links Towan Island to the mainland, allowing the inhabitants of its single house an unrivalled sense of privacy in the heart of a busy seaside resort.
[DP196913]

The threat from the sea

The coastline is dynamic. Sediments from eroding cliffs replenish beaches as they are transported along the coastline by longshore drift (also known as littoral drift), or move in and out to sea, on currents dependent on the shape of the coastline and the form of the seabed.[12] Shingle smoothed by the action of the sea is deposited on some beaches such as Brighton, and perhaps most spectacularly it forms the 29km long Chesil Beach at Portland. However, the dynamism of the coast comes at a high price for settlements on cliffs that are eroding. The east coast of England, and particularly the Yorkshire coast, is prone to erosion.[13] At Atwick, north of Hornsea in the East Riding of Yorkshire, caravan sites increasingly teeter on the cliff edge. The erosion is so severe that since 1066, 26 villages and 8,000ha of land on this coastline have been lost and a plaque on the seafront at Withernsea commemorates its lost mediaeval church, the

remains of which are now apparently a mile out to sea. Much of the resulting sediment created by this erosion has been transported southwards to create Spurn Point, a spit of sand, shingle and boulder clay at the mouth of the Humber estuary.[14] The coastline at Happisburgh, Norfolk, is also eroding quickly (Fig 3.6).[15] Over the next 100 years, a Grade I church, a Grade II manor house and other listed buildings will be lost to the sea.[16] On the Suffolk coast, the most famous victim of coastal erosion has been Dunwich, while nearby Aldeburgh has lost half of its mediaeval area to the sea.[17] On the Isle of Wight, the chalets of Brighstone Holiday Camp, which were built perpendicular to the coastline, have one by one fallen into the sea, new accommodation having wisely been built further inland. In 2014, part of the cliff at the east end of Hastings collapsed on to Rock-a-Nore Road; further west on the Jurassic coast, regular slips of the cliffs frequently expose prized fossils (*see* Fig 1.7).

The coastline is also susceptible to man-made change. This can be caused by structures built in the sea that interrupt, or alter, the natural flow of sediments and by the hardening of stretches of the coast where ports and seaside resorts have been created. At Lyme Regis, the connection of the Cobb to the mainland in the 1750s resulted in the interruption of the longshore drift, causing the build-up of Monmouth Beach on its western side, while Margate's famous sands seem to have been an unintended result of the rebuilding of its stone pier in 1810–15 (Fig 3.7).[18]

The sea is also a threat to property due to flooding. Prior to the creation of sea defences, large areas of farmland would have been regularly prone to flooding, and sometimes were the victim of catastrophic inundations. In 1607, land on either side of the Severn

Fig 3.6 (above)
Homes at Happisburgh in Norfolk have regularly disappeared and others continue to be threatened by regular erosion, punctuated by sudden collapses due to major storms such as in 1953, 1976 and 1993. In this 1947 photograph by Hallam Ashley, a well has been exposed and presumably collapsed soon after. [AA98/16520]

Fig 3.7 (left)
This 1865 photograph of Weymouth's seafront shows that the level of the beach is much lower than today. It also shows the white posts and chains separating the promenade and the road. [BB87/00005; Courtesy of Grahame Soffe]

Estuary was flooded by what may have been a form of tsunami, resulting in around 2,000 deaths by drowning.[19] Some of the worst flooding in recent years has been as a result of storm surges in the North Sea. These occur when high tides, low barometric pressure and strong winds from the north combine to force water southwards down the North Sea. Its shape, with the wide northern gap between Scotland and Norway, but the narrow English Channel at the south, builds up pressure that has to go somewhere, and therefore sea water inundates wherever there is a low-lying, or poorly defended, coastline.[20]

During the storm surge of 31 January and 1 February 1953 the height of the southern North Sea rose by between 2.7m and 3.4m, leading to 800km^2 of land being inundated and causing damage costing £900 million.[21] The east of England was worst affected, especially Essex, where 112 people died.[22] The village of Jaywick was inundated by 9 billion litres of water, causing flooding up to 1.8m deep in places and leading to 35 deaths.[23] At nearby Canvey Island, there were 58 deaths, some of whom drowned while in bed.[24] Gaps were torn in the concrete facing of the promenade at Margate, the railway line flooded, boats were washed into the streets of the Old Town and the lighthouse at the end of the pier fell into the sea.[25] Further north in Lincolnshire, an estimated 860,000 tons (780,175 tonnes) of sand was washed into Mablethorpe, stripping the beach back to its black clay, while near Skegness sea defences were destroyed. Twenty people died in the Skegness area while a further 16 perished in the Mablethorpe–Sutton area.[26] In total, 307 people died and 24,500 houses were destroyed or damaged. Prime Minister Winston Churchill called it a 'National Disaster'.[27]

After World War II, England's coastal defences had been neglected; Hunstanton actually had a hole in its sea wall in 1950 and Canvey Island had no adequate protection for its housing and industry.[28] Sea wall design was poorly understood. Defences were too low in some places and not well built, and many were too vertical to be effective. In many places, bungalows, beach huts and industrial facilities were low-lying and in the way of defences.[29] Additionally, long stretches of natural defences, including beaches and sand dunes, had not been maintained. There was also a lack of coordination; in 1953 defences were looked after by local authorities, river boards and government departments as well as private people and there was no single chain of command to react to events taking place.[30]

The 1953 storm led to immediate and longer-term responses. Remedial works took place quickly, including creating a new sea wall near Hunstanton as well as providing improved defences along the Norfolk and Suffolk coast. However, perhaps the longest-lasting legacy of 1953 was a growing appreciation that sea defences should be a national responsibility.[31] The Waverley Committee was established to consider the country's coastal defences. It concluded that the height of the surge was higher than had been expected and, therefore, the 1953 storm became the new minimum height to which future defences were designed to respond. Monitoring of natural forces, waves, tides, currents and depths of water, was to be improved as were the design and maintenance of defences.[32] After 1953, around 1,200 beaches were replenished, hundreds of kilometres of defences were repaired and improved, walls were raised where needed and early warning measures were put in place.[33]

The next major storm in the North Sea was in 1976, which was less severe than in 1953 and, as the country was better prepared, it was much less destructive.[34] Two years later, another storm hit the North Sea. On this occasion, its lasting legacy was in the severe damage to piers at Herne Hay, Southwold, Skegness and Cleethorpes, and the destruction of those at Margate and Hunstanton.[35]

The winter of 2013–14 was one of the most extreme in British meteorological history and included a major storm surge in the North Sea on 5 and 6 December 2013.[36] As it was comparable in size to the 1953 storm surge, improved defences proved able to withstand the sea, but in a few places, such as at Lowestoft, the pressure of the sea popped off the top of a stretch of the sea wall. Elsewhere, there was considerable damage during that winter. Between October 2013 and February 2014, a series of more than a dozen major storms struck Britain from the south-west (Fig 3.8). At Teignmouth, although it boasted recently upgraded sea defences, the ferocity of an early February storm nevertheless damaged the walls of the seafront gardens on top of the defences and twisted metal signs. The most spectacular damage occurred at nearby Dawlish, where the sea defences were severely damaged, washing away the ground beneath the railway line. The tracks were left hanging in

mid-air, leading to the closure of the main route into Cornwall for two months. The power of the storms was felt in other parts of Britain. In December 2013, the North Pier at Blackpool was damaged and had to close for several weeks, while in early January 2014, Aberystwyth's sea walls were breached and a shelter destroyed.

Holding back the sea

Beaches were not the primary focus of most coastal towns prior to the advent of sea bathing, though they might be places for fleets to land cargo and fish and for people to ride and walk around the coast. At Weymouth, the seafront was unimportant to the town prior to the arrival of sea bathers. A late 18th-century guidebook recalled how 'The Esplanade, which even boys remember to have been nothing but a place where the inhabitants deposited all the rubbish of the town, is in no short space converted into one of the most charming promenades in England.'[37] To the east of Great Yarmouth's historic town wall, there was a largely undeveloped expanse of land leading to the sea that was described in 1777:

> Upon this common are several windmills, there are likewise several detached houses in the humble style, with small gardens belonging to them – and possessed by fishermen, &c. On this common, cattle feed; ropes are made; fishing nets dried and mended; and many other jobs performed.[38]

At modern seaside resorts, after centuries of human occupation and intervention, it is hard to envisage the natural state of the coast as it once existed. However, to get an impression of the original coastline at Brighton or Hastings, a visit to nearby smaller settlements on the Kent and Sussex coastline can be instructive. Similarly, for insights into the original, pre-resort character of small port resorts like Margate or Weymouth, an excursion to more remote, less developed ports in Cornwall or Northern England provides hints of what early sea bathers must have seen and experienced.

Fig 3.8
At Newquay, the damaged defences in front of the aquarium were quickly patched and in 2015 were repaired more permanently.
[DP196919]

There are also some informative historic views of seaside resorts prior to significant man-made intervention on their seafront. Early views of Sea Houses, the settlement soon engulfed by Eastbourne, show a haphazard line of vernacular houses on the seafront.[39] There is some fencing and walling around a few of the houses, more garden fence than sea wall, and the beach has a scatter of boats and capstans on it, evidence of a small fishing fleet. A similar scene is shown in *The Long Painting* of Sidmouth (*see* Figs 1.5 and 9.1). This long panorama shows a similar scatter of boats and capstans with fishermen at work; it also features well-dressed visitors promenading on a simple path at the head of the beach towards Wallis' Marine Library or sitting among the capstans.

Since the 18th century, protection on the coast has come in two general forms. Sea defences are created to prevent the inundation of seafront properties, while coast protection is established to inhibit erosion to the base of cliffs.[40] One scheme can of course be designed to achieve both goals. Coastal works at Scarborough in the 1880s and 1890s were designed to protect against flooding and prevent erosion, while also taking the opportunity to sort out the town's drainage issues and improve the flow of traffic.[41] Walls can also be used to defend land that has been reclaimed from the sea, such as at Weymouth where the site of Devonshire Buildings and Pulteney Buildings was reclaimed from the sea during the early

19th century.[42] In 1878–80, the sea walls at Margate were strengthened, creating Marine Drive along the east side of the beach, linking Buenos Ayres in the west directly to the harbour for the first time.[43]

Sea defences and coastal protection measures fall into two categories, hard engineering, in the form of walls and revetments, and soft engineering, techniques to bolster the natural components of the shoreline. Hard engineering is the solution most often considered to be central for seaside resorts, though often both strategies are used in tandem. Although the hardening of one stretch of coastline might solve an immediate problem, it can also shift the issue further along the coast or lead to the loss of beach materials.[44]

The main hard-engineering solution to prevent incursion by the sea is to build a sea wall that will be durable against wave impact, reflect waves and prevent overtopping and spray. It should be easy to build and maintain, allow access to the sea where appropriate, and be affordable and aesthetically pleasing, the last of these perhaps being the most difficult to achieve.[45] Many schemes include flood gates or barriers that can be closed when a threat is perceived. Automated systems have the advantage of being remotely controllable, but often it is easier to manually swing a gate into place or drop pre-prepared lengths of timber into the gaps left in the defences (Fig 3.9). At Herne Bay, the modern defences have flood gates and the top parts of the sea defences are integrated into the formal gardens laid out on the seafront.

Hard engineering

Since ancient times, landowners have used earth embankments to protect farmland, particularly reclaimed land.[46] Among the examples are a late Saxon Fenland sea bank, which is now inland, and the Roman Bank in Lincolnshire, which has mediaeval origins.[47] The tiny resort of Freiston Shore, originally with its two sea-bathing hotels, is located behind the latter bank.[48] Unfortunately, the sea is now a kilometre away from both hotels.

Earth banks may be the most satisfactory means of protecting reclaimed farmland, but they would be too substantial and intrusive at a seaside resort where access to the sea was essential. Therefore, from an early period wood and stone sea defences were created.

Fig 3.9
At Weston-super-Mare, a low wall alongside the seafront road is the last line in the resort's sea defences, designed to prevent overtopping reaching seafront properties. To provide access to the promenade, long, low gates have been included.
[DP218029]

Setterington's view of Scarborough in 1735 shows timber-piled sea walls and stone inclines for access to the beach. Around the spa there were similar vertical timbers, but after the so-called 'earthquake', a major landslide that engulfed it on 29 December 1737, more substantial defences were established.[49] The cliffs at Scarborough have remained unstable and, on 3 and 4 June 1993, between 60 and 70m of cliff, approximately a million tons in weight, was lost, taking the Holbeck Hall Hotel down with it live on television, an event that must have been like the one in 1737 that destroyed Scarborough's spa.[50]

In 1736, the Reverend John Lewis included a plan/view of Margate in his history of the Isle of Thanet, showing the town clustered around its harbour with its timber pier (*see* Fig 3.19).[51] There is no indication of the existence of the beach, or at least the artist considered it insignificant, but the town's harbourside is shown in some detail. The defences depicted consisted of horizontal timbers apparently reinforced by what appear to be timber props, the same construction technique employed in the pier. In 1810, Colonel Scott, the landowner at Bognor, supervised the erection of 1,200 yards (1,097m) of wooden sea wall, which was named the 'Duke of Kent's Bulwark'.[52] Dymchurch has enjoyed some form of coastal defences since perhaps the Middle Ages and in

1803 the 6.5km-long wall was said to be in a poor condition. An engineer recommended the creation of a new, almost-vertical wall and this clay and wood structure was reinforced with stone for the first time during the 1820s.[53] Before 1840, the only sea defences at Filey were timber piles driven into the sand and clay at the foot of the cliffs.[54] Not all timbers set into the beach may have been used for sea defences. An early photograph of the seafront at Hastings shows the remains of piles set into the beach at what appears to be low tide level, perhaps to prevent boats going on to the rocks beside them.[55] However, timber sea defences did survive into the 20th century on the Lincolnshire coast at Chapel Point where an arrangement of tree branches and timber stakes had been constructed.[56]

Timber may have been cheap and relatively easy to install, but it was far less durable than stone. At St Ives, the renowned civil engineer John Smeaton was asked to design improvements to the town and harbour, including a sea wall along the whole of Porthmeor Beach between 1762 and 1782.[57] A view of Weymouth's seafront in 1789 shows a sloping revetment, a means of consolidating and strengthening the shoreline (Fig 3.10).[58] By 1800, this was deemed insufficient and work began on constructing a stone sea wall.[59] This south–north wall was built by two contractors,

Fig 3.10
This 1789 view of Weymouth by John Crane shows what seems to have been a turf-covered earth bank as the town's sea defence. To the north can be seen Gloucester Row, with the house at the near end in which George III stayed during that summer. [AA050895]

and in 1805 Sir William Pulteney agreed to build a new sea wall running eastwards, parallel to the quay (Fig 3.11). In exchange, he was allowed to erect buildings on the land reclaimed behind it, leading to the construction of Pulteney Buildings and Devonshire Buildings. On 22 November 1824 Weymouth's sea wall was badly damaged by the same major storm that hit Sidmouth, leading to major repairs. G A Ellis vividly recorded the extent of the damage (*see* Fig 3.7):

> whole rows of houses that fronted the foaming, raging, billows, were completely inundated; the pride of Melcombe, its beautiful esplanade, was nearly all demolished, the stone posts and chains (which amount to 336 stone posts, and 4620 feet of iron chain) were rent up and entirely broken, the piers ... also were demolished, vessels, boats, and small craft, were either driven into the centre of the town, sunk, destroyed, or carried out to sea'.[60]

Although responsibility for sea defences is now clearly vested with local and national government, Weymouth's first walls were constructed by private investors. At Teignmouth in 1823–4 there were 'excellent cold, hot and vapour baths' kept by Mrs Hubbard who was responsible for the construction of the first sea wall.[61] At St Leonards, a tall, vertical, stone sea wall was a critical element of James Burton's substantial investment from 1828 onwards.[62] The same major storm that damaged Weymouth's seafront in November 1824 damaged many houses at Sidmouth and prompted the construction of the town's first sea wall.[63] Half of the cost of this project was paid for by the landowner, presumably the rest being funded by the town:

> In 1835, the inhabitants, fearful of the incursions of the sea, which are continually wasting neighbouring parts of the coast, commenced the erection of the excellent *sea wall*, which cost about £2500, of which £1200 was given by the lord of the manor. It was completed in 1838, and affords a dry and very agreeable promenade, upwards of 1,700 feet in length.[64]

At Great Yarmouth, Britannia Terrace and Esplanade, with its accompanying sea wall, were erected in 1847 at a cost of £2,000 by Charles Cory, the owner of the adjacent land and in 1859 the slate-rubble sea wall was erected at St Mawes with funds raised by public subscription.[65]

As well as individuals and groups of property owners, companies also took responsibility for constructing sea defences. In the 1830s, the

Fig 3.11
At the south end of the modern beach at Weymouth there is a stretch of sea wall, largely buried by sand. It is constructed of monumental stone blocks, and is probably a survivor from the early 19th century.
[DP024379]

Herne Bay Pier Company constructed a mile-long sea wall with a parade that visitors paid a small toll to walk or ride on.[66] At Southend, it was the railway company who invested in a promenade and sea wall over a mile in length.[67] The sea wall at Cleethorpes was built in 1884 by the Manchester, Sheffield and Lincolnshire Railway Company, an investment presumably prompted by the presence of its railway station on the seafront (*see* Fig 3.27).[68]

As resorts grew in size, their administration became more complex. Where once a parish council might be the responsible form of local government, Improvement Commissioners, then Boards of Health and, when resorts were large enough, Corporations, would be responsible for sea defences. While Blackpool was a small settlement its governance was in the hands of village institutions, but by the mid-19th century, a new form of governance was required.[69] To administer Blackpool an Improvement Act was obtained in 1853 specifying the powers of the Local Board of Health.[70] Among its provisions was a requirement to improve the sea defences and in 1856 the promenade was repaired and extended. Between 1868 and 1870, an ambitious programme of embanked granite sea defences, stretching from Carlton Terrace in the north to South Shore in the south, was carried out (Fig 3.12).

In 1876, the year that the town became a municipal borough, sloping stone defences were created to prevent erosion to the cliffs on which the Claremont Park Estate was built. In 1896, the local authority acquired the estate and replaced the ineffective earlier defences, a programme that was completed in 1899 at a cost of £145,000. The need to convert the power transmission system of the original seafront trams and the doubling of the tracks meant that Blackpool Corporation obtained an Act of Parliament in 1899, allowing the widening of the promenade and the installation of new sea defences.[71] By 1905, new defences stretching almost two miles (3.2km) from South Shore to Talbot Square had been built. The Princess Parade was completed in 1912 to link the new sea defences to those created to protect the Claremont Park Estate and the programme of providing new coastal protection continued during the interwar years to defend the coastline of the borough as its boundaries were extended northwards.[72]

Blackpool had one of the longest and undoubtedly the most challenging seafronts to deal with due to its easily erodible cliffs, but elsewhere around the coast, local government was assuming responsibility for sea defences during the 19th century. The first sea wall at

Fig 3.12
Vestiges of Blackpool's earlier sea defences in the form of a sloping revetment have been preserved on either side of North Pier, though they have now been engulfed in modern stepped defences.
[DP154884]

Cromer was built in 1836–8 by George Edwards of Lowestoft, but within a decade it had been badly damaged by storms. Therefore, the Cromer Protection Commissioners employed John Wright in 1845–6 to construct a sea wall faced in coursed flint cobbles to the west of the original wall. This was extended again in 1899–1900.[73] At Teignmouth in 1869, the Board of Local Government that had succeeded the Commissioners of Improvement acquired the Den from Lord Devon and created a pleasure ground, necessitating an extension of the sea wall to protect it.[74]

Providing sea walls became a pressing task for a larger number of growing seaside towns during the late 19th century. The Seafront Improvement Scheme of 1883–7 in Weston-super-Mare included the erection of gently sloping, stone-faced sea walls behind which two miles (3.2km) of seafront promenade were created. The work cost about £35,000 and required 1 million tons of stone, 85,000 cubic yards (64,987m³) of earth filling, 9,000 yards (8,230m) of metalling, 49,000 yards (44,806m) of asphalting and 4,000 yards (3,658m) of running fencing.[75] In January 1884, the Mayor of Eastbourne laid the keystone of the sea wall and its overall cost was £49,000.[76] In 1889, the Local Board at Filey agreed a plan to construct a concrete-faced wall and by October 1891 Graham Fairbank of Fairbank & Son had been appointed as engineer.[77] Preliminary works began in October 1892, though the first block was not laid until 24 April 1893 and the wall was ceremonially opened on 9 June 1894.[78]

Early sea walls were vertical, as befits their name, but due to their verticality any such structures had to be very thick. They were built using traditional techniques, materials and thinking, with the disadvantage that they were not always durable and they also led to scouring of the beach in front.[79] During the 19th century, there was a realisation that a gently sloping form using a 1:3 or 1:4 incline would still prevent flooding or erosion, but could reduce the reflected wave energy, resulting in less damage to the beach.[80] Early examples of sloping stone sea defences include at Birkenhead in c 1830–5, Exmouth in 1841–2, Hastings in the early 1850s, Teignmouth in the 1870s and Weston-super-Mare during the 1880s.[81] Gently sloping concrete-faced walls were employed at Cleethorpes in the mid-1880s in defence of the seafront railway station, which opened in 1884 (see Fig 3.27).[82]

An 1885 guidebook contained a description of the first stage of sea defences, which was

composed of solid concrete, with a cemented block facing, which presents a smooth and elegant front, alike impervious to the furious clash of the storm-wave and the languid laving of the calm summer tide. This wall rises six feet above the height of the normal spring tides, and encloses a width of the old beach varying from 70ft. to 100ft; which has been filled up and solidified level with the wall, making a broad even surface, along the centre length of which is formed an imposing promenade, carriage drive, and inner walk.[83]

As well as the use of sloping walls and revetments, there was a realisation during the 19th century that wave-reflecting shapes and stepped forms could be employed to cope with the sea's energy.[84] In 1877, Margate borrowed £140,000 for its sea defences, as well as for street and sewage improvements.[85] The existing sea walls were strengthened and Marine Drive was created in 1878–80 at a cost of £40,000, a reclamation programme that created a new stretch of seafront.[86] The design of the new defences was stepped with a concrete core faced in stone and when challenged by a major storm in 1897 it performed much better and suffered less damage than more vertical walls.[87]

From an early date, engineers realised that to counter scouring of the beach they needed to add protection to the base of the wall, the toe (Fig 3.13). To do this they used stone or concrete steps that helped to reduce the energy of the sea hitting the wall above. In areas where there is limited public access, this can be achieved by using rock or concrete armour, a cheap if somewhat unsightly solution that can be hazardous to any beachgoer (Fig 3.14). A more natural alternative is to stabilise the beach in front of the sea wall to protect the toe and to dissipate the energy of the sea.[88] At the top of a sea wall, a crest was gradually added to reduce overtopping and spray, though in some designs holes are left deliberately to reduce the pressure on the structure.

The material of choice for sea walls was concrete, initially used in the cores or in blocks, but during the 20th century sea defences were increasingly made up of large precast units. As early as 1870 Bognor had a concrete sea wall erected by Robert Bushby of Littlehampton at a cost of £8,000 and by the 1890s a mile-long

Fig 3.13 (left)
At Teignmouth in 2017
a toe was being built to
protect the base of the
sea wall, also providing
somewhere for
holidaymakers to sit.
[DP219535]

Fig 3.14 (below)
Rock armour is used in
front of the sea wall at the
end of the beach in Steephill
Cove at Ventnor.
[DP005487]

concrete sea wall had been constructed.[89] The task of defending Cleethorpes, beginning in the 1880s, was continued in the early 20th century as a result of the Cleethorpes Improvement Act 1902, which led to the creation of a new sea wall 2,000ft (610m) in length. It was 18ft (5.5m) high, 7ft (2.13m) thick at the base and built with 15,000 tons (15,240 tonnes) of concrete.[90] Simple monumental concrete walls were built at a number of seaside resorts during the 20th century. One of the most dramatic was at Jaywick Sands, where its motley collection of chalets and bungalows owes its continued existence to a tall sea wall that limits sea views, but will prevent any repeat of the damage caused by the 1953 storm.

Where the challenge is to prevent erosion rather than flooding, revetments may be employed. These sloping structures reduce the erosive power of waves on cliffs and therefore prevent the landward migration of the beach. Constructed now out of concrete or stone, revetments may be watertight, covering the slope completely, or porous, to allow water to filter through after the wave energy has been dissipated. By the late 19th century, the friable cliffs in central Blackpool were protected using sloping stone revetments, and some coastal towns employ a comparable modern, regular concrete form, Basalton, which is reminiscent of the hexagonal basalt columns of the Giant's Causeway (Fig 3.15, see also Fig 3.12).

Rock armour, also known as riprap, consists of large rocks placed at the foot of dunes or cliffs or in front of sea walls to reduce erosion by absorbing wave energy and holding back some beach material. Delivery of the rock can be by sea or road, though the latter is highly disruptive to a busy town.[91] Although it is an effective technique, it is not popular at resorts as it is thought to be unsightly, potentially dangerous if climbed on and it limits the recreational value of a beach. However, it is found at some resorts in areas where the public is less likely to wish to gain access to the sea. For instance, it is used at Nayland Rock near Margate, but away from the main beach, and at West Bay near Bridport, it is used as part of the harbour defences (see Figs 1.8 and 3.14). A scheme to protect the coastline at Scarborough's spa with a rock revetment was postponed in December 2013.[92] These plans had been criticised by local conservation groups who claimed it was not necessary, as well as unsightly.

Occasionally breakwaters are used to solve a resort's coastal defence issues, such as at Herne Bay, though they are more commonly employed at ports to create sheltered waters for shipping. These sloped or vertical structures broadly parallel to the shore can reduce the energy of incoming waves, preventing erosion by creating calmer waters. They can be constructed of concrete, stone or rock armour.

Fig 3.15
The modern defences at the south end of Blackpool, which were officially opened in September 2001, employ another standard concrete form, the Seabee, which is a larger, precast hexagonal unit.
[DP154881]

The example at Herne Bay consists of a combination of a concrete breakwater with rock armour alongside it. In addition, three new timber groynes have been constructed within the breakwater to stabilise the beach.[93]

Soft engineering

The alternative to hard engineering is to seek a soft engineering solution, though the reality is that the two are often used together and where soft engineering alone is employed, this would be limited to the geographical fringes of resorts. Soft engineering is a more sustainable and, in the long term, potentially cheaper approach to coastal defence, working with natural processes to protect the shoreline. The beach acts as a flexible coastal defence by reducing wave impact and preventing inland flooding.[94] Beaches act like a sponge for wave energy and therefore can help to protect harder defences behind, especially the toe, the most vulnerable lower part.[95]

Some shallow, curved bays have beaches that achieve a natural stability without any man-made intervention, but others may need assistance.[96] Beaches have to be managed to ensure that they are sufficiently wide and high to prevent overtopping during high sea levels. Over time, beach material becomes finer due to the action of the sea grinding it and therefore it becomes easier to wash away.[97] Groynes are a form of hard engineering designed to work as part of a soft-engineering strategy. They extend from the beach into the sea to slow the loss of beach materials through longshore drift as well as to encourage the deposition of new sediments.[98] However, an arrangement that is advantageous for one stretch of coastline may cause problems further along due to changes in the flow of sediments. Groynes can be constructed out of wood, stone, metal or concrete depending on the size of the native beach material, and if required a larger headland might also be employed to alter the littoral transport of sediment. The effectiveness of both groynes and artificial headlands can be easily measured by witnessing how much material builds up against them, the groynes at Tankerton near Whitstable now being almost full to their top (Fig 3.16).

Some beaches require replenishment by the addition of new beach-grade sediments, delivered disruptively by land or more usually by dredging up material from the seabed and pumping it onshore.[99] The earliest example of beach nourishment using a dredge, a technique also known as beach replenishment or beach recharging, occurred in 1922 at Coney Island (USA), but it only became a popular approach in Britain from the 1970s onwards.[100] In the 1990s, the largest soft-engineering projects were on the coast between Mablethorpe and Skegness in Lincolnshire and from Happisburgh to Winterton in Norfolk.[101] In the former scheme,

Fig 3.16
This c 1900 photograph of the beach at Tankerton near Whitstable shows fairly new groynes standing proud of the beach, but in subsequent years the deposition of sand and shingle would significantly raise the beach level.
[OP00692]

between 1994 and 1998, 7.6 million m³ of sand was added to the shore, subsequent regular top-ups taking the total to over 12 million m³. In Norfolk, beach nourishment was employed to protect 14km of coastline on which 6,000ha and 1,150 homes are at risk.[102]

Combinations of soft and hard engineering were already being advocated by the beginning of the 20th century.[103] At Bournemouth, the loss of sand from the beach was a significant problem. A new sea wall from Bournemouth Pier to the Meyrick Steps opened in 1907 at a cost of £16,000, and it was extended to Boscombe Pier in 1911 at a further cost of £45,000.[104] In 1919, the Borough Engineer, FP Dolamore, described how the new walls were causing the loss of beach material and soon groynes 'were constructed on a novel plan in reinforced concrete with sections of railway track at their core'.[105] By 1939, 29 groynes had been erected and a further 19 were added in the 1950s to try to stabilise the situation.[106] Nevertheless, Bournemouth's beautiful beach was still losing sand and therefore in 1970 a pilot replenishment scheme was carried out, involving the placement of 84,500m³ of dredged sand at the mean low-water mark. In 1974–5 the beach was recharged by pumping 650,000m³ of dredged sand onshore, but despite this huge undertaking within a decade the beach level was still falling and a further recharge of a million cubic metres took place in 1988–90 (Fig 3.17).[107]

Sand dunes, which can absorb up to 90 per cent of wave energy, are a key part of the story, though today they are usually only evident on the fringes of resorts, where development has not transformed them.[108] Examples include the southern end of Skegness, an area to the south of the pier at St Annes and at Swansea where they still make up part of the seafront. On St Mary's in the Isles of Scilly, the dunes at Porthloo were heightened at a cost of almost a quarter of a million pounds to protect homes, businesses and the island's boatyard.[109] At a number of seaside towns, a place name may reflect the former existence of dunes where now the resort stands. The Denes at Great Yarmouth or the Den at Teignmouth are now topographically flat, but the names suggest the former existence of dunes.[110]

The promenade, road and circulation

From the outset, visitors to seaside resorts have been able to enjoy more or less formal parades or promenades along seafronts created as part of a programme of sea defences. The promenade is a place for walking, but it is also more energetically enjoyed by joggers, runners, rollerbladers and skateboarders. It provides a flat surface that is good for prams and wheelchair users who would struggle on the beach, and on some of the wider promenades it is possible to include a dedicated lane for cyclists.

Promenades are largely free of vehicles, though there is a need for access across them to reach the beach and the sea for vehicles as diverse as donkey transports, beach-cleaning equipment, lifeboat launching vehicles and, of course, other emergency services. Some promenades are sufficiently wide to cater for some small, wheeled vehicles. In addition to lanes for bicycles, there may be a strip in which a land train might have some notional priority. Ivo Dotto invented his road trains (Fig 3.18) in 1962 'to allow people to enjoy old towns and parks in complete freedom'.[111] They require little infrastructure beyond a long, low garage compared with rival narrow-gauge railways, whose tracks create a separate linear zone along fronts. At St Annes, part of the seafront has a miniature railway creating a barrier between the promenade and the beach in places, and the eastern half of the seafront at Brighton has the world's oldest working electric railway, the Volk's Railway, running along it, necessitating the creation of regular crossing places between the promenade and the beach. Another novelty

Fig 3.17
This photograph shows the beach at Deal in the process of being recharged in 2013. Dredged materials were graded onshore and distributed onto the beach to create a sustainable profile.
[© A Brodie]

Fig 3.18
Land trains ply the fronts of many resorts, such as here at Weston-super-Mare. They offer a relaxing way to travel along a seafront, perhaps back to a car parked at one end of the town, and they are sufficiently widespread now to have their own DVLA regulations.
[DP218044]

wheeled user of the seafront is the horse and carriage or, more elegantly, the romantic, fairy-tale landau. At Blackpool, they share the road with cars and buses, but at Great Yarmouth a dedicated lane has been created alongside the revamped seafront road, a measure designed to increase safety and, by narrowing the main road, it is also part of an attempt to discourage other vehicular use along the seafront.

Although holidaymakers consider seafront promenades simply as a place for socialising and enjoying leisure, this space is also important to make coastal towns work, linking different parts of settlements to each other and often serving as the site of the main road through a resort. Alongside the promenade, there is usually a more or less substantial main road once occupied by horses, carts and coaches, but now the domain of cars, buses and lorries, especially if a major harbour or other industrial facility lies at the end of the resort. What is now absent from the seafront today, with the notable exception of Blackpool, is a tram service. The growth of car ownership required the space once used by trams, and buses proved cheaper and more flexible replacements.

Promenades

Prior to significant investment in resorts, the land simply blended into the beach where there were no cliffs and this arrangement can be seen around the coast where no development has taken place. The original relationship between the land and the beach can also be seen in old depictions of seaside resorts, such as the views of Sea Houses in 1785, where Eastbourne developed, showing people walking along the land at the head of the beach.[112] Setterington's view of Scarborough in 1735 shows that some properties opened directly onto the beach, though one stretch of houses has a road between the houses and the timber sea defences (see Figs 4.12 and 6.1). At Sidmouth, there was a gravel walk and carriageway nicknamed

Fig 3.19
Although Margate may have had a short stretch of road on its seafront, it is likely that the beach remained the main means for many people reaching the harbour from the emerging resort to the west. This map of the town appeared in Lewis 1736. [Courtesy of the Society of Antiquaries of London]

the Mall, a strip of smoother land at the head of the beach according to its depiction in *The Long Painting* (see Fig 1.5).[113]

Some early resorts had seafront roads that became popular promenades because of their geography. By the 1730s, bathing at Margate seems to have taken place from the seafront Parade, a short stretch of road running from the landward end of the pier to the bottom of the High Street (Fig 3.19). This was probably built as part of the sea defences before people came to bathe in the sea and was a vital link between the historic town and the harbour. Like Margate, Scarborough's beach (see Fig 6.1) also seems to have been the main way of moving along the front of the town and at Weston-super-Mare in the early 19th century the firm, sandy beach acted as a facility for walks, carriage drives, horse-riding and 'villagers enjoying the exhilarating breeze after the fatigues of the day'.[114]

Crane's view of Weymouth's seafront in 1789 (see Fig 3.10) shows the presence of a road or walkway separated from the defensive revetment by railings.[115] The earliest seafront roads and walkways were practical devices to give access to the sea and to improve circulation along the front of a town. They were also intended to be spaces for promenading, replicating the types of walks that were a central feature of spa towns. The seafront was the logical place to create a promenade as it was near where visitors would be staying and it offered a relatively straight, flat place with views of the sea. However, there were rival walks at some resorts. At Great Yarmouth, the timber jetty was a popular promenade in the 1770s, at Lyme Regis people walked on the Cobb, the breakwater to the harbour, and a similar walk was favoured along the stone pier at Weymouth (see Fig 4.8).[116] The stone pier at Margate included an elevated promenade along its outside face, for which promenaders paid a small fee (see Fig 2.12). At Brighton, although there had been a narrow seafront road or walk by the mid-17th century, if not before, the main promenade was on the Steyne, an open area at 90 degrees to the sea.[117]

At many resorts a seafront promenade and road had to be created once holidaymakers began to arrive. Blackpool had a small seafront parade by the 1780s, which was 5m wide and 200m long. It was described in 1789 as a 'pretty grass-walk on the verge of the sea bank' separated from the road by white rails (see Fig 3.1).[118] However, as Blackpool has been built

PXVI. *p. 123.*

A VIEW of the PIER of MARGATE

In the Parlor window of
St John's Vicarage in

A *King's Watchhouse & Warehouse*
B *Warehouses*
C *K. George's Stairs*
D *Glasshouse & Storehouses*
E *The Mooring Post*
F *Chalk Clifts*
G *Lamp on the Pier Head*
H *Crane*
I *St John Baptist*
K *The Vicarage*

MANWOOD & COPPINGER

Tenet

I. *Ames delt*

on friable cliffs, this prompted the reconstruction and realignment of the seafront road during the 1820s. At Weymouth a road/walkway had been created along the seafront between the publication of the 1774 map and Crane's view of the seafront in 1789 (*see* Figs 2.2 and 3.10). In mid-19th-century photographs, the new, apparently wider road is seen, along with a separate walkway. The two were separated by a line of small stone posts, painted white with chains between them, a measure to prevent pedestrians and road users from straying into each other's domains (*see* Fig 3.7). Remnants of the little white posts survive at the north end of the resort, in front of the Pier Bandstand.

A surprising place to look for the story of the development of the English promenade is at Nice in the south of France. Struck by the poverty that he witnessed during a harsh winter in Nice, Lewis Way created effectively an early public works programme to provide work for unemployed local people. He approached rich English visitors to subscribe towards the construction of the first seafront promenade, *La Promenade des Anglais* or *Lou Camin dei Ingles*, which opened in 1824 and was further extended in 1844.[119]

Seafront promenades were not only created at sea level, but could also be located on clifftops as geography dictated. At Broadstairs, there is a pedestrian-only walkway along the top of the cliffs, with the road through the town located behind the adjacent line of buildings (Fig 3.20). At nearby Folkestone (*see* Fig 3.2), the Leas was created on the clifftop above the seafront and in 1925 a local guidebook immodestly described it as 'one of the finest marine promenades in the world'.[120]

Seafront roads

The space between the sea defences and the first line of buildings is vital for the circulation of a coastal town, often providing the easiest and fastest route through a town. The seafront is also a convenient way of linking a town to its harbour as at Margate and Scarborough. This is as true today in an era of lorries as when the seafront road was home to horses and carts, though in most resorts lorries can be directed away from the most sensitive tourist parts of the town. Dover is not so fortunate, with a busy dual carriageway running along its front to the ferryport.

Seafront roads were also established for pleasure purposes. In 1840, the seafront at Teignmouth was described as being home to 'spacious carriage drives, promenades, and an extensive lawn'.[121] A seafront road could also be a source of income, The Herne Bay Pier Company charging a small toll to walk or ride on its new promenade.[122] At Blackpool, the

Fig 3.20
Broadstairs has a wide beach with a long 1930s bathing station nestling beneath its cliffs. Above there are gardens and a promenade, with the main road lying behind the first line of buildings.
[NMR 29843/028]

Claremont Park estate was created on the clifftops to the north of the town from 1863 onwards. A toll road was established to limit the number of users passing along the seafront so as to preserve the desired air of gentility for its residents and guests.

Both these schemes were undertaken by private companies, but as the 19th century progressed, resorts grew and local government became more interventionist, including undertaking measures to improve transport. This was usually achieved by sorting out the seafront road to create a single, straight road, sometimes by linking a patchwork of short stretches of road created at different dates. At both Margate and Scarborough during the 1870s, new seafront roads were created, providing an easier way to reach their harbours as well as a convenient space for holidaymakers. During the 1930s, Hastings undertook a major reconfiguration of its seafront, including a revision of its roads, the creation of new tourism facilities and underground car parking (Figs 3.21 and 3.22). Seafronts around the coast were increasingly dominated by roads designed for cars rather than pedestrians (Fig 3.23). However, during

the recent reconstruction of the promenade at Blackpool, the section of the road between the North Pier and the Tower has been reconfigured as a shared space with a 20mph speed limit, a measure designed to allow pedestrians easier access across the road.

The seafront's main road has proved highly adaptable to the changes wrought by the motor car and in fact has sometimes had a pioneering role in promoting the car. The Locomotives on Highways Act 1896 abolished the need for motor vehicles to be preceded by a pedestrian and raised the speed limit to a dizzy 12mph.[123] To mark this event, Harry J Lawson (1852–1925), the founder of the British Motor Syndicate, staged an Emancipation Day Run from London to Brighton on 14 November 1896.[124] The choice of Brighton is significant. It was a popular destination for Londoners and it was sufficiently distant to be an impressive feat for the newly liberated automobile. At Blackpool, an expanded seafront road was created at the beginning of the 20th century as part of the rebuilding of the sea defences. The quality of this new surface allowed it to be used to set speed records for automobiles.[125]

Fig 3.21
At Hastings, a single, wide road was created where previously a patchwork of short sections of road had been constructed to accompany each new development along the seafront. This Aerofilms photograph of 1932 also shows the entrance to the Carlisle Parade underground car park. See also Fig 3.23. [EPW039366]

Perhaps surprisingly, sedate Bexhill-on-Sea, which boasted a wide, smooth seafront road, became the site of perhaps the first prototype Grand Prix race held in Britain in 1902.[126]

Many seafront roads created during the 19th century proved, at least initially, capable of handling the new vehicles. Cars were parked on seafront roads parallel to the pavement and larger charabancs and buses were often catered for in empty spaces back from the seafront. At some resorts with wide seafront roads, it was possible to park large numbers of cars, but the rapid growth in car ownership soon meant that new purpose-built facilities would be required. In 1920, there were 591,000 licensed vehicles in Britain, but a decade later this figure had almost quadrupled to 2.25 million. At Bognor Regis, a large open-air car park was established at the east end of the seafront, the site of which is now occupied by a Butlin's holiday centre, and there were similar examples at Blackpool and Southend.[127] A curious variant of an open-air car park was briefly considered at St Ives in 1931. The idea was to construct a concrete parking raft on pillars on the seafront, but instead a group of fishermen's cottages was demolished in 1936 to provide a new car park.[128] The solution to the growing issue of car parking at seaside resorts was to dig down or build up. At Hastings, the major transformation of the seafront during the early 1930s included an underground car park reached from Carlisle Parade, the first such design in Britain (*see* Figs 3.21 and 3.23). Blackpool soon followed Hastings' example and created an underground car park at Little Bispham close to a new tram station, effectively a proto park-and-ride scheme.[129]

Fig 3.22 (above)
The scheme to remodel the seafront at Hastings was masterminded by the Borough Engineer Sidney Little, who also designed the Carlisle Parade underground car park in 1931. Two other underground car parks further to the west were constructed between 1934 and 1936. See also Fig 3.21. [DP139356]

Fig 3.23 (left)
By the 1970s, the road along the central section of the promenade at Blackpool had become a dual carriageway, with access from the town to the beach being via walkways over the road. This 2005 photograph shows the arrangement before a modern shared-space scheme was introduced, resulting in the demolition of the walkways to the beach. [AA053361]

An alternative parking solution was to create a multi-storey car park. In 1906, Caffyn Brothers opened a three-storey garage on Marine Parade at Eastbourne that could accommodate around a hundred cars.[130] At Bournemouth, a multi-storey car park was built in 1932 a short distance from the seafront, while at Blackpool the continuing shortage of car parking spaces and facilities for buses led to the creation in 1936–7 of a combined bus station and car park on Talbot Road near Blackpool North railway station.[131] These car parks were not located on the seafront, but at Margate, Arlington House included a large car park integrated with flats and shops and at Worthing in c 1970 a multi-storey car park was constructed behind the seafront when space became available (Fig 3.24). In addition to large, public car parks many hotels provided facilities for use by their guests, the earliest examples including one of 1902 at Worthing and the Grade II, Savoy Hotel Garage of 1915 at Blackpool.[132]

Public transport on the seafront

Apart from roads, the largest transport presence on the seafront might be a railway line, sometimes including a seafront railway station. The location of a railway line in a seaside resort was the result of a combination of the geographical form of the coast, the size of the town at the date when the railway arrived and whether the line terminated at the town or continued along the coast. A railway station would normally lie near the edge of the settlement as it existed when the railway arrived. However, at coastal towns, the need to avoid excessive gradients might mean that a station was further from the town centre, and therefore further from the seafront, than expected. Where lines run closer to the coast they might face problems passing through cliffs and running along the edge of the sea (Fig 3.25).[133]

At resorts such as at Dawlish and Colwyn Bay, the town's main railway station was near the seafront, as the railway lines ran along the coast. In 1846, the South-Eastern Railway established a branch line to Margate and the station opened on 1 December 1846.[134] A second through route was opened on 6 October 1863 by the London Chatham and Dover Railway.[135] Both lines took passengers to seafront stations, the former closing in July 1926, leading to the latter station being rebuilt in the same year by Edwin Maxwell Fry. In 1862, the station opened at Hunstanton on a line running parallel to the coast, but terminating in the town, and a similar arrangement was created at Minehead in 1874 (Fig 3.26).[136] At Cleethorpes more than 30,000 people travelled by train to the newly opened

Fig 3.24
Behind the seafront at Worthing there is a substantial multi-storey car park on Grafton Street that serves tourists and people shopping in the town centre.
[DP139248]

Fig 3.25
The Great Western line on the south coast of Devon passes through cliffs, and at Dawlish the sea is so close that trains can be drenched by large waves in stormy weather. [DP217928]

Fig 3.26
The railway line at Hunstanton ended at a large station beside the pier. This Aerofilms photograph of 1920 illustrates the impact that the presence of such a large piece of infrastructure had on the layout of the resort. [EPW001854]

station parallel to the coast on 3 August 1863, a further 4,000 arriving on horse-drawn vehicles (Fig 3.27).[137] Since 1876 the railway line has arrived at Newquay at 90 degrees to the coast-line and terminates at a clifftop station in front of the Great Western Hotel and above the aptly named Great Western Beach.[138] At some resorts, such as Ramsgate (open from 1863–1926) and Cromer (opened 1887), there were separate stations on or near the seafront supplementing the main station serving the town, in the latter case the secondary station now being the only one still in operation (*see* Figs 7.3 and 7.20).[139]

The seafront is also occasionally the location for smaller-gauge railways, sometimes practical, but often to serve as a novelty. On 4 August 1883, Magnus Volk's Electric Railway opened on the seafront in Brighton, the first electric railway providing a regular service in Britain and the oldest electrically driven service still operating in the world (Fig 3.28).[140] Volk wanted to extend his railway to Rottingdean. To achieve this, he needed cars that could go through water at high tide and so he invented the 'Pioneer' or the 'daddy-long-legs', a cross between 'an open-top tramcar, a pleasure yacht and a seaside pier'.[141] It weighed 40 tons and had an elliptical platform deck with a large saloon standing on four, tall, steel legs that each ended in a small truck with four large wheels

and scrapers to sweep seaweed aside. This service was officially opened on 28 November 1896, but it had closed by 1901.[142] Although Volk's Railway is now a novelty, it originally may have been seen as a practical service, but other narrow-gauge seafront railways have more obviously been designed for amusement, such as at Cleethorpes, Hastings and St Annes.

Seafronts have sometimes also been the location for tramways. At Blackpool, an initial two-mile-long (3km-long) tram service running on a single track with a number of passing places was in use by September 1885 (Fig 3.29).[143] Designed by the Halifax engineer Michael Holroyd Smith, it drew its power from a conductor rail in a conduit between the rails. However, sea water caused the electrical supply to be earthed and sand collected in the conduit. In 1897, an extension of the tram system to Lytham took place using Britain's first, short-lived, gas-powered trams and a new line with overhead wires opened in 1898 between central Blackpool and Fleetwood. The switchover of power transmission systems in the original line, which took place as part of the creation of a new promenade and sea defences between 1899 and 1905, was accompanied by the doubling of the tracks. During the 1930s further investment in the system took place, including two seafront tram stations, fragmentary testimony

Fig 3.27
Cleethorpes' seafront station was dramatically enlarged in 1884 as part of the scheme paid for by the Manchester, Sheffield and Lincolnshire Railway Company to improve the town's sea defences and safeguard its investment. This photograph was taken soon after this work took place.
[AA97/05736]

Fig 3.28 (left)
Volk's Railway has been taking passengers along Brighton's seafront since 1883 and remains a popular tourist attraction, as well as a practical means to travel along the eastern part of the seafront. [DP153079]

Fig 3.29 (below)
This late 19th-century photograph from Anon 1926 shows the Blackpool seafront with single tram tracks, as well as one of the tall electric lights installed in 1879. It also shows one of the gardens of the seafront houses already hosting amusements, the roots of Blackpool's celebrated Golden Mile. [Anon 1926 (1)]

Fig 3.30 (above)
Bispham Station, completed
in 1932, was the larger
and more conservative of
the two interwar tram
stations at Blackpool.
The more modernist Little
Bispham Station illustrated
here, further to the north,
was completed in 1935.
[DP157215]

to a comprehensive, but largely unrealised, scheme to modernise the town's transport system (Fig 3.30). By the early 21st century, the tram system, like the town's sea defences, needed investment. Therefore, a four-year programme was launched as part of the prom-enade renewal to upgrade the track, provide new stops and build a new tram depot at Starr Gate

at the southern end of the route. The new service was launched in 2012. Blackpool is now the only seaside resort operating trams, but resorts such as Hastings, Margate and Cleethorpes all once had services running along the seafront (Fig 3.31).

Where a resort has developed in front of cliffs and on clifftops, there is a need for services to connect the two parts of the town. When visitors first arrived at seaside resorts, they made use of existing paths or stairs between the beach and clifftop developments. From the mid-1820s onwards, holidaymakers arriving at Lynmouth on paddle steamers faced a very steep hill to walk up to Lynton. Therefore, ponies and donkeys could be hired at 6d a time, as well as horse-drawn carriages.[144]

Tall cliffs, such as those behind the spa at Scarborough, were a significant reason for slow development in this part of the resort. However, technology in the form of the cliff lift, and the cliff, or funicular, railway, was coming to the aid of holidaymakers who had to trudge up cliffs back to their lodgings and hotels. In 1869, a hoist is mentioned at Saltburn 'for raising and lowering people thus avoiding the toilsome ascent by road' and in the following decades a

Fig 3.31 (right)
The Isle of Thanet Electric
Tramways and Lighting
Company operated a
tramway service between
Margate and Ramsgate
from 1901 to 1937. This
photograph shows the
newly opened tram service
on the incline down to
Ramsgate harbour.
[OP00654]

Fig 3.32
The first, rather flimsy-
looking lift at Shanklin
was built in 1892 but was
demolished in 1957 and
replaced by a new one
that still operates today.
[BB82/13476B]

few resorts installed lifts (Fig 3.32).[145] Ramsgate has two cliff lifts that opened in 1912 and c 1926 and Margate has a cliff lift dating from 1934.[146] At Whitby in 1931, a vertical lift shaft was drilled down through the western cliffs to a horizontal pedestrian tunnel leading out onto the beach and a lift also links the seafront and the cliffs at Marsden Grotto at South Shields and at North Shore at Blackpool (Fig 3.33).[147] Cliff lifts were fairly unusual, but another common feature of everyday life was only used once on a seafront. In 1901, Southend-on-Sea opted for a moving walkway designed by the American engineer Jesse W Reno, a forerunner of the modern escalator.[148] The escalator did not survive long and was replaced by a cliff railway, the most common means of travelling between a seafront and a clifftop.

By 1876, the first cliff railway, the South Cliff Railway, had opened at Scarborough as a result of an initiative by Mr Hunt of the Prince of Wales Hotel for his guests.[149] When the weight of the top carriage of the pair of linked,

Fig 3.33
The Cabin Lift at Blackpool of 1930 was an elegant solution to the problem of linking the cliffs of the North Shore to the sea and the new model boating lake. The lift tower employed classical detailing in faience applied to the stark brick structure, with a copper-clad, pyramidal roof topped with a flagpole. [AA053285]

Fig 3.34 (opposite)
The West Cliff Railway
at Bournemouth, like
Volk's Railway at Brighton,
is both a practical means of
travel and an amusement
for holidaymakers.
[DP001300]

counter-balanced carriages running on parallel tracks was increased by pumping water into a tank beneath the upper carriage, it descended, pulling up the lower carriage on the adjacent track, which had an empty tank. This was the favoured method until the early 20th century, with lifts that ran on this principle still existing at Saltburn (1884), Folkestone (1885, doubled to four cars in 1890), Lynton to Lynmouth (1890) and two at Hastings (1891 and 1903).

By the early 20th century, the water system was being superseded by the use of a counter-weight and electric motors, eliminating the need for a second, counter-balancing carriage. A precursor of this technology was employed by the Central Cliff Railway at Scarborough. It opened on 1 August 1881 and used steam-powered winding gear to raise the cars.[150]

The number of cliff lifts and cliff railways at a resort depended on the height of the cliffs and the length of the seafront; therefore Scarborough had five at one time and Bournemouth three. Bournemouth East Cliff Railway, the oldest of its three funicular railways, opened in April 1908 and is the oldest surviving cliff railway originally powered by electricity. Constructed for Bournemouth Corporation by Waygood and Company Limited, its two passenger cars, running on two parallel tracks, had a 25hp winding motor powered by mains electricity. The second cliff railway at West Cliff opened later in 1908 and originally used the same kind of motor (Fig 3.34), while the third cliff railway at Fisherman's Walk opened in 1935.[151] At Margate in *c* 1912, near the later lido, the country's shortest cliff railway, only 69ft (21m) in height, was powered by a 480v DC 15hp electric winding motor, the 15-seater passenger car being counterbalanced by an iron weight moving up and down a vertical shaft.[152]

Conclusion

Seaside resorts developed around the English coastline, initially at existing ports, but later where a suitable beach provided access to the sea. As these settlements grew, increased investment warranted protection from the power of the sea. Therefore, the natural profile of the coastline was soon replaced by man-made defences designed to protect properties from flooding and prevent coastal erosion. Initially with fairly modest wooden or stone structures, by the 21st century many resorts enjoy the protection of monumental concrete sea defences that will protect the towns from rising sea levels and increased storminess. Behind these defences, a new space was created that offered a location for major transport links through a resort and between clifftop residences and the beach via lifts and cliff railways.

In the next chapter, the role of the engineered seafront in the practical life of seaside towns will be examined. The seafront became the location for much of the vital infrastructure of rapidly growing seaside resorts. Much of this is now unseen, but nevertheless dealing with sewage, water supply and electricity has been a significant preoccupation in the construction of seafronts and their adaptation over the years.

The seafront is also the obvious space in which industrial infrastructure has developed to exploit the sea, though evidence of this has become increasingly scarce as holidaymaking came to dominate the economy. Due to its position in the front line with the sea, the seafront has also been in the front line against Britain's enemies, and therefore retains traces arising from the threats posed by Henry VIII's continental enemies through to the menace of Nazism.

4

The working life of the seafront

In Chapter 3 the story of the seafront as a substantial engineering project was outlined. Unadorned and unadapted, it would offer a harsh and impractical environment, but many specific engineering features were added to make the space work for the various users of the seafront. This chapter will focus on how the seafront has developed to meet the needs of the residents of seaside resorts and the people who work the sea.

Although the seafront is considered primarily as a place for visitors, it must also make a substantial contribution to the function of a successful coastal town. As the 19th century progressed, towns had to provide their residents with a growing number of services. The size of local government therefore increased as populations rose, but it also grew as the utilities and facilities of a town became more numerous and complicated.

Beginning with gas for street lighting, and subsequently home lighting, from the mid-19th century onwards local government began to supply water and electricity, as well as having to deal with the more intractable issue of waste disposal.

The seafront is also the key location for working the sea, some resorts still having beach-launched fleets, while many others have harbours located on, or near, the seafront. To safeguard people working at sea, a complex infrastructure of maritime safety has evolved, including facilities for lifeboats, coastguards and lighthouses, and day marks and time balls to aid navigation at sea.

For the past 70 years the seafront has been a more or less peaceful place of leisure and work, the once-legendary battles of mods and rockers excepted, but it was in the front line of Britain's defences as an obvious place to land enemy forces. Therefore, there may be prominent remains at some resorts of military defences that can date back to the 16th century.

Servicing the seaside resort

The seafront plays an important role in the provision of services and amenities for a resort. Gas street lighting was first installed in towns during the early 19th century, so that by 1821 no town with a population greater than 50,000 was without gas lighting and by 1850, many towns had their own gas works for domestic and industrial users. In old photographs, gas lights are present along seafronts, though it is clear that they were intended to provide minimal illumination for safety purposes, rather than to allow much activity to take place.

With its trams, illuminations and ample street lighting, Blackpool has a greater demand for electricity than any other seaside resort. In September 1879, nine Siemens lamps each producing 6,000 candlepower were placed on each 60ft-high (18.3m) lamp post (18.3m) along the central section of Blackpool's seafront (Fig 4.1 and see Fig 3.29).[1] These tall, plain lamp posts are prominent features in early photographs of the seafront of the resort, alongside the electric trams that were installed in 1885. The trams drew their power from a central conductor rail set within a conduit in the ground between the rails, but the limitations of this system led to its replacement with the more standard overhead pantograph system.

Electricity would also shape another important development at Blackpool. A programme of illuminations, featuring an illuminated tram, was staged to mark the opening of the Princess Parade and the visit of Princess Louise in 1912. A similar display was staged during the following year, but the outbreak of World War I led to the illuminations being suspended until 1925.[2] The illuminations have been a key feature of Blackpool's seafront ever since, apart from during World War II, and today consist of more than 400,000 lamps of various types and

Fig 4.1
This c 1900 photograph
shows the tall electric lights
and the lower gas lamps
lining the promenade.
The Tower, which had
opened in 1894, was
another innovative feature
of the town's seafront.
[CC79/00487]

styles, as well as animated and illuminated tableaux (Fig 4.2 and *see* Figs 10.15(a)–(c)). The example of Blackpool has been followed on a smaller scale at a number of resorts where decorative light displays are switched on for part or all of the year.

Blackpool pioneered the provision of electric arc lighting in 1879 and the electric tram in 1885, though in both cases these premature forms of technology soon had to be replaced. Incandescent lamps replaced arc lights and in 1882, the earliest legislation was passed to deal with the licensing of electric lighting.[3] In the same year, the Eastbourne Electric Light Company was formed and, by the end of that year, it had installed 16 arc lamps along the seafront.

Another power-hungry seafront was at Brighton, where Volk's Railway was powered by its third rail. Its seafront has more than 50 elaborate cast-iron street lamps dating from 1893 and these proudly incorporate the town's coat of arms (Fig 4.3).[4] Such lavish ornamentation was affordable because the cast-iron lamps were mass-produced; on the clifftop Leas at Folkestone there are similarly elaborate lamp standards with the borough's coat of

Fig 4.2
Running from the
beginning of September
until early November, the
illuminations are a creative
way of extending the
tourism season in
Blackpool. They attract
an estimated three million
visitors each year at a
time when trade would
otherwise be decreasing.
[DP129901]

Fig 4.3 (above)
This is one of the highly ornate street lights on the seafront at Brighton, part of the late 19th-century transformation funded by the local authority. As well as lighting, the scheme included railings, bandstands and toilet blocks.
[DP217908]

Fig 4.4 (right)
Blackpool's South Promenade has simple, rather elegant part-circular lamps while around the Festival Headland in front of the Tower there is a row of modern curved lamp posts, each with three spotlights.
[DP154764]

arms moulded into the base. At Southport, in the seafront gardens, beside a municipal lamp post, there is a small, cast-iron box labelled as belonging to the Southport Corporation Electricity Department, presumably for maintenance or monitoring the electricity.

Since the late 19th century, street lighting has been recognised as a necessity, but it was also seen as a way of decorating the seafront. Today's street lighting combines these considerations with modern concerns about energy efficiency and the prevention of light pollution. After a period when the standard streetlight seemed to proliferate along England's seafront, today there has been a return to the use of bespoke designs (Fig 4.4). Brighton has supplemented its more than 50 Victorian lamp posts with short modern lights on Madeira Drive that have been likened to 'Star Wars Battle Droids' (*see* Fig 3.28). At Hastings, the lamp standards themselves have become lit, a feature that allowed them to display the colours of the French flag following the terrorist attacks in Paris in November 2015.[5] At Southend, light has become a fundamental part of the streetscape of the seafront, being incorporated into decorative fountains. There are also 20m-tall towers with LEDs running up them, allowing rainbow patterns and animations to be created. Lasers have been established at Weymouth, but at some resorts the modern preference has been for seafront lights that echo the past, such as at Worthing, where reproduction twin lights have been erected and at Lyme Regis where they refer to the town's past (Fig 4.5).

The most significant utilities located on the seafront concern water supply and the disposal of waste, which became acute problems with the rapid growth of towns and cities during the 19th century. Outbreaks of cholera were eventually attributed to infected water supplies and a heatwave caused London to endure the 'Great Stink' during the summer of 1858. Seaside resorts also suffered from outbreaks of the disease. During the late summer of 1849, Southport reported 26 cholera deaths, Hastings had 65 and Margate recorded 124. Due to health fears, the small resort of Ilfracombe believed that it had lost between £8,000 and £10,000 as a result of the same outbreak.[6] It is ironic that seaside resorts tried to be associated in the public mind with good health, yet many suffered from very poor hygiene standards. This was due to these towns depositing waste in cess pools that seeped

into water supplies or pumping sewage into the sea via outfalls that proved too short, leading to waste being washed back onto the beach.[7] Westward Ho! initially disposed of its sewage on land; when sewers were installed in 1870, untreated sewage was allowed to flow onto an adjacent seafront common, which was turned into a 'pestilential drain'.[8]

The lure of the sea for cost-conscious Victorian local authorities seeking to dispose of sewage may have been welcomed by some ratepayers, but it would not have been appreciated on some days by people using the beaches. As seaside resorts became larger and busier, the problem became more acute and required significant investment from resorts that were still relatively small in size and reluctant to invest in a piece of infrastructure that brought no obvious financial return. The problem was not necessarily that a resort was reluctant to invest; its hoteliers, publicans and shopkeepers would have wanted to improve the salubrity to attract business, but farmers and some local residents with no vested interest in the holiday industry were more resistant to

investment.[9] At Southport, the deficiency of its outfall was thought to be damaging the town's reputation for good health, resulting in an improvised solution consisting of a local outfall into the 'New Hollow' lake. Although the town was willing to invest up to £750,000 by the 1870s in a variety of tourist-related projects, its modest new drainage and sewage system was still contaminating the soil and the town suffered from unnaturally high levels of childhood illness and death.[10] In 1878, a new sewage outfall was proposed at Bournemouth, provoking a furious reaction from a minority who were opposed to what they described as an 'unnecessary and wasteful addition' to local debts.[11]

The Local Government Act of 1858 strengthened and extended the powers of local boards and encouraged many seaside resorts to manage their own affairs, and particularly to deal with the issue of sewage. By the mid-19th century, Blackpool was growing from being a village into a small town and its new local government was faced with meeting the water and sewage needs of the resort's growing population and increasing visitor numbers.

Fig 4.5
At Lyme Regis, modernity and the Victorian past are combined in a design where the brackets are shaped like ammonites, in tribute to the resort's connection with fossils.
[DP083645]

Water began to be provided in July 1864 by the Fylde Waterworks Company and within three years, two-thirds of the town's houses were being supplied by this business. Dealing with sewage proved to be a more intractable problem. In 1850, a government inspector found sewers and drains trickling across the beach and draining into the Spen Dyke, which was the Black Pool that gave the town its name. By 1857, an old watercourse was being used to take the waste southwards where a wood-lined channel took the effluent out to beyond the low-water mark, though it was still prone to being washed back onto the beach. This unsatisfactory arrangement continued to discharge untreated effluent into the sea until the early 20th century, rudimentary screening apparatus not being introduced until 1909. The problems even continued into the interwar years, the sea being described in 1935 as a 'cesspool'. However, in that year measures were put in place to improve the situation, the site of the new, main central beach outfall at the heart of the resort being disguised by Blackpool's famous windmill.[12]

In Devon, local boards were established at Teignmouth in 1859, Dawlish in 1860, at Sidmouth and Paignton in 1863, at Linton and Lynmouth in 1866, and at Westward Ho! in 1867. They soon began to lay new sewers, appointed inspectors of nuisances to eliminate health dangers, and employed scavengers to collect refuse.[13] Torquay, once celebrated for its clear air and pure water, had three sewers spewing their contents across the beach, obliging bathers to dip in diluted sewage, and at low tide

the stench was said to be overpowering. To deal with this issue, the local board agreed in 1875 to spend £65,000 on a new arrangement that would take the waste further out to sea.[14]

The most widely used and cheapest solution to the sewage issue was to construct an outfall, but if it was not long enough, it superficially improved matters without solving the underlying issue. In 1864, the local board at Paignton constructed a sewer outfall to dispose of the resort's sewage, but this emptied onto a coastal park where Mr W R Fletcher, a Birmingham businessman, had hoped to build villa residences. In 1867, he persuaded the board that his development would enhance the rateable value of the resort, and therefore a new sewer outfall was constructed to carry Paignton's waste out into the sea.[15]

Pumping untreated sewage into the sea via outfalls remained a common practice into the 20th century, but there were already many initiatives taking place to improve the waste management of resorts and to treat the sewage before disposing of it at sea. In 1865, work began at Brighton to replace its eight foreshore outfalls by laying 44 miles (71km) of sewer ranging from drainpipes 12in (30cm) in diameter to circular tunnels 8ft-high (2.4m). An intercepting sewer was completed in 1874 to carry waste to discharge into the sea at Portobello near Newhaven, beyond the borough's boundary.[16] At Scarborough, the sewage outfall in the harbour threatened to contaminate the adjacent bays and as early as 1881 Scarborough Council also began to consider how to connect the town's two bays. These two, apparently separate, projects would come together with the laying of the foundation stone of Marine Drive around the Castle Headland in June 1897.[17] Included in the scheme was provision for dealing with Scarborough's sanitation problems and similarly, as part of the recent Marine Drive programme, a modern wastewater pumping station has been erected along with a shelter (Fig 4.6).

A problem that coastal towns face is that lying at sea level they had, like Scarborough, to construct pumping stations as gravity provided insufficient power to discharge the sewage. To solve the sewage problems of Portsmouth and Southsea, a pumping station was constructed at Eastney, a short distance inland from the seafront, but at some distance from the town as it then existed. It opened in 1868 and the James Watt & Co steam engines that were installed in 1887 still run today as museum exhibits.[18]

Fig 4.6
At Scarborough, a new water treatment plant has been created as part of the new sea defences between the harbour and South Bay. This project echoes the scheme a century earlier that linked the town's two bays.
[DP006231]

It is surprising how long it took to sort out sewage issues at many seaside resorts. In 1970, sewage from about six million people was being discharged into the sea or estuaries.[19] However, in 1957, only 15 out of 97 seaside towns had taken steps to supplement outfalls with treatment works and even nine years later only 22 out of 148 local authorities discharging into the sea had done so.[20] In 1955, Bournemouth began to discontinue using sea outfalls altogether, instead building a new water purification plant and a sewage treatment works.[21] At Brighton during the 1990s, a major engineering programme drove tunnels beneath the beach and the promenade to intercept wastewater and carry it to treatment plants before discharging the cleaned waste into the sea.[22] Despite this type of initiative, in 1994 more than 80 per cent of larger coastal towns still dumped some untreated sewage into the sea, a total of around 220 million gallons of effluent being discharged daily.[23]

As well as dealing with waste, it was important for seaside resorts to be able to proclaim the purity of their drinking water. At Westward Ho! short-sightedness had endangered its water supplies, though most resorts relied on water drawn from sources further inland. Desalination, which inevitably requires the presence of some infrastructure on the coast, is rare in Britain. However, the Isles of Scilly rely on this method for their drinking water, an inland plant treating the salt water that is pumped from the sea using small, underground pumps beside the coastal path.

Today, some seafronts boast significant water treatment plants (Fig 4.7). A substantial pumping station was erected a few years ago to the north of the harbour at Folkestone, its seafront location prompting its architect to incorporate a shelter into its design. Local wastewater from the Blackpool South area is pumped to a facility on the seafront at Manchester Square, from where it is pumped through a 14km-long tunnel to Fleetwood Wastewater Treatment Works.[24] All that is obvious to the public now above the surface is a small brick building resembling a large garage set within an embankment with vertical ventilators resembling lorry exhaust pipes.

Working the sea

Harbours and shipping

Harbours may be considered as natural or man-made; in fact 'natural' anchorages have usually been enhanced through man-made intervention for centuries. This term might be applied to coastal harbours such as St Ives, Newquay or Scarborough where the geography of the coastline provided a natural bay that could be adapted, but there are also some seaside resorts, such as Great Yarmouth, Teignmouth

Fig 4.7
On the seafront at Ventnor, a water pumping station has been constructed as part of new sea defences. On top, a structure reminiscent of a bandstand echoes a key feature of holidays of the past.
[DP005456]

and Weymouth where the harbours are located a short distance up a river, and consequently are much less visible to holidaymakers. These natural harbours are in contrast to towns such as Lyme Regis and Margate where there is no natural bay and therefore the harbours are entirely man-made through the construction of the former's famous Cobb (Fig 4.8) and Margate's stone pier of 1810–15 (see Fig 2.12).

Long before becoming a focus for leisure, coastal towns depended on their commercial connection to the sea. Their economies relied on exploiting the sea to import goods and export raw materials and produce. In 1586, William Camden described the people of the Isle of Thanet as 'excessively industrious, getting their living like amphibious animals both by sea and land'. Depending on the time of year 'they make nets, catch codd, herrings and mackerel, &c. make trading voyages, manure their land, plough, sow, harrow, reap, and store their corn, expert in both professions'.[25] The harbours at Bridlington and Scarborough, now celebrated for their fishing vessels and tourist boats, were key stops in the trade moving coal from the north east to London.[26] In 1734, *A Journey to Scarborough* described how some visitors to

the spa from London travelled on the colliers sailing along the east coast, and Margate's early popularity was due to its convenient links by cargo ship from London.[27]

Although sea bathing and holidaymaking would today seem to be in conflict with commercial activities taking place in a modern harbour, during the 18th century they were often closely associated. At Margate, sea bathing took place beside the harbour, where bathing machines were entered from stairs descending from the rear of the bathing rooms on the High Street. Thomas Barber's first bathhouse of 1736 and Mitchener's New Inn, the principal place of entertainment before Cecil Square was built, seem to have been located down on the seafront parade beside the harbour (see Fig 3.19). Early sea bathing at Weymouth took place on the beach, but the earliest baths were located on the quayside and the floating bathhouse used by the Royal family at the end of the 18th century was moored beside the stone pier at the harbour mouth.[28]

The harbour remains an important part of the character and economy of many modern seaside resorts. They vary in shape and size depending on the geography of the coastline,

Fig 4.8
This Aerofilms photograph of 1925 shows the Cobb at Lyme Regis, an arrangement that has its origins in the Middle Ages. Complete rebuilding took place between 1783 and 1829, especially after the great gale of 1824 that also damaged Sidmouth and Weymouth.
[EPW013476]

Fig 4.9
At Brighton, a huge modern marina is the centrepiece for a large commercial development also containing shops, entertainment venues, apartments and places to eat and drink.
[NMR 33051/018]

the industries using them, the commodities traded and the dates of their development. Declining fisheries have contributed to a transition towards the leisure market, a process that has been under way since the mid-18th century, when the failing herring fishery in the North Sea caused such a shift at Margate.[29] Although harbours such as Bridlington and Scarborough are still the home ports of small fishing boats, the largest trawlers now operate from a few larger, purely commercial harbours.[30] At Weymouth, the harbour still accommodates a busy fishing fleet, while a large marina has been established in the backwater on the inland side of the Town Bridge and a new one created along the coast from the centre of Brighton (Fig 4.9).

A key function of some harbours is as a transportation hub, Dover being the largest. In 1794, Weymouth became the departure point for a packet service to Guernsey and Jersey, and in 1827, a steam packet was introduced.[31] At Yarmouth on the Isle of Wight, the ferry terminal is located next to the seafront Tudor castle looked after by English Heritage.[32] Elsewhere in the Solent, the facilities for a hovercraft link between the mainland and the Isle of Wight are located on the seafronts of Southsea and Ryde. A route across the Solent began operating from Stokes Bay to Ryde on 24 July 1965, the first in the world, but soon the mainland departure point became centred on the seafront at Southsea (Fig 4.10).[33]

It is also possible to have a port without a harbour; the most famous instance is perhaps Brighton where the town's economy was dependent on its beach-launched fleet of fishing and cargo vessels, an activity that continued even after the first aristocratic sea bathers arrived.[34] A late 18th-century view of Dr John Awsiter's seafront bathhouse includes a series of small fishing boats and capstans occupying half of the engraving, and Victorian photographs often romantically provide glimpses of the hard life of working fishermen (*see* Fig 6.13).[35] Like Brighton, Hastings once had an estuarine harbour that had been abandoned for some time by the 18th century.[36]

Fig 4.10
Once seen as the transport of the future, the route from Southsea to Ryde is now the sole hovercraft route operating in England, the monumental vehicle that once crossed the Channel having long since gone into retirement.
[DP196971]

A number of other smaller seaside resorts on England's south coast also have a few working vessels operating from their beaches, such as Deal, Greatstone-on-Sea, Bognor Regis and Budleigh Salterton (Fig 4.11). There may still be vestiges of the industry where fishing fleets once operated from beaches, such as the three 19th-century capstans at Worthing that were used to draw boats up on to the shore. On the beach at Eastbourne there is still a motorised capstan and a wheeled gangplank, a traditional way to gain access to a boat for a short pleasure trip.

Active harbours are now seen as tourist attractions, part of Britain's rich industrial heritage. Painters, photographers and jigsaw makers have long been smitten with the colours, the textures and the light of ports such as St Ives and Newlyn in Cornwall, while harbours such as Padstow, Scarborough, Whitby and Whitstable are interesting places to amble around and buy seafood. They were also technological and historical curiosities, unfamiliar territories for inquisitive tourists. Dr Richard Pococke (1704–65) visited the dockyards at Plymouth and Portsmouth, as well as the harbour at Ramsgate while it was being constructed in 1754.[37] In the diary of his Kent holiday in 1829, Daniel Benham described his visit to the steam engine that opened Ramsgate's harbour sluices.[38] West Bay developed around Bridport Harbour, which is used by working vessels and leisure boats.

Here the harbour is at the heart of resort, with entertainments, terraces of houses and flats around it, including a block of 10 terrace houses built in 1884–5 by the architect E S Prior.[39]

Shipbuilding and maintenance were key functions at many coastal towns. Scarborough was a major shipbuilding and ship-owning port. It was one of only seven ports with more than a hundred ships, and in 1702, 606 men were recorded as working on ships registered there.[40] In 1730, there were 20 ships weighing over 200 tons and about 70 were between 60 and 100 tons.[41] Most of Scarborough's ships had been built in its own shipyards, which stretched from the Old Pier to King Richard III's house. These are shown at work in John Setterington's view of the town in 1735, the same engraving that illustrates sea bathing for the first time (Fig 4.12). On beaches as different as Hastings and Hugh Town in the Isles of Scilly boat maintenance is a regular necessity. However, as boats have become larger and more complex, specialist shipbuilding facilities have taken over seafront space or occupy new areas at the peripheries of coastal towns.

Shipwrecks have always been an unfortunate consequence of Britain's island geography, and, occasionally, they take place at seaside resorts. The wreck of *Amsterdam* is a notable feature on the beach at Bulverhythe, near Hastings, the tops of its ribs being exposed in the sand at low tide, coincidently near the remains of

Fig 4.11
This c 1900 photograph by W & Co, perhaps intended to be used as a postcard, shows working boats drawn up on the seashore at Deal, while holidaymakers stroll past and sit on the beach. [OP00540]

a prehistoric forest (Fig 4.13).[42] *Earl of Abergavenny* was also an East Indiaman, which had been launched in 1796. It was wrecked in Weymouth Bay in 1805, resulting in the loss of 263 lives out of the 402 people on board, including its captain John Wordsworth, brother of William Wordsworth.[43] This vessel enjoyed a brief moment as a popular tourist attraction; Abigail Gawthern recorded in her diary that

during her holiday in Weymouth in June 1805 her husband Frank took a boat trip to the wreck site.[44] Visitors to Scarborough during the 1860s were treated to two shipwrecks on the beach. On 2 November 1861, the schooner *Coupland* struck the shore in front of the south end of the Spa Promenade and on 26 October 1869 *Mary* was wrecked on the beach, attracting crowds of people to watch its plight.[45] At Blackpool on

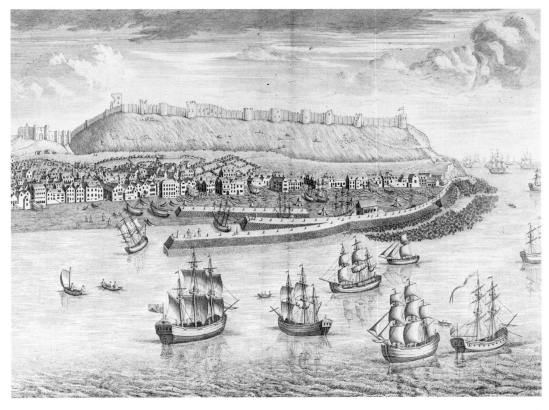

Fig 4.12
The right-hand half of John Setterington's 1735 view of Scarborough shows the busy harbour and the shipyards at work on the seashore. This print is more widely known for its depiction of the spa and sea bathing to the left. See also Fig 6.1.
[CC80/00145]

Fig 4.13
Amsterdam ran ashore on Bulverhythe beach at St Leonards in a severe gale on Sunday 26 January 1749. It is reputedly the most intact East Indiaman known in the world.
[DP140008]

9 October 1892, the aptly named Norwegian ship *Sirene* ran aground on the beach, causing a small amount of damage to the North Pier.[46] Five years later, HMS *Foudroyant* met a similar fate, also on the beach beside Blackpool's North Pier, a sad ending for a ship that had once served as Nelson's flagship.[47] Not all stranded ships remained so; *Manaav Star* is one such success story, (Fig 4.14).

Industry and the seafront

Fish and seaside holidays are inextricably linked, not only geographically, but also gastronomically. The origins of fish and chips can be traced back to two separate traditions: fried fish businesses that appeared in London as early as the 1830s, and the chipped potato that became popular in Lancashire during the mid-19th century. By the 1870s, the fortuitous geographical coincidence of fine fish from the Irish Sea and plentiful potatoes from the Fylde soon combined to create Blackpool's celebrated fish and chips.[48] As well as takeaways and conventional fish and chip restaurants, there are now many celebrated fish restaurants around the British coast and Padstow has become famed for its connection with the chef Rick Stein. At Padstow, Scarborough, Whitby and Weymouth fishing fleets still operate from their harbours (*see* Fig 2.4). On the south coast, fishing fleets once operated from many beaches, the largest probably being at Brighton, though today only vestiges of this heritage survive. The largest beach-launched fleet still operating today is at Hastings (Fig 4.15). Old maps and photographs show that there were fish markets on the seafront at Hastings and at Brighton, and the last vestige of this function can be seen in the stalls selling freshly caught fish at Hastings.[49] Fishing is now predominantly an industrial rather than an artisanal function at most ports, for instance the Birds Eye processing plant on the seafront at Lowestoft to the north of the harbour.

The collection of seafood takes place on some beaches. An engraving of Blackpool beach in 1842 shows people who had been collecting shrimps, while William Freeman, who spent his summer holiday at Tenby in 1868, described the women shrimpers in perhaps unrealistically romantic terms (*see* Fig 2.5).[50] At the other extreme is the tragic event of 5 February 2004 when at least 21 undocumented Chinese migrant labourers were drowned by an incoming tide while cockle picking in Morecambe Bay.[51]

Some seaside resorts have become specifically linked with seafood delicacies. Morecambe Bay is renowned for its shrimps, Cromer is celebrated for its crabs and Whitstable for its oysters. Less well known today is the close link between Newquay and pilchards and at nearby St Ives huge hauls of the fish were also taken at one time; in October 1767 one catch is supposed to have netted 245 million pilchards (Fig 4.16).[52]

Fig 4.14
The cargo ship Manaav Star *ran aground at Jurys Gap near Camber on 11 September 2004 but was successfully refloated later in the month and is still at work.*
[MF99/0789/24]

Fig 4.15
At Hastings, tall, wooden net lofts survive on the section of the beach from where the beach-launched fleet still operates. As well as being used for storing and drying fishing gear, some have been converted to other uses, including hosting fish sellers on their ground floor.
[DP139405]

Fig 4.16
A huer's hut on the clifftop at Newquay was used as a lookout to alert fishermen to nearby shoals of pilchards.
[259A/00020]

A vital accompaniment to any fish and chips is salt, one of the oldest coastal industries. Salt-water baths were a prominent feature of many seaside resorts and at Southwold, a sea-water bathhouse was erected in 1766 and used waste heat from the salt pans to warm its water.[53] The 1884 Ordnance Survey map shows that these were a short distance inland at the south end of the resort, just behind the reading room, but salt production ceased there in 1894.

In recent years, the coast has become associated with energy production. The sites of nuclear power stations such as at Dungeness, Heysham, Hinkley Point and Sizewell were chosen for their relative remoteness, but also because the sea could supply the huge quantities of water needed for cooling. With the discovery of oil and gas deposits around the British coast, the sea assumed greater importance, delivering much of the country's power requirements. Most of the infrastructure for this industry lies beyond the horizon, but the Morecambe Bay gas fields are close enough to the shore for rigs to be visible on the horizon. The two fields lie approximately 40km to the west of Blackpool and at peak production account for 15 per cent of Britain's supply.[54]

If nuclear power plants were inevitably controversial, there is also some public concern about wind farms.[55] These were initially located on land or in inshore waters where the technological challenges were easier to overcome, but the energy yield was less as the individual turbines were smaller. Scroby Sands was one of Britain's first commercial offshore wind farms when it was commissioned in March 2004. The project involved the construction of 30 turbines off the coast of Great Yarmouth, each measuring 68m from sea level to their hub and generating up to 60MW, sufficient to supply over 30,000 homes (Fig 4.17).[56] Teesside Wind Farm is a 27-turbine, 62MW capacity offshore wind farm constructed approximately 1.5km off the Teesside coast.[57] Officially opened in April 2014, it is visible from the seafronts of Redcar and Seaton Carew. When the Kentish Flats Offshore Wind Farm in the Thames to the north of Herne Bay was proposed, there was local concern about its visual intrusiveness. However, as it is located approximately 8.5km to 13km from the coast, its 30 wind turbines have had considerably less visual impact than at Great Yarmouth (Fig 4.18).[58] The honour of being the world's largest offshore wind farm in 2018 was held by Walney Wind Farm, a complex of 189 turbines generating 1026MW of electricity.[59] As it is located 14km off the Cumbrian coast, it has only an occasional and negligible impact on the visual setting of the seafront, a significant advance aesthetically and technologically in only a decade since Scroby Sands was constructed.

Safety at sea

Seafronts have also made a significant contribution to the safety of seafarers. Lighthouses have been the inspiration for souvenirs, obstacles on crazy golf courses and, perhaps most touchingly, a gravestone in the cemetery overlooking the sea at St Ives commemorating a person who died at Longships lighthouse. In fact, most seaside resorts do not boast an iconic lighthouse, the tall tower set on a lonely

Fig 4.17
What the energy generating company's highly informative webpage does not mention is that the turbines on the Scroby Sands sandbank are a mere 2.5km offshore. They are therefore visually highly intrusive from anywhere on the seafront at Great Yarmouth.
[DP217496]

rock out at sea. Most lighthouses at seaside resorts instead provide guidance and location information to direct ships into a port or harbour. For instance, a small lighthouse on the seafront at Teignmouth alerts boats to the location of the adjacent harbour, while many harbours have small lighthouses at the ends of their piers to guide ships in safely.[60]

When larger lighthouses are constructed at seaside resorts this may be to take advantage of a suitable clifftop location. A chapel on the clifftop at Ilfracombe had a light in its window to serve as a simple form of lighthouse at least from the 16th century.[61] At Lowestoft, there is a small, mid-19th-century lighthouse on the clifftop behind the seafront and a 20ft-high (6m-high) weatherboarded light of 1851 was erected on the cliffs behind the Old Town at Hastings (Fig 4.19).[62] The tower originally built in 1759 by John Smeaton on the Eddystone Rocks was re-erected on Plymouth Hoe in 1882.[63] Some lighthouses were located lower down, on, or near, the seafront. The former, small, Georgian light on the seafront at Hastings was beneath the high light on the cliff above and a small lighthouse was added to Southsea

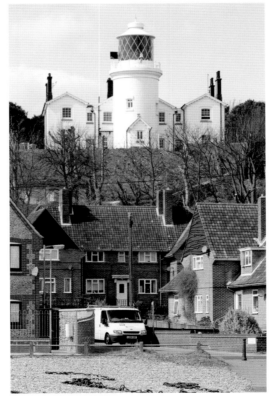

Fig 4.18 (above)
When the Thanet Offshore Wind Farm became operational in 2010, its 100 3MW wind turbines made it the largest offshore wind farm in the world. It is located approximately 13km off the coast at Margate and is visible on the horizon from the resort.
[NMR 26605/014]

Fig 4.19 (left)
This lighthouse and accompanying accommodation at Lowestoft takes advantage of the town's cliff to allow its light to be seen further out to sea. The first light on the site was constructed in 1676, but the present building dates from 1853.
[AA053470]

Castle on the seafront in 1823.[64] At Fleetwood, Sir Peter Hesketh-Fleetwood provided a pair of elegant stone structures in 1840 designed by his architect Decimus Burton alongside his prestigious but incomplete new town (Fig 4.20).

The distinctive silhouettes of seafronts, and some of their larger buildings, have served on charts to aid navigation. At some coastal locations, away from the hearts of seaside resorts, day marks may be provided on prominent headlands to assist navigation. For instance, the twin west towers of the church at Reculver near Herne Bay have been maintained to serve as a navigational aid after most of the church had been demolished. A day mark would be difficult to see against the backdrop of a coastal town, but a number of seaside resorts have buildings that incorporate time balls. These consist of a large ball on a shaft that is dropped at a predetermined time to allow navigators on ships to check their marine chronometers. The seafront Jubilee Clock Tower at Margate of 1889 incorporates a time ball, as does a building on the seafront at Deal (Fig 4.21). Like the Greenwich time ball, it fell at 1pm, triggered by an electric signal sent directly from the Royal Observatory.[65]

Since the 18th century, provision has been made to save lives at sea. Today, the search and rescue infrastructure of the United Kingdom is complex and involves a large number of bodies ranging from government agencies and military personnel and assets, to charities and volunteer organisations. The main organisations that have left their mark on the seafront are the Royal National Lifeboat Institute (RNLI) and HM Coastguard. While these are wholly separate organisations, they do occasionally share facilities; Cleethorpes has a modern combined lifeboat and coastguard station on the seafront.

The RNLI has a fleet of more than 340 lifeboats, ranging from just under 4m to just over 17m in length, as well as a relief fleet and seven hovercraft.[66] The likely need for rescue determines the type of boat and therefore the size and form of any lifeboat station. Most lifeboat stations at seaside resorts are to meet local safety needs. Inevitably, they will be located on or very near the seafront, the lifeboat being launched from a slipway or towed out into the sea by a tractor, though some large lifeboats are now kept at moorings in harbours, such as at Weymouth and Hugh Town in the Isles of Scilly. In both instances, the modern lifeboat is too large for the historic lifeboat station, which is now used as a base for the lifeboat crew. At other locations, the small, historic lifeboat station can now be used as the base for smaller inshore lifeboats. At Cromer and Southend-on-Sea, the lifeboat stations are at the end of the pier, an arrangement that still exists at Birnbeck Pier in Weston-super-Mare, though the dilapidation of the pier means that it can no longer be launched from there.

The earliest dedicated lifeboat was based at Formby in the 1770s, but the first purpose-built boat for lifesaving was built by Henry

Greathead at South Shields in 1790 and was stationed there until 1830 (Fig 4.22).[67] Greathead was the leading lifeboat builder in his lifetime and therefore, when Cromer wanted one in 1804, the money raised by public subscription was used to purchase a boat from him in the following year.[68] Scarborough's lifeboat station may be the oldest in existence in Britain; in 1801, a Greathead boat was housed near the Mill Beck underneath the present Spa Bridge and in 1826 it was transferred to a site beside the West Pier where it remained for almost a century.[69]

Leaving the provision of lifeboats to local communities led to a haphazard deployment of boats around the coast. Therefore, in 1824, the Royal National Institution for the Preservation of Life was established, its name being changed to the Royal National Lifeboat Institution 30 years later.[70] By 1851, there were 95 boats located around the coast, many of which were in a poor state of repair and in need of buildings to house them. In 1858, Charles Cooke was appointed as the RNLI's first architect, leading to the creation of a distinctive building type resembling a church hall with large doors.[71]

Fig 4.21
This seafront building at Deal was originally a semaphore tower built or rebuilt in 1821 on the site of an earlier telegraph station. The time ball was added in 1855 and the building is now a museum.
[DP217401]

Fig 4.22
Henry Greathead went on to build 31 boats of this design, the only surviving example being the 1802 Zetland which is housed in a dedicated museum at Redcar.
[MF99/0804/10]

Within a few years, new lifeboat stations began to become prominent features on many seafronts. As the first lifeboats were relatively small and unpowered, the buildings housing them did not have to be very substantial. The lifeboat house at Teignmouth of 1862 is a simple stone building with large doors in the gable end, but little lighting of the interior.[72] During the following year, the lifeboat station at Lytham St Annes was built and, while it shares the same relative lack of lighting when the main doors are closed, it has a more elaborate gabled roof line (Fig 4.23).[73] In 1864, Blackpool's first lifeboat house was constructed to the south of where Central Pier would be built a few years later and a short distance inland.[74] This lifeboat station survives as a rock shop and a play facility, while Skegness' former station of 1864 has become the Smuggler's Den souvenir gift shop.

Although many lifeboat stations have ceased to be used or have been rebuilt, some still occupy their original building. Swanage's station was built in 1875 and had been kept in continuous use through adaptations, though a new station was completed in 2016 to house a new lifeboat.[75]

Minehead's station was constructed during 1901 and remains in use today now as the base for two inshore lifeboats due to an extension in 1950 and recent modifications.[76]

The first steam-powered lifeboat was introduced in 1890, followed by petrol engines added to existing boats in 1904 and purpose-built, internal combustion-engined boats in 1908.[77] Changes in boat design and their increasing size had a major impact on seafront lifeboat houses, rendering smaller ones redundant or requiring major alterations. With the widening of Blackpool's promenade at the beginning of the 20th century and the increasing size of boats, the small lifeboat station of the 1860s was replaced in 1937 by a larger one immediately on the widened seafront with its own slipway into the sea. This lifeboat station was demolished when the new sea defences were created between 2005 and 2012 (see Fig 11.5).[78] Scarborough had a new lifeboat house built on the promenade in 1914 and this remained in use until 1940 when a new lifeboat station and slipway was completed. The older lifeboat house became a store and a tractor house, and has subsequently become an amusement arcade.[79]

Fig 4.23
Prior to Charles Cooke's appointment, lifeboats had been kept on beaches, in harbours or in any large building near the seafront that could be adapted for the purpose. This c 1900 photograph shows the lifeboat station at Lytham beside the windmill, the only buildings beside the seafront promenade.
[OP00450]

In 1958, the first self-righting boat was introduced and in the 1960s a new class of lifeboat, the inshore lifeboat, began to appear.[80] With the appearance of these smaller, inshore lifeboats a new life for old lifeboat stations was secured. At Teignmouth, the 1862 lifeboat house had been forced to close in 1940 and was sold off for use as a cafe, but in 1991 the RNLI re-acquired and renovated it to house a new inshore lifeboat.

The modern approach to lifeboat station design has ranged from reinterpreting Cooke's original formula to ultra-modern high-tech forms (Fig 4.24). At Filey, the lifeboat station of 1991 evokes something of the designs of the 1860s, consisting of two brick gabled blocks facing the sea.[81] Morecambe's 1998 lifeboat station is almost a hybrid of the old and the modern, using the broad design of Victorian stations but reinterpreting it using late 20th-century detailing.[82] Blackpool's 1937 station was replaced in 1998 when a new inshore lifeboat station was built a short distance to the north (Figs 4.25 and 4.26).[83] These stations are all firmly planted on the seafront, but at Cromer the new lifeboat station and slipway

Fig 4.24 (above)
The present boathouse at St Ives opened in 1994 and although it is traditional in its overall form, the large windows and door reveal its modern date. It is arranged with the main Shannon class all-weather boat in the central bay and a smaller inshore lifeboat in the right-hand bay.
[AA052788]

Fig 4.25 (left)
As Blackpool's modern lifeboat station is a prominent feature on the seafront, showers and other washing facilities for use by bathers were included on the exterior of this building, which was built in a contemporary, post-modern style.
[AA053316]

Fig 4.26
In contrast to more traditional designs, Aldeburgh's new lifeboat station of 1993 houses an all-weather boat and an inshore lifeboat in two high-tech buildings reflecting the sizes of each boat.
[DP217342]

Fig 4.27
At South Shields, the Volunteer Life Brigade Watch House of 1867 survives on the seafront beside the pier. This timber-framed structure with a brick extension is single-storeyed, but has a small, taller lookout tower at its north-east corner.
[MF99/0796/09]

of 1998–9 was added to the end of the pier.[84] Although these stations have attempted to provide distinctive, if different architectural forms, many recent lifeboat stations are more utilitarian. The buildings constructed at Margate in 1978 and Skegness in 1990 are simple industrial boxes, highly practical, but not aesthetically pleasing.[85]

The coastguard service is also a crucial part of the search and rescue infrastructure, particularly for emergencies on and near the coast. In 1809, the Preventative Water Guard was established to combat smuggling, but with this activity decreasing during the mid-19th century, the organisation began to function like an auxiliary naval service. Although responsibility for revenue protection was retained, rescue services began instead to be undertaken by Volunteer Life Brigades and by the lifeboats of the RNLI, with the coastguard acting in a support role (Fig 4.27). In 1923, the coastguard was re-established as a coastal safety and rescue service, and also dealt with salvage from wrecks and the administration of the foreshore. In 1931, there were 193 stations and 339 auxiliary stations in England. However, from the 1960s onwards the service's priority shifted again from maintaining coastal lookouts to the provision of coordinated search and rescue services. Old watch houses, with their on-site accommodation and annexed boathouses, were superseded by fewer Maritime Rescue Co-ordination Centres. During the 1990s, HM Coastguard became a government executive agency and in 1998, the Marine Safety Agency and the Coastguard Agency were merged to become the Maritime and Coastguard Agency (MCA).[86] Today, the agency is not only responsible for search and rescue, but also for much of the regulation and licensing of shipping and maritime activity.[87]

In the past coastguards operated from watch houses, some of which survive, such as the small octagonal lookout hut on the headland at Newquay.[88] While these are normally on a clifftop to maximise the area of sea that can be observed, any boathouses that the service used were inevitably at sea level. At Seaview on the Isle of Wight, the Old Boathouse is dated 1557

Fig 4.28
The Life Brigade Watch
House at Tynemouth
occupies a prominent
clifftop location to increase
the distance that volunteers
could see out to sea. It was
built in 1886–7 by the
Borough Engineer
C T Gomoszynski.
[MF99/0752/28]

above its door, but it was heavily restored and altered in c 1840–50.[89] Coastguards re-employed other suitable coastal structures, such as the Martello towers at Felixstowe and Folkestone.[90] The modern service operates from larger, purpose-built stations, some of which are at seaside resorts such as at Hastings and Margate, respectively located on the seafront and on the clifftop. A similar, modern Marine Rescue Centre was built in 1980 on the clifftop at Tynemouth Priory beside the c 1900 coastal battery and remained in use until the beginning of the 21st century.[91] The service also provided its staff with housing, which would not necessarily be located on the seafront. One of the most ambitious sets of coastguard cottages can be found on the cliffs at Ramsgate, where three terraces of two-storeyed brick houses of 1865 are placed around an open courtyard, an arrangement comparable to contemporary almshouses.[92]

Some of the watch houses and rocket stations operated by Volunteer Life Brigades have survived. The country's first Volunteer Life Brigade was established at Tynemouth in 1864 to rescue people from close to the shore rather than out at sea and within a few years there were a number of similar brigades nearby (Fig 4.28).[93] At Cullercoats near Tynemouth, the former 1867 clifftop garage of the Life Brigade was originally the base for this brigade, which pioneered using rocket-fired lifelines to ships to rescue victims (Fig 4.29).[94] On the

clifftop nearby, there is also a Life Brigade Watch House of 1879 by F W Rich, which now houses a community centre and exhibition space.[95] This sandstone building has a wooden veranda around it, providing a pleasant shelter while looking out to sea.

Another volunteer organisation today makes a contribution to safety around the coast. The National Coastwatch Institution (NCI) is a voluntary organisation that keeps watch on parts of the coast from 50 stations. It was established in 1994 when two fishermen lost their lives off the Cornish coast below a recently closed coastguard lookout. More than 2,000 volunteers watch for signs that people are in trouble, and on days with poor visibility their monitoring of radio channels can also save lives.[96]

Fig 4.29
The Cullercoats 'Rocket
Garage', later aptly used
as a garage, is a small,
stone building for storing
equipment. Similar to a
small version of a lifeboat
station, its clifftop location
would have prevented it
from serving that function.
[DP174961]

The seafront at war

As Britain is an island the coastline is the key location for military defences to prevent invasion. Some of these are found at seaside resorts, as there were times when it was feared that enemies would invade via a beach. The location of military defences also depended on who was perceived to be the current enemy. During the 16th and 17th centuries, Britain feared attack from the continental Catholic powers France and Spain, prompting the construction of Henrician forts principally along the south coast of England. Briefly during the 17th century, the Dutch were an active enemy attacking the Medway and the Suffolk coast in 1667 and this potential threat was behind the maintenance of Landguard Fort, a short distance to the south of Felixstowe.[97] Through the 18th and 19th centuries, France was the threat to Britain. This prompted sporadic fortification construction in the 18th century and the major campaign of Martello tower construction on the east and south coasts.[98] With the signing of the Entente Cordiale in 1904, the orientation of Britain's defences began to shift towards the east coast in preparation for two world wars against Germany.

The location of anti-invasion fortifications and resorts often reflected two sides of the same geographical equation, namely access between the sea and land. When designing military defences, their location was chosen where there was easy access from the sea to the land, while seaside resorts were established to achieve the converse. Before the 16th century, responsibility for any defences near the coast lay in the hands of major landowners, acting to safeguard their own local interests rather than protecting the country *per se*. By the reign of Henry VIII, the Crown began to undertake national initiatives.[99] England faced invasion in 1538, and consequently, coastal fortifications were constructed from Hull to Milford Haven as part of an underlying plan, the Device, which was drawn up by February 1539. The fortifications constructed ranged from small blockhouses with a few guns defending the Thames, to the largest castles, such as those on the seafronts at Deal, Walmer and Sandgate, with dozens of gun positions, structures costing up to £10,000 (Fig 4.30).[100] Defence spending continued into the reign of Edward VI, during which time new architectural forms were introduced from the continent. The earliest angled bastions in England may have been at Southsea Castle

Fig 4.30
Deal Castle was one of the largest fortifications built during the reign of Henry VIII. The income raised by the Dissolution of the Monasteries partly funded his monumental construction programme.
[NMR 27308/005]

in the mid-1540s and at Yarmouth Castle in c 1547.[101] Southsea Castle lies at the heart of the seafront and, although there have been major additions in subsequent centuries to upgrade the defences, the original form of the Tudor building is still clear.[102]

When the first people came to bathe in the sea, the presence of military establishments, and sometimes detachments of soldiers, would not have been uncommon. Scarborough was threatened during the 1740s, not by invasion from the sea, but from the Jacobite Uprising of 1745. A map of that year, which was published in 1747, suggests that 99 guns manned by 400 men were deployed to defend the town with a further 400 infantrymen in batteries around the town's defences.[103] By 1750, Brighton's unused Elizabethan blockhouse was falling into the sea, but with the outbreak of the Seven Years War, five new coastal batteries were built in 1759 on the Sussex coast.[104] In 1762, Thomas Turner described a visit to the seaside and for him the only notable event of the day was his inspection of two of the newly built forts at Seaford.[105] A new blockhouse at Brighton was built of brick and armed with a dozen rather ancient guns, which by 1779 were rusting and their wooden carriages were beginning to rot. The battery succumbed to encroachment by the sea and finally collapsed during a severe storm in November 1786.[106]

Maps often reveal the presence of military installations close to where sea bathing was taking place. In Hutchins' map of 1774, two forts are shown on the seafront at Weymouth. Mount Joy Fort was at the north end of the town, approximately where George III's statue now stands, and Block House Fort was a short distance to the south, in the same location as the 'Smal Platforme' depicted in a late 16th-century map (Fig 4.31).[107] This structure was described in 1790 as being square in shape and built of stone, having embrasures for eight guns, although only five were mounted at this time. It has had a small, but noticeable effect on the arrangement of the terraces on the Esplanade, interrupting the line of Georgian seafront terraces. In 1793, two new batteries were built at Brighton; the West Battery, which stood near the site of the present Grand Hotel, and the East Battery at the southern end of the New Steine overlooking where the Chain Pier would later be built. Both were designed by Captain William Twiss of the Royal Engineers, who would later be involved with the construction of Martello towers.[108]

An 1858 photograph shows the demolition of the West Battery. The Grand Hotel was built on the site of the old Battery House, where the naval lieutenant in charge of the battery was stationed.[109]

At some resorts, names may reveal the location of former military fortifications. For instance, the clifftop above the harbour at Margate is still known as the Fort. It was once the site of an earthwork defence, which during the Napoleonic wars boasted 'eight pieces of iron ordnance, – four 24 pounders and four 18 pounders, which with two others on the Pier, constituted the security of the town and harbour'.[110]

Fig 4.31
On Hutchins' map of Weymouth in 1774 'b' marks the location of the Mount Joy Fort and 'c' the Block House Fort. This area became a key part of the seafront for tourism, the Theatre Royal being marked 'd' on this map. [DP022292]

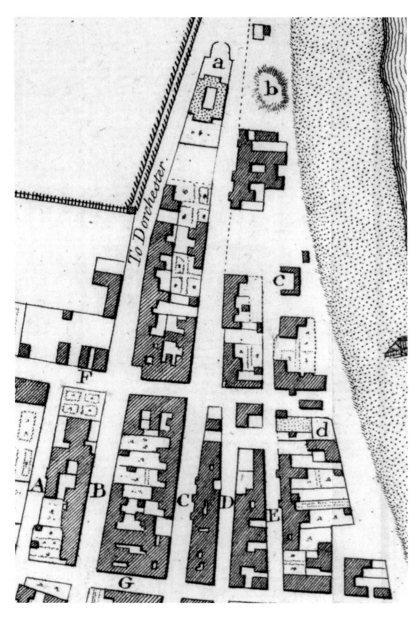

In the south and east of England, a more concerted approach to anti-invasion defences was taken at the beginning of the 19th century.[111] The threat of a huge French army assembling near Calais after 1803 prompted the government to build a network of 73 Martello towers on the south coast between 1805 and 1808, followed by 29 on the east coast from 1809–12 (Fig 4.32).[112] A further tower was built on the south coast at Seaford in 1810 and two other forts were built at Dymchurch and Eastbourne to serve as control and supply points (Fig 4.33).[113] Since 1815, the towers have largely been redundant, though some were reused as coastguard lookouts, signal stations and, during World War II, as observation posts and radar stations. Today, some of the surviving examples are used as museums, while others have been converted into desirable seafront homes.[114]

Signal stations were also established during the war against France. A series of shutter telegraph stations began to be set up in Sussex in 1794 and similar lines were constructed subsequently to connect the Admiralty in London to Portsmouth, Deal and Great Yarmouth.[115] The final station of the Portsmouth Line was located on Southsea Common and as late as 1823 the hut was still standing, though the system had long been abandoned.[116]

There may seem to be a certain incongruity between preparation for war and bathing in the sea, but these contrasting activities seem to have co-existed happily. An early form of 'dark tourism' involved people visiting active military defences, much as they toured prisons and lunatic asylums. An anonymous tourist travelling around Kent in 1809 was able to see the recently erected Martello towers, Shorncliffe Barracks and the Royal Military Canal, which had been constructed between 1804 and 1809.[117] Thomas Lott also travelled around Kent in July 1815, a month after the final French defeat at Waterloo. Although Dover Castle was still an active military site, Lott was shown around its barracks, bake houses and cannons.[118] It remained a popular destination through the 19th century and a number of guidebooks included detailed descriptions of visits to the site.[119]

At the height of the conflict with France, many leading seaside resorts would have been busy with military activity. An 1806 guide to Great Yarmouth described how an armoury was being constructed using designs provided by 'the celebrated Mr. [James] Wyatt': 'the whole is an edifice assuming a just and becoming importance, proportionate to the magnitude of the undertaking, and to the munificence of the Board, by whose orders it is erected'.[120]

Fig 4.32
Martello towers were constructed to defend against landings on vulnerable beaches, but by the early 19th century a number of these sites were already popular with people bathing in the sea, such as at Clacton, Jaywick, Folkestone and here at Eastbourne.
[DP059979]

Plans were also afoot to establish a Naval Hospital on the South Denes, which was constructed shortly after the guidebook was published. There was also a barracks that was described as 'not far distant from the Beach; the buildings are capable of accommodating upwards of 1000 men, with all the requisite conveniences and appendages'. The guidebook goes on to describe how the town was defended by a fortification at the mouth of the river and by 'three forts, on the verge of the Beach, mounted with 32-pounders, (erected during the American war) to defend it from the privateers which at that time infested the coast'.[121] The first edition one-inch Ordnance Survey map of 1837–8 shows this military infrastructure of the seafront still in place, a noticeable presence on a seafront that would have been busy with visitors during the summer months.

The construction of fortifications may have had a visual and practical impact on a small number of seaside resorts, but more often it was the presence of soldiers that contributed to the town's character and economy (see Fig 2.6).

They reassured holidaymakers and were major contributors to local businesses.[122] The presence of King George III at Weymouth between 1789 and 1805 led to the military occupying buildings and camps in and around Weymouth, helping to make the town lively at a period when war with France could have discouraged some visitors.[123]

World War I saw the shelling and bombing of east coast seaside resorts with working ports, particularly Scarborough, Whitby and Great Yarmouth.[124] Most damage inflicted on English seaside resorts was caused by Zeppelins, the earliest raid being on Great Yarmouth in January 1915, and later by twin-engined Gotha bombers.[125] In 1917, an air raid on Folkestone damaged and destroyed buildings, killing 33 people.[126] At Ramsgate, holidaymakers could purchase a postcard boasting that the town had suffered 119 air raids, killing or injuring 138 people and causing nearly £108,000 worth of damage.[127] At vulnerable resorts, anti-invasion defences were installed, such as at Felixstowe, where a contemporary photograph shows a concrete pillbox alongside tangles of barbed wire.[128]

Fig 4.33
Also at Eastbourne, this Aerofilms image of 1920 shows the larger Redoubt Fort that was built in 1806 as part of the fortification programme to prevent Napoleon from landing in England.
[EPW000101]

During the late 19th century, many coastal batteries were constructed on cliffs, and by 1914, they had been rationalised according to gun types, calibres and mountings, and armed according to the expected weight and type of attack (Fig 4.34). From 1893 onwards, new purpose-built batteries were constructed at Tynemouth Castle, the defences being further updated during World War I.[129] The construction of a battery and searchlight positions at Blyth began in August 1916 and in 1925 they became incorporated into the development of the South Beach amenities when two of the buildings were converted into public toilets (Fig 4.35). A coastal location also allowed for long-range detection of any enemy coming by sea or air (Fig 4.36). During World War I, sound mirrors began to be constructed to provide early warning of an approaching enemy, and they continued to be built until they were superseded by coastal radar stations just before the outbreak of World War II. The earliest radar system was the Chain Home system, consisting of around

20 stations running from the Tyne round to Southampton, using 250ft-high (76m) masts, examples of which can still be seen on the clifftops at Dover.[130]

During World War II, there was a genuine threat of invasion from the sea and therefore it was vital to defend the beaches of the east and south coasts of England. By the summer of 1940, the most vulnerable beaches were lined with barbed wire, landmines and scaffolding poles, maps of some resorts showing the multiple layers of defences that had been hastily assembled.[131] At Blackpool, an air-raid shelter was constructed on the promenade opposite the Golden Mile in 1939, along with large concrete blocks designed to thwart invading vehicles, and ferro-concrete posts protruding from the sands to prevent aircraft landing.[132] Tanks and other vehicles were to be countered by concrete defences, including dragon's teeth and tank traps, and these survive in places such as Bude and Winterton Beach as they were too difficult to remove after the war. At Aldeburgh, a coastal

Fig 4.34
On the headland between the harbour at St Ives and Porthmeor Beach, beside the mediaeval chapel of St Nicholas, there are the remains of a c 1900 former gun battery and semaphore station. [NMR 23931/001]

Fig 4.35 (left)
At Blyth, this World War I gun emplacement was reused during World War II. It is now one of a number of structures in a seafront area that have been adapted to meet the needs of holidaymakers. [DP169963]

Fig 4.36 (below)
This clifftop World War I lookout tower at 47a Percy Gardens in Tynemouth would have provided early warning of approaching enemy ships, weather permitting. Built in c 1916 for the army, it also had a gun emplacement on its roof. [DP169954]

battery has been converted into a seafront shelter.[133] Pillboxes were also constructed at some seaside resorts during both world wars, some of which survive (Fig 4.37). However, many, particularly those on the Yorkshire coast and at Camber, Hemsby and Walton-on-the-Naze, have succumbed to the sea, the last of these having fallen down on to the beach.

Preparations to counter a threatened invasion by Nazi Germany had a dramatic impact on the archaeology of seafronts, including the removal of what survived of almost 200 years of sea-bathing heritage. Sections of piers were blown up to prevent them being used by an invading force. At Bognor Regis, the eastern bandstand of 1910 was demolished as it was in the way of a strong line of military defences and nearby Shoreham Bungalow Town was largely demolished in 1940.[134] As well as being made ready for invasion, many seafronts suffered from enemy action, the worst being Dover, an easy target for long-range guns on the French coast. The Imperial Hotel was reputedly the place that Nazi gunners aimed at, and therefore it and adjacent Regency houses, were destroyed and replaced by the Gateway Flats after the war.[135] The parish church at St Leonards was destroyed on 30 July 1944. A V1 rocket exploded in front of the church door, bringing down the tower and leading to the demolition of the church along with five houses in the vicinity (see Fig 9.46).[136]

Fig 4.37
At Swanage, a type 25
pillbox has survived on a
stretch of the seashore that
is not used by tourists. With
a diameter of 8ft (2.4m)
and walls just 12in (30cm)
thick, they would have been
very vulnerable to heavy
enemy weapons.
[MF99/0725/06]

Not all resorts and seafronts suffered from the threat of enemy action during World War II. At Douglas on the Isle of Man, seafront guest houses were used as an internment camp for foreign nationals considered to be potential enemy agents. It was chosen as it was remote from the continent. However, the similarly distant seaside resorts on the Lancashire coast remained open for business during the war. Blackpool was still able to function as a resort, but it also benefited from an influx of military personnel who worked, and lived, in the town during the conflict. At one time, up to 45,000 RAF recruits were lodged there and there were also substantial numbers of evacuees, not just children, but also civil servants from London.[137] Far from being denuded of its populace as Margate suffered, it was estimated that Blackpool's population grew from 128,200 in 1939 to 143,650 in 1945.

Conclusion

Small coastal settlements that welcomed hundreds of holidaymakers in the 18th century soon had to deal with thousands and later millions of tourists. The seafront has been created or adapted to house some of the major services of the town, particularly to deal with water treatment and the disposal of sewage. Seafront lighting and trams required a reliable electricity supply and its presence subsequently stimulated the development of the illuminations at Blackpool. This example demonstrates how the provision of services is integrated with catering for tourists, and features such as harbours, now considered as practical work-places, were subject to the curious tourist gaze from the 18th century onwards. At Brighton, there are only faint reminders of the town's seagoing history, but Hastings has managed to retain a beach-launched fleet, albeit corralled into a small area at one end of the resort.

In recent years, energy generation has assumed a greater significance, and while much of its infrastructure may lie over the horizon, some features are visible from seafronts. There is also necessarily archaeological concern about any route of a power line bringing electricity onto the land. With activity at sea inevitably comes danger and the seafront has many struc-tures associated with safeguarding seafarers. These are designed primarily for peacetime use, but the same accessibility to the sea prized by holidaymakers is also potentially a vulnerability in time of war. Since the 16th century, much effort has been expended to prevent enemies from landing on beaches where holidaymakers would rather be sunning themselves.

Having considered how the engineering projects that have formed seafronts have been designed and used for the benefit of the resident population and national security, Chapter 5 will consider how the same space has been adapted to meet the specific needs of tourism. Consider-ation will be given to a range of large-scale and small-scale, hard and soft features ranging from bins, benches and bandstands to gardens with fountains and flowerbeds. It will also tackle the thorny issue of providing toilets for holiday-makers, a rarity before the late 19th century, suggesting that while people may have sought the seaside for their health, this may have been a far from healthy location to pass a few weeks away from home.

5

Preparing for tourists

The construction of substantial man-made sea defences created a large space that became the key location for facilities needed by residents of seaside resorts. The seafront is also the shop window for a seaside resort, a key driver for the economy of the town. Therefore, investment has been needed to transform the potentially harsh, functional space created behind sea defences, and over the past 200 years it has been embellished with the facilities that visitors would enjoy and require during their visits.

By the late 19th century, local authorities had begun to actively invest in the detailing of the seafront. For residents and visitors, a series of hard and soft features were developed on the seafront to make the space work. Among the former might be railings, street furniture including seating, shelters and beach huts, as well as vital toilet facilities and rubbish bins. The soft dimension is a seafront's gardens, with carefully chosen plants and trees adapted to deal with the particular conditions of wind, sea and salt.

The form and detailing of the seafront's architecture and infrastructure has changed dramatically during the past 300 years. While little may survive from the 18th century, the successive styles favoured by architects and engineers since the late 19th century are still well represented today. These range from ornate, exotic cast-iron features, ultimately inspired by the Royal Pavilion at Brighton, through interwar classicism and art deco to the late 20th century, where an eclectic mixture of the modernist and the old, often seen through a nostalgic lens, may be combined to create the facilities for modern holidaymakers.

Landscaping the esplanade

Once visitors began tentatively to transform the natural form of the seafront into a practical but pleasant space in which to bathe, socialise and relax, there was a need for places to sit and shelter.

Physical evidence for this early transformation is limited; the dynamic nature of tourism, as well as the challenging environment of the seafront, means that the lifespan of early investments was limited. Visual evidence is now restricted to paintings, engravings and early photographs. In *The Long Painting* of Sidmouth, many elegantly clad tourists shelter on the veranda of the library, while others promenade and one couple sit on the base of a former capstan (*see* Fig 1.5). From the second half of the 19th century onwards, more begins to survive, in part due to the widespread use of iron and steel, materials that can, with care, resist the harsh climate of the English seafront.

Tourist infrastructure ranges from the mundane to the luxurious. One of the most important practical features is the humble rubbish bin. The scale of dealing with huge seasonal influxes of visitors is often reflected in the provision of industrial-size bins. Although these are very necessary, they are unfortunately large and unsightly, and on a warm summer's day it is not unusual to find people sitting in deckchairs beside them. If a resort chooses not to install large bins, it therefore incurs the additional cost of having to provide a greater number of small bins, which need to be emptied more frequently (Fig 5.1).

Fig 5.1
A bench and an adjacent bin at Blyth are two of the vital, but unglamorous, features that tourists expect on the seafront. A plaque commemorates the donor of the bench, who would have sat and admired the view out to sea.
[DP087762]

Signs are perhaps more important and more plentiful on seafronts, as it is a space that caters for people who are not residents and therefore they may be unfamiliar with the location of its facilities and landmarks (Fig 5.2). Seafronts are also often the location for information boards explaining the history and heritage of an individual resort: Margate, for example, has a series of signs proclaiming it to be Britain's 'Earliest Resort'; Sidmouth uses the familiar blue plaque formula to deliver information about key buildings; at Fleetwood detailed information panels illustrated with attractive old photographs lead visitors through the history of the resort along the seafront (Fig 5.3). Seafronts also have poster display units advertising current and future shows or entertainments. These may be fixed to bus shelters and other structures, but frequently take the form of freestanding cylindrical pods.

Railings are a necessary safety measure to prevent falls from a raised promenade. Old photographs of seaside resorts also show

Fig 5.2
Signs can also add to the merriment of the seaside holiday. This sign directed prospective customers to the Joke Shop that was formerly located in Arlington Square at Margate.
[DP140193]

Fig 5.3
At Whitby on the clifftop there is a signpost pointing to distant destinations once discovered, or visited, by Captain Cook, who is also celebrated with a statue looking out over the harbour.
[DP175063]

that railings were once common between the promenade and the road that ran along the seafront to prevent pedestrians straying in front of a passing coach. At Weymouth, there were white-painted, small stone posts linked by chains between the promenade and the carriageway, and these were reinstated after the 1824 storm (Fig 5.4 and *see* Fig 3.7), while at Brighton by the 1860s there was a light set of railings in this same location.[1]

Railings separating the promenade from the beach were first erected during Victorian campaigns to install sea defences or secure cliffs; early examples include those at Brighton dating from 1886 and 1894 (*see* Fig 4.3).[2] Old photographs show that prior to this, there was, at least in places, a lightweight wooden handrail supported on thin timber uprights.[3] William Miller, who visited Brighton in the autumn of 1886, recorded how the promenade was being widened and improved, including by 'placing on it an ornamental rail or balustrade'.[4] Railings typically consist of more or less elaborate cast-iron uprights with rails or panels between and a wooden or metal handrail on top. They usually employ geometric forms as the panels are produced in such large quantities, leaving more

elaborate, and more expensive, detailing to be used where smaller amounts of casting is required, such as decoration to seafront shelters or the uprights of benches (Fig 5.5). At Swanage, there are attractive moulded uprights with leaf and rope motifs linked by long, plain metal poles that look too modern for the composition.

Fig 5.4 (left)
A number of the original small stones have survived at the northern end of the seafront at Weymouth. A 1990 plaque on one of the posts celebrates this remarkable survival. [DP055531]

Fig 5.5 (below)
At St Annes, solid metal sheeting is used in place of open railings between the beach and the promenade. This has the advantage of preventing sand from blowing onto the promenade. [OP00445]

North Promenade, St Annes on Sea.

At Blackpool, railings employed to delineate the tram route to the north of the resort consist of cast concrete panels, a form favoured in some interwar gardens. The tendency in modern railings is to replicate existing forms and patterns to match older designs, but at Weston-super-Mare, where there were no pre-existing railings, a thoroughly modern approach has been adopted, using shiny stainless-steel uprights with tensioning wires between, above the low sea wall (Fig 5.6).

Seating has been provided on seafronts at least since the 19th century; in the 1880s, William Miller recorded how 'From seats, provided in liberal number about Torquay, we had a fine view of the bay and coast.'[5] Municipally provided seats range from embellished cast-iron framed benches, like elaborate garden furniture, to Southampton seats with cast concrete uprights with timber planks between them.[6] Seating may be built into features such as low garden walls; at Weymouth the coping stones topping these walls have been set at a height to serve as seating. Swanage also has a long,

moulded concrete bench with a tall back to protect seated holidaymakers from wind and splashes from the road beside it.

Today, seaside resorts adopt a wide range of approaches to providing seating. Great Yarmouth has created long, curving benches divided into units for couples, an arrangement that also serves to prevent them being used by skateboarders. At Littlehampton, a long, colourful bench has been constructed, perhaps inspired ultimately by the seat designed by Antonio Gaudí for the Parc Güell in Barcelona (Fig 5.7).[7] At Worthing, a range of approaches to seating has been taken in recent years. On part of the seafront there are reproduction Victorian cast-iron benches, presumably now made of steel. However, on another part where money was provided from the Commission for Architecture and the Built Environment's (CABE) Sea Change fund, there are fountains set into the ground amid large blocks of stone, with the accompanying seating taking the form of cast concrete shapes similar to those at Blackpool (Fig 5.8).

Fig 5.6
A modern approach has been taken at Margate, as part of the public realm works. A new ramped access to the beach was created at the same time as part of the seafront was provided with modern seating and railings.
[DP032165]

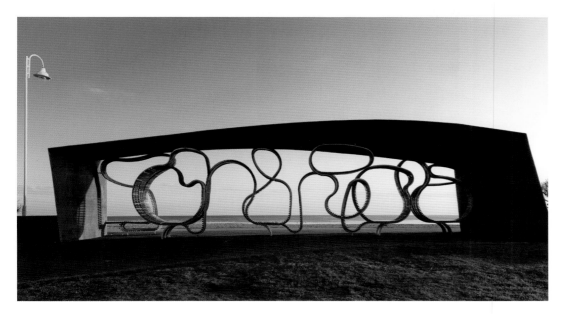

Fig 5.7
The long bench at Littlehampton, which was opened to the public in July 2010, runs into a shelter on the seafront where most of it cannot be used as a seat. It creates a dramatic design on a seafront with other striking design features including a modern cafe. See also Fig 9.44.
[DP139416]

Investment in shelters also begins to be obvious by the late 19th century. William Miller, writing in 1888 about his visits to resorts during the previous few years, regularly mentions shelters, perhaps due to their novelty, but also because he was sitting in them when he was writing his notes. He included a sketch of a thatched shelter at Bournemouth in 1887 and noted that similar 'dos a dos' (back-to-back) shelters were available at Hastings.[8] Iron was by far the most common material used. With proper maintenance, it was modern, durable and cheap to construct. Its flexibility allowed the creation of complex, yet cheap, roof forms and elaborate detailing, ranging from classical columns to panels decorated with ornate foliage, all made possible by mass production.

Brighton was at the forefront of providing shelters between *c* 1883 and 1887, as part of a major scheme to widen and improve the seafront.[9] These were part of a programme undertaken by Philip Causton Lockwood, Brighton's Borough Surveyor for over 25 years. It also included the 'Birdcage' bandstand, a combined shelter and bandstand with public toilets beneath (*see* Fig 5.17). The standard shelters are rectangular in form with seating on four sides and a wide roof carried on stylised square columns from which vault ribs spring. Constructed using timber and moulded cast-iron detailing, and manufactured by John Every, these were clearly standard designs selected from a catalogue (Fig 5.9).[10] In 1889, a set of shelters was added to the seafront at Weymouth and some of these had balconies projecting over the sands (Fig 5.10). At Bexhill-on-Sea, among its varied collection of seafront shelters, is a timber-framed example with an elongated decahedronal plan dating from 1896. Other examples dating from *c* 1900 are also timber framed, but are rectangular in form.[11]

Seaside shelters typically provided seating perhaps for a handful of people, but some examples can be larger. On the Fort at Margate, there is a long, rectangular, concrete shelter with nine compartments, each probably for one family (Fig 5.11). Overlooking the east side of

Fig 5.8
On the renewed public realm of the central seafront at Blackpool there are giant pebbles, moulded concrete shapes that serve as seats as well as decorations.
[DP140686]

Fig 5.9 (right)
Proof of the assertion that the Brighton shelters came from a catalogue can be found on the clifftop at Whitby, where almost identical shelters obviously came from the same source. [DP006145]

Fig 5.10 (below)
Blackpool's seafront shelters of 1905 are similar in overall form to the Brighton ones, but like the Weymouth examples they have more elaborate cast-iron detailing and more complex roof forms. [AA053296]

the main beach, on the landward side of Marine Drive, there is a long shelter with cast-iron columns supporting the roof. At the other end of the beach is Britain's most celebrated seaside shelter, a large structure of *c* 1900 reputed to be where T S Eliot (1888–1965) wrote some lines from *The Waste Land* in 1921 (Fig 5.12).[12]

The classic materials for seaside shelters were wood, cast iron and stone, but during the interwar years concrete became the favoured material. At Spittal, at Berwick-upon-Tweed, there is a large 1930 concrete shelter that is nevertheless quite traditional in its design. However, at Deal, Hastings and New Brighton something of the geometric potential of concrete is used to create modern designs beneath interestingly shaped roof structures (Fig 5.13). At Hastings, two concrete shelters on Carlisle Parade echo the traditional rectangular Victorian form, but actually disguise ventilators for the

Fig 5.11
At Margate the shelter, which now overlooks the Turner Contemporary gallery, as well as the adjacent Fort Green, was a post-war replacement of an earlier shelter. [MF99/0777/29]

Fig 5.12
The Nayland Rock shelter at the east end of Margate's main beach is reputedly where T S Eliot wrote 'On Margate Sands. I can connect Nothing with nothing.' [DP139577]

Fig 5.13
This shelter at Deal illustrates how an architect could comprehensively rethink a familiar design object. A circular shelter in this location appears on the 1938 Ordnance Survey map and therefore this could be a radical interwar design rather than a more standard 1950s work. [DP217404]

subterranean car park beneath. At Trusthorpe, near Mablethorpe, its post-war shelters in the seafront gardens take thinking about concrete further by creating moulded shells with seating within. In contrast to the use of modern materials, thatch still makes an occasional appearance, such as at Cromer. Another shelter there makes use of red tiles, while at some other resorts slate is employed rather than the more common sheet-metal roof covering.

As well as individual shelters, some resorts have colonnades or covered promenades serving as places to shelter and a means of walking along a seafront. The earliest is the long iron structure running along Madeira Drive to the east of the Palace Pier at Brighton. Almost half a mile long, this cast-iron and brick structure was constructed between 1890 and 1897 by the Borough Surveyor Philip Causton Lockwood (Fig 5.14). The cast-iron arcade has round arches carried on single columns of a fanciful marine order, with spandrels formed from quatrefoils to create a pierced sun screen.[13]

In 1912, at Blackpool, a curved shelter was created in an arcade along the seaward side of the Metropole Hotel as part of the Princess Parade, while at Eastbourne, colonnades with terracotta-clad columns provide a promenade around the bandstand, but also serve as a shelter along the

seafront, a similar example was built at Bexhill (Fig 5.15). At Hastings, the transformation of the seafront in the early 1930s, masterminded by the Borough Engineer Sydney Little, led to the creation of a double-height promenade, with part of the lower storey serving as a long shelter and covered walkway. The scheme was executed in concrete, the material so favoured by Little that he earned the local title of the 'Concrete King'. A similar double-decker promenade was created at South Shields during the 1980s, the lower part being glazed to counter cold winds from the North Sea. Occasionally a shelter may be created from a pre-existing structure, such as at Aldeburgh or Blyth where a potentially unsightly former military defence emplacement has received a new lease of life (see Fig 4.35).

Many seaside resorts have sought to embrace modernity when constructing new shelters in recent decades (Fig 5.16). At Lowestoft, shelters have been created in the form of what might be described as a jellyfish on stilts, with a tri-radial arrangement of seating beneath this canopy. At Blackpool, as part of the revamping of the southern part of the seafront completed in 2001, a shelter was constructed that can be rotated to follow the sun and avoid the wind, recalling the revolving shelters pioneered at the sanatorium at Mundesley c 1900.[14]

Fig 5.14
Brighton's Madeira Drive consists of an arcade with a walkway above, associated buildings and a lift tower connecting the seafront to the cliffs above. It provides both shade and shelter depending on the weather and was an elegant place to promenade.
[Author's collection]

Madeira Walk, Brighton.

Fig 5.15
At Bexhill, the King George V Colonnade of 1911, designed by J B Wall in a classical style, provided an arcaded shelter looking out to sea in front of where the De la Warr Pavilion would later be constructed. This 1920 Aerofilms photograph shows the coastguard station behind that was demolished in the 1930s.
[EPW000120]

Fig 5.16
A competition was held at Bexhill-on-Sea to design new shelters, leading to a wealth of modern proposals ranging from the practical to the fantastic. In the end, this elaborate timber geometric form was chosen and has featured in a recent set of stamps celebrating the heritage of the seaside.
[DP217862]

The bandstand

The bandstand has been a central feature in many seaside resorts for over a century and often has a leading place in the elaborate ironwork essays that grace seafronts. Their origins can be traced back to the structures erected in London's pleasure gardens for music performances during the 18th century and to facilities provided for music in spa towns, the best surviving example being the Georgian music gallery on the Pantiles at Tunbridge Wells.[15] The seafront bandstand, or the band house as it was often known, also owed its origins to the need to provide a music venue in the growing number of municipal parks being established from the 1830s onwards. The first bandstands appear to have been erected in the Royal Horticultural Society Gardens in South Kensington in 1861.[16] These were designed by Captain Francis Fowke of the Royal Engineers, who was also the architect of the main quadrangle of the Victoria and Albert Museum and was one of the designers of the Royal Albert Hall. These first bandstands were circular, domed pavilions supported on slender cast-iron columns, resembling *chatri* from Indian and Islamic architecture. Similar designs were exhibited at the Paris Exposition Universelle in 1855, on which Fowke worked. When the gardens closed in 1882, the bandstands were bought by the London County Council and re-erected in Southwark Park and Peckham Rye.

One of the earliest bandstands to be erected on a seafront was the elaborate 'Birdcage' bandstand at Brighton (Fig 5.17). Designed

Fig 5.17
Brighton's Birdcage Bandstand consists of a stone basement housing public lavatories with a cast-iron and timber bandstand above with oriental detailing and the town's signature dolphins in the spandrels.
[DP217905]

in 1883 by Philip Causton Lockwood, and manufactured by Walter MacFarlane and Company of the Saracen Foundry in Glasgow, it is the sole survivor of eleven constructed in the town during the Victorian period.[17] Its exotic detailing was a clear nod to the nearby West Pier and to the Royal Pavilion, which was ultimately responsible for the infusion of exoticism into the mainstream of seafront architecture. Other seaside resorts soon followed Brighton's lead, including a bandstand on the Leas at Folkestone, which was manufactured by the Elmbank foundry and erected in 1886, and Clevedon's of 1887. There were also formerly examples at Worthing in 1897, a Walter MacFarlane bandstand that opened at Clacton-on-Sea in 1899 and another at Bognor Regis (Fig 5.18).[18]

Most bandstands were established on sea-fronts, usually in carefully manicured gardens, but some were erected on piers. Among the earliest examples erected anywhere in Britain was a bandstand placed at the end of the pier at Llandudno, which had opened on 1 August 1877.[19] Other examples were on the South Pier at Lowestoft of 1884, beside a large pavilion, and at Southsea where a bandstand with an enclosure around it was the main occupant of the pier head when it opened in 1879.[20] At Weston-super-Mare, an octagonal bandstand dating from the early 20th century was erected in front of the entrance to the pavilion of the Grand Pier.[21]

In 1914, a new Band Pavilion was opened at Clacton-on-Sea as a part of the town's General Beautifying Programme. The polygonal bandstand was set within a sunken pavilion with a glass front protecting the band and audience from sea breezes. A number of other seaside resorts employed this formula of setting a bandstand within an enclosure. The Marine Parade Bandstand at Eastbourne in the 1920s had glazing around it to protect the musicians from the elements. It stood on slender iron columns at the top of the beach and this meant that the musicians were above their audience on the beach, but level with people in the seafront gardens. During the mid-1930s, a new band-stand was built in the vicinity of the seafront redoubt, replacing a Victorian one. It consisted of a central, circular bandstand finished with classical detailing, along with a two-storey curved structure to the east providing shelter and seating on the lower deck. The other new bandstand at Eastbourne, which dates from 1935 and survives, was erected in the centre of the main beach. It was designed by the Borough Council Engineer, Leslie Rosevere, and is an example of a bandstand combined with an enclosed seating area (Fig 5.19).[22]

At Weymouth, the pier bandstand opened in May 1939.[23] This was effectively an enclosed bandstand that projected across the beach to the sea and provided seating for 2,400 people. Despite its vulnerability to poor weather, it was

East Parade Bandstand, Bognor

Fig 5.18
This postcard shows what appears to be a military band playing in the bandstand on the seafront at Bognor Regis.
[PC10835]

used for concerts, dances, wrestling, rollerskating and the Miss Weymouth Bathing Beauty Contest (Fig 5.20). At the end of Blackpool's North Pier, there is a sun deck that includes a stage for musical performances, a form analogous to some of these bandstand enclosures.[24] The Floral Pavilion at Bridlington was another, but different, example of expanding the idea of the bandstand, in this instance into something akin to a diminutive version of a winter gardens. Built

in 1904, and extended around three years later to include an adjacent bandstand, it has a cast-iron framework that is largely glazed. In *c* 1960 it was extended further towards the sea and the Victorian bandstand was rebuilt (*see* Fig 9.33).[25]

The shift at some resorts from a freestanding bandstand to a more complex provision for music on the seafront during the first decades of the 20th century coincided with a move away from using iron to brick, stone and tile. This

Fig 5.19
The Eastbourne bandstand eschews the use of elaborate iron detailing, this time employing a neo-classical style, finished in cream faience with some decorative blue, green and black faience. A glazed screen surrounds the enclosure, sheltering concert-goers from breezes off the sea.
[OP13142]

Fig 5.20
Only the landward end of the 1939 Weymouth Pier Bandstand survives today. Most of the events that it hosted took place in the enclosure that existed until 1986, a structure that straddled the beach and ended over the sea.
[DP055535]

period also marked a shift from lavish Victorian exoticism to more classical forms and some art deco-inspired detailing, such as at Eastbourne. At Bexhill-on-Sea, an Edwardian bandstand with classical detailing was constructed as part of the development of the Central Parade in 1910–11.[26] At Blyth in Northumberland a rather lonely bandstand in the seafront gardens was added during the late 1920s in a similar, rather conservative classical style.[27]

World War II, changes in musical tastes and a reduction in the number of people visiting the seaside have all contributed to the decline and demolition of many, or perhaps most, seafront bandstands.[28] By the end of the 20th century bandstands were usually largely decorative items with only occasional use, though some resorts, such as at Eastbourne, still have a strong programme of musical entertainment. However, one seaside resort dared to create a new bandstand in the early 21st century. At Bexhill-on-Sea, between the De La Warr Pavilion and the Edwardian colonnade and bandstand, a new bandstand has replaced 'The Bus Shelter', an unsympathetic 1970s brick bandstand. The award-winning replacement was designed by Niall McLaughlin and was officially unveiled on 8 December 2001 (Fig 5.21).[29]

The beach hut

The beach hut can range in form from single timber sheds to multi-storeyed complexes of chalets, the exact configuration depending on the shape of the seafront and the number of anticipated customers. A line of timber beach huts along the seafront is the most common arrangement, echoing the lines of bathing machines from which they originate. At some resorts these small chalets have pitched roofs that might project in front of the cabin to create a sort of veranda, as at Southwold (Fig 5.22). Lining the bottom of the cliffs at Shanklin are white gabled beach huts, the doors and the barge boards of the roofs being painted in a variety of colours to provide a colourful backdrop to the resort's beach. At Bournemouth, following the creation of the new sea defences in the early 20th century, a line of beach huts was established and survives today, though only one or two probably date from 1909, a few from the 1930s, with the majority having been built during the 1950s and 1960s (*see* Fig 3.34).[30] At Scarborough, some of the chalets added beside the South Bay Pool between the wars share a common roof, the veranda area in front being defined by a light timber-framed arch, uprights

Fig 5.21
Beside the De La Warr Pavilion at Bexhill-on-Sea, steel, plywood and fibreglass were used to create the curved shell of the bandstand's canopy, which provides fine acoustics, as well as echoing the changing shape of the sea behind. [DP073065]

Fig 5.22 (right)
A row of classic beach huts at Southwold, with small verandas at the front, have been painted in a wonderfully haphazard kaleidoscope of colours. [K030616]

Fig 5.23 (below)
In 2007, Jabba the Hut, a modern take on the beach hut, was erected on the beach at Mablethorpe. It was one of five huts on the Lincolnshire coast featured in the Bathing Beauties festival, Britain's first beach hut festival. [DP139820]

and side panel. A similar arrangement had first been used in a simpler form by Scarborough's Borough Engineer Harry W Smith at the town's North Bay in 1910.[31] An unusual arrangement exists at Frinton-on-Sea, where the line of beach huts is raised above the beach on a tall timber deck, meaning that they are entered from the landward side and have no access at sea level, and at Mablethorpe a definitely one-off approach was taken to beach hut design (Fig 5.23).

Timber is the most common material for individual cabins, but some lines of beach huts are constructed of brick or concrete. At Weymouth, the two lines of 1920s chalets at Greenhill Gardens have part of the tennis courts and bowling greens above them. A post-war line of chalets at Lowestoft has verandas partly

enclosed by a brick wall and their more substantial construction has allowed the creation of
a sun deck above. The desire to have individual
beach huts in a more focused arrangement led
to terraces of beach huts (Fig 5.24). At Saltburn
during the 1920s two tiers of 10 chalets
were created on terraces cut into the cliff.[32]
At Swanage, there are various arrangements of
beach huts, including single stand-alone cabins,

lines of chalets, a terraced arrangement of
timber huts created, unusually, on the landward
side of the main road and tiered terraces of
beach huts on the seafront. A similar arrangement can be found at Porthmeor Beach at
St Ives and at Folkestone, where tiers of white
concrete beach huts resemble lookout towers.[33]
Some resorts invested in more substantial
complexes (Fig 5.25). In 1935 at Broadstairs,

Fig 5.24
At Tolcarne Beach
at Newquay, simple
rectangular concrete
beach huts dating from
1936 are arranged in
four tiers, predominantly
in long terraces and with
doors of the assigned
colour for each tier.
[AA052657]

Fig 5.25
The Overstrand building at
Boscombe is a substantial
three-storeyed, concrete
block built in 1958. As well
as chalets on the upper
floors, the ground floor has
various facilities, including
some now aimed at surfers,
as well as the universally
welcome toilets.
[DP114039]

the Urban District Council erected a two-tier bathing station at the base of the cliff. Constructed of reinforced concrete, it provided 66 bathing cubicles and 32 chalets, while the flat roof acted as a promenade and sun deck.[34]

Spending a penny, and washing your hands

The provision of toilets remains a major commitment for local authorities today, who have to maintain facilities beyond the level that would be required for their resident population. At many resorts, some of the main facilities used by holidaymakers are incorporated into the large, publicly accessible entertainment venues such as piers and amusement arcades, and even the railway station at Cleethorpes, but most seaside resorts also have stand-alone toilet blocks provided by the local authority.

Public toilets were beginning to become available even before main sewers had been constructed. Large cities started to install them during the early 19th century, beginning in Paris, then in Berlin in 1820 and finally reaching London by 1851.[35] One of the unsung features of the Great Exhibition of 1851 was the presence of 'Monkey Closets' designed by George Jennings (1810–82), who contributed a number of improvements to the design of sanitary engineering.[36] A penny was charged to use the retiring rooms apart from the men's urinals and by the time the event closed in October 1851 receipts totalled £2,441, income

that guaranteed that the principle of paying to use public toilets would continue.

Although seaside resorts had small populations compared to major cities, the annual influxes of holidaymakers, including trippers with no overnight accommodation, meant that there was pressure to provide public conveniences. An issue to ponder is the impact that a lack of toilets had on the sight and smell of the seafront in the early days prior to purpose-built facilities being available. One of the first seafront public conveniences was housed in the octagonal stone basement beneath the elaborate 1883 'Birdcage' bandstand at Brighton (see Fig 5.17).[37] The same combination of a basement public lavatory with a bandstand above appears at the southern end of the seafront at South Shields, in a structure probably dating from the 1930s (Fig 5.26). The decision to convert it into a fish and chip shop by constructing a modern addition was greeted unfavourably by many local residents, though it afforded opportunities for the local newspaper to indulge in headlines such as 'Batter future for South Shields seafront'.[38]

Toilets combined with bandstands were a rarity, the most common approach being to create a self-contained toilet block, often set in front of, or into, any cliffs or slopes. Examples include blocks at Eastbourne, Bournemouth, Scarborough (Fig 5.27) and Brighton, while a toilet block is set into the cliff beneath the entrance to the 1930 Cabin Lift in the North Shore at Blackpool (see Fig 3.33).[39] At Great Yarmouth, where the seafront is entirely flat, the main central toilet blocks of 1900 employ some

Fig 5.26
At South Shields, the brick podium housed toilets, including original toilet stalls and urinals. Above, the elegant colonnade of Tuscan columns could serve either as a viewing platform or a bandstand. It is now part of the fish and chip restaurant.
[DP175003]

modest Edwardian detailing to soften their visual impact (Fig 5.28). At Weston-super-Mare, where there is a similarly flat seafront, the freestanding public lavatories bear the date of 1905. They are in an eclectic Edwardian style with plasterwork and timber framing providing a hint of the Tudor in a building that is far from being ashamed of its function.[40] At Withernsea, a dated brick toilet block of 1909 is embellished with pilasters, finials and a small clock tower. The block stands in the Memorial Gardens, but also serves the seafront across the road.

As well as historic toilet blocks, some seaside resorts have modern facilities in car parks, such as the large block in the car park near the old town at Hastings, while at some resorts, such as at Southport, they are in the seafront gardens. A toilet block is also a design feature of the

Fig 5.27
At Scarborough, a 1900 brick toilet block with elaborate detailing and tiling inside was constructed into the hillside beside the central seafront. [DP175001, DP175002]

Fig 5.28
Coincidentally, this is another dated toilet block of 1900, though this example at Great Yarmouth is freestanding. Created beside the site of the former jetty, it incorporates the remains of an earlier fountain of 1859. [DP217470]

Fig 5.29
At Cowes, in the seafront
gardens, there is a lavish
cast-iron c 1890 drinking
fountain supported on four
pillars with a domed and
fretted canopy.
[DP004978]

recent revamping of the seafront at Bridlington, a scheme that also features outdoor showers and beach huts, treated in a modern style (*see* Fig 5.31). Purpose-built toilet blocks can also be incorporated into larger structures, such as the clock tower at Morecambe, which also includes a shelter and a kiosk selling food and drink.

Public conveniences have also been created by converting other buildings. At Weymouth, toilets are housed in the ground floor of an elaborate red-brick building with Portland stone detailing that was formerly occupied by the Westminster Bank.[41] On the seafront links at Blyth, public toilets have been created in the engine house that supplied power for a World War I Defence Electric Light installation.[42] The arrangement of some seafronts permits the creation of underground toilets as part of a town's sea defences such as at Bognor Regis, Margate and Weymouth. These provide practical facilities without creating a potentially unsightly block.

As well as toilets, the provision of clean water is necessary for drinking fountains and showers (Fig 5.29). The 1900 toilet block at Great Yarmouth has the remains of a drinking fountain attached to it, a marble commemorative stone recording that it was a gift from Robert Steward in 1859 (*see* Fig 5.28). A short distance to the north of Eastbourne Pier there is a cast-iron drinking fountain erected in 1865 by local resident Elizabeth Curling (1790–1873).[43] It was restored in 2000 after having been moved to its current location and old photographs show it originally had a gas lantern on top. To commemorate Queen Victoria's Diamond Jubilee, a clock tower was erected on the seafront at Shanklin on the Isle of Wight, which incorporates a drinking fountain with the inscription 'KEEP THE PAVEMENT DRY' (Fig 5.30). The provision of showers is a more modern phenomenon and usually takes the form of a purely utilitarian facility, a vertical pipe with a showerhead and a tray or drain to capture the water. However, in the gable end of the modern lifeboat station at Blackpool there are two moulded concrete alcoves, one containing a drinking fountain, the other a foot washing shower, and Bridlington has integrated showers into its modern promenade (Fig 5.31 and *see* Fig 4.25).

Although provision is inevitably focused on the needs of people, animals were also considered at some resorts. Water troughs survive on the seafront at a number of resorts, including

Fig 5.30
The combined clock tower
and fountain at Shanklin
was felt to be both a fitting
tribute to Queen Victoria
and a means to provide
residents and visitors
with practical facilities.
[DP005437]

Fig 5.31
At Bridlington, the new facilities created to the south of the harbour include three sets of showers within artworks employing decorative motifs designed to alert visitors to the function of the facility.
[DP006329]

a cast-iron example at Scarborough and the stone one near the Trocadero, opposite Central Pier at Blackpool (Fig 5.32). There is also a granite trough at Great Yarmouth provided by the RSPCA in 1912 and this has been incorporated into the modern public realm as a practical drinking trough for the horses that still pull carriages along the seafront.[44]

Parks and gardens

The creation of public parks and gardens was an act of philanthropy or an initiative taken by a local authority concerned with the welfare of its citizens and visitors. By 1850, 18 municipal public parks had been established, but it was not until the Public Health Act 1875 that local authorities were given statutory powers to acquire and maintain land for recreation.[45]

At seaside resorts, the pressure to provide a healthy place for recreation was perhaps felt less acutely as residents and visitors had access to the beach and the sea. The commercial drive of resort development meant that there was little space for non-profit-making features on the seafront, such as civic halls, churches and parks. However, at some resorts the character of the land behind the beach precluded large-scale construction, leaving this area free for less intensive use. Therefore the existence of gardens on the seafront at seaside resorts, and their size and character, will depend on the particular geography of an individual settlement (Fig 5.33). Along most of the seafront at Blackpool and Brighton there are no gardens, but at North

Shore and Hove respectively the geography of the seafront changes, leading to the incorporation of some gardens in the former case, and open lawns in the latter. At Weymouth, the main part of the resort has a thoroughly man-made seafront, with just one small triangular garden, Alexandra Gardens, though this is now dominated by a large amusement arcade. At Eastbourne, there is only room for a narrow strip of formal garden, a small area of grass and colourful flower beds (*see* Fig 1.9).

On some stretches of seafront, the lack of space has encouraged local authorities to install hanging baskets or create planters. One stretch of the seafront at Weymouth has raised flower-beds, the coping stones of the surrounding walls also serving as seating. Some resorts have what amounts to vertical gardens. In the centre of

Fig 5.32
This drinking trough at Blackpool was provided by the Metropolitan Drinking Fountain and Cattle Trough Association, which was established in 1859. At most resorts, such troughs have now been converted into planters.
[AA060304]

Fig 5.33
This view of the gardens and seafront at Herne Bay was taken from the clock tower, which is illustrated in Chapter 10. The gardens are narrow, hemmed in between the beach and the main road. They are arranged with decorative planting within small, grassy areas.
[DP076205]

Scarborough, the hillside from the beach up to the town is partly devoted to a public garden and there is a vertical garden in the centre of Ventnor. Along Madeira Drive at Brighton there is a green wall, which is up to 20m high. Over 90 different species once grew on this retaining wall along the eastern part of Brighton's seafront, and it has been a curiosity since the first half of the 19th century.[46]

In contrast, the natural topography of resorts such as Southport, Skegness and Great Yarmouth with a sandy foreshore or reclaimed land has led to the creation of wide seafront gardens incorporating more or less substantial water features (Figs 5.34 and 5.35). Great Yarmouth has a public seaside park designed by the Borough Engineer S P Thompson in 1926 and the Venetian Waterways that it incorporates were constructed in 1928 as part of relief work for the unemployed.[47] At the edges of some resorts, there are areas of more or less untouched sand dune, and one such area to the north of Great Yarmouth is designated as a Site of Special Scientific Interest. At other resorts, the arrangement of a narrow beach in front of cliffs might prompt the development of clifftop gardens, such as at Clacton, Filey, Folkestone and Scarborough.

As well as being designed to fit with the geographical space available, seafront gardens have to combine the enjoyment of residents and visitors with the challenges of wind, sea and salt.

In formal gardens, such as those at Herne Bay or Eastbourne, lavish displays of colourful annuals in well-prepared flowerbeds delight holiday-makers during the summer, but perennials have to be chosen to cope with climatic conditions. A firm favourite, and a symbol of sun and seaside holidays, is the palm tree and where climatically possible it is a conspicuous feature of many seafronts, particularly in the southern part of England.

At some resorts, themes for gardens have been introduced, with Clacton and Hunstanton both providing sensory gardens. The most famous example of a garden exploiting a shingle beach is the late Derek Jarman's highly influential garden at Dungeness. At Worthing, the Waterwise Sculpture Garden on the beach, designed by John Marder and installed in 2006, was commissioned to raise awareness of ways of conserving water.[48] Marder is a freelance horticulturist and garden designer who provided the plans for this shingle garden.

At some seaside resorts there are also more or less private gardens on the seafront, green oases in an urban environment to be enjoyed by residents in the houses surrounding them. An inspiration for this comes from the Steine in Brighton, originally an undeveloped area leading inland from the seafront, which gave its name to planned developments elsewhere in Brighton and at other Sussex resorts such as Bognor Regis and Worthing. The land that

Fig 5.34 (above)
This modern aerial photograph shows the Marine Lake at Southport that now separates the town from the sea. In the distance can be seen some seafront development of retail units and entertainment facilities, but most construction is back behind the Marine Lake.
[NMR 28774/050]

Fig 5.35 (left)
Skegness has a small canal system that snakes along much of its seafront, a feature made possible by significant reclamation.
[DP175104]

would form the gardens of Kemp Town to the east of Brighton was enclosed by Thomas Read Kemp in 1823 when building work first began. Responsibility for these gardens was entrusted to Henry Phillips (1779–1840), who would later audaciously erect the ill-fated Anthaeum to the west of Brunswick Town, an unsuccessful attempt to provide an enclosed oriental garden in a conservatory.[49] This garden at Kemp Town is probably the earliest example at any seaside resort of a private, enclosed garden. It would inspire later developers over the subsequent decades to include gardens within their prestigious developments, one of the first being James Burton's St Leonards where a subscription garden was created behind the seafront.

Conclusion

With sea defences, services and basic tourist facilities in place, the seafront is ready to welcome tourists. In subsequent chapters, the focus will shift from the practical, sometimes large-scale infrastructure and smaller-scale, but necessary facilities, to looking at the activities taking place on seafronts. Today the seafront is associated with fun, play and relaxation, but in the 18th century the seaside resort had a strong association with health. Bathing in the sea was the reason that seaside resorts came into existence and before any local government bodies began to invest in the structure and facilities of seafronts, private investors had been providing basic facilities designed to improve visitors' health. The first of these, arguably the most curious, is the bathing machine, an invention of the early 18th century but one still found on the seafront of many resorts in the early 20th century. During 200 years of changing practices regarding health, the seafront has also witnessed the construction of facilities such as bathhouses and swimming pools, the latest examples of the latter type now being more commonly associated with entertainment and leisure. In Chapter 6, the changing attitude towards the sea, sea bathing and health will be described and the various manifestations on the seafront of changing practices and attitudes will be outlined, before turning in later chapters to the equally serious business of fun.

The pursuit of health

Prior to the 18th century, the sea was usually seen as a source of food and salt, and as a natural defensive barrier. It was home to monstrous creatures and was feared because it could devastate communities, taking lives and destroying a local economy by smashing harbours and inundating land.[1] However, by the beginning of the 18th century, a few people were embracing the sea in a new way. It was becoming England's bath, where physical and mental ills could be washed away, and the seafront, inevitably, has been at the forefront of delivering this treatment. Bathing machines were a constant presence on seafronts around the coastline for almost 200 years. Many resorts also provided bathhouses, heating seawater for bathers who did not want to endure the cold of England's seas.

During the 19th century, swimming for exercise and pleasure became more important. Larger pools were added to existing bathhouses and new purpose-built indoor and outdoor facilities were established across the country, not only in seaside resorts, but also in every major town and city. The culmination of this programme was in the interwar years when vast, elaborate indoor and outdoor facilities were provided at some resorts.

Although the sea has always been at the heart of the seaside holiday, the health-giving character of the environment of coastal towns was also recognised to be important. The bracing fresh air, filled with the scent of the sea, salt and seaweed, was thought to be beneficial for improving a person's health, including patients recovering from illnesses and operations. From the late 19th century onwards, the sun became a more significant factor in the seaside holiday. A suntan became associated with good health, but it was also increasingly a status symbol, a demonstration that a person had the time and wealth to enjoy a long, and later a foreign, holiday.

The origins and science of sea bathing

Although there are occasional, scattered references to sea bathing and the use of sea water during the 16th and 17th centuries, its widespread use, and therefore visits to the seaside, began to emerge in a more concerted way in the early 18th century. This is in part a result of the development of medical science after the Restoration, but is also a reflection of the growing amount of published and unpublished material that survives from this period. Sir John Floyer recognised that 'Since we live in an Island, and have the Sea about us, we cannot want an excellent Cold Bath, which will both preserve our Healths, and cure many Diseases, as our Fountains do.'[2] In this simple statement he made the explicit, logical link between cold-water bathing and sea bathing, ushering in the new, national vogue for the sea.

While Floyer and other medical writers were well versed in classical scientific works, it was the emerging scientific culture that encouraged them to make their own observations about the impact of sea-water bathing on ordinary people. At Brighton, Dr Richard Russell (1687–1759) used women working on the seashore to demonstrate that the sea and sea air was good for health.[3] He is celebrated for his influence on the popularity of sea bathing during the mid-18th century, but at Scarborough by the 1730s the naval surgeon John Atkins (bap 1685, d 1757) and the physicians Thomas Short (c 1690–1772) and Peter Shaw (1694–1763) were already advocating the use of sea water.[4]

The scientific consensus of Georgian medical writers was that people should bathe in cold water; Floyer explained that hot things did not agree with the English constitution.[5] However, as early as 1768, Dr John Awsiter at Brighton suggested that a warm bath might more effectively open the pores and allow salt water to penetrate the skin.[6] His thinking was undoubtedly influenced by the prospect of his new bathhouse that opened in the following year on the seafront at Brighton, but his ideas also found support from Dr Thomas Reid in Kent (*see* Fig 6.13).[7]

There was, however, agreement that sea bathing should take place during the morning, before any food was consumed. Interestingly, a version of this medical opinion or myth has survived in popular culture as a cautionary for children to avoid swimming on a full stomach. Scientific explanations might be medical, but bathing before breakfast seems to have had a commercial motive, leaving the remainder of the day for 'patients' to enjoy the pleasures of the entertainment facilities. Dr Belcombe at Scarborough in the early 19th century believed that 'The morning, however, in general is the most convenient time for bathing; as it leaves the rest of the day for other exercises and amusements.'[8]

By the mid-18th century, there is evidence that ordinary people were beginning to follow doctors' advice. Sea bathing was common on the Lancashire coast at the August spring tide, when it was believed that the waters had special powers of purification and regeneration.[9] Nicholas Blundell bathed in the sea near his home at Little Crosby, near Liverpool. The first reference to this occurs on 5 August 1708, six years after his diary begins, suggesting that it was still only an occasional and novel activity: 'Mr Aldred & I Rode to the Sea & baithed ourselves ... it was extreamly hot as were also the two preceding days, the lick hardly ever known at this time in these parts' (*see* Fig 2.1).[10] A year later, Blundell's family bathed for medical reasons, probably to cure a skin disease: 'I went part of the way towards the Sea with my Children but turned back, my Wife & Dorothy Blundell went with them, they were put into the Sea for some out breacks.'[11] In 1718, Samuel Jones, a customs officer at Whitby, wrote a poem praising the spa water and the sea for curing jaundice and in Lincolnshire in May 1725 'Sr Hardolf Wastnage & his lady come in Whitsun week to a farmhouse in this neighbourhood to spend three months in order to bath in ye sea'.[12]

By the 1720s, a distinctive bathing culture seems to have been beginning to emerge, and perhaps implausibly the earliest town with clear evidence of this is Liverpool, where there was a seafront, or technically a riverfront, bathhouse and bathing machines.[13] At Scarborough, there is plentiful evidence of a lively sea-bathing culture by the 1730s. A book that was effectively Scarborough's first guidebook in 1734 described how sea bathing was undertaken (Fig 6.1):

It is the Custom, for not only the Gentlemen, but the Ladies also, to bath in the Sea: The gentlemen go out a little way to Sea in Boats (call'd here Cobbles) and jump in naked directly; 'tis usual for Gentlemen to hire one of these Boats, and put out a little a way to Sea a fishing. The ladies have the Conveniency of Gowns and Guides. There are two little Houses on the Shore, to retire to for Dressing in.[14]

By 1750, a small number of other coastal towns were following Liverpool and Scarborough's lead. Ports such as Liverpool, Portsmouth, Southampton and Margate were hosting sea bathers and at Brighton in 1736, a family was 'sunning ourselves on the beach' after their 'morning business' of 'bathing in the sea'.[15] The earliest reference to sea bathing at Weymouth occurs in 1748, where a document records the erection of 'two wooden bathing houses on the N. side of the Harbour.'[16] When Dr Richard Pococke and Reinhold Rucker Angerstein were travelling around England during the 1750s, they recorded sea bathing and bathing machines at a handful of places, suggesting the spread of the new fashion was still slow, but would gather pace during the second half of the 18th century (Fig 6.2).[17]

The absurdity of bathing machines

Between the 18th and the early 20th centuries, a more or less strict etiquette governed bathing in the sea. In the 18th century, men bathed in the nude and women wore thin linen slips that would cling to their bodies when wet. Setterington's view of Scarborough suggests that women were on the beach while men bathed, but usually some form of separation was enforced. At Blackpool in the 1780s, men and women bathed at different times during the morning, the changeover being marked by the ringing of a bell, but at more popular Brighton each sex had its own section of beach.[18] A 1770 guidebook tells of a man who 'accidentally' turned up to bathe in the area reserved for

Fig 6.1
John Setterington's View of the antient Town, Castle, Harbour, and Spaw of Scarborough in 1735 includes a depiction of sea bathing. Men are shown entering the sea from a cobble, and he also illustrated a single primitive bathing machine. [CC80/00145]

Fig 6.2
The Swedish industrial spy Reinhold Rücker Angerstein visited Scarborough in 1754 and observed that the bathing and spa industries were the principal sources of income for the town. Angerstein's view of Scarborough echoes the scene depicted by John Setterington some 20 years earlier, including the spa building and 'bathing houses'. [Courtesy of Jernkontoret]

women at the end of the Steyne and a dipper, one of the guides for bathers, drove him off to the stretch of the beach devoted to male bathers.[19] At Ilfracombe, the Tunnels Beaches, reached from the bathhouse via a tunnel through the cliff, were treated as separate male and female beaches until 1905.[20]

The bathing machine was a way of monetising the sea, canny entrepreneurs using it, as well as bathing rooms and bathhouses, to profit from an entirely natural phenomenon. The naval surgeon James Rymer bemoaned this fact: 'For my own part, for the sake of exercise, pleasure and health, I would prefer the "crystal pool" and salubrious sea to all cisterns and reservoirs whatever. But delicacy and the valetudinarean state are here excepted: to such we recommend bathing houses, machines, and such like.'[21]

Although a bathing machine may seem an absurd contraption, a hindrance to sea bathing rather than a way of promoting it, it nevertheless remained at the heart of the seaside experience for almost 200 years. Its origins can be traced back to the 1720s, before the term 'bathing machine' had been coined.[22] On 2 August 1721, Nicholas Blundell wrote that 'I went with Pat: Acton to Leverpoole & Procured him a Place to Lodg at & a Conveniency for baithing in the Sea.'[23] The term 'Conveniency' was being used for something that had not yet acquired a name, in this instance probably a primitive bathing machine. A similar use of the word appears in 1735 referring to sea bathing at Scarborough:

Bathing in the Sea, is, of late Years, at Scarborough, with the Spaw, grown into great Credit, frequented by both Sexes, and those of the best distinction, as a pleasant, and a medicinal Exercise; there being few Cases, wherein a moderate use of it, cold or warm, that is, Morning, or After-noon, when the want of the Sun has chill'd, or his lucid beams beat for hours on the Surface. They have a fine long Sand from the Town to the Cape, commodious for Gentlemen to retire and undress at any Distance from Company, or to push a little off the Beach in Boats; and the Ladies have Guides, Rooms, and Conveniences for it, under the Cliff.[24]

John Setterington's view of Scarborough in the same year depicts the small boats used by male bathers and shows a naked man emerging from a primitive four-wheeled bathing machine,

probably one of the 'Conveniences' to which Shaw referred (see Fig 6.1).[25] In 1753, Benjamin Beale at Margate revolutionised its design, adding the concertina canvas hood to the rear of the vehicle to allow a modest bather to enter the sea unseen, as well as providing some protection from wind and waves.[26] Dr Richard Pococke, who visited Margate in September 1754, provided the first description of sea bathing using these machines:

This is a fishing town, and is of late much resorted to by company to drink the sea water, as well as to bathe; for the latter they have the conveniency of cover'd carriages, at the end of which there is a covering that lets down with hoops, so that people can go down a ladder into the water and are not seen, and those who please may jump in and swim.[27]

The earliest depiction of Beale's bathing machine is on a sheet of paper inserted into a copy of the 1736 edition of Reverend John Lewis' *The History and Antiquities, Ecclesiastical and Civil, of the Isle of Tenet* in the Society of Antiquaries in London.[28] James Theobald's drawing (Fig 6.3) is accompanied by a description of how 'Bathing Waggons' operated:

The above is a View of the Machine to bath with, it contains a Room to undress and dress in with Steps to go down into the Sea [. It] will hold 5 or 6 People. There are men and Women Guides who if desired attend. The price is 4

shillings a Week or £1 1s for Six Weeks and you pay your Guide for every attendance. They drive into [the] sea till it is about breast high and then lets down the Screen which prevents being seen under which you go down the Steps into a fine sandy bottom.

Typical 18th-century bathing machines were usually designed for one, or perhaps two bathers, though by the late 19th century larger, multiple-occupancy saloons had appeared at a number of resorts, including Weymouth (Fig 6.4 and *see* Fig 2.16). However, if more than one bather was determined to use a machine this could be accomplished as Dickens described in his 1836 essay, 'The Tuggses at Ramsgate':

And, sure enough, four young ladies, each furnished with a towel, tripped up the steps of a bathing-machine. In went the horse, floundering about in the water; round turned the machine; down sat the driver; and presently out burst the young ladies aforesaid, with four distinct splashes.[29]

By the mid-18th century, the number of resorts with bathing machines was growing and the number of machines was increasing. In 1745, Samuel and Nathaniel Buck's engraving of Scarborough depicted five bathing machines in the sea with a further five on the shore and Angerstein's sketches showed nine in use in 1754 (Fig 6.5).[30] By the end of the 18th century between 30 and 40 were catering for bathers, a reflection of the growing popularity of sea bathing.[31] Margate witnessed a similar expansion; the handful of bathing machines available during the early years of the resort had risen to 11 by 1763, 30 in 1790 and 40 by 1793.[32]

Nevertheless, bathing machines were still sufficiently rare and strange to merit discussion in guidebooks and comment by authors. Margate's guidebooks from the 1760s onwards provided visitors with helpful and practical information about how to use bathing machines, accompanied in one case by a handy annotated diagram.[33] Descriptions of bathing machines even appeared in literary works. Tobias Smollett's *The Expedition of Humphry Clinker*, published in 1771, includes a lengthy description of a bathing machine.[34]

'Patients' using bathing machines could also rely on the support of guides, often described as 'dippers'. Fanny Burney recorded George III's

Fig 6.4
This 1930s postcard of Weymouth, advertising the restaurant in the Clinton Arcade, shows how the remaining bathing machines were used to enforce the separation between the male and female saloons.
[DP024380]

1750   WEYMOUTH. Aerial View showing position of
THE CLINTON RESTAURANT
AERO PICTORIAL LTD.
136 REGENT STREET. W.1.

first dip in the sea at Weymouth in 1789: 'The King bathes, and with great success; a machine follows the Royal one into the sea, filled with fiddlers, who play "God Save the King," as his majesty takes his plunge.'[35] John Nixon's contemporary depiction of the event suggests that a number of female guides also accompanied the bathing machine and royal personage into the sea. At Scarborough in the 1780s, each lady bather was attended by two guides and gentlemen had one guide.[36]

Although bathing machines are long gone, they have left a slight legacy at some resorts. The shape of 19th- and early 20th-century sea defences was conditioned by the need for them to gain access to the sea. Sloped access to deploy them, as well as other beach attractions and boats, was needed at regular intervals. At some resorts there were fixings in sea walls, probably

to secure the bathing machines. There are metal loops set into the sea wall every few metres on a stretch of the seafront at Bournemouth, which may have been used to tie up boats or bathing machines and a similar arrangement can be seen at Shanklin and Seaton (Fig 6.6). At some seaside resorts there may have been rails to take bathing machines into the sea. In 1784, at Lowestoft a bathing machine with an attached crate and hood was deployed on tracks.[37] The New and Improved Safety Carriage at Folkestone, patented in 1888, consisted of 'a number of cabins on an iron frame fitted with wheels, running on a tram line ... The carriage is drawn up and let down by a wire rope, and can be worked by hand, gas or other power.'[38]

By the late 19th century, the beaches of larger resorts were dominated by dozens of bathing machines, but bathing cabins and tents were beginning to appear. In the 1880s, there were around 60 bathing machines on Weymouth's beach, but by the 1920s bathing saloons and beach huts had gradually replaced them (*see* Fig 6.4).[39] At Southend-on-Sea, almost new bathing machines were already being sold off in 1920 and in the same year the local authority at Broadstairs replaced 'old-fashioned' bathing machines with tents and huts.[40] The need to clear beaches to install anti-invasion defences during World War II dealt the final blow to the few bathing machines that had survived as bathing cabins.

The decline of the bathing machine corresponded with a liberalisation of bathing practices, resulting in bathing from the beach becoming the norm for both sexes. At Bournemouth in 1883, the Improvement Commissioners published bathing rules:

Fig 6.5 (above)
This engraving by Samuel and Nathaniel Buck of Scarborough in 1745 is from a similar viewpoint to Setterington's work of 10 years earlier. It also shows bathing machines and a busy harbour, and depicts the rebuilt Spa after the landslide of 1737.
[BB86/03835]

Fig 6.6 (below)
At Seaton there are a regular line of rings fixed to the sea defences, which may have been for boats or bathing machines.
[DP196950]

It is recommended in all cases of bathing [that] suitable bathing drawers be insisted upon. That persons be allowed to bathe from the landing stage of the Pier between the hours of 6am and 8am. That no bathing whatever be allowed from the shore between the Steps Chine to the East of the Pier and Joseph's Steps to the West of the Pier, except from bathing machines. That beyond the shore limits to the east and west boundary of the District persons be permitted to bathe from the shore up to 9am and after 7pm. That bathing be allowed within the last mentioned limits up to 11am and after 6pm from tents or from inclosing screens.[41]

The prudery once enforced by local bylaws was increasingly being replaced, if not always in law, at least in reality, by what came to be known as 'Mackintosh bathing', namely turning up at a beach with a swimming costume beneath a coat. This began before World War I, Bexhill-on-Sea being one of the first resorts to allow, officially, mixed bathing.[42] This new bathing practice encouraged the provision of alternative, temporary structures on beaches and more permanent ones on the seafront. In 1906, a bathing-machine operator in Hastings replaced some of his machines with canvas bathing cabins inspired by the colourful tents that were common on continental beaches. At Thorpeness, 'Dhoolie bathing cabins', portable canvas cabins, took the place of the 'old-fashioned, unwieldy bathing machines of other days' (Fig 6.7).[43] Another solution to providing changing facilities on the seafront, derived from Mediterranean resorts, was the bathing platform, a small-scale pier on which there were changing cubicles and an opportunity to jump or dive into the sea. Thomas Pettman leased part of the foreshore at Cliftonville beside Margate and erected a bathing platform (Fig 6.8).[44] At Herne Bay, at the base of the East Cliff, a bathing station was opened in 1912.[45] It consisted of a row of fixed cabins on the promenade, divided into male, female and family sections. Bathers would enter the water via narrow, horizontal gangplanks that extended out over the beach towards the sea and a water chute allowed bathers to slide into the sea, at least when the tide was in. The limited popularity in Britain of bathing platforms was probably due to the difference between the small tidal range in the Mediterranean and the often much higher ones in the seas around Britain.

Fig 6.7
This Walter Scott photograph of Filey in September 1934 shows a line of canvas cabins on the beach above the high tide mark, much as bathing huts now line the seafronts of many resorts.
[WSA01/01/17504]

Fig 6.8
This Aerofilms photograph
of 1933 shows the Marine
Terrace Bathing Pavilion
on the seafront at Margate,
with Dreamland behind.
In 1937, an open-air
bathing pool would be
opened in front of it.
[EPW042850]

Bathing rooms – a solution to local problems

At Margate in the mid-18th century, a distinctive bathing procedure developed in response to the town's sudden popularity, but consequent shortage of bathing machines. On 9 October 1753, a group of local men signed a 21-year-long lease 'to build and erect a waiting Room for Bathing in the sea at his and their own Expense, Cost and Charges'.[46] Two years later, a similar lease was signed for another plot and by the time that Margate's first guidebook was published in 1763, three bathing houses were available:

> The bathing Rooms are not large but convenient. Here the company often wait their turns of bathing. The guides attend, sea water is drank, the ladies' dresses are taken notice of, and all business of the like kind is managed. There are three of these rooms, which employ 11 machines till near the time of high water, which, at the ebb of the tide, sometimes runs two or three hundred yards into the bay.[47]

By the early 19th century, a number of local and national guidebooks explained how bathers were expected to use the bathing rooms.[48] Between 6am and noon, when bathing machines operated, a prospective bather arrived and chalked their name on a blackboard. While waiting for a bathing machine they could read the latest newspapers, drink coffee or sea water, look out to sea, enjoy conversation and even play a piano. A later guidebook recorded how the bathing rooms were 'filled with every luxury, including yesterday's newspaper, and a piano with a rich banjo tone'.[49] Later, the bathing rooms served as entertainment venues: 'in the evening, parties assemble in the different rooms, and, what is seldom found in other places of the kind, accord in amity, and find an innocent and laudable entertainment for themselves'.[50]

By 1797, there were seven bathing rooms on the west side of the High Street and at least one provided heated salt-water baths, as well as serving as a waiting room.[51] A major storm in 1808 destroyed many seafront buildings, but by 1822 there were still six bathing rooms at the foot of the High Street (Fig 6.9).[52] They

Fig 6.9 (left)
The rebuilt High Street
bathing rooms at Margate,
with their perilous stairs
down to the sea, are clearly
shown in this engraving of
1812. The return elevation
of Philpot's establishment
advertises 'warm salt
water baths and machines
for bathing' and the large
building beyond is the
circulating library at the
foot of the High Street.
[DP022308]

Fig 6.10 (below)
The low height of the
bathing rooms can be seen
on the left side of the High
Street at Margate. Legal
covenants prevented taller
buildings obstructing the
views from properties on
the west side of the street.
[BB67/08933]

provided customers with warm and cold baths, as well as one or two shower baths and a vapour bath; they had effectively evolved from being waiting rooms into bathhouses. The bathing rooms were entered from the High Street, but at their rear there were stairs down to the sea below where bathing machines waited. However, with the creation of Marine Drive along the seafront in 1878–80 a row of buildings was erected on reclaimed land, thus isolating the bathing rooms from the sea.[53] Although these buildings have now gone, they have left their imprint on the street (Fig 6.10).

The term 'bathing room' was used in other resorts, though in most cases it seems to have simply referred to another place for bathing. However, around 1795, improvements were made at Ramsgate 'for the accommodation of the company, while waiting for their machines'.[54] *The Bathing Place, Ramsgate*, a 1782 engraving, indicates that this accommodation comprised simply a few weatherboard huts at the base of the cliff to the north of the harbour.[55] From here, bathers passed via wooden gangplanks to the beach where they could board bathing machines. At Broadstairs there were waiting rooms at the bathing place beside the harbour, while at Hastings, the waiting room in 1797 was described as 'a small box, called the bathing-room, for the use of the company while waiting for the machines.'[56]

Bathhouses – for invalids, for everyone

An almost universal feature of seaside resorts was the bathhouse, which was logically, though never exclusively, located on the seafront. The first 'seafront' bathhouse that is known was in Liverpool. In 1728 Samuel and Nathaniel Buck published *The South-West Prospect of Liverpoole*, an engraving showing the river frontage of the rapidly expanding town.[57] In the bottom left corner, there is a small, undistinguished rectangular building, standing on its own beside the river (Fig 6.11). A late 18th-century view shows this same modest Georgian building with extensions at either end.[58]

In 1736, a bathhouse on the seafront Parade at Margate was advertised in local newspapers:

> Thomas Barber, Carpenter, at Margate in the Isle of Thanett, hath lately made a very convenient Bath, into which the Sea Water runs through a Canal about 15 Foot long. You descend into the Bath from a private Room adjoining to it.
>
> NB There are in the same House convenient Lodgings to be Lett.[59]

In 1737 another advertisement provided more detail about the bathhouse, which was described as being accompanied by 'Lodging Rooms, Dressing Rooms, and a handsome large sash'd Dining Room' and 'a Summer House, ... which affords a pleasant Prospect out to Sea.'[60] In 1740, an article in a local newspaper described it again:

> 'tis quite enclosed, and covered by a handsome Dining Room; and that there is a neat Dressing Room, and Dresses, adjoining to the Bath; and as the House fronts the Sea, there is a most delightful Prospect; and the Number of people that have received Benefit from Bathing, sufficiently demonstrates its Usefulness.[61]

Quebec House beside the docks at Portsmouth is a weather-boarded bathhouse dating from 1754, mentioned in that year by Dr Richard Pococke: 'The town of late has been resorted to for batheing and drinking the sea-water, and they have made a very handsome bathing-house of wood, at a great expence, with separate baths and apartments for men and women.'[62] (Fig 6.12).

Fig 6.11
Samuel and Nathaniel Buck's view of Liverpool of 1728 includes an isolated building at the far left side. A comparison of this building's location with the position of the bathhouse on the 1765 and subsequent maps demonstrates that this was the town's early riverside bathhouse. [BB86/03830]

In 1768, Dr John Awsiter at Brighton, who advocated bathhouses for use by invalids all year round, published a blueprint for a small purpose-built one. He stated that any prospective bathhouse should be situated near the sea for the convenience of collecting sea water and that

A building whose area is thirty feet, and twelve feet high, will admit of four rooms, with a bath in each, a lobby for servants to wait in, with a space behind them the whole length of the building, for the copper, the fuel, and cold bath, which must be kept supplied with fresh sea-water pumped out of the sea at half tide ... here it is necessary to observe, unless ordered otherwise by the physician, that a hot bath should never exceed the natural heat of the body, and any medium between 50 and 80 degrees of Fahrenheit's thermometer will be a good standard.[63]

In the following year, Awsiter built the first bathhouse on the seafront at Brighton close to the established sea-bathing section of the beach (Fig 6.13).[64] In 1780, it was described as follows: 'On one side of a spacious vestibule are six cold-baths; and on the other side are the hot baths, sweating bath, and showering-bath. The baths are supplied with water from the sea

by means of an engine.'[65] This small bathhouse survived until the 1860s and although it was raised and extended it was still recognisable through the period when the Prince Regent was holding court nearby and even survived the arrival of the railways.[66]

By 1776, Sidmouth was beginning to be visited by 'company resorting hither for the benefit of bathing and drinking the waters' and therefore Mr Taylor, a local surgeon, 'erected conveniences for warm sea-bathing and the cold shower bath', the site of which is now part

of the seafront Mocha cafe. At Teignmouth by the 1820s, Mrs Hubbard kept the baths located on the beach and constructed the town's first sea wall to protect her investment.[67] Southend-on-Sea had a small, probably late 18th- or early 19th-century bathhouse on the seafront; a photograph of *c* 1865 shows Ingram's Warm Water Baths to be little more than a single-storeyed, weather-boarded shack.[68] However, Great Yarmouth's first bathhouse may have been a larger building. Built in 1759, it was described by James Rymer in 1777: 'This Bathing House is built of brick ... and divided into three chief parts. The first whereof, is the bathing place where the reservoir is: The second is the tea room – alias dressing room, for ladies; and the third is do. for gentlemen.'[69] Rymer later provided more detail:

The vestibule is a neat, and well proportioned room. On the right of the entrance are four closets, having each a door into the bath-room. This bath is 15 feet by 8, and is appropriated for gentlemen. A similar one is assigned for the use of the ladies ... A hot salt water Bath is lately fitted up, with a convenient waiting and dressing-room; and there are Machines, equally commodious, on the Beach.

Rymer could also boast that 'In short, the accommodations here are perfectly adapted either to the bather for health, or pleasure: the attendance is good, and the charges are reasonable.'[70] At the north end of the bathhouse, a public room was added in 1788 for tea and coffee, breakfasts, balls and concerts.[71]

By the 19th century, bathhouses were beginning to diversify into a wider range of treatments, which might be medical in character, but often were edging towards modern pampering. In the early 1820s, Deen Mahomed opened a large bathhouse on the seafront at Brighton in which he practised shampooing, using oils to massage patients.[72] In his 1822 book, Mahomed claimed that the herbs in his baths had been brought from India and in a secret process he prepared a special concoction to treat patients with a huge range of illnesses.

By the first half of the 19th century, Hastings and St Leonards had a number of competing seafront bathhouses. The Marine Warm Baths had been constructed on the Parade near the Royal Marine Library between 1800 and 1804 and new warm baths were erected in 1815 to the east of the Battery, near the fish market.[73] The large Pelham Baths was erected alongside Pelham Crescent during the mid-1820s: 'The Entrance is by a spacious stone hall, which leads into two handsome saloons, of an octagonal form and decorated with beautiful Chinese scenery ... Here are eleven warm baths – two vapour – two shower – and a fine plunging bath.'[74] By the 1830s, the bathhouse in nearby St Leonards in front of the hotel offered eleven baths, shower baths and a plunging bath.[75]

During the early 19th century, other resorts experienced a similar expansion in their facilities to cater for increasing numbers of visitors. William Fry, visiting Margate in August 1826, recorded in his diary that 'Just before breakfast had a dip in the warm salt water Bath, the heat thereof 96 degrees, for the good of my Lumbago'.[76] These were presumably still baths on the seafront, somewhere on the Parade or in the bathing rooms on the High Street, as he then went on to describe the Clifton Baths that were being hewn out of the nearby cliff at the time. These new baths, begun in 1824 and completed by 1831, combined a range of health and leisure facilities with storage for bathing machines (Fig 6.14).[77]

As well as combining baths with rational genteel entertainments, another way to generate income was to accommodate visitors. In July 1820, Howe's Baths in Weston-super-Mare opened on Knightstone Island.[78] The site was purchased in September 1830 by Dr Edward Long Fox (1761–1835) and his son, who developed the island as a place for hydro-therapeutic treatment.[79] Their new bathhouse, which survives today, was built in 1832. The ground floor contained hot and cold shower baths, dry hot and vapour baths, which could be medicated with sulphur, iodine, chlorine and douches. The other rooms in the building included three sitting rooms, seven bedrooms and suites of service rooms and water-heating apparatus (Fig 6.15).[80]

The ultimate expression of the multi-functional nature of 19th-century bathhouses was the Bathing Establishment at Folkestone opened in July 1869.[81] It was designed by Joseph Gardner with a swimming pool and plunge bath and a variety of medicated baths and invalid baths at beach level. On the first floor, there were warm and cold baths, and on the top floor there were separate Subscription and Assembly Rooms (Fig 6.16).

Swimming

As early as 1878, the lack of a large swimming pool was recognised by the Directors of the Folkestone Bathing Establishment Company at their Annual General Meeting.[82] Therefore, an extension was added to the front to provide a larger swimming pool, a recognition of a changing attitude to the sea and an acknowledgement of a new activity that would be at the heart of people's relationship with the sea in the late 19th and 20th centuries.

By the early 18th century, bathing in the sea usually involved a short trip out in a bathing machine and a brief dip in the sea. Swimming did not play a reported role in the standard Georgian health regimen, but this did not mean that it did not take place. In *Robinson Crusoe*, published in 1719, the hero's native companion Friday was an excellent swimmer and Edward Baynard, the physician and poet who collaborated with Sir John Floyer, published *Health A Poem* in 1716 in which he proclaimed that

Of Exercises, Swimming's best,
Strengthens the Muscles of the Chest,
And all their fleshy parts confirms,
Extends, and stretches Legs and Arms.[83]

Fig 6.14 (above)
Clifton Baths at Margate was constructed in a circular form and topped with a domed room that contained newspapers, an organ and, by 1851, a billiard table. The large entrance in its ground floor was for storing bathing machines.
[BB85/02168A]

Fig 6.15 (left)
Knightstone Island at Weston-super-Mare still retains the Georgian bathhouse looking out to sea. An Edwardian swimming pool and pavilion, as well as modern blocks of flats, now also grace the island.
[NMR 33066/014]

Fig 6.16
The Bathing Establishment
was constructed on the
seafront at Folkestone,
a short distance from the
cliff lift shown to the left.
This Aerofilms photograph
of 1920 shows the extension
in front for a larger
swimming pool.
[EPW000080]

In Setterington's view of Scarborough in 1735, rightly celebrated as the earliest depiction of sea bathing and a bathing machine, men are shown swimming in the sea, an activity entirely ignored in the contemporary literature concerning the emerging seaside resort function of this port (*see* Fig 6.1).[84] However, in Tobias Smollet's *The Expedition of Humphry Clinker*, Jeremy Melford writes to Sir Watkin Phillip that 'I love swimming as an exercise, and can enjoy it at all times of the tide, without the formality of an apparatus' and in the early 19th century, Lord Byron was known to have been a very capable swimmer.[85]

The earliest examples of purpose-built pools were in major towns and cities, or at places of learning.[86] Spa towns and seaside resorts were well supplied with bathhouses and, while these were usually equipped with small or individual baths, some did have plunge pools that would have allowed some swimming. The Cleveland Baths at Bathwick to the east of Bath had a D-shaped pool measuring 137ft (41.8m) by 38ft (11.6m) with a crescent of changing rooms surrounding its curved end.[87] In 1832, an indoor tepid bath was erected beside the Hot Bath in the centre of Bath providing a larger

pool than bathers had enjoyed at any of the Georgian baths in the town.[88] Seaside resorts also began to provide visitors with baths large enough in which to swim, despite having the sea on hand. In 1823, a building opened at Brighton containing a large, circular, public bath that was used for swimming, and the baths on Knightstone Island at Weston-super-Mare included an outdoor tidal pool by the mid-1820s.[89]

In the first half of the 19th century, new baths were predominantly provided by private investors, Liverpool's St George's Baths of 1829 being a rare example of local government involvement. Some major settlements had few or no facilities and stimulated by growing concern for public health, the government passed the Baths and Washhouses Act 1846.[90] In the following year, a second act extended local authority powers to be able to charge for outdoor swimming pools, though it would be some time before any provision was made for similar indoor facilities.[91] By 1870, at least 49 public baths had been erected in England and Wales and by 1901 there were 210.[92]

During the 1870s, swimming came to the forefront of the public imagination and featured explicitly in legislation for the first time. In August 1875, Captain Matthew Webb successfully swam the English Channel and duly became a national hero (Fig 6.17).[93] The Public Health Act of 1875 included clauses allowing funding for swimming pools, while the 1878 Baths & Washhouses Act empowered local authorities to provide covered swimming baths.[94] The growing interest in swimming was also reflected in the establishment of swimming associations and clubs from the late 1860s onwards and by 1896 it was one of the core elements of the inaugural Olympic Games in Athens.[95]

During the same period, some pools were beginning to be built at seaside resorts with swimming in mind (Fig 6.18). In 1859, sea-water baths were built on Blands Cliff at Scarborough, while a decade later at Brighton, Brill's Baths were built on the site of Awsiter's old Georgian bathhouse in a seafront block near where the Palace Pier would later be erected.[96] It had a circular pool 65ft (19.8m) in diameter, a rare example of a non-rectangular pool.[97] Designed by George Gilbert Scott, it resembled a Gothic, polychrome-brick version of the Pantheon, an epic structure costing an epic £90,000. Near the seafront at Blackpool, swimming baths on Cocker Street opened at the beginning of the 1870s. In the early 1880s, the Prince of Wales Baths was created on the seafront between the North and Central Piers, providing bathers and performers in aquatic shows with a plunge pool 103ft (31.4m) long by 35ft (10.7m) wide beneath a glass roof supported on stone pillars.

Fig 6.17
Captain Matthew Webb (1848–83) reached Calais on 25 August 1875 after 22 hours in the sea. This monument on the seafront at Dover was funded by public subscription and was unveiled in 1910. [DP217428]

In May 1878, a large swimming bath opened on the seafront at Hastings. It contained a pool measuring 180ft (54.9m) by 40ft (12.2m) and another smaller one half the length for ladies opened during the following year. William Miller saw the men's pool during the 1880s, which was 'refilled with water from the sea three mornings in the week, when an admixture of hot water or steam is injected in order to remove

Fig 6.18
At Southport, the Victoria Salt Water Baths opened in July 1871 on the promenade and the largest of its six baths was large enough for swimming. [AA053222]

any chill, but one morning going in after it had been so refilled I found the water uncomfortably hot'.[98] The building closed in 1911, but was revived in the early 1930s as part of the comprehensive transformation of the seafront by the Borough Engineer Sidney Little.[99]

The 1870s also saw the beginning of the appearance of aquaria at seaside resorts, the earliest being at Brighton, which opened in 1871 (*see* Fig 9.30). The aquarium at Scarborough, which was nestled beneath the Valley Bridge, was designed and built in 1877 by Eugenius Birch, who had also designed Brighton Aquarium. The largest tank in the building, which was the largest in the world at the time, contained over 75,000 gallons of water and was sometimes used for swimming exhibitions.[100]

Diving also featured at some pools. As early as 1837, the National Swimming Society had added diving boards to its six swimming pools in London and the profile of the sport was raised when it was included in the 1904 Olympics.[101] To cater for diving required investment in diving boards and towers; the most striking example was at Weston-super-Mare where an elaborate, concrete art deco structure was created (Fig 6.19). Wicksteed and Co, renowned for producing playground rides, also manufactured more affordable, tubular steel, diving stages that were installed at many pools. The other expense caused by diving was due to the additional depth required in a pool, high boards needing around 5m-deep water.

Some pools encouraged playing by providing chutes. One had been erected at the Knightstone Swimming Pool at Weston-super-Mare as early as 1913 and by the end of the 20th century such simple pleasures had given way to the elaborate flumes of water parks and leisure centres (*see* Fig 6.29).[102] Playing was not left solely to children; at a number of seaside resorts 'professors' carried out daring displays of aquatic and diving skills, such as Professor Harry Parker who did imitations of sea life, lit cigars, drank champagne and even escaped from handcuffs.[103] The feats of professors are celebrated in sculptures on the seafront at Southport, including Professor Gadsby, a one-legged diver, and Professor Osborne, who frequently plunged off the pier on a bicycle or dived from a high board.[104]

After an initial burst of enthusiasm for providing pools for swimming during the 1870s, there appears to have been little appetite for providing new facilities by either seaside local authorities or private investors. Examples include the Medina Baths on the King's Esplanade at Hove of 1894 and in 1902 a large swimming bath was added alongside the Georgian bathhouse on Knightstone Island at Weston-super-Mare (*see* Fig 6.15).[105] When new baths were built at Brighton and Eastbourne in 1903 and 1905 respectively they were a considerable distance from the seafront, and, therefore, were designed for the resident population rather than visitors.[106]

Fig 6.19
The bathing pool at Weston-super-Mare, designed by the Borough Engineer H A Brown, opened in 1937. The elaborate diving-board structure was at the seaward side of the pool, where the water was at its deepest. Unfortunately, the temporary closure of the pool in 1982 led to the demolition of the diving platform.
[BB81/08493]

Indoor pools were erected in great numbers in large urban conurbations and, while some seaside resorts such as Blackpool and Brighton might be in that category, the availability of the sea, and the existence of early baths, seems to have been sufficient to limit later expenditure on covered pools. However, seaside resorts invested in outdoor pools, especially between the wars, as they could provide facilities for hundreds, or even thousands, of people. They also fitted in with the emerging interest in sun worship and the body beautiful and they allowed people to play in the water, as much as formally swimming.

One of the earliest outdoor pools was far from a grand facility designed for thousands. The Table Rock Bathing Pool at Brown's Bay, Whitley Bay was first developed in 1894 and extended to 70ft (21.3m) in length in 1896. It was again increased in size around 1908 after Whitley and Monkseaton Urban District Council took it over and until the 1950s there were also modest changing facilities for bathers.[107] This outdoor pool was presumably created by exploiting a natural hollow in the rocky foreshore and enlarging and regularising it into a rectangle.

The pool at Whitley Bay was scarcely more than a hole in the rocks, but by the outbreak of World War I, a much more ambitious outdoor pool was being created at Scarborough. The South Bay Pool was the brainchild of Harry W Smith, the town's Borough Engineer from 1897–1933. He believed that the provision of outdoor swimming pools might improve Scarborough's image and in 1900 he explained the advantages of an outdoor bathing pool:

A reduction of the risk of sea bathing to a minimum: bathing is possible at times when, owing to the rough seas, it would be risky to do so; more commodious accommodation and comfort can be provided for the bather than is possible in a bathing van; facilities for the holding of swimming galas and carnivals, with the attendant revenue to be obtained therefrom.[108]

Construction began on the South Bay Pool in April 1914 and it opened on 21 July 1915 (Fig 6.20).[109] This pool, and some of the subsequent interwar open-air pools, were huge compared to the Olympic swimming pool, which is 50m long by 25m wide. Work continued despite the war as the pool's monumental concrete wall also served as a sea wall to protect the cliffs from erosion. Initially the pool was provided with 137 dressing cubicles, hot and cold showers, first aid rooms and a separate block housing the pumping plant and laundry. Between the wars the Corporation added a cafe, restaurant and more seating for spectators on a

Fig 6.20
Harry W Smith,
Scarborough's Borough
Engineer, created an oval
pool at a cost of £5,000
measuring 350ft (106.7m)
by 180ft (54.9m). The South
Bay Pool closed in 1989
and after many years
of being left to decay it
was infilled and its site
incorporated into the park
at the foot of South Cliff.
[AA038528]

terrace hewn out of the cliff face, while further up the cliff three blocks of holiday bungalows for rent were created.

Although large and well-built, the South Bay Pool was nevertheless a fairly simple structure, but the same could not be said of the open-air pool that opened at South Shore in Blackpool. The baths, which opened on 9 June 1923, were reputedly the largest such facility in the world. They cost £80,000, 16 times as much as the pool at Scarborough, despite having a pool approximately the same size [376ft (114.6m) by 172ft (52.4m)].[110] The price difference was a reflection of its lavish architecture (Fig 6.21). Around the pool there was a colonnade of Doric columns flanking a central, Beaux Arts domed entrance and a cafe with a pergola-style roof terrace, open to the elements. There were 574 dressing rooms for bathers accessed from a concourse a third of a mile long around the pool, and tiers of seating could accommodate around 3,000 spectators on three sides (Fig 6.22). Between the wars, other

new lidos made extensive provision for spectators and in many places more people watched than swam.[111] In one period during August 1933, Scarborough's baths sold 31,000 tickets for bathers while 114,000 went to spectators. However, by the 1960s the popularity of the open-air pool at Blackpool, and outdoor pools in general, was in decline and so it closed in 1981 and was demolished in 1983. Its site is now occupied by the Sandcastle Waterworld indoor leisure centre (see Fig 6.29).

During the 1920s, around 50 outdoor pools were built, while in the following decade another 180 were opened, predominantly in large towns, with only a few being on the seafront of seaside resorts. In 1928, the Sea Bathing Lake at Southport opened at a cost of almost £70,000, its form, scale and style being inspired by Blackpool.[112] During the 1930s, Blackpool's and Southport's monumental classical style was replaced increasingly by moderne versions of art deco (Fig 6.23). In 1934, this was adopted

Fig 6.21
The open-air pool at Blackpool of 1923 was designed by Francis Wood, Blackpool Borough Engineer and Surveyor and his chief architectural assistant JC Robinson. It was located at the south end of the town, close to the South Pier and the Pleasure Beach.
[EPW029209]

Fig 6.22
On some days at the height of the season there were over 20,000 visitors to Blackpool's open-air pool and by the end of its first full season in 1924, more than 500,000 people had gone through the turnstiles. Only 94,403 were actual bathers, the remainder being happy to pay to sit, watch and relax.
[AFL03/Lilywhites/BLP43]

Fig 6.23
St Leonards Bathing Pool, which opened in 1933, was designed by the Borough Engineer of Hastings, Sidney Little. It had tiered seating for 2,500 spectators around the curved, landward side of the pool and beneath this was a gymnasium, and some underground parking.
[EPW042843]

for the pool at New Brighton; Morecambe's Super Swimming Stadium of 1936 was on a similar scale to Blackpool's baths of a decade earlier, but was effectively a moderne version of the earlier design.[113]

In 1935, Plymouth opened a lido on its rocky shoreline.[114] In this case, and at Penzance, these open-air pools provided access to the sea on a rocky, and therefore, otherwise largely inaccessible stretch of coastline (Fig 6.24). In 1937, the bathing pool at Weston-super-Mare opened, and like Morecambe it had a very large pool [220ft (67m) by 140ft (42.7m)] (Fig 6.25 and see Fig 6.19).[115] Many of these pools were on an enormous scale, much larger than Olympic-size pools, but at Saltdean, the last of the interwar moderne seaside lidos, the pool was a mere 140ft (42.7m) by 50ft (15.2m).[116] What distinguished this design was the elegant, curved structure that embraced the pool's landward side. Designed by R W H Jones, its centrepiece is a semi-circular central block, reminiscent of the stair tower on the De La Warr Pavilion at Bexhill-on-Sea.

While the interwar years saw the creation of monumental, elegant and architecturally sophisticated pools at some resorts, there was also a desire to provide more utilitarian pools to enable bathing more cheaply (Fig 6.26). At Weston-super-Mare, the distance from the beach to the sea at low tide prompted the establishment of the Marine Lake, created by constructing a concrete wall between Knightstone Island and the seafront to trap water within the enclosed area (Fig 6.27). At Margate in 1927, an open-air pool was built beside the century-old Clifton Baths (see Fig 6.14).[117] To provide further facilities, three simple tidal pools were created in 1937, two on the main beach and one at Walpole Bay (Fig 6.28).[118]

During the 1930s, a few seaside resorts decided that they required an indoor pool. Just behind the seafront, the SS (Super Swimming) Brighton was erected on West Street in 1934, with an indoor pool with seating for 1,900 and a pool measuring 165ft (50.3m) by 80ft (24.4m), which was claimed to be the world's largest indoor sea-water pool.[119] Another indoor pool opened on the seafront at Bournemouth in 1937, designed by the architect Kenneth Cross.[120] Blackpool's Derby Baths, which unofficially opened in 1939, contained a competition-sized pool at which swimming events were held after the war. Designed by JC Robinson, this stark moderne art deco structure cost an eye-watering £270,000; it was unfortunately demolished in 1990.[121]

In 1960, Lord Wolfenden highlighted the lack of sports facilities in Britain.[122] His report ushered in the era of the sports centre,

Fig 6.24
The Lido at Penzance, which opened in 1935, was designed by the Borough Engineer and Surveyor Frank Latham apparently to reflect the shape of a seagull alighting on water. It closed in 1993, but happily reopened after refurbishment during the following year.
[AA031412]

Fig 6.25
Although Weston-super-Mare had a long beach, the pool served a similar function to those at Penzance and Plymouth, allowing people to swim when the sea was unavailable, in this case because it had receded so far at low tide.
[EAW025157]

Fig 6.26
At Tynemouth, a small rectangular pool with some terraced seating beside it, more a large paddling pool than a lido, was built in 1925. By 2017, a community regeneration programme was raising funds to revive this facility.
[MF99/0753/28]

Fig 6.27 (above)
The Marine Lake at
Weston-super-Mare was
created through a job
creation scheme for Welsh
miners who were employed
to build the causeway in
the late 1920s.
[EPW039937]

Fig 6.28 (right)
This tidal pool at Margate
was constructed on the
beach beneath the
Edwardian Walpole Bay
Hotel. It provided a huge
area for swimming and
playing regardless of
the state of the tide.
[NMR 33057/038]

combining a range of sports and community facilities under one roof. Inevitably, these would be located to suit a town's populace, but at some resorts a seafront location proved to be appropriate. The Worthing Aquarena, which opened in 1968, cost £377,000 and was likened to a power station because of its stark lines and tall chimney.[123] It has recently been replaced by the Worthing Splashpoint on the same site, the name change reflecting a stronger emphasis on fun rather than sport. Blackpool's open-air pool was replaced in 1986 by the Sandcastle Water Park (Fig 6.29) and a similarly prominent seafront location was chosen for Great Yarmouth's Marina Centre, with impressive facilities in an unimpressive building. At Southsea, the seafront Pyramids was opened to the public in July 1988 providing a leisure and entertainment facility combining swimming, play activities, gym facilities and spa treatments inside a modernist, unsurprisingly pyramid-shaped structure.

Today, the vast majority of resorts have their swimming pool and leisure facilities inland, convenient for residents rather than visitors.

However, 'pools' still have some presence on seafronts, often in the form of small paddling pools and boating pools and even lakes, as was discussed in Chapter 5 (Fig 6.30). These successors of the large tidal pools of the 1930s provide safe places for small children of all ages to play and sail their skilfully made pond yachts without fear of danger from the sea.

Fig 6.29
Flumes mean fun!
Blackpool's Sandcastle
Water Park has colourful
flumes on its outside to
allow people to slide into
the pool on the inside.
[DP154865]

Fig 6.30
This 1959 Hallam Ashley
photograph shows the
paddling pool at
Bridlington. Although it
would only have required
a modest investment by the
local authority, it provided
a valuable year-round
attraction for paddling
and pond yachts.
[AA99/00311]

Cure and convalescence – the sea, climate and health care

Many doctors and medical writers also recognised that fresh air, a mild climate and, later, sunshine would also be beneficial to a patient's well-being. During the early 17th century, doctors in Cambridge were already sending patients to Great Yarmouth to enjoy the air blowing in from the sea.[124] Many local histories and guidebooks also included discussions of the climate of resorts, often praising the virtues of a particular location and noting its superiority to rival towns. The earliest was probably Dr Anthony Relhan's description of Brighton in 1761; although it was a history of the town, it also offered a medical appraisal of the resort due to his professional interest.[125]

A popular interest in climate was stimulated by an emerging scientific literature, led by Sir James Clark (1788–1870). He published two major books during the 1820s: a work on the relationship between the climate of southern Europe and pulmonary consumption and his major study of the influence of climate on health.[126] The latter work examined the impact of climate in general, rather than specifically seaside resorts, but for Brighton he did make observations about the relative merits of the climate of different parts of the resort.[127] In the 19th century, books were also published on the climate of stretches of the coastline and some works focused on the virtues of the climate of individual resorts, such as Bournemouth and Worthing.[128] There are also references to climate in general surveys of popular watering places; Augustus Bozzi Granville's *Spas of England and Principal Sea-bathing Places* in 1841 frequently mentions the temperature, rainfall and hours of sunshine of an individual resort.[129]

Consideration of climate was one factor in the decision to establish the Royal Sea Bathing Hospital at Margate during the 1790s, though the existence of a well-established sea-bathing culture and infrastructure, an available site and good transport links to London along the Thames were also significant. This initially modest institution was internationally influential during the 19th century, serving as a model for similar sea-bathing hospitals around the coasts of Europe, particularly in France and Italy.[130] On 2 July 1791, Dr John Coakley Lettsom (1744–1815) convened a meeting to discuss the foundation of a hospital to treat London's poor who were suffering from scrofula (tuberculosis of the glands, joints and bones). The seafront hospital was ready to receive its first 30 patients in May 1796.[131]

Designed by Reverend John Pridden, the hospital incorporated open loggias called piazzas beside the small wards that were located on either side of a two-storeyed staff and administration block. The loggias anticipated by a century the open-air treatment of pulmonary tuberculosis. Although exposure to sunshine and fresh air contributed to the treatments, sea bathing was the main way of curing patients. The physician at the hospital, Dr John Anderson, claimed that a wide range of conditions could be treated by bathing in the sea, including scrofula, rheumatism, scurvy, leprosy and rickets.[132] In 1820, a new wing was added with a Greek Doric portico, which local tradition says included reused columns brought from nearby Holland House (Fig 6.31).[133] The hospital was enlarged again in 1837, so that by 1841 it was treating 214 patients on the day the census was enumerated.[134] It was further extended during the 1850s by adding two wings, transforming it into a uniform piece of Greek Revival Classicism and in 1858 indoor baths were provided with salt water pumped up from the shore, replacing sea bathing as the main treatment.[135]

Over time the sea-bathing hospital at Margate was increasingly used for convalescence and a similar, but slightly later, facility at Scarborough enjoyed a similar transformation.[136] A sea-bathing hospital was first contemplated there in 1804 and, following fundraising by a number of local gentry and the support of local MPs including William Wilberforce, the Royal Northern Sea Bathing Infirmary was established in 1812 to cure 'sick poor who were proper objects for warm sea bathing' (Fig 6.32).[137] The infirmary's building still survives on the seafront near the harbour; unusually for a medical facility it was located near the heart of the historic town. It is more common for medical institutions, such as at Margate, to be located at the margins of resorts, on less commercially desirable sites. If sea water was not a major part of the treatment, they could be inland on a cheaper site where the air and climate was still therapeutically beneficial. However, a seafront site was early recognised as appropriate for convalescence and the treatment of tuberculosis due to the bracing, fresh sea air.

The earliest part of the Promenade Hospital at Southport was built at the north-eastern end of the seafront in 1852–3, by Thomas Withnell

Fig 6.31 (above)
The Royal Sea Bathing Hospital at Margate closed in July 1996, and after many years unoccupied, work began to convert it into flats. However, the project fell victim to the 'credit crunch' and other problems, and is still incomplete.
[DP219033]

Fig 6.32 (left)
A new building was constructed for the Royal Northern Sea Bathing Infirmary at Scarborough in 1858–60 to the designs of William Baldwin Stewart. Sea water was delivered to the infirmary in wooden barrels by horse and cart until 1888, after which it was pumped by gas engine from the adjacent public baths.
[DP006183]

for the Southport Strangers' Charity, to act as a convalescent hospital and sea-bathing infirmary (Fig 6.33).[138] At Whitley Bay, the Prudhoe Memorial Convalescent Home, built in 1867–9, faced east towards the sea; it was 'conveniently placed for sea-bathing purposes', being located on the seafront a short distance from the northern limit of the town.[139] The bathing facilities in the building included salt-water as well as fresh-water baths.[140]

Although Prudhoe was a convalescent home, the presence of bathing facilities suggests that medical treatments were part of the regime. However, purely convalescent facilities were also sometimes established on seafronts to exploit the sea air, sometimes adapting or incorporating existing buildings until a new purpose-built facility could be built. The Bartlet Convalescent Home at Felixstowe was built between 1923 and 1926, designed by H Munro Cautley (1875–1959), on top of the remains of a Martello tower. Some convalescent homes were created for specific types of patients. The Hornsea Children's Convalescent Home (Humberside) was built on the seafront to the north of the resort in 1907–8 for children recovering from bone diseases. The Children's Convalescent Home for Surrey was in Clarence Road on the seafront at Bognor Regis. It was donated by Sir Max Waechter in 1906 and

rebuilt in 1930 by Sir Jeremiah Colman to accommodate 40 children and two mothers with babies in a separate flat.[141] Nearby, the Convalescent Home for Women of Surrey was founded in 1897 in Surrey House on the Esplanade. This two-storey red-brick building was opened by the Duchess of York in 1900.[142]

Some convalescent homes were established by organisations representing specific industries and two of the miners' homes were built on the seafront. The Lancashire and Cheshire Miners' Convalescent Home was built in Blackpool in 1925–7 to house 132 men on a 7½ acre (3ha) site (Fig 6.34).[143] A second purpose-built convalescent home for Derbyshire miners, built in 1928 on a 4-acre site at Ingoldmells, near Skegness, could accommodate 124 male and 34 female patients. The ground floor contains communal recreation rooms at the front of the building with adjacent open-air rooms, sheltered from the coastal winds by larger billiard and recreation rooms on their east sides (Fig 6.35).[144] Charities were also active in the provision of convalescent facilities. The London Samaritan Society and Homerton Mission, founded by John James Jones, opened the Beach Rocks Sea-Side Convalescent Home at Sandgate near Folkestone on 25 June 1892 in a new purpose-built building, previously having used existing buildings.[145]

Fig 6.33
The Promenade Hospital at Southport was extended in 1862 and the substantial Hanseatic-influenced Gothic Revival front range was added in 1881–3 by Paull & Bonella. The building has been converted into flats.
[OP00600]

Fig 6.34
The Lancashire and Cheshire Miners' Convalescent Home in Blackpool contained a range of facilities. These included a smoking room, reading room, billiards room, winter garden, concert hall, retiring rooms and cinema. [DP174868]

Fig 6.35
The Derbyshire Miners convalescent home at Ingoldmells is arranged with its wings around two courtyards that act as sheltered sun-traps where patients could rest and exercise. [AA93/01438]

Although convalescent homes were set up to allow patients to recover in an environment offering fresh sea air, exposure to sunshine was increasingly being recognised as having medical properties. By the late 19th century, heliotherapy had become a well-recognised medical treatment in Alpine hospitals and at some seaside facilities, including at open-air schools, such as the one established at Hayling Island.[146] Exposure to the sun did not require patients to be on the seafront, but this new interest did have a wider impact on the architecture of the seaside, particularly in the interwar years. The new architectural vocabulary ushered in between the wars was perfectly suited to allowing light, as well as air, to flood into modernist houses, hotels and hospitals, and the new interest in sunbathing for pleasure, and to improve well-being, led to the creation of sun terraces, sun decks and sun lounges. One of the most useful, and most common, instruments to allow people to bathe in the sun was the humble deckchair, cheap, light and easy to move to follow the passage of the sun across the sky.

Another impact of the new ideas about embracing fresh air and exposure to the sun was the spread of naturism. It originated in Germany in the late 19th century and, by 1905, there were around 100 nudist societies in Germany, Austria and Switzerland.[147] By 1937, Britain's National Sun and Air Association had 2,350 members.[148] During the interwar years, naturists would use a secluded garden or a quiet part of the coast to meet, camp and enjoy games, sports and bathing.[149] After the war, consolidation of the various naturist groups took place and the Central Council for British Naturism, now known as British Naturism, was formed in 1964. In 1978, the first public naturist beach was established at Fairlight Cove, with the approval of Hastings Borough Council.[150] There are now dozens of places where naturism is tolerated including a few specially designated nudist beaches, the most prominent one being Brighton East Beach where the steep shingle of the beach screens nude sunbathers from the public riding past on Volks Railway.[151]

Conclusion

In the 18th century, the widespread belief that the sea could cure almost every ailment caused annual migrations of people afflicted with largely self-inflicted conditions caused by lifestyle and diet. By the 19th century, some form of break at the seaside was becoming available to most of the population, the more or less fresh sea breezes and, unfortunately often, polluted seawater offering some respite from the harsh living conditions of industrial cities. And during the 20th century, exposure to the sun was becoming part of the arsenal of treatments available to doctors, as well as a way of achieving a suntan.

While the seafront might seem the obvious place for purely medical facilities, there are relatively few examples in central parts of resorts because there was less money to be made from using a valuable seafront plot of land for a hospital than a hotel, a lodging house or an entertainment venue. Siting medical facilities on the margins of seaside resorts meant that the prestigious, central stretch of the seafront could be left to the serious business of entertaining holidaymakers and helping them to part with their hard-earned money. In the next two chapters, the ways that the seafront evolved to entertain and amuse visitors will be explored. In Chapter 7, the natural and sociable pleasures of the seaside holiday will be described, encompassing activities as varied as sandcastle building and donkey rides to Punch and Judy and pierrots. Chapter 8 will then look at how entertainment on the seafront was affected by the introduction of new technology, creating many of today's favourite activities, such as walking on a pier or riding a rollercoaster.

7

Fun and games

Entertainment was a major attraction for the first visitors to seaside resorts. With sea bathing taking place during the morning, there was a need to fill the remainder of the day socialising in entertainment venues. These could be set within the first line of buildings along the seafront, and examples will be examined in Chapter 9, but in most cases they were in the heart of the town, located where most people would be spending the majority of their day. The seafront during the 18th century was a place to walk, ride, race horses on the beach and admire the view; it was not at first an obvious place for wider leisure activities. However, by the 19th century, the beach and the land along the seafront behind increasingly became areas for relaxation and play. One of the catalysts for this was the erection of piers, initially constructed to facilitate the landing of passengers from ships, but they were soon in use first as a fashionable promenade, and later as a venue for entertainments.

By the end of the 19th century, the family beach holiday was well established, children and their parents enjoying a range of games, spectacles and activities, some of which have continued to the present day, such as riding a donkey or building a sandcastle. The seafront is also a place for sports and novelty forms of transport, and from the 19th century, it has been the venue for seasonal entertainers ranging from minstrels and pierrots to modern DJs. As well as activities on the land, the beach is the the departure point for people wanting to enjoy a trip round the bay, or, if more excitement is required, a trip on a jet ski.

As well as man-made pleasures, the beach is a place to relax, walk and contemplate. However, beaches can still be crowded, limiting the activities that can take place at busy times of the day. Crowds permitting, the beach provides opportunity to enjoy wonders of nature. The level of interest stimulated by popular Victorian science writers was feared to have destroyed the natural character of many beaches, but today people are still drawn to the beach to explore rockpools, find shells and, in some places, to discover fossils that reveal the planet's history.

In this chapter, the leisure pursuits of people on the beach and on the seafront will be examined. Broadly speaking, the focus will be on the fun and games that tourists practise while on holiday, particularly those relying on the natural quality of this distinctive space. New technology from the mid-19th century onwards transformed the nature of the leisure experience on the seafront and this will be examined in Chapter 8.

On the beach

The nature of any day spent on the beach will depend on the weather. A day with large seas and breaking waves may prove appealing to surfers but would be unsuitable for small children wanting to play in the shallows. Apart from weather, the most important factor conditioning a day on the beach is probably the tidal range of a resort. Tidal range, the vertical difference between high tide and low tide, has an impact on the nature of the beach activity and the facilities on the beach. At Weston-super-Mare, for example, provision has to be made for people wishing to swim and play in sea water when the tide has retreated almost to the horizon. In contrast, Weymouth's limited tidal range means that permanent, albeit small, fairground rides can be left on the beach all year round.

Any photograph of a beach is a snapshot of a moment. Every day a seaside resort will experience changing tides, so that at high tide the beach might almost entirely disappear, relegating sunbathers to the sea defences or the promenade. Modern stepped sea defences can provide ideal seating areas; this function was designed into the new coastal protection scheme undertaken at Margate to protect the old town in 2011–13.

The character of the beach also changes according to the time of day, the time of year and whether schools are on holiday. In the morning, it may be the place for a vigorous walk, but as the day heats up during the summer months of the year it will gradually be filled with people seeking to relax, enjoy a paddle or eat a picnic. On a hot day in midsummer, English beaches can still be packed with holidaymakers, just as they were in the 1950s or 1960s (Fig 7.1). In winter, a beach that might welcome land yachts and parasailing will be too busy for such activities during the summer and therefore they will be relegated to quieter beaches or to the less popular edges of main beaches. As night falls, families pack up to head home or to their bed-and-breakfast, to be replaced sometimes by younger people hanging out. The seafront in general, but the beach in particular, has long been recognised as a liminal space in which the restrictive norms of home can be, and often

were, relaxed. This might range from a Victorian gentleman daringly kicking off his shoes and rolling up his suit trousers to paddle in the sea to what euphemistically might be called holiday romances and their consequences (Fig 7.2). Similarly, while topless and entirely nude sunbathing might be practised on some beaches, this would not be an appropriate behaviour even in most people's backyards. At night, a few people might sleep on the beach, an experience fuelled by alcohol, a lack of money or a lack of accommodation. Bathing machines were sometimes colonised by people unable to find or afford rooms, while rough-sleeping at seaside resorts is a common sight and problem today, homeless people often finding a place to sleep in a seafront shelter or beneath a pier.

The experience of the day at the beach will also vary according to the age and gender of the holidaymaker, an energetic child having a very different experience from a tired mum

Fig 7.1
In the post-war years, the main beach at Blackpool between North Pier and Central Pier must have been the busiest in the country on a hot day. The resort attracted millions of visitors arriving by train at its two stations each year, sometimes disgorging tens of thousands daily onto this beach.
[AA047912]

and dad who would relish lying down for a few hours. People with physical and learning disabilities will also experience a day at the seaside differently, potentially facing challenges of access, familiarity and safety. For most adults enjoying a beach holiday, the key aim is to sit down, lie down and relax. This is not an activity that features much in Georgian writing about the seaside, the beach being a place to traverse, to enter the sea or to walk or ride along. However, by the early 19th century, spending a day sitting on the beach was becoming a standard part of the seaside holiday. In *The Tuggses at Ramsgate*, published in 1836, Charles Dickens describes the family's first day at the beach:

> If the pier had presented a scene of life and bustle to the Tuggses on their first landing at Ramsgate, it was far surpassed by the appearance of the sands on the morning after their arrival. It was a fine, bright, clear day, with a light breeze from the sea. There were the same ladies and gentlemen, the same children, the same nursemaids, the same telescopes, the same portable chairs. The ladies were employed in needlework, or watch-guard making, or knitting, or reading novels; the gentlemen were reading newspapers and magazines; the children were digging holes in the sand with wooden spades, and collecting water therein; the nursemaids, with their youngest charges in their arms, were running in after the waves, and then running back with the waves after them; and, now and then, a little sailing-boat either departed with a gay and talkative cargo of passengers, or returned with a very silent and particularly uncomfortable-looking one.[1]

An illustration of this type of day first appears in John Leighton's *London Out of Town* in 1847, a cartoon story that is highly derivative from Dickens' short story. It shows the Brown family wearing smart everyday clothes, father and mother sitting on lightweight chairs, with one daughter sitting beneath a parasol and one son using the telescope. In the distance, a donkey walks along the edge of the sea, and the family look on at two bathing machines and some boats further out to sea.[2] Limner's depiction predates any photographs illustrating a seaside holiday, but when these become commonplace towards the end of the 19th century, the same elements that Dickens and Limner record are evident. The chair shown in Victorian images is usually

Fig 7.2
This John Gay photograph of Blackpool after World War II shows an elderly man with rolled up trousers and his wife, presumably with a grandchild in tow, enjoying a paddle.
[AA047927]

a lightweight type of chair, something like a campaign chair used by military officers on their journeys.[3] Some of these chairs may have come from the lodgings in which people were staying, but chairs were available to hire on the sands of Ramsgate as early as 1829.[4] Photographs of the beach at Ramsgate during the last quarter of the 19th century suggest that the chairs and some small benches were still being provided on the beach by enterprising local businessmen (Fig 7.3).[5] These small chairs were fixed rather than folding, although folding wooden chairs, known as 'steamer chairs', began to be used on the decks of oceangoing liners from the 1860s.[6] Although these were sometimes known as 'deck chairs', the portable, folding chair with canvas seating was only patented during the 1880s and a number of photographs dating from *c* 1900 onwards show these chairs being employed in growing numbers.

The deckchair was the key piece of portable equipment required for a day at the beach during the 20th century (Fig 7.4). It was often supplemented by large sun umbrellas, which replaced the individual parasol as a means of preventing excessive exposure to the sun.

Fig 7.3 (above)
*That seats are being
rented out at Ramsgate is
suggested by the uniformity
of design of the chairs and
benches. Also, so many
appear in one photograph
to be entirely unoccupied,
as if waiting for customers
to pay for their use. In the
background is Ramsgate's
long-demolished seafront
railway station.*
[OP29135]

Windbreaks, screens to protect families from wind and blowing sand, are unfortunately also a requirement on many holidays. These accoutrements may be brought to the beach by holidaying families, but they can also often be rented from local authority staff, who may also provide larger sun loungers. Today, these are often supplemented by small pop-up tents that can protect against sun and wind, as well as

*Fig 7.4 (right)
John Gay's photographs
of Blackpool beach after
the Second World War
illustrate the central role of
the deckchair in the seaside
holiday. Amid all the fun
and games, older family
members can relax and
enjoy the sun.*
[AA047917]

providing a weatherproof storage facility and even a changing room for small children. Larger versions of such tents, inspired by Continental bathing practices, have appeared at English seaside resorts since the beginning of the 20th century (*see* Fig 6.7).

Having secured a patch on the beach, the relaxation can begin. Adults on holiday often face the regular commute between the sun lounger, deckchair or towel and the sea, alternately heating up and cooling down. However, a day at the beach is also a chance to read a novel or a newspaper, and, when bored, enjoy a saunter along the beach, perhaps in shallow waters on a hot day (Fig 7.5). A relaxing day at the beach also offers an opportunity to admire the view out to sea. Normally this is dominated by fairly prosaic activities and events, such as people playing in the sea, distant pleasure boats sailing by or the launch of the lifeboat on a training exercise. However, the beach is also an ideal place to see planned major events; these include regattas, most famously the event held annually at Cowes, and air shows such as the one that takes place each year at Bournemouth. Among the planned spectacles that beachgoers could have enjoyed in the past were reviews of the fleet in the Solent. In 1735, John Whaley (bap 1710, d 1745) undertook a summer tour of England. His letters to his pupil Horace Walpole and his notes record a visit to see the fleet at Portsmouth.[7] The last formal review of the fleet occurred on 28 June 2005 to celebrate the 200th anniversary of the Battle of Trafalgar. This attracted huge crowds to Southsea Common and Gosport Sea Front to witness the largest gathering of naval vessels in the Solent since 1977.[8]

The beach is also an ideal place to watch impromptu events; from 1789 until 1805 George III spent most of his summers at Weymouth, sometimes bathing in the sea accompanied by servants and a band of musicians, events that attracted crowds of onlookers.[9] Visitors to the beach near the North Pier at Blackpool in June 1897 would have been saddened by the site of the wrecking of HMS *Foudroyant*, Lord Nelson's former flagship, while at the same location in June 1938 spectators would have seen the seaward end of the pier on fire.[10] The beach may occasionally become an attraction when something monumental and interesting is washed up onto it. In the past, creatures that were washed up onto beaches were viewed as sea monsters.[11] A whale was washed onto the beach near Boscombe Pier in January 1897, and as well as providing spectacle for the curious, disposing of its 39-ton (40-tonne) carcass provided a significant challenge for the coastguard and the local authority. After stripping its flesh and dumping it at sea, its skeleton was displayed on Boscombe Pier until 1904.[12] In January 2016, five sperm whales were washed up on the Lincolnshire coast, the worst sperm whale stranding on the English coast since records began in 1913.[13] This event prompted thousands of visitors to come to see the whales and take selfies in front of the huge carcasses, but it also afforded scientists an opportunity to take samples and study the creatures.

By the mid-19th century, some holidaymakers assiduously collected samples of seaweeds and shells, much as they would collect insects and butterflies while in the countryside. This had been spurred on by the works of a number of Victorian naturalists, including Philip Henry Gosse, whose research into nature included guides to the seashore. In these works, he discussed the wildlife to be found there, including detailed consideration of the less glamorous invertebrates that occupied rockpools and beaches.[14]

However, by the late 19th century, it was feared that the collecting of shells and other specimens had caused irreparable damage to the coast.[15] Gosse's son recorded that the unforeseen consequence of this new interest was damage to the very environment that his father had lovingly documented.[16] One of the factors behind damage to seashores was the Victorians' new ability to create aquaria at home and the beach proved an ideal place to pick up specimens.

Another strand in the story of people's interest in nature at the seaside is fishing, apparently Britain's most popular pastime. At the seaside, this may take the form of fishing from the beach, from the end of piers or from boats. Almost every pier has a fisherman at the end of it at some point during the day, but Deal Pier actively promotes fishing with a tackle shop and a lively website dedicated to fishermen and their catches.[17] For children, the first introduction to angling might be through using a small net in a rockpool or a luminous orange hand-line dangled off the edge of a harbour. And no seaside holiday would be complete without a small fish or a crab being temporarily on display in a plastic bucket previously used for sandcastle construction.

Fig 7.5
Promenading was a popular activity in Victorian resorts. This early photograph of Broadstairs shows well-dressed people walking along the beach while a few children venture into the sea.
[BB70/01563; Courtesy of Alan Howarth Loomes]

By the early 19th century, fossil hunting was already a pursuit at some resorts. Lyme Regis became a destination for people interested in the activity, guidebooks celebrating it as the pre-eminent place for people, including members of the Royal family, to search for samples.[18] This was due to the interesting geology of the Jurassic Coast that was being promoted by a local woman, Mary Anning (1799–1847), a renowned collector and dealer who ran a fossil shop in the resort (*see* Fig 1.7).[19] During her lifetime fossils went from being a curiosity requiring explanation from biblical scholars to being at the heart of modern science as many scientists, the most celebrated being Charles Darwin, explored the origins and evolution of life. Today the beach at Lyme Regis is still popular with professional and more casual fossil hunters, particularly after a major storm, but for the unsuccessful there are also a number of fossil shops in the town. A comparable interest has developed around Whitby Jet, which has been used for making jewellery since the mid-19th century. It became particularly popular after Prince Albert's death in 1861 drove Queen Victoria into a continual state of mourning.[20]

People are also drawn to beaches to pick up bits of driftwood for art projects or simply to burn on their fires, but sometimes they may come in search of interesting, even potentially lucrative, flotsam and jetsam. Perhaps the most famous case of flotsam is the wreck of SS *Politician* that ran aground on Eriskay in the Outer Hebrides and became the inspiration for the 1949 Ealing comedy *Whisky Galore*. In November 2015, part of an unmanned *SpaceX Falcon 9* rocket drifted into the Isles of Scilly, while in January 2016 thousands of pink detergent bottles appeared on Cornish beaches.[21] The stricken container ship MSC *Napoli* spilled cargo from around 40 containers onto beaches on the south Devon coast in January 2007.[22] Although the police soon secured the unopened containers, around 50 motorbikes were carried off, as well as exhaust pipes, steering wheels and beauty cream. This scavenging may have caused amusement in the media, but oil spilling from the ship also caused difficulties for many seabirds, though this was on a small scale compared to the devastation caused by *Torrey Canyon* running aground off the Cornish coast in 1967.[23] The 700km² slick contaminated about 190km of the Cornish coast, killing around 15,000 sea birds along with huge numbers of marine organisms.

As well as the beach providing a place to find man-made and natural treasures, it is also the perfect place to sit and look out to sea, a telescope or a pair of binoculars allowing holidaymakers to improve their view of scenes at sea. In Charles Dickens' *The Tuggses at Ramsgate*, a telescope was an essential part of the family's equipment on holiday; in John Leighton's cartoon book, *London Out of Town*, Mr Brown, the father of the family, insists on purchasing a telescope before leaving home.[24] Today, some tourists in search of interesting ornithology bring their binoculars, to quieter beaches, where interesting migrants may alight en route to summer or winter feeding grounds.

As well as relaxing on a beach, many people, and particularly families with younger children, come to play. This can be gentle or energetic, informal or formal, friendly or highly competitive, and a range of fun and games possible on the beach can be enjoyed by children or adults, and by men or women (Fig 7.6). On sandy beaches, a popular pastime is to construct sandcastles, a task sometimes involving elaborate water engineering to create a moat (Fig 7.7). Probably the earliest reference to 'sandcastle' construction comes from Giraldus Cambrensis in the late 12th century, describing how during his child-hood he built churches and monasteries while his older brothers built towns and palaces in the sand.[25] While most sandcastle builders are content to create simple structures, some craftsmen have turned a simple pastime into an art form. At Weymouth, a small structure on the beach contains the latest works of Mark Anderson, whose grandfather Fred Darrington began sand sculpting in the 1920s.[26] Among their works have been a depiction of the Last Supper and a display celebrating the film ET (Fig 7.8). At Weston-super-Mare, for over a decade, there has been a sand sculpture festival; Brighton, despite not having a sandy beach, has also held a festival and a competition has been held on the Devon coast for many years.[27] A less ambitious use for a sandy beach is to bury a parent or a sibling, thankfully not permanently.

One thing missing from the central seafront of popular resorts during the middle months of the year will be dogs, these pets being rele-gated to the edges of beaches or to less popular stretches of coastline. However, from time to time, other animals appear on beaches: at Blackpool and Great Yarmouth it was once a fairly common sight to see elephants bathing in the sea near their respective circuses and in

Fig 7.6
This Walter Scott photograph taken at Filey in August 1930 shows a game of beach cricket, with batsman, wicketkeeper and a crowd admiring the spectacle. Two of the portable beach tents for changing and storage stand on the beach.
[WSA01/01/G0584]

Fig 7.7 (far left)
A 'child' has sought inspiration for his sandcastle from Bamburgh Castle behind or can the hand of a parent be detected in this work?
[MF99/0759/20]

Fig 7.8 (left)
On the seafront at Weymouth, most of Mark Anderson's works elicit a smile, but to commemorate the centenary of World War I he created this poignant war memorial in sand.
[DP219577]

143

the Isles of Scilly, until recently, a pair of reindeer enjoyed a regular dip in the sea, amusingly on a beach where dogs were banned.

The most common animal seen on many beaches during the summer is the donkey. They are now only associated with short rides for small children on the beach, but the earliest references to donkeys at the seaside suggest a wider usage such as in racing, trotting on the cliffs and as a practical means of getting around a resort. Fanny Burney went to see the races at Teignmouth on 2 August 1773, which began 'with an Ass Race. There were 16 – some of them really ran extremely well – others were indeed truly ridiculous: but all of them diverting.'[28] In August 1793, a similar sports day took place at Margate: 'we had, for the gratification of the amateurs of the grotesque and ridiculous, the following elegant sports: A Donkey Race, on which there was much betting – a Pig Hunt – men grinning through horse collars, and running in sacks.'[29] At Brighton in 1805, there is a reference to 'donkey-trotting on the cliffs' and in 1822 donkeys were available at Margate for one shilling per hour.[30] The Brown family on holiday in 1847, at a fictional version of Margate, hire donkeys to ride out into the countryside and a woman is shown guiding a donkey with a small child on it along the beach.[31]

Donkeys were also used for transport at some resorts. At Weston-super-Mare in 1822, donkeys were available for hire alongside 'Jaunting cars, wheel and sedan chairs, ponies', while at the end of the 19th century, in Margate a donkey chaise could be hired for 1s 6d for the first hour while the first hour in a goat chaise cost only 9d.[32] A writer in 1820 described the dual purposes of donkeys at Margate, providing fun by day and carrying smuggled goods at night.[33] Although donkeys might have at one time been involved in activities on the wrong side of the law, today their activities are very much governed by regulations to protect their welfare. The operators of donkeys now require licences and are regularly inspected, and Blackpool has a 'donkey charter' enshrining their rights.[34] Their working hours are from 10am to 7pm with an hour off for lunch at 1pm, and Friday is their designated day off. No person aged over 16, or weighing more than 51kg, is permitted to ride them and the animals and their harnesses must be kept clean (Fig 7.9).

Entertainers on the beach

The beach has also long been a place where people could be amused by professional entertainers. From the mid-19th century onwards, beaches were home to a range of musicians, acrobats, jugglers and banjoists.[35] These performers, who might be making their living on the streets of London and other major cities during the winter months, would migrate to the seaside during the summer.[36]

Punch and Judy is synonymous with beach entertainment. Glove puppet shows in a small booth had appeared in England by the mid-14th century and by the 1660s these were probably Punch and Judy shows, though initially they used marionettes rather than glove puppets.[37] Samuel Pepys went to see a performance by the Italian puppet showman Pietro Gimonde from Bologna in Covent Garden in 1662 and regularly records seeing puppet shows during the 1660s,

Fig 7.9
A drove of donkeys has obligingly lined up at Bridlington in size order for Hallam Ashley to take their portrait. Apart from the mother making sure her child remains on, these well-trained animals have remained in this pose without handlers.
[AA99/00354]

while by 1710 a marionette theatre had been established in London.[38] The earliest-known reference to puppets in a coastal town dates from 1710 when a puppet show was held in the Tolbooth at Whitby.[39] During the 19th century, the Punch and Judy show added features that make the modern show so distinctive; the glove puppet superseded the marionette, the dog Toby appeared around 1830, the Crocodile replaced the devil during the 1860s and by the mid-19th century, the swizzle stick was being used to create Mr Punch's voice.[40] These changes marked a shift from Punch and Judy being aimed at adults to an entertainment for children. Old photographs suggest that there were Punch and Judy shows at many, if not all, larger seaside resorts by the end of the 19th century, but their popularity gradually declined during the 20th century. Many of the 'professors', as Punch and Judy showmen are known, continued oral traditions begun by their fathers or grandfathers, including the Staddons of Weston-super-Mare, the Maggs of Redruth and Bournemouth, and the Smiths of Poplar. Albert Smith worked in London during the 1930s and his brother Charlie finally gave up his Margate pitch in 1963 (Figs 7.10 and 7.11).[41]

Fig 7.10
Today, there is only a handful of Punch and Judy shows still operating on beaches during the summer. This portrait shows Professor Davey at Lyme Regis with Mr Punch and the crocodile. [MF99/0672/35]

Fig 7.11
At Weymouth, the Punch and Judy booth is a semi-permanent feature on the beach and on the promenade there is a plaque commemorating Professor Guy Higgins (1933–2007) who was Weymouth's punchman from 1976 until 2004. [AA036100]

Punch and Judy is aimed at children, but some former beach performers for adults now seem equally politically incorrect. Black-faced minstrels and black American performers both arrived in London during the 1830s and 'Ethiopian' acts had appeared at the seaside by the 1840s.[42] The first of these performers were solo artists, echoing a longer, British tradition of acts that mimicked African characters. However, by 1843 the earliest minstrel troupe, an 'Ethiopian band' called the Virginian Minstrels, was appearing on British stages and was similar to that first depicted at the seaside by John Leighton in his cartoon book *London Out of Town*.[43] The mid-19th century was the period when music hall was evolving into a distinctive art form, but there was nevertheless a lingering feeling about the vulgarity of this new type of entertainment. Westward Ho! boasted in 1872 that visitors would never be 'annoyed by the vulgar discordant songs of Ethiopian 'serenaders'.[44] In 1877, Blackpool tried to banish minstrels and itinerant musicians, raising fears that the town was getting too grand, and the pierrots at Seaford were evicted in 1894 though they came back in later years.[45] As late as 1926 a guidebook published by the London Midland and Scottish Railway Company (LMS) assured holidaymakers that 'The pierrot has taken the place of the raucous nigger minstrel.'[46]

Nevertheless, the minstrel show was beginning to gain a reputation for being a decent and proper form of entertainment, just at the point when it would be supplanted by pierrots.[47] Pierrots were introduced from France in 1891, the first group being Clifford Essex's Pierrot Banjo Band; such performers soon came to dominate beach and seafront entertainment at some resorts.[48] The *Official Guide to Morecambe* of 1906 informed visitors that 'the Corporation license respectable troupes of Pierrots and "niggers" to give entertainments daily'.[49] However, minstrels were increasingly being displaced (Fig 7.12) and in 1904 the *Daily News* announced that 'niggers at the seaside have given place to pierrots'.[50]

By the late 19th century, a number of larger seaside resorts were sufficiently busy to support permanent troupes of entertainers. Margate had a minstrel troupe in the late 19th century called Uncle Bones' Margate Minstrels, while one of the last was Uncle Mack's Minstrels in Broadstairs, founded in the 1890s and lasting for 40 years.[51] Will Catlin operated troupes of pierrots at Scarborough, Great Yarmouth, Bournemouth, Whitley Bay, Bridlington, Colwyn Bay and Llandudno.[52]

Photographs taken during the late 19th and early 20th century often show these types of entertainer performing on the beach with a

Fig 7.12
Margate's sandy beach, easily accessible from its railway stations, was often packed with trippers. Here, men, women and children, sporting hats and bonnets, are entertained by a minstrel show in c 1900. [OP00621]

crowd gathered around them. However, at some resorts, such as Bognor, Mablethorpe and Morecambe, small stages were erected for use by entertainers (Fig 7.13). Before World War I, Scarborough Corporation charged £600 for a season's pitch, and early photographs and postcards show entertainers performing on a temporary stage (Fig 7.14).[53] Catlin's troupe of pierrots played on the beach at Scarborough, but

by 1906, as he was finding the rent to be too high, he bought some land near the seashore on which to erect a stage with a canvas top.[54] He later moved into the Arcadia, which had opened in 1903 which subsequently became the Futurist Cinema.[55] As well as small stages, the beach at one resort had a more substantial theatrical venue on it, if only probably briefly. A photograph taken in September 1904 from the

Fig 7.13
This photograph of Burnham-on-Sea in August 1909 shows pierrots performing on a simple platform set above the high tide mark. The audience sits on deckchairs on the sloping sea defences. [CC76/00328]

Fig 7.14
In the foreground, two minstrels on a makeshift wooden and canvas stage at Scarborough entertain visitors sitting on deckchairs. In the background, dozens of bathing machines are joined by a few people paddling in the sea. [DP022316]

Warwick Revolving Tower at Great Yarmouth shows a large circular theatre enclosed within a timber board wall, an arrangement suggesting a temporary, though perhaps summer-long creation by a visiting theatre company.[56]

As well as private provision of seafront and beach entertainment, some local authorities invested in music and entertainment. Seaside resorts found various ways to provide holiday-makers with musical performances. In Devon, the earliest bands were local, amateur groups, but as resorts became busier there was pressure to provide more professional performers. For instance, at Torquay a local band led the entertainment from the 1840s, but once the resort could offer a financial guarantee, it was able to attract more accomplished bands, for instance securing the services of a group of Italian musicians in 1871 (Fig 7.15).[57] In some towns, there was a resident, semi-professional band; at Clacton-on-Sea the town band under the conductor George Badger consisted of 10 members who were each paid £1 per week.[58] Initially, the provision made by local authorities for music was very limited, but in 1893 Bournemouth Corporation leased the existing winter gardens and established the country's first municipal orchestra.[59] Torquay, Brighton, Hastings and Margate followed suit and by World War I Margate Corporation ran the winter gardens, the orchestra and its concerts.

As well as small-scale sedate performances by a local band in a bandstand or on a beach, the seafront has occasionally been used for pop concerts, perhaps most famously the one staged by Fat Boy Slim at Brighton in July 2002. A free event entitled the 'Big Beach Boutique' was designed for 60,000 fans, but in the end a quarter of a million people crammed onto the beach. At Blackpool, the Tower Festival Headland on the promenade regularly hosts performances in a temporary arena that can be erected on top of the Comedy Carpet. Not all encounters between pop music fans and seaside resorts have been as positive. The beaches and seafronts at Brighton and Margate were regularly battlegrounds between mods and rockers during the 1960s.

The impact of major amusement parks on seafronts will be described in Chapter 8, but smaller rides may be located on beaches beyond high tide level where local conditions allow semi-permanent structures to remain in place for some, or all, of the year. Old photographs also show that suitable resorts up and down the country have had small rides on the beaches since the 19th century and among the resorts where this still occurs are Brighton, Cleethorpes, Margate and Weymouth (Fig 7.16). There are also more substantial single rides on seafronts such as larger carousels and observation wheels. Ordnance Survey maps and a photograph of *c* 1900 of Southport show that there was a version of a zip wire running across the Marine Lake (Fig 7.17).[60] At Folkestone, a full-sized switchback was erected on the beach to the west of Victoria Pier in 1888, which succumbed to a major fire in 1919–20 (Fig 7.18).[61] While major amusement parks were built on the seafront and Blackpool Pleasure Beach was established in the sand dunes behind the beach, the first ride at Great Yarmouth, an L A Thompson Switchback Railway, was erected on the beach to the north of the resort in 1887 and remained there until the early 20th century.[62]

Commerce on the seafront

At the height of summer, a beach may be a temporary home for thousands, or even tens of thousands, of holidaymakers, and consequently offer a potentially lucrative market for vendors. These can be broken down into broad categories

Fig 7.15
By the end of the 19th century, a number of bands, including military ones, would tour seaside resorts during the summer, their cost usually being met by the sale of tickets. This postcard of the elaborate new bandstand at Southend-on-Sea shows a concert in full swing.
[PC10136]

Fig 7.16
At Weymouth, where the tide is less of a threat, there are rides that remain in situ throughout the year. They are predominantly for small children and include swing boats, carousels, merry-go-rounds, bumper cars and trampolines. [DP054534]

Fig 7.17
The Aerial Flight at the Marine Lake at Southport, which was built in 1895 and dismantled in 1911, was a system on which a small car seems to have run on a system of wires. [OP00610]

Fig 7.18
At Tynemouth, a photograph of c 1900 shows a set of swings beside an incomplete, more substantial, early rollercoaster; this was probably a switchback in the process of being dismantled or simply abandoned. [BB65/01705]

such as providing food, equipment to deal with Britain's capricious weather, playthings for the beach, services and souvenirs. Late 19th-century photographs show vendors on beaches selling a range of treats such as ice creams, fresh fruit, shrimps and oysters from baskets and barrows, later to be succeeded by rock, candy floss and ice creams sold from seafront kiosks and cafes (Figs 7.19 and 7.20).[63] During the 20th century, the thrifty sand-sprinkled sandwich picnic and cups of tea dispensed from a hamper onto a rug on the beach have waned in popularity in the face of competition from hot dogs and Coca Cola. Despite the influx of popular foods from across the Atlantic, the humble British fish and chips remains supreme at the seaside and has even been the subject of serious academic study.[64] These foods may be bought and taken back to the beach, but the increasing prominence of a more sophisticated cafe culture, perhaps first evident on the seafront, means a cold beer and a ciabatta on a terrace may now be the meal of choice.

The need to deal with the capricious British climate sustains many beach and seafront vendors. The same shop or kiosk may sell sun

Fig 7.19 (above)
This photograph shows a seafood seller on the beach at Blackpool. Why a serviceman in full uniform and a policeman are under the parasol is unclear, but there was obviously a story that John Gay wished to capture.
[AA086146]

Fig 7.20 (right)
This lively scene at Ramsgate includes an ice-cream vendor, souvenir sellers and a Punch and Judy booth amid the throng of tourists, some of whom may have come out of the seafront station behind.
[OP32694]

hats, sunglasses and suntan lotion one day, while supplying windbreaks and umbrellas the following day. They may also sell basic items needed for a day at the beach ranging from towels and swimming costumes that were forgotten to body boards, buckets and spades, Frisbees and footballs. Architecturally, kiosks and small retail units are modest structures, often incorporated into the landward ends of piers or set into blocks lining the seafront, that also contain toilets, bathing cabins, eateries and lifeguard offices. At Weymouth, to mark the Olympics in 2012, new, bespoke kiosks were created on the seafront as well as a matching structure to exhibit the works of the sand sculptor (*see* Fig 7.8).

Seafront shops also provided rolls of film to capture those precious holiday moments, but that technology now seems as ancient as the honourable art of 'smudging'. Since the late 19th century, photographers have regularly been present on beaches and seafronts offering to capture holidaymakers for posterity, perhaps with a monkey or a parrot (Fig 7.21). At some resorts there were photographic studios in which families could pose for portraits. In old photographs of Uncle Tom's Cabin on the cliff-top at the north of Blackpool an American photographer's studio appears beside it and in a photograph of *c* 1900 an 'American studio' appears on the beach at Weymouth, America at this date being a fashionable, exotic name used

to sell many things (*see* Fig 2.16).[65] This tradition continues today at some seaside resorts where small studios still exist in which families can have their portraits taken in Wild West costumes. As well as photographers, a host of other 'services' were available on the Victorian beach and seafront, ranging from quack doctors and phrenologists to palmists and fortune tellers. Today, fortune tellers are still a regular and popular feature of many piers and seafronts.

Increasing visitor numbers and the consequent growth in the number of people trading on the seafront caused problems at some resorts. During the late 19th century the reach of local government was extending to the regulation of bathing, stalls and entertainments, with the growing number of tradesmen requiring regulation and supervision. The extreme example was Eastbourne where bylaws inherited from the Devonshire Estate forbade all kinds of hawking and unofficial outdoor entertainment.[66] At most resorts, the issue was to find a balance that allowed legitimate traders to continue while regulating the actions of the less respectable. Blackpool faced a particular problem due to the size of its tourist market. In 1895, the Town Clerk compiled a list of 316 people who had 'standings on the foreshore', including 62 fruit vendors, 57 selling toys, general goods and jewellery, 52 ice-cream vendors, 47 sellers of sweets and 21 seafood vendors. There were also 36 photographers, 24 ventriloquists and

Fig 7.21
This c 1900 photograph shows the Marine Lake at Southport with donkeys taking a break from the beach. At the right-hand side, there is a photographer with his monkey firmly on a chain.
[OP00602]

Fig 7.22
Old photographs often show businesses with their names emblazoned across their roof. One of the most dramatic is the combined library and bathhouse of the late 19th century on the seafront at Bournemouth.
[BB98/05750]

Fig 7.23
Advertising for food often takes the form of grotesque, giant hot dogs smothering themselves in tomato ketchup, and substantial 99 ice-cream cones, such as this one on the beach at Ramsgate.
[MF99/0785/27]

phrenologists, 6 quack doctors, 6 musicians and 5 conjurors.[67] Stalls had been spreading rapidly through the central entertainment district during the 1890s and by 1901, there were 700. The 1901 Improvement Bill sought the power to prevent any further spread of stalls and tried to suppress existing ones, but Parliament believed that these stalls were legitimate and instead vendors had to submit plans for any new stalls over 4ft (1.2m) high.[68]

Advertisers can also exploit the presence of a large audience and since photography began to record the seafront, the existence of advertising has been obvious. Advertising may come in two broad categories. Businesses based on the seafront have proclaimed their presence through advertisements since the 18th century, from painted signs through to modern illuminated neon displays (Figs 7.22 and 7.23). Today no seafront is free of adverts for boat trips, future tribute act shows and pantomimes starring former soap-opera stars and fondly remembered children's entertainers. The other kind of advertising is the use of the beach to promote local or national brands. A common sight in 19th-century photographs are bathing machines with adverts on their sides, not for their operators, but for brands with a link to health and hygiene, such as Beechams' medicines and Pears or Sunlight soap. From time to time, aeroplanes have flown above beaches trailing advertising slogans aimed at a captive audience below. After the war, beaches were sometimes the location for fun and games, sponsored by local or national newspapers. At Broadstairs, the *Daily Mail* organised a sandcastle competition, while the *Sunday Pictorial* arranged a beauty contest under the heading of 'Are you the Venus of Broadstairs?'.[69]

Fun on the esplanade

At high tide on a sunny day, many holiday-makers retreat from the beach on to the land, where they seek opportunities to continue their fun day out. The extent to which facilities for fun are provided on seafronts partly depends on the extent of the flat area between the beach and the beginning of the town; the larger this area, the more facilities can be provided if there are customers for such investments. Therefore, at a busy resort, or a resort where access to the sea can be problematic, there may be a demand for small bathing or paddling pools, as well as playgrounds and similar facilities. At Weston-super-Mare, the Marine Lake provides bathing facilities when the sea is out, while further along the beach a large paddling pool has also been created for younger children. A similar paddling pool was built at Burnham-on-Sea in 1921 by Mr and Mrs JB Braithwaite in thanks for the safe return of their five sons from World War I.[70] At Whitley Bay, there is a large paddling pool on the lower promenade, allowing children to play in water on this rocky coastline, much as other resorts provided lidos to overcome similar geographical challenges. At resorts such as Sheringham and Whitby where most development has taken place on the clifftop, there would be a demand for facilities from families who did not always want to head down onto the beach, and therefore a paddling pool and play facilities are available on the cliffs. As well as catering for children, these paddling pools were sometimes used to sail model boats (see Fig 6.30). At Felixstowe, a large boating pond was created beside the pier pavilion, allowing adults to enjoy a paddle while children played with the pond yachts.[71] Southend-on-Sea also had a large boating pool on the east side of the pier, matching the Marine Gardens that had been created on the west side. Probably the largest paddling/boating pools constructed at Blackpool were part of the creation of new sea defences during the mid-1920s. The 1932 Ordnance Survey map labels the former pool at the southern end of the resort as a 'Model Yacht Pond', though an interwar photograph clearly shows it in use by children.[72] The larger pool at the north of the resort was a 'Boating Pool' according to the same Ordnance Survey map though again dual usage is likely (Fig 7.24).

Even larger pools were created by a combination of reclamation and intervention, creating a marine lake at Southport in 1927 at a cost of £70,000, as well as miniature canal and river systems at Great Yarmouth and Skegness.[73] At Fleetwood there is a large boating/paddling pool and an adjacent, larger marine lake also serves as a place for practical training for students at the nearby Fleetwood Nautical College.

As well as providing opportunities for wet play, the land on the seafront is a popular location for activities such as trampolining, skateboarding and go-karts. The promenade is popular with people rollerskating for exercise and for pleasure. If these activities prove too energetic, a feature of a few seafronts is the model village. The earliest example in the world, Bekonscot in Beaconsfield in Buckinghamshire, opened to the public in 1931.[74] This quintessential depiction of England spawned many followers, including one at Bourton-on-the-Water of 1936–40, which was the first to become a listed building.[75] Some model villages at seaside resorts are at some distance inland, such as at Blackpool and Skegness, but a few still occupy sites on the seafront where they make an ideal distraction from the daily routine of the beach. Merrivale at Great Yarmouth combines a model village with crazy golf, a miniature railway and the Penny Arcade. Among the scenes in the village are recreations of the Victorian seaside, a sports stadium, Merrivale Castle and an airship taking off.[76] The model village in the gardens beside the Marine Lake at Southport opened to the public in 1996.[77] It covers approximately 0.61ha and includes over 200 models in local architectural styles along the 500m of model train track running through the village.

Fig 7.24
Paddling pools are normally given a simple geometric form. However, at Whitby, the clifftop paddling pool has an elegant curvilinear form, while here at Ventnor this pool contains a model of the Isle of Wight. [DP005465]

Unfortunately, many seaside model villages have closed in recent years (Fig 7.25). The example at the Eastbourne Redoubt was in existence between 1957 and 1975, while the village at Ramsgate, which was known as 'Castlewode', opened in 1953 and closed half a century later.[78]

Sport on the seafront

Sport on the seafront can range from children playing a game of football and a family playing tennis or cricket on the beach to organised sports including bowling, tennis and golf (*see* Fig 7.6). Informal games once enjoyed by families have even become codified into international sports, leading to the creation of formal beach football and beach volleyball competitions, the latter appearing in the Olympics and enjoying an international competition circuit.[79] At some seaside resorts, beach volleyball nets are a fixture, at least during summer months. Another family holiday pursuit enjoyed around the coast has also spawned its own world championship. Crazy golf, although usually considered a family pastime, has its own national association and Britain has been the host for its world championship, the

2014 event having taken place on the course on the seafront at Hastings (Fig 7.26).[80] Courses no longer just challenge crazy golfers to pass a windmill or traverse a dogleg in a course branded using the name of Arnold Palmer; they are now often themed as adventure courses with palm trees, fountains, pirates and monsters of the deep, and Great Yarmouth has an indoor adventure crazy golf course located in one of its former seafront cinemas.[81]

The natural geography of the coastline, with significant man-made intervention, has meant that the seaside has been ideal for some sports. Large, flat areas of seafronts that might be unsuitable for the erection of buildings have proved ideal locations for bowling, croquet, putting and lawn tennis. The Victorian preoccupation with personal improvement, and the improvement of others, by means of 'rational recreation', included advocating wholesome sporting activities, and seaside resorts provided an ideal opportunity to seek to achieve this 'improvement' while people had the time and opportunity for leisure.

Bowling has been recorded in England since the Middle Ages and was certainly being played on the coast by the end of the 16th century.

Fig 7.25
The model village in the White Rock Gardens behind the seafront at Hastings opened on 19 February 1955 after three years of work. Designed by Stanley Deboo, it featured models of classic Sussex buildings including oast-houses and timber-framed houses, but sadly it had to close in December 1998 after vandalism.
[PC07834]

Bowling greens started to be a feature in urban pleasure gardens and in spa towns during the 17th century and Great Yarmouth was described by Thomas Baskerville as 'a place to bowl in on the greens of the shore' during the 1680s.[82] John Cossins' map of Scarborough of 1725 shows the Old Bowling Green just inside the town walls and a new one beside the church of St Sepulchre.[83] By the 19th century, bowling greens were commonplace at seaside resorts and while many were in inland parks, some were established on the seafront. These might be located within seafront parks, as at Southport, or take the form of a self-contained bowling club or facility, such as the Britannia Bowling Greens at Great Yarmouth. Since 1945, these greens have been the site of the annual Festival of Bowls, which attracts over 1,800 participants each year, making it Britain's largest bowling tournament.[84] At Eastbourne the parkland to the west of the seafront Redoubt was used as a performance area with a bandstand, while the large flat area to the east was turned into a bowling green (Fig 7.27).[85]

Fig 7.26
A couple on holiday at Cleethorpes are putting out after having negotiated the obstacle provided by a miniature Italian mediaeval tower.
[DP174949]

Fig 7.27
As part of a concerted programme of improvement to the seafront at Greenhill to the north of Weymouth in 1923, new seafront shelters were erected with gardens above that included tennis courts and bowling greens.
[DP055432]

Bowling greens were also prominent features on clifftops at some resorts. On the West Cliff at Ramsgate, large areas of land between the Royal Esplanade and the cliff edge were divided into public lawns for croquet and for bowling, as well as a bandstand area, now converted into a boating pond.[86] Indoor bowling facilities also appear on some seafronts. At Margate, there is a modern indoor bowling facility beside the outdoor bowling greens opposite the Walpole Bay Hotel.[87] Potters Leisure Resort near Great Yarmouth offers year-round indoor bowling as one of its main attractions and hosts the world indoor bowling championships each year.[88] The provision of facilities for bowling, putting and lawn tennis have gone hand in hand since the 19th century, potentially appealing to a similar clientele and requiring a comparable flat, firm surface. At some resorts, two or three of these activities may be co-located, as at Great Yarmouth, where there are seafront tennis courts and bowling greens.

The area of the seafront that might be unsuitable for buildings has also been adapted for pitch-and-putt golf, while the wilder dunes and heathland on the peripheries of resorts have sometimes become homes for links golf courses. This was the kind of land on which golf originated on the east coast of Scotland during the late Middle Ages and prospered during the following centuries before arriving in England with the Scottish court at the beginning of the 17th century.[89] Scotland led the way in codifying the rules of the sport in 1744 and in creating golf clubs. By the late 19th century, golf was an essential part of many people's seaside holiday by the Scottish coast: a visitor to Elie in Fife in 1873, when asked what they did on holiday, replied 'We golf' and when a Glaswegian visiting North Berwick in 1881 asked what there is to do, he received the terse reply 'golf'.[90] England was slow to follow Scotland's example, but by the 19th century, golf courses were appearing at many English seaside resorts. In 1850, England boasted only one golf club, Blackheath (founded in 1766), but the situation changed dramatically during the late 19th century. By 1880, there were around a dozen golf clubs, rising to 50 by 1887 and to over 1,000 courses by the outbreak of World War I (Fig 7.28).[91]

Fig 7.28
The Burnham and Berrow Golf Club was founded in 1890. This photograph of September 1921 shows the late Victorian clubhouse and part of the course.
[CC76/00402]

One of the earliest golf courses in England was established at Westward Ho! in 1864, coinciding with the creation of this new resort, and within two years, tournaments were being staged on the course, attracting players from all over the country.[92] The Open Golf Championship, first staged in 1860, has four English golf links on its schedule of active venues. Royal St George's at Sandwich was first used in 1894 for the competition and there are three courses in the north-west of England, at Hoylake on the Wirral (established in 1869), and two on the Lancashire coast, at Birkdale and Lytham St Annes (Fig 7.29).[93] These links courses take advantage of dunes on the coastline, though the last of these is a short distance inland from the sea.[94]

Conclusion

This chapter has focussed on people enjoying fun in the natural environment of the seafront. The beach has been at the heart of the seaside holiday since the 19th century; it is an ideal place to sit in a deckchair or build a sandcastle, depending of course on your age and the British weather. It is also a place for family games and more or less organised sports and, while on the beach, people have wanted to be entertained and to buy food and novelties. Since the late 19th century, photography has recorded in detail the life of the beach, its simple and often natural pleasures. It has also recorded changes in costume, people now sporting bikinis and leisure wear where once they wore dresses and suits.

While there is something both ever-changing, yet unchanging, about sitting on a beach and looking to sea, turn the deckchair landwards and the story is quite different. In the next chapter the impact of technology on entertainment on the seafront will be examined, beginning by describing the story of the seaside pier, perhaps the single element of British seaside that separates it from resorts anywhere else in the world. The story of fairgrounds and rollercoasters will also be considered, as well as novelty forms of transport on land, on the beach and at sea. What these features share is that they embraced new technology from the mid-19th century onwards and contributed significantly to the process of transforming seafronts from natural to man-made environments.

Fig 7.29
The Royal Birkdale Golf Club is located on the seashore near Southport and its art deco clubhouse still welcomes amateur and professional golfers. The course has hosted the Open Championship 10 times, most recently in 2017.
[MF99/0817/10]

8

New technology and fun

New technology has had a dramatic impact on the seafront, through the provision of utilities ranging from lighting and sewers, to trams and road transport. Technology has also made a major contribution to the holiday experience in terms of entertainment. From the mid-19th century onwards, a major presence at most seaside resorts has been the pier. Jetties had been part of harbours for centuries, and once holidaymakers arrived at coastal towns, they began to walk along them. Spotting an opportunity to make money, the stone pier of the harbour at Margate, completed in 1815, included a raised promenade for which a fee was charged (*see* Fig 2.12). However, a concerted programme of pier building had to wait until the middle years of the 19th century, when engineers mastered the use of cast-iron piles. As well as being practical transport facilities, the first new piers served as elegant promenades, but by the 1860s and 1870s, piers were beginning their transformation into pleasure piers, with pavilions, kiosks and other entertainments, such as fairground rides, becoming important features of the design. Eugenius Birch, an accomplished civil engineer, emerged as England's leading designer and he also created two of the country's most significant seaside aquaria, at Brighton and Scarborough.

By the end of the 19th century, technology was also being applied to fairground rides. Initially, this meant steam engines powering small carousels, switchbacks or scenic railways, but with the introduction of the internal combustion engine and electric power, fairground rides grew in size and increased in speed and cost. This led to a concentration of larger rides in distinctive areas of the seafront, usually towards the periphery where land was still plentiful. Leading the way was Blackpool Pleasure Beach, which is the world's most important historic amusement park, boasting many rides that predate World War II.

The seaside pier

On 26 July 1814, the pier at Ryde on the Isle of Wight opened to boats landing passengers, but it was also used by promenading holiday-makers.[1] Its simple wooden deck was carried on brick arches at the shoreward end with driven wooden piles further out to sea. It was, therefore, very different from the fully developed, iron pleasure pier that would become so familiar later in the 19th century. Ryde is celebrated as the first seaside pier, but it was also a confirmation of a practice that had been taking place at some resorts since the first visitors arrived. Most early resorts were ports, some of which had jetties and harbours with stone piers that visitors could walk along; at Scarborough the harbour was improved and enlarged in the 1730s, the same decade in which the first documented influx of sea bathers occurred. In the late 18th century, a stone pier at Weymouth separated the mouth of the harbour from the beach. A 1789 drawing suggests that it had been extended and was a place for well-dressed visitors to promenade (*see* Figs 2.2 and 3.10). The Cobb at Lyme Regis, which was rebuilt during the late 18th and early 19th century, offered shelter for working boats, but it also served as a walk for visitors, including Jane Austen while on holiday there in 1804, as immortalised in *Persuasion* in 1817 (*see* Fig 4.8).[2] Some resorts had timber jetties that were also used for promenading; on the beach at Great Yarmouth there was a wooden jetty for small boats to moor alongside, though it was also used by visitors:

The Jetty, close to the Bath-House, is 110 yards in length, and 8 in breadth, at the outward extremity; it is a lively and interesting scene, and was it under proper regulations, no place would be better calculated to afford a relaxation from the severe application of the mind; and the heat of summer softened by the refreshing breezes from the sea.[3]

These structures were primarily for commercial use and were adopted by holidaymakers as a fashionable promenade, but at Margate the new harbour pier was constructed between 1810 and 1815 specifically with visitors in mind (Fig 8.1). By the early 19th century, the town's timber pier may have been reclad in stone, but even this reinforcement did not prevent it from being damaged by the devastating storm of 1808. A replacement stone pier, constructed by the engineers John Rennie (1761–1821) and Josias Jessop (1781–1826), was completed in time for steamers to begin to ply the Thames in 1815.[4] It has a raised promenade around its seaward side that visitors paid 1d to walk along, though the introduction of this toll sparked a near riot.[5] In 1823, 'A Cockney' described walking along the pier: 'sallied out for a walk on the Pier – beauteous dames, and gentlemen with reputable calves to their legs'.[6]

The new stone pier, despite having facilities for landing passengers from steamers, still could not cope with steamers at low tide and therefore a timber jetty, similar in form to the pier at Ryde, was erected. Jarvis' Jetty, also known as Jarvis' Landing Stage, was named after Dr Daniel Jarvis, Chairman of the Pier and Harbour Company, and was constructed in 1824 at a cost of £8,000.[7] Although it was over 1,000ft long (305m) to allow steamers to land their passengers, it still proved too short at low tide and therefore sometimes holidaymakers still had to land, as before, by rowing boat. William Fry, who visited Margate in August 1826, described how at low tide 'it is quite a favorite promenade, but at high water the Sea washes all over it', and therefore steamers still used the earlier stone pier.[8] The jetty offered its customers some entertainment; Fry's manuscript describes how 'When the Company are walking on the Jetty, the Margate-Orpheus serenades them with Tunes on a Violin of his own manufacture'.[9]

A visually more ambitious approach to pier design was pioneered by the civil engineer and naval officer Captain Samuel Brown (1776–1852).[10] The cables for the steamship *Great Eastern* were manufactured at his works in Pontypridd and because of this expertise he became involved with the construction of suspension bridges, including the 1820 Union Bridge across the Tweed near Berwick-upon-Tweed. In the following year, he erected the Chain Pier at Granton near Edinburgh, followed

in 1823 by another pier with a suspension structure in the centre of the seafront at Brighton (Fig 8.2).[11] Both his chain piers were destroyed by storms, in 1898 and 1896 respectively. Two other examples of this type were erected, at Greenhithe on the Thames in the 1840s (demolished in 1875) and at Seaview on the Isle of Wight in 1880 (demolished in the 1950s).[12]

As well as providing promenades, piers were critical for resorts wanting to attract visitors arriving by steamer in the years before railways. In 1802, a landing jetty had been erected by Sir Thomas Wilson for boats to land passengers at Southend-on-Sea, and in 1821, people wishing to disembark from steamers at low tide had to use 'two gravelled causeways, the one begun, and the other finished' to reach the shore.[13] Therefore, in 1829 construction began

Fig 8.2
Although the chains and the upright elements of the superstructure of Brighton's Chain Pier were made of iron, the pier was still constructed on wooden piles.
[BB85/01743b]

Fig 8.3
Completed in July 1834,
Gravesend's Town Pier
consisted of three graceful
arches carried on 26 iron
columns, anticipating the
elegant design of Clevedon
Pier three decades later
(see also Fig 8.7).
[DP217462]

on a wooden pier and the 600ft-long (183m) structure opened in June 1830.[14] However, it proved to be too short for steamers and was first lengthened to 1,500ft (457m) in 1833 and then to a mile and a quarter (2km) in 1846.

Driven wooden piles remained the mainstay of pier construction until the 1850s. Wood was prone to decay and to damage by small, wood-boring marine creatures; the new piers at Southend-on-Sea and Herne Bay both required significant repairs within a few years of their construction. The earliest surviving iron pier in the world, the Town Pier at Gravesend, was designed by the engineer William Tierney Clark (1783–1852) (Fig 8.3).[15] Another iron pier opened at Sheerness in 1835 and in 1842 the timber Royal Terrace Pier at Gravesend was replaced in iron.[16] However, the definitive shift to using iron piles only took place in the 1850s with the construction of the new jetty at Margate by the distinguished civil engineer Eugenius Birch (1818–84).[17] This was his first pier and eventually he would be responsible for 14, a career that helped to define the essential characteristics of the seaside pier. His first contribution to pier design was to employ the screw pile, which was patented by Alexander Mitchell (1780–1868) in 1833 (Fig 8.4).[18]

Fig 8.4
Alexander Mitchell's new
system involved using
a screw on the end of an
iron rod to fix the pile into
the seabed. This screw
pile from Bournemouth
Pier is now located
at Amberley Museum
and Heritage Centre.
[MF99/0680/31]

Mitchell used it in a number of lighthouses before constructing his first jetty at Courtown Harbour in County Wexford in 1847.[19] The first pile of Margate's new jetty to replace Jarvis' Jetty was driven in May 1853 and it opened in April 1855, although the 1,240ft-long (378m) structure was not finally completed until July 1856 (Figs 8.5 and 8.6).[20]

At Margate, Birch had placed the use of iron and the screw pile at the heart of thinking about pier construction, though other engineers used alternative techniques, sometimes to overcome particular local problems. By the end of the 1860s, more than 20 piers had been built or were under construction and a similar number were constructed during the following decade, a boom based on a belief that there was money to be made from piers. In 1875, Brighton's West Pier entertained 600,000 visitors and, by 1890, Blackpool's Central Pier welcomed around a million visitors annually, figures that guaranteed profits for investors.[21] Blackpool's first pier yielded 12 per cent annual profits for its investors during most of the 50 years before World War I and other piers regularly yielded between 6 per cent and 10 per cent.

Fig 8.5 (above)
This photograph shows Margate's jetty before its extension in 1875–7. Eugenius Birch designed it to be a very simple promenade pier capable of landing passengers from steamers.
[BB88/04260]

Fig 8.6 (left)
This photograph of c 1900 shows Margate's jetty after the construction of the polygonal extension at its seaward end. This increased the number of landing stages and provided space for a bandstand, kiosks and shelters.
[OP00650]

Profits depended on local financial circumstances, especially the size of the resort's market, but some piers proved to be less successful, including perhaps surprisingly the pier at Scarborough, where the company formed in 1865 was wound up in 1889.[22] One problem facing promoters of new piers was the complexity of getting permission to erect the structure. As a pier crossed from the land over the beach into the sea, consent was required from Parliament and from the appropriate foreshore authority, which might be the Board of Trade, the Office of Woods and Forests, the Duchy of Lancaster and sometimes the lord of the manor.[23] Nevertheless, despite these potential economic and financial problems, most resorts of any size had a pier by the end of the 19th century.

Margate's jetty, like other piers being built during the 1850 and 1860s, had a plain, uncluttered superstructure that maximised the area for promenaders and passengers disembarking from steamships (Fig 8.7). However, changes were already under way in the detailing of the seaside pier. At Blackpool, Eugenius Birch erected the town's first pier, which opened in 1863, and he included a series of kiosks on its deck (Fig 8.8). Three years later, he completed Brighton's West Pier using a similar formula, but included the first hint of exotic forms inspired by the nearby Royal Pavilion. This 'oriental' vocabulary would come to dominate the detailing of piers for several decades and culminate in the extravagance of Eastbourne (revamped at the end of the 19th century),

Fig 8.7
The uncluttered elegance can still be appreciated today while walking along the piers at Saltburn-by-the-Sea and here at Clevedon, both of which opened in 1869.
[DP081829]

Fig 8.8
Originally, the North Pier at Blackpool was a simple promenade pier with two pairs of square, wooden buildings with pyramid-shaped roofs at the landward end of the pier. On the rest of the pier, there were three pairs of octagonal, wooden kiosks with another at the pierhead.
[BB88/00110]

Brighton's Palace Pier (1899), the Grand Pier at Weston-super-Mare (1903–4) and Blackpool's Victoria Pier (1893) (Fig 8.9).

Increasingly, piers sought to increase their income by offering more facilities and entertainments to their customers to raise income including, by the 1870s, some large pavilions. Hastings Pier opened in 1872 on the first ever August Bank Holiday and incorporated a pavilion able to seat 2,000 people.[24] Existing piers were also expanded and extended to include large venues. In 1874–7, the Indian Pavilion was constructed at the seaward end of Blackpool's North Pier, an extravagant building apparently inspired by an Indian temple.[25] Some piers also included fairground rides and today some are largely dedicated to them. As early as 1876, Birnbeck Pier at Weston-super-Mare provided its customers with swings and by the early 20th century, it hosted a range of entertainment facilities as the pier included an island in its structure (Fig 8.10).[26]

Fig 8.9
In 1893, Blackpool's new Victoria Pier (now South Pier) would personify the new lavish taste and inspire the detailing of the enlarged and transformed North Pier a few years later. [OP00487]

Fig 8.10
This old postcard shows a busy Birnbeck Pier in Weston-super-Mare with a variety of amusements, which included a switchback, a water chute, a helter skelter and a short-lived flying machine. [PC48002]

Less substantial piers might also contain rides, such as Ramsgate Pier where a switch-back filled most of the deck from 1888 until 1891. There was also a short-lived water chute attached to Southend Pier in 1901 and the spinning Joy Wheel had been added to Hastings Pier by 1911.[27] Many piers also provided amusement arcades with novelties such as the newly invented mutoscope (for example the What-the-Butler-Saw Machine), rifle-shooting galleries and stalls with other opportunities to win prizes.[28] The pier at St Leonards, erected in 1888–91 and rebuilt in 1938, included on its deck a ballroom, amusement arcades, dodgems, skittles, bars and shops.[29]

As well as providing a variety of novelties, some of the longer piers incorporated miniature railways to shuttle their customers to the end of the pier. Herne Bay's pier in the 1830s led the way with a sail-powered car for transferring luggage, which had to be pushed when the wind was light; inevitably, Southend Pier at more than a mile long, and Southport Pier, which was almost as long, had to provide rail links to the pier head.[30]

By the outbreak of World War I, Britain had more than 100 piers, ranging from the quiet, plain promenade pier to the fully developed pleasure pier with pavilions, rides and amusements. A small number of new piers were constructed or rebuilt during the 20th century, with steel and concrete usually replacing iron as the main structural materials. Burnham-on-Sea's pier, which opened in 1911 and was therefore the last pier erected before war broke out, was built using concrete piles and like the 1939 Pier Bandstand at Weymouth, which also employed concrete, it scarcely projected into the sea.[31] After World War II, Deal Pier, which opened in 1957, was designed by Sir William Halcrow using concrete piles, while the piers at Boscombe and Bournemouth were also rebuilt in the same material.[32] There was also a shift from exuberant, oriental-inspired Edwardian detailing, drawing ultimately on the exoticism of Brighton's Royal Pavilion, to art deco detailing of the mid-1930s, such as in the pavilion on the Grand Pier at Weston-super-Mare prior to the disastrous fire in 2008 (Fig 8.11).

Despite some additions and replacements, the 20th century was dominated by loss, through fire, the power of the sea and neglect. Although piers have substantial and largely non-flammable structures, the decks and the superstructures are predominantly wooden and easily succumb to flame. Since their creation, piers have suffered from fire damage, stretching from the era where open flames and gas lighting inevitably contributed to fire damage, to modern

Fig 8.11
A fire in September 1933 badly damaged the superstructure of Worthing Pier. As part of the reconstruction, a new art deco-style pavilion was built in 1935 and an amusement arcade added in 1937.
[DP018030]

times where electrical fires have struck buildings on piers. Perhaps most spectacularly, the pavilion on the Southsea South Parade Pier was destroyed by fire during the filming of the Pinball Wizard scenes for The Who's rock opera *Tommy*, footage that was included in the final film (*see* Fig 1.1).[33] Piers have also proved susceptible to damage from storms and boats colliding with them, but the most systematic programme of damage took place in 1940 when sections of many piers on vulnerable coastlines were removed, often with explosives, to prevent use by the enemy. As with other aspects of seaside resorts, some piers have suffered in recent years from economic difficulties, underinvestment and neglect. Weston-super-Mare has two piers, both of which have faced significant challenges. After World War II, Birnbeck Pier passed though the hands of a number of owners who failed to maintain it. The pier closed in 1994 and it has continued to decay, despite ambitious schemes and considerable public concern about its future (Fig 8.12). In contrast, Weston-super-Mare's other pier, the Grand Pier, is prospering, despite a catastrophic fire in July 2008 that destroyed its art deco pavilion. Decisive action by its new owners saw a new pavilion erected in just over two years, creating a new, exciting attraction containing, among other features, a hi-tech indoor amusement park.

Fairgrounds and amusement parks

Apart from piers, the largest seafront entertainment facilities were fairgrounds. In terms of geography, these have very different presences on the seafront. Piers require little land and therefore can be in central locations, but the largest amusement parks being later in origin, and requiring a significant footprint, are usually found at the peripheries of resorts, where affordable, undeveloped seafront land can be found. Examples include Blackpool, Southport and Great Yarmouth, but where particular circumstances allowed some amusement parks could be more centrally located, such as at Margate and Southend-on-Sea.

In the 1820s, Margate apparently had 'Russian Mountains', an early gravity-powered form of rollercoaster, on the Fort, a low cliff overlooking the harbour.[34] At Folkestone, a switchback was erected on the beach in 1888, but it succumbed in 1919–20 to a major fire.[35] The Switchback at Bridlington, which was in existence between 1898 and 1912, is shown on the Ordnance Survey map in a field on the seafront to the north of the growing resort. Blackpool has been offering visitors fairground rides since at least the early 1890s, with switchbacks on the south side of Rigby Road and at Uncle Tom's Cabin to the north of the resort, while in 1896 a large Ferris wheel opened at the winter gardens.[36] The tradition of single rides or small clusters in prominent locations continues at seaside resorts. On the seafront at Southport Herbert Silcock's Golden Gallopers has become a semi-permanent feature of the resort (Fig 8.13).[37]

Fig 8.12 (left)
Birnbeck Pier lies to the north of Weston-super-Mare and therefore has had less of a visual impact on the overall appearance of the resort, though its decline may be causing some neglect and underinvestment in that part of the resort. [DP083541]

Fig 8.13 (below)
Herbert Silcock's Golden Gallopers at Southport was built in c 1900 by Savages of King's Lynn and was purchased by Silcock's in 1989. [DP175034]

Fig 8.14
The i360 at Brighton is the world's slenderest tall tower, the world's first vertical cable car and the world's tallest moving observation tower. It has been constructed where the West Pier used to be located. [NMR 33048/049]

A number of seaside resorts, including Brighton and Weston-super-Mare, host, or have hosted, large Ferris or observation wheels, descendants of the wheel at Blackpool's winter gardens, but also a phenomenon stimulated by the success of the London Eye. Blackpool Central Pier also boasts a Ferris wheel that is faithfully erected and dismantled each year.

The latest revival of an old idea on the seafront is the tall observation tower. The British Airways i360 at Brighton, with its 161.75m-tall central tower, raises a pod to 138m and offers unrivalled views out to sea and inland since it opened in August 2016 (Fig 8.14).[38] This novel structure echoes the types of tower that have graced seafronts since the late 19th century, such as at Blackpool (1894) and originally at New Brighton (Fig 8.15; see also Fig 9.36).[39] A tower was also built at Morecambe in 1898 and there was a plan to erect a 530ft-high tower at Southend's Kursaal, but this was never built. Most similar to Brighton's i360 was the Warwick Revolving Tower, which was built first at Great Yarmouth in 1897, followed by those that at Morecambe, Douglas, Scarborough and probably Margate.[40]

By the early 20th century, the first amusement park had been created. The site of Britain's first enclosed seaside amusement park evolved from the mid-1890s onwards on a stretch of sand dunes at the south end of Blackpool, an area that was becoming increasingly accessible due to the southward extension of the tram network. This area was occupied by a gypsy encampment; in 1906 there were 20 permanent gypsy households in residence with others arriving during the summer, but they were served with an eviction order in 1910, although the last families did not finally leave until 1926 (Fig 8.16).[41] The first attractions were small-scale rides, fairground booths and stalls, similar to those found further north at Central Pier where the Golden Mile was developing.[42]

Fig 8.15
New Brighton Tower was 567ft (173m) high. It was the tallest building in Britain between when it opened in c 1900 and its dismantling, which began in 1919. [OP00587]

The men behind the creation of the Pleasure Beach were William George Bean (1868–1929), a Londoner who had become involved with the emerging American amusement industry, and John William Outhwaite (c 1855–1911) from Shipley in Yorkshire.[43] In 1903, they bought 30 acres of the Watson's Estate and the title of 'The Pleasure Beach' first appeared on advertisements in 1905, indicating that the process of consolidating the ownership of the plots and rides into a single entity was under way.[44]

The idea of the amusement park can be traced back in Britain to the annual fairs that took place throughout the country and to the pleasure grounds that evolved during the 18th century. In addition, there is a clear debt to developments taking place across the Atlantic at Coney Island in Brooklyn, New York, where the earliest self-contained amusement parks established from the mid-1890s onwards provided the most direct model for Blackpool Pleasure Beach and subsequent amusement parks. A further influence on the creation of the amusement park was the success of national and international exhibitions, many of which included amusements among their displays.[45]

Blackpool Pleasure Beach incorporated a number of rides that had already been erected in the sand dunes. Sir Hiram Maxim's Captive Flying Machine, the oldest ride in continuous use in Europe, first operated on 1 August 1904, early photographs showing it standing among the sand dunes (see Fig 8.16).[46] The ride consisted of 10 steel arms, from which cables

hung to support cars in the shape of boats each holding several people. The original gondolas were replaced in 1929 by aeroplanes, and then rockets in 1952, updates designed to keep the ride's appearance in step with new technology. The arms rotate around a central 30m-high vertical driving shaft, allowing the cars to fan outwards as they turn, and they could achieve a terrifying maximum speed of 105kph (Fig 8.17).

In 1905, the River Caves opened.[47] The ride became popular in 1904 in America and first came to England at Earl's Court. It consisted of a series of boats passing through 'caverns' with tableaux lit by electric lights. The ride has survived though the interiors have been updated. Before its removal in 2007, there was a similar one at Pleasureland at Southport, which had been at the White City at Southport since 1908 and was relocated to the new park in 1922.[48]

Fig 8.16
This photograph of the site of Blackpool Pleasure Beach, probably in 1905, shows the gypsy encampment. To the left can be seen a switchback, while the River Caves of 1905 is in the middle of the shot and Sir Hiram Maxim's Captive Flying Machine of 1904 is on the right side of the photograph.
[Anon 1926 (1)]

Fig 8.17
In 1934, Joseph Emberton designed a new building at the base of Sir Hiram Maxim's Captive Flying Machine on Blackpool's Pleasure Beach as part of his concerted reinvention of the townscape of the park. To the left is his Fun House of 1934.
[AFL03/Lilywhites/BLP39]

In 1906, over three million people visited the Pleasure Beach and in the same year, the first element of theming appeared with the creation of the Spanish Street of buildings, though in 1912 it was revamped as Ye Olde Englysche Street.[49] John Henry Iles (1871–1951) erected the Scenic Railway in 1907, which he owned until his bankruptcy in 1919.[50] A 65ft (19.8m) water chute was also erected in 1907, propelling 55 boats per hour, each with their own gondolier, down a 267ft-long (81.4m) chute.[51] In 1909, the Velvet Coaster was built by William H Strickler, a ride named after its velvet seating. It remained in use until 1932 when it was dismantled, though elements of it were incorporated into the Roller Coaster of 1933.[52] The most important development before World War I was the creation of the first casino in 1913 by the local architect R B Mather.[53] Modelled on some of the exotic orientalism of continental casinos, such as Monte Carlo, and echoing the style of the nearby Victoria Pier, it contained a billiard hall, the park's first cinema, a grill room, a restaurant and a shop behind a white ferro-concrete facade decorated with white electric lights.

During the interwar years the programme of providing new rides for the Pleasure Beach continued. Noah's Ark of 1922 allowed visitors to take a trip in a boat to Mount Ararat, walking past animals on moving platforms with a rocking motion to simulate the sea voyage.[54] It still survives today and is a key feature near the main entrance to the park. The Big Dipper was added to the Pleasure Beach in 1923.[55] It was the first ride in Britain to use John A Miller's under-friction system in which wheels beneath the track held the car on to the ride.[56] By the mid-1930s, extra land was available to the south of the Pleasure Beach and so the ride was lengthened, rearranged and provided with a new station created by Joseph Emberton in 1936. In 1933, the Roller Coaster (now the vibrant-orange Nickelodeon Streak) was built reusing the lift hill and other parts of the Velvet Coaster.[57] The Little Dipper (later known as the Zipper Dipper, now the Blue Flyer) opened in the following year and, in 1935, the Grand National was constructed, a ride with a Möbius Loop track that allows competing cars to race around a circuit with features named after famous jumps on the Aintree racecourse.[58]

The 1930s also saw the Pleasure Beach undertake a major programme of modernist theming, inspired by parks in America. Between 1933 and the outbreak of World War II, Joseph Emberton was employed to give the park an overall visual unity.[59] He gave existing rides a moderne facelift and created a number of modernist structures, including the Fun House of 1934 (Fig 8.18).[60] In July 1937, the 2,000-seat Ice Drome opened, but a fire in July 1949

Fig 8.18
The Fun House at Blackpool Pleasure Beach, which was the largest in the world, was on two levels, with moving platforms, cylinders, dark corridors, a rocking floor, an ice walk, a drop floor and centrifugal drums. In 1958, its facade was altered by Jack Ratcliff, but the main internal and external elements were retained. Unfortunately, it burned down in 1991. [CC47/01518]

caused considerable damage, leading to extensive repairs that were completed by 1951.[61] Once the Ice Drome was completed, work began on a new casino; the 1913 casino was demolished by the end of 1937 and the new building opened officially on 26 May 1939 at a cost of £300,000 (Fig 8.19).[62]

Blackpool Pleasure Beach remained open throughout the war and although it suffered from issues such as backlogs in maintenance and a lack of suitable labour, it was well placed to take advantage of people's desire for fun when peace returned.[63] Investment in new rides continued, leading to the erection in 1958 of the Wild Mouse rollercoaster, with the Derby Racer, a fast carousel set within a modernist, polygonal shell lit by a thousand light bulbs, first running in the following year.[64] A monorail was established in 1966, a year after one first appeared at Butlin's Ingoldmells Holiday Camp, and in 1967 the Log Flume was built, the longest outside the USA.[65] Investment continued through the 1970s and 1980s, but the largest ride, and the most substantial investment, was the Pepsi Max Big One, now the Big One, which opened in 1994 (Fig 8.20).[66] As well as investing in new rides, the Pleasure Beach has also been improving visitor facilities. In 1991, the new Ocean Boulevard development of shops, restaurants and a *Ripley's Believe it or Not* opened at a cost of £9 million.[67]

Fig 8.19 (above)
The new casino at Blackpool contained a series of restaurants and bars including a grill room, an American-style soda bar, a banqueting hall seating 700 and a luxurious restaurant called the Savarin. In addition, the building incorporated the company offices and a flat with art deco detailing and furniture. [DP154856]

Fig 8.20 (left)
The Big One at Blackpool is 71.5m high, 1.5km long and reaches a maximum speed of 119kph. In 2003, the Big Blue Hotel opened at the south side of the park, offering high-quality hotel accommodation for holidaymakers in general and visitors to the park. [DP154887]

Blackpool Pleasure Beach was an inspiration for many seafront amusement parks, located where customers can be most easily attracted from the beach. The Kursaal at Southend-on-Sea evolved from the pleasure grounds at Marine Park that had opened in 1894.[68] It opened in July 1901, with enlarged gardens, amusements, a cycle track, a cafe, a menagerie and a circus.[69] The public face of the Kursaal was a large, red-brick structure with ashlar detailing, dominated by a tall, Wrenaissance-style dome (Fig 8.21). In 1909, the Pleasure Beach was established at the southern end of the seafront at Great Yarmouth with a Scenic Railway set within a plaster mountainous terrain (Fig 8.22). The park expanded during the 1920s, but in 1928, the lease of the Scenic Railway ended and the ride was transferred to Aberdeen. However, a new Scenic Railway was purchased from Paris and opened in 1932. It originally had an alpine landscape that entertained riders to mountains and fairy-tale castles on the circuit, but the ride was reclad in the 1960s (Fig 8.23).

Apart from Blackpool Pleasure Beach, Dreamland at Margate is the amusement park with the most famous history. The park, which opened in 1920, was established on a large site behind Marine Terrace, a line of seafront buildings that was built during the 1820s and 1830s.

On 5 October 1863, the London, Chatham and Dover Railway opened its line into Margate and, in 1867, its unused booking hall opened as the Hall-by-the-Sea entertainment complex.[70] It was subsequently sold to Thomas Dalby Reeve, Mayor of Margate, who also acquired the land beside it.[71] By 1874, the site was in the hands of Britain's leading circus menagerie proprietor, the self-appointed 'Lord' George Sanger who converted the Hall-by-the-Sea into a restaurant and ballroom.[72] He developed the land to include ornamental pleasure gardens and to serve as the headquarters for his circus and as a place to lodge his animals when he was not travelling.[73] The original converted booking hall was replaced in 1898 by a large purpose-built ballroom, designed by Richard Dalby Reeve.[74] Sanger was murdered on 28 November 1911, but after his death the increasingly old-fashioned Hall-by-the-Sea managed to remain open throughout World War I (*see* Fig 9.34).[75] The site was sold to John Henry Iles in November 1919, reopening on Boxing Day 1919 as the Palais de Danse, though it closed again after two months. Iles had created his first Scenic Railway at Blackpool and in 1909, he established the amusement park at Great Yarmouth.[76] He also marketed roller-coasters for L A Thompson's Scenic Railway Company in Britain and Europe.[77]

Fig 8.21
The site of the Kursaal at Southend-on-Sea changed ownership in 1910 and became Luna Park, a dedicated amusement park. It provided holidaymakers with the Harton Scenic Railway and a Figure of Eight coaster, a miniature railway, Astley's Circus and a cinema. This shot was taken in 1920. [EPW000443]

Fig 8.22
The Scenic Railway at
Great Yarmouth was
destroyed by fire in 1919,
but rebuilt quickly. This
Aerofilms photograph of
1920 shows the new scenic
railway devoid of any
scenery, standing alone
on the sand.
[EPW001875]

Fig 8.23
This 1949 photograph of
the Pleasure Beach at Great
Yarmouth shows a helter
skelter, swings and the
Scenic Railway in the
distance, still clad in
mountain scenery.
[AA98/14647]

The Margate site was soon renamed Dreamland, a name chosen to reflect the glamour of Coney Island, where there was a park known as Dreamland from 1904 to 1911.[78] In the 1 May 1920 edition of *The World's Fair*, the trade paper of the amusement industry, the advert for the recently opened Dreamland states that it includes 'THE LARGEST SCENIC RAILWAY IN EUROPE now nearing completion' and Iles' Scenic Railway finally opened on 3 July 1920, three months after the park itself (Fig 8.24).[79] During the 1920s and 1930s, many new rides were created and in 1923, the existing ballroom was reused as a 900-seat cinema and a new ballroom, the Palais de Danse, was created in the former rollerskating rink.[80] In 1935, the present Dreamland Cinema was completed according to designs by Julian Rudolph Leathart (1891–1978) and W F Granger, leading cinema architects of the period (*see* Fig 9.39).[81] The park remained under the control of the Iles family until 1968, but over the subsequent years it passed through a number of hands until its closure in 2006, by which time all the fixed rides, with the exception of the Scenic Railway, had been removed. Dreamland has now reopened as an amusement park with heritage rides drawn from a number of sites around the country.

In the late 20th century, seaside amusement parks have been in serious decline in England; Blackpool and Great Yarmouth are the only traditional parks that have remained open. Southport's park reopened after a brief closure and the loss of major rides, while Margate's Dreamland has been reinvented as a heritage park. The decline in the popularity of seaside amusement parks has been partly caused by lower numbers of visitors at the seaside, but can also be explained by competition from major inland rural parks that are now often more exciting, more modern and more conveniently located for large population centres. Nevertheless, there are also some modern seaside amusement parks, most notably the large Fantasy Island Park at Ingoldmells and the Brean Leisure Park near Weston-super-Mare. These are not in the main parts of seaside resorts, but in recent years there has also been a trend towards providing smaller parks nearer the heart of resorts, such as in the centre of the seafront at Skegness or near the pier at Southend-on-Sea, where younger children are the main customers (Fig 8.25). Some seaside piers are now also home to fairground rides; with the restriction in space available these are inevitably aimed at younger riders, but Blackpool's South Pier offers the Sky Coaster and the Sky Screamer, rides that catapult daring customers high into the sky.

Fig 8.24
In April 2008, an arson attack destroyed about a quarter of the Scenic Railway at Margate including the two 'pull-up' inclines and the workshop containing the cars. Fortunately, the motor room containing the winding gear was not affected. The ride has become the centrepiece of Dreamland Margate, a heritage amusement park. [DP032138]

Fig 8.25
There is a small amusement park at Scarborough, beside the harbour, convenient for holidaymakers on the beach, though its compact footprint limits the thrills/ terror on offer.
[MF99/0708/20]

Novelty transport

The seafront is also a location for novel forms of transport, ranging from practical but fun types such as land trains, miniature railways and horse-drawn carriages, as discussed in Chapter 4, to the entirely frivolous pedaloes and swans on boating ponds. These forms of novelty transport are at the safe, fun end of the spectrum, but for the more adventurous many resorts offer go-karts, that range from being suitable for children to ones designed for teenagers and adults. The seafront is also a place to experience events involving transport. The creation of promenades with their long, flat surfaces prompted drivers to seek to break speed records in cars, as well as being the location for motor sports events ranging from the earliest Grand Prix in Britain at

Bexhill-on-Sea to being the destination for the London to Brighton Rally each year, the World's Longest Running Motoring Event.[82] At Weston-super-Mare, the beach is used for a motocross gathering, an event that attracts thousands of visitors; for over 30 years the beach has been transformed into a difficult track created using giant mountains of sand.[83] A similar event is also held at Margate, the virtue of the beaches at both resorts being their plentiful sand.

Helicopter flights could be enjoyed at Weston-super-Mare and the seafront also makes a dramatic place for airshows, the first of which was held in Blackpool in October 1909.[84] The idea was inspired by a similar event that took place in August 1909 at Reims in Champagne, as well as a growing interest in flight that had culminated in Louis Blériot's successful crossing of the English Channel in July 1909.[85]

The organisers at Blackpool had less than two months to raise funds and construct the grandstands and hangars for planes. It was scheduled for the week beginning Monday 18 October, but a hastily arranged event at Doncaster began on the previous Friday to claim the accolade of being Britain's first aviation meeting.[86] Blackpool was quick to embrace the possibilities of flight, little knowing that it would ultimately be a contributing factor to its decline during the late 20th century when travel abroad became affordable to the mass market that had once flocked to Blackpool.

As well as land and air transport, the seafront is often a launching point for many forms of seaborne transport. The smallest and safest form of sea-going transport are the lines of pedaloes that operate from beaches such as at Weymouth (Fig 8.26). In many historic photographs, a predecessor of the pedalo, the small rowing boat, can be seen on beaches waiting to be used or to provide access to a larger boat at sea. At some seaside resorts small sailing boats have been, and are still, kept on beaches (Fig 8.27). Today, larger sailing boats and powerboats are kept in harbours or marinas, though some seafronts are still the location for yacht clubs, such as at Bexhill-on-Sea and at Cowes.

One feature visible in some old photographs is a long mobile gangway on wheels that could be positioned to take holidaymakers from the beach on to waiting boats for a trip around the bay. These potentially perilous structures no longer feature at most seaside resorts. Alternatively small boats may take paying customers out to pleasure boats, but Allchorn Pleasure Boats at Eastbourne have found a much more exciting way to ferry passengers from the shore to their pleasure boats at low tide, by using a World War II DUKW amphibious vehicle (Fig 8.28).[87]

Today's holidaymaker is no longer simply restricted to the simple wooden boat, with plastic and fibreglass canoes and kayaks being popular to hire or bring to the seaside. For the more adventurous some resorts provide trips out on banana boats, unpowered, inflatable boats resembling a banana designed for towing behind a speedboat. These are particularly popular in warmer climes, such as in the Mediterranean and the Caribbean. However, the arrival of the wetsuit at an affordable price has increased the use of the sea all year round, allowing people to enjoy exciting watersports such as wind surfing, jet skiing and parasailing. It has also been responsible for the widespread popularity of diving and the huge growth of

Fig 8.26
At Weymouth there are also craft with amusing names such as Carnival Queen, Thomas Hardy *and the more familiar 'come in number 47'. Here two pedaloes commemorate local attractions.*
[DP219584]

Fig 8.27
One part of some beaches
may be reserved for small
private boats, alongside
working boats, and such
an arrangement can still
be seen on the beach at Beer
in August 1950.
[AA98/09373]

Fig 8.28
In the past, DUKWs were
more common at seaside
resorts and were ideal for
a novelty trip 'around the
bay'. This 1950s photograph
shows one at Hunstanton
with passengers embarking.
[AA98/17564]

surfing, particularly at seaside resorts in the South West (Fig 8.29). The pre-eminent surfing resort is Newquay, the 'Surf Capital of the UK', where a range of purpose-built facilities have been established in recent years on Fistral Beach at the west side of the resort, while other nearby beaches often have people learning to surf.[88] The impact of this activity can be felt in Newquay throughout the year, with a number of shops providing surfing equipment and 'surf dude' ephemera for old and young. To exploit this growing interest, particularly among younger people at the university, Bournemouth has invested in an artificial reef to create surfing conditions that have resulted in the opening of surfing shops and hip cafes on one part of the seafront, a short distance to the east of the traditional family beach. The Boscombe Surf Reef, the first surfing reef to be constructed in the northern hemisphere, has provided a unique focal point for the town's multi-million-pound waterfront redevelopment and has helped to give this part of the seafront a distinctive brand (*see* Fig 5.25). First proposed as early as 1993, the general development scheme got the go-ahead at the end of 2003, though the reef was only finally approved by DEFRA in October 2007. Its construction was completed in September 2009, but it closed at the end of March 2011 for safety reasons that required repairs. The reef reopened in April 2014 when it was rebranded as a Coastal Activity Park focusing on diving, snorkelling, wind and kite surfing rather than just surfing.[89]

Fig 8.29
'Surf's Up'! The wide beach in front of the Fistral Beach Surf School at Newquay is a popular place for surfing, one of many locations on the north coasts of Devon and Cornwall where this pastime is practised.
[DP219529]

Conclusion

In the early 21st century, millions of visitors to Britain's seaside resorts are still fortunate to be able to experience many of the promenade piers and pleasure piers of the 19th century. While still providing something of the original thrill of walking on water, holidaymakers can see how these more than a century-old structures have been updated and refreshed to cater for modern tastes. However, piers today face the twin challenges of the sea and finding ways to maintain and renew their fabric and facilities. To secure their future they must remain popular and despite all the competing modern, exciting attractions of today's seaside, holidaymakers still flock to them to fish, breathe in the sea air and look out to sea. And if this can be combined with a bag of chips, a ride on a helter skelter or being catapulted into the sky, then the pier is perhaps the consummate destination during a day at the seaside.

Piers have graced seafronts for over 150 years and, as relatively old arrivals that demand little prized land along the shoreline, they are more or less centrally located, where the concentration of tourists is greatest. Amusement parks began to be created about 50 years later, when major resorts were considerably more developed. In addition, they require a large area of land on which to create their magic and therefore in many seaside resorts they are found on the peripheries of the seafront. While they may not be close to the central entertainment facilities, the main beach and the main railway station, amusement parks are such an attraction that they still draw huge crowds.

When the day at the beach, on the pier or riding a rollercoaster is over, people return to their lodgings, bed-and-breakfasts and hotels, before perhaps heading out again to enjoy the entertainments and the bright lights of the seafront. While the beach, in good weather, is at the heart of a day at the seaside, the first line of buildings along the seafront are often central to the night-time life of the seaside resort, providing the lodgings, hotels, restaurants, bars, theatres, cinemas and amusements. This line of buildings has been at the heart of the seaside industry since the 18th century and has changed dramatically, and regularly, over the decades to cater for growing numbers of tourists and their changing tastes. In the next chapter, the range of buildings lining the seafront will be described in search of common themes and styles that help to explain how this remarkable architectural essay evolved.

The buildings of the seafront

This chapter is devoted to the first line of buildings on the seafront. These are the primary economic drivers of tourism and, if tourism is considered as an industry, they are the productive machinery of the leisure business. This line of buildings is one side of a seaside street, and depending on the particular geography of the resort, it will normally be on the seafront, though it sometimes can be on clifftops. Compared to streets further inland, or in other types of town, this is the location for a bewildering variety of buildings carrying out a broad range of tasks. Most streets simply contain housing, perhaps a combination of housing, shops and occasional entertainment venues or a series of industrial works. However, the central section of the seafront may contain hotels, houses, shops, flats, bars and restaurants, a range of entertainment buildings and buildings associated with the working life of coastal towns.

The seafront tells the story of development and frequent redevelopment. In the central parts of resorts, the pressure to meet the changing tastes and the growing numbers of holiday-makers prompted regular and repeated change. As the 19th and 20th centuries unfolded, there was often economic pressure to replace small non-specialist buildings; the house that once interchangeably provided lodgings, a circulating library or a bathhouse was replaced by larger, more elaborate and more specialised structures. Moving out from the centre of seaside resorts there is a tendency towards more uniformity in date and function, and sometimes there are distinct zones providing terraced housing, villas, bed-and-breakfasts, flats and hotels. In terms of date, areas of development further from the resort centre will normally be later and are more likely to be for the provision of residents, rather than tourists.

This chapter will examine how and why seafront buildings are prone to change and the reasons for the variety in their form, function and date. It will also consider whether any other generalisations can be used to help to understand the complex history and architecture of the first line of buildings. There has been a belief that the seaside has a style, some kind of melange of the nautical and the exotic, but does an occasional porthole and an oriental arch amount to a seaside style?

The first line of buildings – an overview

At a handful of seaside towns, a small number of buildings survive on their seafronts that predate the settlement's identity as a resort. Until the 18th century, the view out to sea was not a prized commodity, most coastal settlements having their buildings orientated towards inland streets or their harbour. Where there were seafront buildings, these were often perpendicular to the sea, rather than facing it. Today, the seafront of seaside resorts, irrespective of their origin, will be dominated by a major road where once there was an undeveloped beach or clifftop. At a few of the first resorts early views give some impression of the direct connection between the first line of buildings and the beach and sea before a road intervened (Fig 9.1). Early views of Sea Houses, the settlement soon engulfed by Eastbourne, show a haphazard line of vernacular houses, ranging from low small houses to two-storeyed buildings with tall roofs containing two storeys of attics.[1] The timber-framed Moot Hall at Aldeburgh of the early 16th century, despite significant later alterations and repairs, is the earliest recognisable building on the immediate seafront at any current seaside resort (Fig 9.2).[2] At Swanage, the Royal Victoria Hotel is a complicated building with its origins as a house probably in the 16th century, though its most striking feature is its main elevation that dates from the early 18th century.[3]

Fig 9.1
The Long Picture (1814)
of Sidmouth shows the
circulating library at
the centre of a largely
undeveloped seafront.
To the right a few houses
and a simple promenade
can be seen, but with no
road along the shoreline.
[DP021042]

Fig 9.2
The Moot Hall on the
seashore at Aldeburgh is
now a museum and so it
can be said to have been
adapted to meet the
demands of tourists.
[DP217351]

Although effectively on the seafront and seaward facing, it is actually located at the coastal end of the High Street and should be considered as having originated in that context, rather than being orientated to the sea.[4]

A road normally separates the promenade and beach from the first line of buildings, but some resorts had, and still have, buildings between the road and the beach. However, many have been lost due to their vulnerable location near the sea or because they were in the path of development. At Hastings, Beach Terrace was a line of three- and four-storeyed late 18th- and early 19th-century houses located in front of the main road (Fig 9.3). A short distance to the west, Ordnance Survey maps show that

there were two other clusters of buildings standing directly on the seafront where no major seafront road existed, but a number of Aerofilms photographs taken in 1931 and 1932 show the current configuration, all the early buildings having been demolished.[5] At Eastbourne, to the north of the pier, the 1876 Ordnance Survey shows the working area of the seafront where there were capstans for hauling boats up onto the beach, as well as boathouses and the lifeboat station. Just behind the beach, before a seafront road was created, there were a number of houses orientated towards the sea, some of which may be the early houses of Sea Houses shown in 18th-century views of the seafront.[6]

Fig 9.3
This 1929 Aerofilms photograph shows Beach Terrace in front of Pelham Crescent at Hastings. It survived until Sidney Little's wholesale reconfiguration of the seafront in the early 1930s, in which a single major road was created along the whole length of the resort. The site is now a car park.
[EPW000111]

Fig 9.4
These seafront houses at Bexhill-on-Sea were home for the Maharajah of Cooch Behar who occupied 22 Marina Court in 1911 to recuperate after attending George V's coronation. Adjoining houses shown here were occupied by his retinue. Unfortunately, he didn't recover and he died there on 18 September 1911.
[DP217880]

At Blackpool, the early resort had no significant seafront road, and therefore all the early buildings were effectively located directly on the low clifftop and at the head of the beach (*see* Fig 3.1). A map of the resort dating from 1870 shows that by this date a road had been established along most of the seafront.[7] Some new buildings were located on the seaward side of this road, particularly to the south of Central Pier, and Bailey's Hotel to the north of North Pier, now the Metropole Hotel, still lies on the seaward side of the main road. The character of this arrangement is shown clearly in James Mudd's photographic panorama of Blackpool in the mid-1860s, a photograph taken from where Blackpool's second pier would soon be constructed.[8]

As the Edwardian Metropole Hotel at Blackpool demonstrates, sites located between the main seafront road and the beach can still be desirable locations for buildings where geography permits. At Bexhill-on-Sea, there are two sets of cottages sitting at the top of the beach, including a row of bungalows built in a Moghul style between 1903 and 1907 by various architects (Fig 9.4).[9] A key requirement for such later examples of seafront development in the centre of resorts was for the buildings to be low, so as not to impede the view of the buildings behind. Therefore, the Bexhill houses were bungalows and in James Burton's scheme for St Leonards in the late 1820s his seafront baths, library and reading rooms could only be single-storeyed, so that people staying in the hotel behind would have an uninterrupted sea view. In contrast, such concern was not in the thinking of Earl de la Warr and his architects Serge Chermayeff and Erich Mendelsohn in the mid-1930s when conceiving the design of the De La Warr Pavilion beside the earlier seafront cottages. At Hove, there is a large area of seafront development between the main road and the beach, including 19th- and 20th-century housing, flats and a 20th-century leisure centre. As at Bexhill, these have been designed without considering the view from properties behind the main seafront road.

Immediate seafront locations may be desirable for their view, and convenient for sea bathing, but the virtue of proximity to the sea can also be a significant drawback. These locations endure the harshest weather, making them difficult and expensive to maintain, and they could be very susceptible to storms and high tides, as some of Blackpool's earliest sea-front buildings proved. They could also be inconvenient for a town seeking to maximise

its access to the beach and the sea; as occurred at Hastings, the buildings were swept away to streamline the seafront during the early 1930s.

Buildings located immediately on the seafront can be a testimony to the early date of the town that became a seaside resort, but the character of the first line of buildings in general may also be dependent on the date of the establishment of that resort. Where a pre-existing historic settlement existed, its plan form and piecemeal development over centuries can be reflected on the seafront; it often expresses this history, almost serving as a cross-section through an old town. The pre-resort town normally covered a small area, with small plots, narrow streets and a dense pattern of relatively small-scale buildings (Fig 9.5). Development, which may have taken place over several centuries, was piecemeal, with buildings varying in size, height and date. This variety is also an expression of the lack of single ownership, but also reflects periods when regularity and uniformity were not required objectives of patrons or builders.

Fig 9.5
At Margate, the densely packed streets of the Old Town are clear beside the harbour. Above and to the left more spacious streets and squares can be seen laid out after tourists had arrived in sufficient numbers to justify such investment.
[NMR 33057/018]

Another factor shaping the general form and character of the first line of seafront buildings is the presence of a harbour. At Scarborough, the pre-18th-century focus of development was the harbour and, therefore, today this stretch of the seafront has a rich heritage of early buildings. Margate had similar origins, the historic town developing behind the harbour. While many early buildings survive in the Old Town, the narrow section of the seafront that survives between the stone pier and the base of the High Street has been rebuilt, though it still reflects the earlier, dense street pattern. At Weymouth, seafront development occurred in front of the historic town, new buildings being erected at the rear of the plots of buildings that had previously faced inwards and towards the harbour, rather than towards the sea (*see* Fig 2.2). By the 1780s, the seafront was becoming the focus for new development, initially single buildings such as Harvey's Circulating Library of the early 1780s. It was briefly freestanding before two short terraces were built adjacent to it during the 1780s. The character of the seafront development of this early part of the seafront at Weymouth was defined by the piecemeal character of the plot system of the mediaeval town (Fig 9.6).

Fig 9.6
At Weymouth, the dense, mediaeval street pattern and the triangular shape of the original settlement of Melcombe Regis is clear. The main tourism development is on the seafront to the north of the town, where there is a long line of terraced houses.
[NMR 21660/05]

The first new buildings stimulated by the arrival of tourists were effectively grafted on to the back of the mediaeval town of Weymouth and a similar process occurred at Great Yarmouth, but with a different outcome. Both towns had harbours located on their rivers, but, at Great Yarmouth, the distance between the rear of the historic town and the beach was sufficient to allow the growth of its resort function, unencumbered by having to fit in with the historic town. In contrast, Brighton had no harbour, but the section of the seafront between West Street and the Steine, where the remnants of the narrow historic town still exist behind, has clearly been influenced by the town's long history. The position and size of some of the plots, and the frequent, narrow streets, reflect the dense urban development of the historic town behind. By the time that the railway arrived in 1846, Blackpool had the plan of a small town with a handful of streets leading to the sea and a haphazard row of houses along the seafront. This small settlement would condition the later development of the central part of the resort, rather than any ancient town (Fig 9.7). At Great Yarmouth, the distant historic town was a less significant factor in the pattern of growth than its early jetty, the earliest, new urban development taking place on either side of it and on the road leading from it to the historic town. At seaside resorts where there was no pre-existing historic coastal town or just an inland hamlet or village, architects and developers were similarly free to lay out developments to meet the demands of the market as it existed at the date of construction. For instance, the heart of the initial development at Southport was Lord Street, parallel to, and now fairly distant from, the sea (Figs 9.8 and 9.9).

Fig 9.7
This 1920 Blackpool Aerofilms photograph shows Church Street, which was the main axis of the town before the railway arrived. With its arrival, Talbot Road, further to the north (left), became more significant, especially once North Pier was established at its end.
[EPW002057]

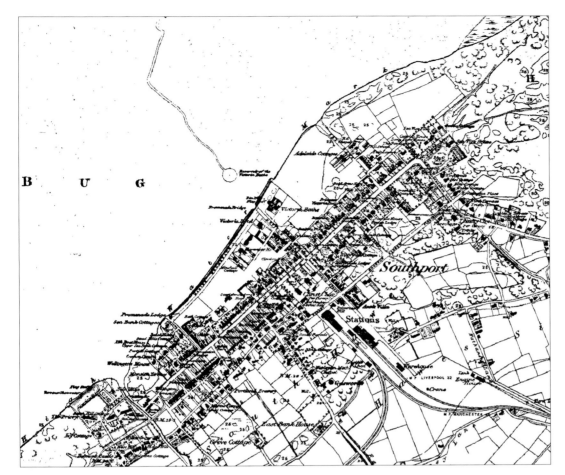

Fig 9.8
The Ordnance Survey
map of the mid-1840s
shows that Lord Street
at Southport was then the
main line of development
running along the shoreline.
This map predates any
significant reclamation
on the seafront.

Fig 9.9
Although the form of
Southport seems to have
the regularity of a planned
development, and more
order than nearby
Blackpool, this was largely
due to the practice of the
two principal landowners,
Miss Bold and Mr Hesketh,
who controlled the leasing
out to developers of parcels
of former 'waste land'
along the seashore.
[EPW018660]

Buildings along the seafront

Having discussed the general character of the first line of buildings on the seafront, consideration is needed of the variety of buildings on what is effectively one side of a street. But what a street! This is no monoculture simply of housing, shops or industrial units, but a highly elaborate collection of purpose-built buildings and structures that have perhaps been adapted to serve many purposes in the tourism industry over the past three centuries.

Houses

The most common type of building to be found on a seafront is the house. These can range in date and character from small pre-resort, vernacular buildings using traditional materials to modern concrete, glass and steel constructions. At most older resorts, the earliest buildings are unlikely to be found on the immediate seafront as historic buildings were not necessarily orientated towards the sea and, if they did

originally enjoy such a prominent location, their valuable site would lead to their replacement by larger, more prestigious and more valuable structures. However, Scarborough has some early buildings facing on to the harbour, which owe their existence to the town's commercial function. In the 17th century, the town's architecture consisted of a mixture of timber-framed, brick and an occasional stone building and by the mid-17th century, any thatched roofs were giving way to slate or pantiles.[10] The Newcastle Packet Inn (13 Sandside) was mediaeval in origin, but underwent a major refurbishment in 1898–9.[11] Behind the modern seafront road is the original Quay Street, which contains a number of timber-framed structures that would have once been close to, or on, the harbourside. Stone was much rarer than timber-framing, but the King Richard III's house appears to be a 17th-century stone building, though it may contain some earlier fabric (Fig 9.10). By the early 18th century, brick houses were being built for prosperous local people, but many were probably being planned with the expectation of providing accommodation for visitors. One of the largest, and oddest, new brick buildings is 33 Sandside, a large building originally on the quayside. Although superficially now domestic, an impression increased by its refenestration, it probably also originally had a commercial function.

Immediately behind the seafront in the old towns of Margate and Brighton a range of timber-framed, brick and stone houses can be found that date from between the 16th and the early 18th century. At such early resorts, any buildings on the seafronts were built in unplanned rows and once visitors arrived these began to be refurbished and replaced to maximise the rental income to be made from providing lodgings. Dr Anthony Relhan in 1761 documented the start of this process at Brighton: 'The town improves daily, as the inhabitants encouraged by the late great resort of company, seem disposed to expend the whole of what they acquire in the erecting of new buildings, or making the old ones convenient.'[12] At a similar date, East Cliff House (1760–2) on the seafront at Hastings was being constructed for Edward Capel, a Shakespearean scholar who spent his summers there.[13] This building is located in the first line of buildings behind the famous net lofts and the beach-launched fishing fleet and has for many years been used as a restaurant (Fig 9.11). East Cliff House

Fig 9.10
The King Richard III House at Scarborough now opens on to the roadside, but in the 18th century it would have stood immediately on the quayside. It now houses a restaurant.
[WSA01/01/05923]

is an exceptional house in its context and location, most early seafront buildings being architecturally unremarkable and necessarily small-scale due to restrictions imposed by pre-existing buildings and the ownership of plots. However, as it was built on the site of a former fortification, the usual restriction on space was not a factor. It is England's earliest dateable surviving house built on a seafront for someone coming to spend summers by the sea.

From the late 18th century onwards, the seafront came to be increasingly dominated by terraces and, on some occasions, crescents of new housing. The earliest phase of seafront development at Weymouth from the 1780s onwards was beginning to appear to the north of the historic town, on previously undeveloped land (see Fig 3.10). According to early maps, this was once no more than a spit of sand, but by the late 18th century it was clearly sub-stantial enough to allow the construction of long tall terraces, beginning with Gloucester Row, with Gloucester Lodge at its southern end (Fig 9.12).

In most instances, new terraces are a long line of identical houses, but at some resorts where they were built speculatively, rather than by one developer, individual houses of new developments may share overall characteristics, but vary in detail. For instance, the seafront terrace Buenos Ayres at Margate and Nelson Crescent at Ramsgate are each clearly part of single developments in terms of their layout and general disposition. However, while they may share the same number of storeys, and sometimes the same number of windows, the overall height of the buildings and the heights of individual storeys vary (Fig 9.13).

This arrangement resulted from builders interpreting the overall brief differently and not caring about the resulting variation, but another type of terrace resulted from exactly the opposite process. Palace fronts are an arrangement in which a terrace, or a crescent, has a pronounced central block, which is matched with similarly treated end pavilions. This served to disguise the humble nature of the individual buildings by suggesting the existence of a more palatial

Fig 9.11
Behind the modern extension to East Cliff House at Hastings is an outstanding building, a large and elegant Georgian house with polygonal bay windows and originally elaborate panelled interiors.
[DP018019]

Fig 9.12 (right)
Gloucester Row, with
Gloucester Lodge at its
southern end, was the home
of the Duke of Gloucester
where King George III
stayed during his visits
between 1789 and 1805.
The King purchased the
house in 1801 and renamed
it Royal Lodge. It was
badly damaged by fire
in 1927 and rebuilt.
[DP219594]

Fig 9.13 (below)
Originating from 1803,
though still incomplete in
1821, haphazard Buenos
Ayres was the earliest
development near the
Royal Sea Bathing
Hospital at Margate.
In the early 19th century,
the terrace of 13 houses
was apparently used as
lodgings for holidaymakers.
[AA049285]

structure and this form enjoyed its brief heyday during the second quarter of the 19th century (Figs 9.14 and 9.15). In the south-east, Brighton, St Leonards and Ramsgate had the most substantial schemes, the prestigious developments at Kemp Town and Brunswick Town both providing large terraced houses behind the grandest palace fronts found on the seafronts.

A handful of similarly elaborate schemes appeared elsewhere around the coast, some of which were on the seafront. Britannia Terrace at Great Yarmouth was built in 1848–55 as a palace-fronted terrace of 20 four-storeyed houses, but later painting and alterations to the individual houses disguise the fact that it is a single design.

Fig 9.14 (above)
Hesketh Crescent, built in 1848 on the coast to the east of Torquay, has three-bay-wide end pavilions and a five-bay centrepiece, which marks the central location of the hotel. [DP001355]

Fig 9.15 (left)
Bizarrely, the central section of Fort Crescent in Margate of c 1825 may be a hybrid of two types of housing development. It has the haphazard nature of speculative development, yet it also has what appears to be the central block and end pavilions of a palace-fronted scheme. [DP219019]

With the arrival of railways, and what was perceived to be a deluge of unwashed trippers, the same wealthy visitors who had once been content to occupy terraced houses began to shift into what amounted to early self-contained seafront communities, such as on the Leas at Folkestone or the Claremont Park Estate in Blackpool. Increasingly, they also began to move towards staying in individual villas, which required more land than was usually available on the seafront, and, therefore, instead colonised the extremities of the settlement. In most, but not all seaside resorts, villa developments occur inland, away from the seafront and the influxes of visitors. However, some of the later resorts to develop, with space to expand, have seafront villas set in large gardens enjoying wonderful views of the sea (Fig 9.16).

Apartments

A development of villas, despite the high cost of the individual buildings, would yield less income for an investor than a more intensive development, such as a terrace or a crescent. By the 20th century, although resorts were spreading outwards due to changes in transport infrastructure, the desire for a seafront location also prompted development upwards, in the form of blocks of flats. Perhaps the earliest is the Grand on the clifftop Leas at Folkestone, which opened on 12 September 1903. It is now a hotel, but it was built as a block of 'gentleman's residential chambers'.[14] The block had communal facilities on the ground floor and apartments on the upper floors. Gentlemen had the rooms around the outside of the building, while their servants were in rooms around an inside courtyard, across the corridor from their masters (Fig 9.17).

Modern blocks of flats first appear during the 1930s, the two most dramatic examples announcing the arrival of this new form being Embassy Court, Brighton and Marine Court at St Leonards. Embassy Court is a 12-storey reinforced-concrete block that was erected in 1934–6 by Wells Coates. Each of the nine types of flat provided residents with an open balcony and an enclosed sun-room that could be reached through the living room and bedrooms. The original windows to the sun-room had sliding, folding windows to create an open-air room, and there was a sun terrace on the roof (Fig 9.18).[15] After World War II, new development at seaside resorts was a lower priority than the reconstruction of heavily damaged cities, but new apartment blocks were built on, or near, the seafront at a number of resorts from the late

Fig 9.16
One of the resorts with extensive seafront villa development is Ventnor, where, despite modern seafront development, it is still possible to appreciate the original scatter of villas, houses and hotels on the hillside overlooking the beach.
[OP06129]

Fig 9.17 (above)
At Folkestone, the Grand,
the smaller building, is
four-storeyed with attics
with a long palm court in
front. In style, it is designed
to be sympathetic to, yet
distinctive from, its larger
neighbour, the Metropole.
[EPW000594]

Fig 9.18 (left)
Kenneth Dalgliesh and
Roger K Pullen's Marine
Court at St Leonards had a
dramatic visual impact on
the historic seafront. Its sleek
modern lines, evocative
of an ocean-going liner,
visually crash into the
terrace from James Burton's
1820s development.
[DP018000]

1950s onwards. The seafront at Dover, which had suffered so badly during the war, was identified as a suitable location for new apartments during the 1940s. Various schemes were proposed, but it took until October 1959 for the Gateway Flats to be completed (Fig 9.19).[16] Some industrial towns and cities have clusters of tall tower blocks, but seaside resorts almost exclusively have single, seafront point blocks. Examples can be seen at Margate, Blackpool, Brighton and Great Yarmouth, while Bournemouth has a tall clifftop block of flats (Fig 9.20).

During the 1960s, lower-rise clusters of apartment blocks were favoured in new seafront areas of development on the peripheries of resorts. Examples include a group of six seven-storeyed blocks at Bexhill-on-Sea, the blocks of four-storeyed flats that complete the footprint of the Crescent at Hayling Island and the groups of three-storeyed blocks that were built at Bispham to the north of Blackpool. These are fairly conservative buildings, typical of developments taking place throughout the country at the same period. At the end of the 20th century, the

Fig 9.19
Dover's Gateway Flats is a long, seven-storeyed block with public gardens in front. It provides 221 flats, all of which have sea views, a compensation for having the main dual carriageway from the ferry port as a neighbour behind.
[NMR 33065/024]

Fig 9.20
Arlington House and Square at Margate was designed by Russell Diplock Associates and opened in 1963. It provided shops and car parking around its base. Being perpendicular to the seafront allows all the flats to have views of the coast.
[AA050585]

preference in central parts of resorts was for low-rise developments. New blocks of contrasting design include Charleston Court at Broadstairs in 1995, which has a stepped layout and a fairly conservative style, while the Van Alen Building of 2001 in Brighton is built in a contemporary version of art deco moderne.[17] By the early 21st century, there had been a revival in interest in high-rise buildings nationally, but there has been no significant return to constructing tall blocks at the seaside. However, in 2017, Worthing Borough Council approved plans for 140 new homes, including a 'curvaceous' 15-storey tower that will stand on the seafront.[18]

The increase in the number of flats available at seaside resorts is in part fuelled by the general growth in the housing market, but it has also been stimulated by people wishing to retire there, second-home ownership and the popularity of buy-to-let properties. Scarborough's North Bay has new flats and even a small resort like Westward Ho! now has a prominent six-storeyed apartment block, as well as many other lower, modern blocks of flats (Fig 9.21).

Fig 9.21
At Boscombe, the hillside above the pier is now lined with blocks of flats, at least some of which are second homes.
[DP114044]

Hotels and holiday accommodation

Since the early 19th century, the seafront has also been a marketable asset for hoteliers. Hotels, in the modern sense, began to appear at seaside resorts in the early 19th century as what would become a luxurious alternative to taking lodgings in a house. At the seaside, the word 'hotel' by the 1760s was in use in its older sense, describing a large house with catering provided. Examples include the sea-bathing hotels on the Lincolnshire coast and Fox's Tavern in Cecil Square in Margate, built in 1769, which was renamed the Royal Hotel in honour of the visit of George Prince of Wales in 1794. The first full-scale, purpose-built hotel was probably the Royal Hotel at Plymouth, which was completed in 1819.[19] During the 1820s, a number of substantial purpose-built hotels began to be built on the seafront of new and leading resorts (Fig 9.22). The development of Hayling Island in the mid-1820s included a new hotel, the foundation stone of which was laid on 16 December 1825.[20] At Teignmouth, Andrew Patey built Cockram's Hotel on the Den in 1825 and, in 1826, the Albion Hotel opened on the site of Dr Russell's house at Brighton.[21]

The next major step in the story of hotel development on the seafront came during the 1860s, with the creation of grand hotels, grand both in terms of scale and name. The Grand Hotel du Louvre in Paris, which had opened in 1855, gave its name to some of these vast, luxurious hotels. However, English seaside resorts were soon matching it in quality and outstripping it in size. Brighton's Grand Hotel, with 260 bedrooms, opened on the seafront in 1864 and was the first English seaside hotel to adopt the name that associated it with its Parisian counterpart.[22] The Grand Hotel at Scarborough opened in 1867 and was designed by Cuthbert Brodrick (Fig 9.23). These hotels became increasingly important for wealthier visitors seeking to withdraw from the busy centres of resorts. They formed small, self-contained communities and, when hydropathic facilities were added, they almost became small exclusive resorts in their own right. The Imperial Hotel at Blackpool was built in 1866–7 by the Manchester architects Clegg and Knowles. Its original capacity was said to be 100 bedsteads in 120 rooms as well as restaurants, dining rooms, billiard rooms and coffee rooms, a substantial investment for a town that still only numbered a few thousand inhabitants. A new wing was added in the mid-1870s, providing 39 additional bedrooms and six sitting rooms, as well as a new restaurant and smoke room, and in 1881 a company was formed to convert it into a hydropathic hotel (Fig 9.24).[23] As the hotel was set within the Claremont Park Estate to the north of North Pier, it initially benefited from the limiting of traffic along the seafront as a result of charging tolls.

From the late 19th century onwards, substantial hotels appeared on the seafront of any self-respecting seaside resort, the prestige of the sea view guaranteeing premium rates. Some hotels continued to adopt a style and form that would echo their cosmopolitan, European roots, but more often they employed the currently fashionable style, using Italianate, baroque and Gothic forms. Examples include the 1891 Hotel de Paris on the cliff above the pier at Cromer, the Metropole Hotel on the Leas at Folkestone 1895–7 and the Savoy Hotel at Blackpool of 1915 (*see* Fig 9.17).[24] By the 1930s, art deco forms were being used for hotels, the leading example being Oliver Hill's Midland Hotel at Morecambe (Fig 9.25).[25] After World War II there was a shift away

Fig 9.22
The Royal Victoria Hotel was at the heart of the seafront of St Leonards in the late 1820s. It acquired its name from a visit there by the 15-year-old Princess Victoria in 1834.
[DP217957]

Fig 9.23
The Grand Hotel at
Scarborough of 1867
contained 300 bedrooms,
meaning that when it was
built it was reputedly the
largest hotel in Europe.
It stands on a low clifftop
overlooking the South Bay,
a monumental presence
at the heart of the resort.
[DP006187]

Fig 9.24
Although not a grand hotel
in name, the choice for the
Imperial Hotel at Blackpool
of a French Renaissance
style and its scale echoes
grand hotels being built in
Paris, London and at other
leading seaside resorts.
[DP154924]

Fig 9.25
The Midland Hotel at
Morecambe of 1933 was
built for the LMS Railway
and was one of the first
Modernist buildings erected
at the seaside. It replaced
a Victorian hotel that had
been built by the railway
company for passengers
travelling by ship from
Morecambe.
[DP056382]

from staying in some hotels as historic ones grew older and their once modern facilities increasingly seemed out of date. In some resorts, historic hotels have successfully been updated and still cater for the wealthiest holidaymakers and business people. Alternatively, others prefer to cater for the coach-party market, which guarantees large numbers of guests at cheaper room rates. However, many resorts have lost their historic hotels as the shape and size of the tourist market changed during the late 20th century. Margate once boasted several large hotels on the clifftops at Cliftonville, but today only the 1914 Walpole Bay Hotel survives.[26] Clacton's Royal Hotel, built in 1872, has recently been converted into a pub and flats and Worthing's Warnes Hotel burned down in 1987 and was replaced with a block of flats.

Some new hotels with modern facilities have been built in recent years, often created by modern chains with the money to invest in new facilities; examples include the Premier Inns on the seafronts at Dover and Margate. At the Butlins site at Bognor Regis, three new hotels have been built recently, including one on the immediate seafront. There has also been a growth in the number of boutique hotels, and highly rated bed-and-breakfasts, predominantly in existing buildings, and sometimes in seafront locations. And at the edges of resorts, the seafront may be home to chalets or caravans, properties that may serve as both holiday homes and places for people to rent for a holiday. Holiday camps are also a significant seafront presence at some seaside resorts, again at the peripheries where land was available and affordable.

Health buildings

Structures associated with sea water had to be on the seafront, at the top of the beach or set within the first line of buildings. Early examples on the seafront have not survived, but at Cromer a building that began as a subscription reading room in *c* 1814 had bathing facilities added in *c* 1824. The present building near the pier dates from 1836 when it was rebuilt following destruction by a storm; it was converted into a hotel in 1872.[27] At Southport, the Victoria Salt Water Baths opened beside the approach to St Anne's Pier in July 1871. The Fylde Borough Council offices occupy the site of this building that combined smaller offices with a substantial sea-water bathhouse (Figs 9.26 and 9.27; *see also* Fig 6.18).[28]

Fig 9.26
This c 1900 photograph shows the pier approach at St Annes looking from the seafront across the lawns towards the public baths on the right.
[OP00453]

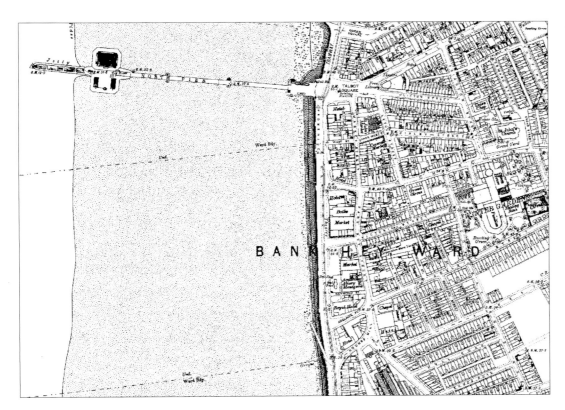

Fig 9.27
The 1893 Ordnance
Survey map for Blackpool
shows that, prior to the
construction of the Tower
and Alhambra, two
substantial bathhouses,
hotels and lodging houses
occupied the central section
of the seafront.

Like bathhouses, sea-bathing hospitals also required a seafront location. While the pioneering Royal Sea Bathing Hospital at Margate stands away from the heart of the resort, Scarborough's sea-bathing hospital, rebuilt in 1858–60, is set in the buildings lining the beach at the heart of the resort (*see* Figs 6.31 and 6.32). Access to a plentiful supply of water was also a factor in the siting of early swimming pools, as was the desire to place such a facility near where likely customers were spending their days. As was discussed in Chapter 6, seafront swimming pools were once common though few have survived, but the modern successor to swimming pools, the pool in the multi-functional leisure centre, may, as in the case of Great Yarmouth, Blackpool, Felixstowe and Worthing, be located on the seafront if there is a suitable site and a desire to attract tourists, as well as residents, to the facility (*see* Fig 6.29).

Entertainment venues

Entertainment venues do not have to be located on the seafront, though this location is desirable to maximise the number of customers. The earliest entertainment facilities – circulating libraries, assembly rooms and theatres – were often created in existing buildings and, therefore, these were inevitably within the footprint of the historic town. By the end of the 18th century, seaside resorts were sufficiently busy to justify investment in purpose-built facilities and a number of these were located on seafronts. Margate was well provided with circulating libraries, most of which were in the town, though one of the purpose-built examples was created at the foot of the High Street, on the junction with the seafront Parade facing the harbour (Fig 9.28).

Fig 9.28
Similar to the example
in Margate, the former
Powell's Library in
Hastings was built on the
seafront in the early 19th
century. It originally had
a bow-fronted shopfront
to the ground floor library
and a room above with
a billiard table. It is now
a fish and chip shop.
[DP018008]

On the seafront at Lyme Regis, Library Cottage was the site of the Marine Circulating Library, established in 1839. In 1826, the ambitious Den Crescent at Teignmouth was constructed with an assembly room at its centre looking out to sea (*see* Fig 2.10). At Weymouth, the Theatre Royal was established in 1771, while nearby Harvey's Circulating Library was constructed around a decade later (*see* Fig 2.2). In 1896, a theatre was built on the seafront at Morecambe alongside the now-demolished winter gardens and through patient work by volunteers it is being kept running.[29]

The entertainment facilities of the first century of seaside resorts were primarily based on the model of charging high fees to a small number of wealthy people. This led to the creation of small-scale, sociable, elite venues, the exception during the Georgian era being theatres, where varying ticket costs meant that different classes of patron enjoyed different experiences. From the mid-19th century onwards, there was a significant change in the model of funding entertainment facilities, the arrival of thousands, and later millions, of holidaymakers prompting the creation at larger resorts of more substantial facilities charging small fees to large numbers of tourists. The best example is Blackpool Tower, a building providing millions of tourists with opulence for 6d (Fig 9.29). To create large-scale facilities required considerable economic courage, but it also required a suitable site, a significant challenge in a well-developed resort. The Ordnance Survey map published in 1893 reveals that the Tower was being constructed on the site of housing, a market and an aquarium that had begun life as the house of Sir Benjamin Heywood MP in the 1830s. The site of the adjacent Alhambra was achieved by aggregating three main sites containing a hotel, baths and the market and theatre (*see* Fig 9.27).

Blackpool Tower illustrates the shift towards large-scale, occasionally industrial-sized, venues in the busiest resorts. It also illustrates that there had been an extension in the character of entertainment, from sociable and personal activities to entertainments based on emerging technologies, necessitating purpose-built facilities. Piers had led the way from the 1850s onwards and by the 1870s, a visitor to the first line of buildings on the seafront might also be entertained at an aquarium, in winter gardens and related entertainment venues or at a rollerskating rink.

In 1853, the world's first public self-contained, self-sustaining, marine aquarium opened in Regent's Park and by the 1870s, the first aquaria had opened at seaside resorts.[30] Brighton Aquarium was designed by Eugenius Birch, the pier engineer and designer of Brighton's West Pier (opened 1866), who conceived the idea following a visit to Boulogne Aquarium.[31] It was built close to the Chain Pier and its construction required the creation of a new sea wall and an extension of the promenade to create Madeira Drive. The Brighton Marine Aquarium Company was formed on 2 January 1868 and, in the following year, an Act of Parliament was obtained to allow work to take place.[32] The whole project was completed in 1872 at a cost of £130,000.

A description of the building appears in a book designed to celebrate the building and to promote interest in the emerging science of home aquaria.[33] This and early photographs show that it was a large, complicated structure finished with highly decorative architectural detailing. Modern visitors to seaside resorts are used to seeing aquaria as modernist, streamlined structures. However, Brighton's aquarium had a lavish Victorian interior, with polychromed brick terracotta vaults and fine stonework (Fig 9.30). Where Brighton led, other resorts followed. Aquaria were built in Southport in 1874 in the winter gardens complex, followed by others at Blackpool and Tynemouth in 1875, and Great Yarmouth in 1876 (now a cinema).[34]

Fig 9.30
The largest tank in Brighton's aquarium measured 103ft (31.4m) by 40ft (12.2m) and held 110,000 gallons (500,069 litres) of water, making it the largest display tank in the world at that time. This photograph shows a hall with the tanks accessible through the arches on each side. [BB78/07043]

A large, but short-lived, aquarium was also built at Scarborough in 1877, in an Indian style with caves and grottos complementing the fish tanks.[35] Today, the seafront is a common place to find modern aquaria; their strident high-tech style means that they are usually stand-out, if not outstanding, buildings with a key visual impact on the seafront (Fig 9.31).

Although sea water was not needed for winter gardens, visitors were, and if a suitable seafront site could be found, this would strengthen their economic viability. The roots of seafront winter gardens can be traced back to Henry Phillips' Anthaeum, a large glass conservatory housing palm trees as well as a literary institute.[36] Abandoned due to a lack of funds, the idea was revived in 1833 when the Anthaeum was built on the seafront at the west end of Hove.[37] Unfortunately, this glazed, domed structure had serious design flaws and collapsed. However, the success of the Crystal Palace in 1851 demonstrated that the technology could be mastered and during the 1870s a number of large examples were created in resorts in north-west England, as well as at Bournemouth, Torquay and Tynemouth (Fig 9.32).[38] Torquay's winter gardens were erected in 1878–81 on an inland site, but were dismantled and reconstructed on the seafront at Great Yarmouth in 1903. Later examples of winter gardens erected on a seafront were at Margate in 1911 and at Weston-super-Mare in 1924–7. At some resorts, alternative names were employed for what was becoming simply a multifunctional entertainment venue; the Kursaals at Southend (1898–9) and at

Worthing (1911, now the Dome Cinema) are still prominent features in the first line of buildings.[39]

The first line of buildings was also a location for smaller pavilions, essentially a large hall, with some accompanying facilities for social, musical and theatrical events (Fig 9.33). The Royal Victoria Pavilion on the seafront at Ramsgate was built as a concert hall and assembly rooms in 1903 by S D Adshead 'in the style of a Robert Adam orangery'.[40] The Spa Pavilion in Felixstowe originally opened as the New Floral Hall in place of a bandstand and it was extended and refurbished in the late 1930s, reopening as a large theatre and music hall in April 1939. The building was damaged in 1941 but was rebuilt to reopen in May 1950.[41]

These general entertainment buildings on the seafront assumed the role once the preserve of the assembly rooms, but, rather than paying one season-long subscription, these venues relied on charging entrance fees for single events. Examples of purpose-built, stand-alone ballrooms and dance halls are relatively uncommon, this role being fulfilled by these pavilions or hotels with large function rooms, as a dedicated dance hall faced significant economic challenges in the face of such strong competition (Fig 9.34). The years immediately before and after World War I were probably the high point for the construction of seafront music venues and entertainment complexes, but the tradition continued through the 20th century, the 1935 De La Warr Pavilion at Bexhill-on-Sea being the outstanding example of a modernist solution to entertaining residents and tourists (Fig 9.35).

Fig 9.31
At Weston-super-Mare, the modern aquarium stands on the beach and is almost a third pier near the heart of the resort.
[AA049330]

Clockwise from top left:

Fig 9.32
Southport's winter gardens were built on the seafront in 1874 and the concert pavilion could hold 2,000 people. This photograph of 1878 shows the scale of these new arrivals on the seafront.
[BB83/05801]

Fig 9.33
The cast-iron Floral Pavilion at Bridlington was constructed on the seafront in 1904, and was extended in 1907 and again in c 1960, before undergoing late 20th-century alterations.
[BB98/16307]

Fig 9.34
The most famous purpose-built seafront ballroom was another creation of Lord George Sanger at Dreamland at Margate. The original Hall-by-the-Sea ballroom and this Edwardian successor was sustainable as they were one of a suite of attractions on the site.
[BB84/00899]

Fig 9.35
In December 1935, the future George V opened the De La Warr Pavilion in Bexhill-on-Sea. This image shows the central staircase tower of Serge Chermayeff and Erich Mendelsohn's design.
[DP217884]

The third of the new entertainment phenomena of 1870s was rollerskating, but few buildings designed to cater for this short-lived fad have survived. It reached Britain during the early 1870s, prompting 'rinkomania' or 'rollermania', so that at its height in spring 1876 Brighton had six public rinks.[42] Combining skating with other uses, such as being concert venues, would prove to be a saviour for some rinks as within a couple of years the craze had passed, though there were regular, if usually short-lived, revivals in subsequent decades. Lord George Sanger's development of the Hall-by-the-Sea at Margate included a rollerskating rink after he acquired the site in February 1874, as he had a plentiful supply of undeveloped land.[43] On the central parts of other resorts, it would prove more difficult to find a suitable site for an activity that proved short-lived and not particularly lucrative, but in June 1876, the terrace of Brighton's Aquarium was extended and a rollerskating rink was one of the new facilities created. Margate's recently reopened Dreamland has even revived rollerskating as part of its modern offer.

A rollerskating rink need only be a fairly modest structure, but a large winter gardens was technologically ambitious and financially adventurous. However, Blackpool Tower of the early 1890s was on an altogether different scale and ushered in a rapid growth in the town's entertainment venues (Fig 9.36).

Fig 9.36
At 518ft 9in (158m), Blackpool Tower was Britain's tallest structure when it was built, and it epitomised the new devotion to technological entertainment.
[AA058315]

The Tower was economically possible because the resort was welcoming around two million visitors per year to a town with a population of fewer than 40,000 residents. Technologically, the inspiration was the Eiffel Tower, but unlike its French counterpart, around the base of the Tower there is a cluster of large-scale entertainment facilities.

Blackpool Tower opened to the public on 14 May 1894.[44] It offered visitors a range of entertainments for 6d, including a visit to the aquarium, a menagerie holding big cats and other creatures, the Monkey House and Aviary, the Seal Pond and Bear Cage, and Roof Gardens. The Tower's elevator hall was treated as a picturesque English village and there was also a Grand Saloon, refreshment bar, billiard saloon and the Grand Pavilion that would soon be reinvented as the celebrated Tower Ballroom (Fig 9.37). If visitors paid extra, they could ascend the Tower or enjoy a show in the 3,000-seat circus. Its floor could be lowered to reveal a 6ft 6in-deep (1.95m) water tank to stage aquatic performances; the same arrangement was incorporated into the Hippodrome at Great Yarmouth in 1903. Between 1898 and 1904, Frank Matcham was employed to transform the main venues in Blackpool Tower. This involved extending and raising in height the ballroom and altering the layout of the circus. These measures were in response to the recent enlargement of the winter gardens, and the construction of the adjacent lavish Alhambra and the nearby Hippodrome.

Fig 9.37
The interior of Blackpool Tower Ballroom, a key venue in each series of 'Strictly Come Dancing', is a shrine to ballroom dancing, with its adjustable, sprung floor and its famous Wurlitzer organ that rises up from beneath the floor of the stage.
[AA048180]

By the early 20th century, the introduction of new forms of technological entertainment was resulting in the creation of important new buildings and structures on many seafronts. Electricity and the invention of practical systems for projecting moving pictures came together to create cinema. The earliest purpose-built cinema at a seaside resort is probably the Gem Cinema at Great Yarmouth, though it was apparently originally designed to be a venue for a wild-animal show.[45] It was a simple structure with a large open hall behind an elaborate facade, a formula that remained a standard approach for cinema design until the 1930s. Prior to World War I, Blackpool had more than a dozen venues showing films, a mixture of cinemas within existing complexes such as the Alhambra, theatres and other buildings showing films occasionally, as well as a few purpose-built cinemas (Fig 9.38). Margate still boasts two early, surviving cinemas; the Parade Cinema, which opened in 1911, is located on the seafront. Its facade has panels decorated with masks and musical instruments, suggesting that the building could have been conceived as a music hall. Cinemas reached the peak of their popularity during the 1930s when resorts such as Brighton and Bournemouth could each boast 16.[46] As primarily evening entertainments, they did not necessarily have to be situated on the seafront, but the Dreamland Cinema of 1935 at Margate

enjoys such a prominent location (Fig 9.39). Some modern multiplexes can also be found on seafronts and Bournemouth had a short-lived, now demolished, IMAX cinema on a site beside its pier.

In the late 19th and early 20th century, a wealth of technological amusements developed for individual players to enjoy. These ranged from the mutoscope and the automated phonograph (the future jukebox) to early arcade games such as the Penny Falls, bagatelles that would morph into the modern pinball machine, and athletic testing machines, such as the boxing bag.[47] The rapid proliferation of such novelties prompted the creation of amusement arcades, though in most cases machines were initially simply placed in any convenient location where they might catch the eye of a player. This could be outside as long as the machine was mechanical or well waterproofed. By the mid-20th century, purpose-built arcades were beginning to be created. Among the earliest was Joyland at Bridlington, originally named Luna Park after the Coney Island amusement park. It originated during the 1930s and in its heyday was the largest privately owned amusement arcade in Britain.[48] During the 1930s, prior to his involvement with holiday camps, Billy Butlin pioneered the creation of small seafront amusement parks with arcades, such as those at Littlehampton and Felixstowe (Fig 9.40).[49]

Fig 9.38
One of the three early, surviving cinemas in Blackpool is located on the seafront. The former Princess Cinema on the Promenade originally opened in 1912 and was significantly enlarged when it reopened in 1922.
[DP154943]

Fig 9.39
Margate's Dreamland
Cinema was completed
in 1935 to designs by
Julian Rudolph Leathart
and W F Granger, leading
cinema architects of the
period. The slim fin tower,
which was also adopted
by cinemas in the Odeon
chain, was styled on Berlin's
1928 Titania Palast.
[OP13149]

Fig 9.40
On the former site of a
Butlins Amusement Park
at Felixstowe is Mannings
Amusements. It bears the
date 1945 and the names
of Manning and Sons,
and Charles Manning,
who took over the site.
[MF99/0675/12]

Fig 9.41
The exotic style of this Scarborough amusement arcade is due to the building being the original Victorian sea-water baths, though much of its original exotic detailing has been pared back.
[DP006178]

The Coney Island arcade on the seafront at Scarborough, which was Corrigan's until 2009, is a fairly simple building, though its facade has a series of blind arches and there is a corner turret with Mozarabic blind arches to impart a hint of the exotic (Fig 9.41). Later amusement arcades are essentially small industrial units with highly illuminated and lavishly decorated fascia that announce their name and function. Names are likely to evoke a Las Vegas casino or a Coney Island amusement park. They might also celebrate the Wild West, pirates and exotic foreign resorts or proclaim a long-established family brand such as the Silcock's facilities at Blackpool and Southport. Some recent arcades have adopted a more comprehensive high-tech style, rather than simply applying a fascia to a box. Following the fire on the Grand Pier at Weston-super-Mare in 2008, the centrepiece of its new pavilion is a high-tech arcade with state-of-the-art rides and amusements.

Shops

Since visitors have been coming to the seaside, they have been buying goods from traders in streets, on the seafront and on the beach. Shops originally existed in the historic towns that welcomed sea bathers, and while these originally supplied basic goods, Georgian trade directories indicate that new shops soon provided visitors with luxuries and fancy goods. In 1824, Teignmouth, a town of just 4,000 inhabitants, could boast 2 booksellers, 5 drapers, 13 milliners, 4 tailors and 8 bootmakers.[50] Food was provided by 5 bakers, 3 brewers, 3 confectioners, 7 grocers and 19 general merchants.[51] There were also 4 cabinet makers and 2 perfumiers. Markets were also important from the outset as this was where visitors often purchased the ingredients that they provided to their landlord or landlady to prepare their meals. Mary Figgins' wonderfully humdrum diary of her stay at Margate in *c* 1828 regularly describes visiting the market in the morning to buy her family's food for her landlady to prepare.[52] Markets and shops providing provisions did not need to be on the seafront. Furthermore, until the 19th century, there was probably little economic reason to open businesses there as most of the social timetable of the day involved people using facilities within the towns, rather than on the seafront. However, as the seafront became more developed, shops occupying the ground floor of buildings became commonplace, though the pressure to continually adapt to changing tastes and growing visitor numbers has precluded the survival of interesting, intact, early shopfronts on seafronts.

Some bazaars and shopping arcades were created on seafronts, though most have also succumbed to subsequent redevelopment. Bazaars were large spaces with counters that could be rented out by traders offering pre-dominantly expensive fancy goods to visitors. The earliest examples appeared at the beginning of the 19th century in London and were soon appearing at seaside resorts (Fig 9.42).[53] There was a seafront parade of shops, including a bazaar, at Herne Bay by 1835, a development that also included a circulating library, assembly rooms and baths.[54] On the seafront at Great Yarmouth, a pair of Edwardian shopping arcades dated 1902 and 1904 have been converted into an amusement arcade and at Morecambe there are a pair of late 1930s buildings on the seafront beside the winter gardens that were designed as shops for Littlewoods and Woolworths (Fig 9.43).[55] At Blackpool, a new Woolworths building of 1938 was built on a prominent position beside the Tower. It blends a stripped classical style with some more geometric moderne touches and is finished in cream-coloured faience (*see* Fig 1.6). A modern Woolworths store opened a short distance northwards. This had been the location of the Alhambra, which was demolished and replaced in 1964 by the strikingly modern Lewis's department store, which closed in 1993 to be replaced by the new Woolworths building. However, the honour of being the largest shop on the sea-front is enjoyed by the nondescript light industrial shopping units of Ocean Plaza at Southport. While they may be meeting a commercial need, they do nothing to enhance the beauty of the seafront.

Fig 9.42 (above)
Pelham Bazaar on the seafront at Hastings, which opened in August 1825, was built in front of Pelham Crescent. It consisted of two rows of shops flanking a central corridor top-lit by a glazed roof. In the centre of the crescent is St Mary-in-the-Castle, a rare example of a seafront church.
[DP163922]

Fig 9.43 (left)
This rare example of a late 1930s department store on a seafront can be found at Morecambe, one of a pair of highly distinctive designs a short distance from the slightly earlier Midland Hotel.
[AA93/04450]

Food outlets

As many seaside resorts are co-located with more or less active harbours, these towns have a long tradition of providing high-quality, fresh seafood and fish. Residents of Hastings are particularly well provided by a series of fish stalls among the net lofts of the Old Town selling fish landed by local boats. Cooked food outlets may be in kiosks, booths and small cafes on the seafront. As part of the preparation for hosting the sailing events of the 2012 Olympics, Weymouth constructed new kiosks for food sellers, minor works of art rather than just simple boxes. When a new cafe building was needed at Littlehampton, the owners had the foresight to engage a talented young designer, Thomas Heatherwick (Fig 9.44). What is missing today is the purveyor of seafood and snacks on the beach, a feature that was common in historic photographs of seaside resorts (*see* Fig 7.19).

There is also a need at seaside resorts for restaurants for more substantial meals. These range from small bistros and fine dining establishments to the large facilities within hotels catering for residents and visitors. Blackpool's Alhambra's restaurant and lounges could house 4,000 people at a time, while nearby the British Workman Company offered teetotal visitors the Station Temperance Hotel opposite Central Station and the British Workman on South Beach. These two restaurants provided seating for 1,000 diners at a time and in 1889 dinners cost between 8d and 1s 6d, meaning that 'Visitors lodging in private houses will find it more convenient and economical to dine here than to provide for themselves.'[56]

The most distinctive forms of food outlet on seafronts are the fish and chip shop and the ice-cream parlour. The former is housed in a mixture of adapted ground floors of houses and some modern, purpose-built structures, particularly when a restaurant is included as well as a take-away facility. The Harry Ramsden chain of fish and chip shops can be found at many resorts, but seaside resorts are rightly celebrated for the variety of local businesses selling locally produced food.[57] Ice cream has been on sale at British seaside resorts since the 18th century; the Reverend John Swete described buying it at Sidmouth in 1795.[58] Ice-cream parlours were often the creation of Italian families and some have left a legacy of mid-20th century architecture in their seafront parlours. The Morelli family introduced their recipes into Britain in 1907 and the first Morelli's ice-cream parlour opened on the seafront in Broadstairs in 1932.[59] The Macari family opened their first ice-cream parlour on the seafront at Herne Bay in 1931, while the Rossis started making ice cream at Southend-on-Sea during the following year and opened a seafront parlour soon after.[60] And special mention has to be made of Scotland's most famous seafront ice-cream parlour, the art deco Nardini's on the seafront at Largs in Ayrshire, which originally opened in 1935 and has recently been refurbished.[61]

Fig 9.44
The East Beach Café at Littlehampton by Thomas Heatherwick is more than just a cafe; it is a work of art and a reason to visit the resort. It has inspired the creation of Britain's longest bench nearby. See also Fig 5.8.
[DP139417]

Places of worship

If surviving purpose-built shops and restaurants are rare on the seafront, places of worship are even scarcer, because few were built. Nevertheless, many diaries reveal that religious worship was a key part of a god-fearing Georgian or Victorian visitor's week. Initially, holiday-makers made use of an existing church, which was usually inland at the heart of the original town or in a nearby historic village. As making money was the driving motivation of owners of plots of land on the seafront, they would not normally wish to provide a site for an activity that would yield no earthly profit.

At Margate, worship was at the mediaeval parish church about half a mile inland, up the High Street. Despite having hosted visitors for almost a century, it was only in 1825–8 that Holy Trinity Church was built in the centre of a piecemeal development on three sides of an irregular 'square' just behind the seafront Fort Crescent (Fig 9.45). At Hastings, between 1824 and 1828, Thomas Pelham employed Joseph Kay to build a crescent of houses with a large parish church at its centre.[62] The foundation stone of the church, St Mary-in-the-Castle, was laid on 21 September 1825 (see Fig 9.42).[63] This scheme was more than just a housing development, as the presence of the church, a shopping bazaar and baths demonstrates. For similar reasons, churches were features of Kemp Town and Brunswick Town at Brighton, though they were not afforded seafront locations. However, at St Leonards, James Burton's scheme for a new town included a church on the seafront, but at the western periphery of his development. It was completed in 1832, though it was only formally consecrated on 22 May 1834. However, in 1837 a sudden fall of the cliff damaged the church and the new chancel had to be much shorter. The church remained in use until it was destroyed by a flying bomb on 29 July 1944 (Fig 9.46).[64] These examples were initiated, and funded, by prominent landowners or successful developers, wealthy men developing prestigious and expensive schemes, who included a church to meet the demands of their prospective customers. Morecambe is unusual because it has three seafront churches dating from the late 19th and early 20th century. While the visitors and residents of the town might be God-fearing folk, it is more likely to be a result of its long seafront and relatively late date of development, meaning that profitable seafront space was not at a premium.

Fig 9.45
Holy Trinity Church at Margate was one of the largest seaside churches ever built. It is almost the size of a small cathedral with a nave 57ft high (17.4m) and a tower that rose to a height of 136ft (41.5m). [EPW000636]

Although lack of profitability was one reason for the absence of seafront churches, a second consideration is the cultural clash between acts of worship and the potential hedonism of activities on the beach. The seafront might be perceived to be at the heart of irreligious behaviour and while churches in seaside resorts may commemorate the heroism of seafarers, it is rare for them to acknowledge the existence of holidaymaking; a window in the Roman Catholic Church at Blackpool is exceptional in its depiction of the seafront of the town. The church's contribution to bridging the gap between worship and hedonism on the seafront will be examined in Chapter 10.

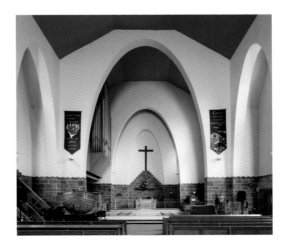

Fig 9.46
At St Leonards, a new church was built between 1953 and 1961 by Sir Giles and Adrian Gilbert Scott. It is on the site of the 19th-century one that was badly damaged during World War II. [DP162492]

In search of a seaside style

Any efforts to identify overarching characteristics shared by the first line of buildings occupying the seafront may be doomed to fail. The reason, as has been outlined, is the incredible complexity of its architectural story. The seafront is unlike any other street in a town; it is much more complex in terms of its dates, functions and forms. Therefore, instead of seeking universal factors and features that all types and dates of buildings share, a seaside style, it is perhaps more realistic to seek to identify some broad characteristics that they share.

Diversity

The first factor to recognise is the diversity of the buildings along a seafront, functionally and visually. Broadly, these can be summarised as being buildings created for residents, for tourists, and to work and exploit the sea. The central part of a resort's seafront, which once would have been home to the people living in the town and working at sea, has now become the preserve of tourists, residents being displaced inland, or outwards, over the past 200 years. Buildings associated with working the sea have similarly become marginalised, sometimes being entirely displaced to a nearby settlement where tourism is a less significant factor.

The seafront hosts a range of accommodation including houses used as lodgings, bed-and-breakfasts, hotels and holiday camps, as well as a wide range of entertainment venues and health facilities. As was discussed in Chapter 4, the working buildings found on seafronts may include lighthouses, lifeboat stations and a range of utilities for the town that take advantage of, or rely on, a location by the sea. At Hastings, the first line of buildings on the seafront beside the Old Town is particularly varied in size, shape and current function, and even includes a former timber-framed lighthouse among a host of cafes, chip shops and pubs. It also has a lifeboat station and its net lofts lie alongside an art gallery and public toilets. At the edge of this historic area is the 1820s Pelham Crescent, providing high-class homes and lodgings, a bazaar and a chapel. Within a half a mile of the seafront there are also two cliff lifts, some modern offices and an old street of shops. Pelham Crescent aside, it is rare to find adjacent matching buildings in terms of size, colour and function.

The need to change

The variety in terms of date, size and shape may also be due to a second factor that needs to be considered when examining the seafront. Change occurs particularly swiftly on seafronts, requiring fundamental alteration or replacement of existing buildings. The reason for such rapid and dramatic change is primarily economic. Regular change of use over the life of a historic building was more frequent where the demands of tourists had to be met. A house built inland from the seafront would probably remain a house throughout its history, but a building on or near the seafront that originated as a house might then see service as a circulating library, a bathhouse or lodgings and by the 19th century might have a shop on its ground floor. By the 20th century, the same building may have even enjoyed, or perhaps endured, life as a shop, cafe, milk bar, chip shop or amusement arcade. The possibilities are almost endless, but it is likely that its upper floors will have ceased to be used for anything beyond storage. Some buildings are more fortunate as their upper floors have a separate access, meaning that they can continue in use as apartments, prized for their sea views, if not for the cooking smell wafting up from the ground floor.

Although the humble house proved highly adaptable, by the 19th century it was usually too small to be economically viable and profitable and therefore older, smaller buildings built in vernacular materials were increasingly replaced by taller houses on the same plot, or plots if common ownership of adjacent properties had been achieved. Buildings also needed to be altered or replaced to meet the changing tastes and demands of holidaymakers, sometimes in response to advances in technology that led to new forms of entertainment. During the 19th century, there was a greater need for specialised, purpose-built buildings to accommodate and amuse holidaymakers, the humble house being no longer capable of adapting to meet the needs of more demanding visitors.

Numbers

While tastes and needs undoubtedly drove change on the seafront, it was the rapid growth in visitor numbers that accelerated the pace of change, especially after the arrival of the railways from the 1840s onwards. Railway stations were usually located near the heart of resorts, on a site near the edge of the town as it existed when the railway arrived. They inevitably concentrated tourists in the heart of resorts and the arrival of railways sometimes led to a realignment of towns and the creation of new links to the seafront. A good example is at Blackpool where the main access inland from the seafront shifted from Church Street to Talbot Street and the creation of this new road conditioned where Blackpool's first pier was built in 1863 (see Fig 9.7). The opening of the railway stations at Margate in 1846 and 1863 had two major impacts on the seafront of the town. Little development had taken place to the west of the historic town before the opening of the stations. The other impact was at the east end of Margate, far from the stations, where new clifftop residential development took place at Cliftonville for displaced middle-class holidaymakers.

The impact of railways on most seafronts was to increase the pace of change in the central core, accelerating the replacement of old buildings with new larger structures. And any change that may have taken place in the immediate aftermath of the arrival of railways would not necessarily be a permanent one, many seafront plots, and sites, being redeveloped regularly over the coming 150 years. Visitor numbers once measured in hundreds grew to thousands and subsequently millions annually, meaning that the small-scale, sociable and expensive facilities once enjoyed by wealthy Georgian visitors were not able, or appropriate, to meet the demand of new holidaymakers. The circulating library occupying the ground floor of a Georgian house was a distant memory by the time that winter gardens and Blackpool Tower were being constructed on an industrial scale. In the centre of seaside resorts, the pace of change was rapid as this was the area that had to cater for visitors, but further out along the seafront residential accommodation becomes the dominant type of building. While there may be a need to update these houses, or subdivide them to provide flats or holiday accommodation, there has been less need to replace them entirely and, therefore, any changes over time may be less dramatic.

Status

The influxes of millions of working-class tourists had a marked impact on the social tone of areas of resorts within easy reach of railway stations. However, even before railways, genteel visitors, who had once sought the sociable atmosphere of the centre of resorts, were increasingly retreating to new developments further from the busy town centre. The large-scale developments at Brighton, Kemp Town and Brunswick Town look today much as they did 200 years ago (see Figs 2.8 and 2.9). Their status, and the quality of their architecture, has meant that they have continued to meet the needs of residents almost unchanged. They have also remained largely unaltered, at least externally, as they still serve broadly the same purpose today, namely providing accommodation for residents and visitors. However, on some parts of some seafronts, there may be distinct changes in character, areas once populated by middle-class residents and holidaymakers having declined in status. The status and function of a key part of the seafront at Blackpool changed dramatically during the 20th century. In front of the working-class Bonny's Estate, beside Central Station, there was a stretch of middle-class housing on the seafront to the north of Central Pier (see Fig 3.29). These houses provided lodgings and were blessed with long gardens, but by the early 20th century these were beginning to host small fairground rides, fortune-telling booths and a variety of stalls, and were a key part of Blackpool's celebrated Golden Mile. This distinct decline in the status of the buildings led to their comprehensive redevelopment during the second half of the 20th century, the large footprint of individual plots when combined allowing the development of large entertainment complexes. An area that might have once been characterised as middle-class and domestic has been transformed into one dedicated entirely to pleasure and leisure.

In other seaside resorts, the change in status may be less dramatic architecturally. Houses, once the homes of respectable middle-class townsfolk providing lodgings for genteel visitors, may now be bed-and-breakfasts or have been sympathetically subdivided into flats. However, a key problem in modern seaside resorts is the prevalence of Houses in Multiple Occupation (HMOs). HMOs have two architectural characteristics: a large number of doorbells flanking the front door of the property and a generally poorer standard of maintenance. This is why local authorities try to prevent this form of unsympathetic subdivision happening on seafronts, but the profitability of such use makes it irresistible to property owners.

Durability

The owners of seafront buildings can adopt two approaches, either creating buildings that are lightweight and cheaply built, with the expectation of being regularly replaced, or building substantial permanent structures. On seaside piers, both approaches are found. The superstructure often contains lightweight buildings that have proved susceptible to storms and fire, but can be cheaply replaced, whereas the substructure, the costly part of the pier, has to survive everything that man and nature can throw at it. On seafronts, there are cafes, booths and kiosks built cheaply to last at most a generation, but the main line of buildings along the seafront is predominantly built to last, even though it has had to be responsive to changing tastes. Seafront buildings also have to endure harsher weather than those in more sheltered locations inland and therefore they suffer from the requirement for more regular and more costly maintenance.

Location

A seafront location will lead to houses being taller and larger compared with examples on inland streets. As the numbers of tourists grew, the height of buildings increased as the greater likelihood of a good return made larger initial investments worthwhile. This is because the sea view is at a premium, and therefore the property owner could charge more for accommodation (Fig 9.47). Proof of the economic benefit of a seafront location is provided by the fact that immediately behind, houses step down in height from having four or five storeys until a short distance inland they reach the regular two-storey domestic form to be expected in any comparable town. The same factors also condition the size and form of hotels, larger, more expensive ones being sustainable on the seafront because of the prized sea views.

As well as being taller and larger, seafront houses and hotels are more likely to have large windows and balconies to make full use of the sea view. At different periods, there were different solutions to maximising the sea view, ranging from balconies during the Georgian period, to adopting bow and bay windows, sometimes combined with balconies, during the 19th century. In modernist, and modern architecture, large expanses of sliding glass windows in blocks of flats turn rooms into sun lounges.

Competitiveness

Another factor in determining the character of seafront buildings is economic competitiveness. The owner of a seafront property will seek to maximise the income that it can provide, and therefore, it may be worthwhile replacing a small house on a plot with a larger building. Modernising, or replacing a building in a more up-to-date style, may also be responding to fashion and taste, and presenting a modern face is good for business. The seafront's customers increasingly have sought novelty, which is why this location has hosted some notable examples of modernism between the wars, ranging from the Midland Hotel at Morecambe and the De La Warr Pavilion at Bexhill-on-Sea to Canvey Island's Labworth Café (Fig 9.48; *see also* Figs 5.21, 9.25 and 9.35). A century earlier it would be the elegant, classical inspired elevations of major terraces and crescents, such as those in Kemp Town and Brunswick Town

Fig 9.47
To be profitable, enlargement normally takes place upwards, meaning that many seafront terraces and crescents have unfortunately enlarged attics. Claremont Crescent, a palace-fronted crescent at Blackpool, has succumbed to a new roofline and some vivid paint.
[DP154932]

at Brighton, that would have attracted wealthy customers. However, the seafront is more often associated with lavishness and even excessiveness, embracing oriental and exotic forms, Gothic detailing and classical motifs, sometimes on the same building. To attract customers, seafront buildings need to be eye-catching, not only in terms of architecture, but often through bright colours, elaborate signage and vivid illumination and lighting schemes. Visual restraint would be lost in the carnivalesque playground of the seafront and, perhaps more importantly, unprofitable.

Conclusion

This chapter has outlined the complexity of the first line of buildings on the seafront in terms of their function, date, style and, therefore, their appearance. At the core of a settlement with a sometimes complex, and long, pre-resort history there is likely to be some vestige of that early story, not necessarily in the buildings, but in the size and piecemeal character of the town plan. Consequently, this is also the area that is the most haphazard in terms of date, form, size and function as buildings responded to changing tastes and growing numbers of visitors. The slightly more anarchic quality of this part of the seafront may also apply in towns that did not have a historic core but have been subject to the impact of the proximity of a railway station and the rapid growth of tourism.

Further out from the historic core, the first line of buildings usually has more coherence, more uniformity and less variety in the buildings, most being houses, or houses used as lodgings. In terms of the date of development, buildings near the core are likely to be early or later replacements on earlier plots, while those further away tend simply to be later. Therefore, a person travelling along the seafront from the historic core would first pass late Georgian and Victorian urban housing, then witness suburban development of the first half of the 20th century and later blocks of flats. Some version of this pattern of development can be seen on the seafronts of resorts as different as Margate, Worthing, Blackpool or Bexhill-on-Sea.

Although any attempt to define a seaside style may be unsuccessful, seafront buildings do share certain characteristics. The most obvious is their diversity, in part due to their complicated origins, but this is also a result of the considerable and constant pressure to change and to respond to new fashions quickly and to cope with growing numbers of tourists. Another key trait is the distinctiveness of seafront buildings, in terms of their architectural styles, but also frequently their extravagant detailing and bold lighting and signs. In the central part of seaside resorts the seafront is dominated by businesses, ranging from bed-and-breakfasts and hotels to cinemas and large entertainment complexes. What they have in common is that these buildings have to make money and to do so they have to meet the needs and tastes of current customers and be more eye-catching than nearby rival businesses.

The need to make money from a seafront property and a tendency for these buildings to be lavish, even excessive, goes a long way to explain the relative absence of churches from the seafront. Reluctance to commit a potentially valuable site to a non-profit-making institution is commonplace at seaside resorts. However, the next chapter will explore the almost polar opposite aspect of the seafront, its more altruistic, civic and cultural dimension. People rather than profit will be the focus of Chapter 10, which describes how the seafront has served the residents of seaside resorts as a park and as a place to celebrate and commemorate.

Fig 9.48
Canvey Island's Labworth Café was built in 1932–3 by the engineer Ove Arup. Built in reinforced concrete, it was a pioneering building in the promotion of the modernist International Style.
[MF99/0636/05]

10

A civic and cultural space

The seafront serves its community as a key civic amenity, an antidote to the highly urbanised character of seaside resorts. It was often a town's only 'park' for many years and is still likely to be a key location for public events. These may range from the frivolous and entertaining, such as carnivals, shows and races, to more sombre occasions marking jubilees, the death of a monarch or the loss of life during wars.

There is also a spiritual and reflective dimension to the seafront. Churches may be largely absent, but there have been attempts to reconcile faith and fun through the sterling work of church missions and the Salvation Army. In the face of the power of nature, and supplied with time to stop and think, the seafront has become a place of memory. Tangible reflections of remembrance may range from a brass plaque on a bench recalling family and friends who admired the view to monumental war memorials commemorating the millions who have died for their country.

The seafront can also be a cultural space where the public can enjoy museums, art galleries and monumental works of art aimed at enriching the life of residents and tourists, as well as expressing the town's civic identity. Some memorials and works of art may be similar to standard ones found in towns all over the country, but coastal life and seaside history is also strongly reflected in the range and form of memorials and public art found on seafronts. A coastal location provides artists with a physically challenging environment, but an ever-changing canvas of sky, sea and sun can provide a perfect backdrop for works of art. The seafront also has something very important for art; during the summer it can provide a substantial audience, one with the time and inclination to admire art, rather than simply walking past it unacknowledged while hurrying through their lives.

The people's park

The seafront can serve as a town's park, its main street and its square. Some resorts are blessed with seafront squares, spaces that may be private or public, and, depending on the geography of the seafront, there may also be public gardens behind the beach on the clifftop. The existence of such large spaces meant that they have had a leading, though not necessarily exclusive, role in the civic life of seaside resorts, hosting events not just aimed at visitors, but more importantly for the local community. These gatherings and ceremonies might be annual events, such as town pageants or the switching on of Blackpool's illuminations, or they can be special occasions, such as the marking of VE Day, coronations and royal jubilees. Events may mark national occasions, such as the Armistice and subsequent Remembrance Days, or they can be more parochial occasions, such as the honouring of local dignitaries.

The most prestigious events that take place on seafronts are royal visits and celebrations to mark major national royal occasions. The first monarch to spend time at the seaside was George III (Fig 10.1). His presence seems to have been a major attraction for visitors and therefore was important to the local economy. The king's younger brother Prince William, Duke of Gloucester and Edinburgh had already spent a number of years visiting Weymouth and was the reason for the king choosing this resort. The future George IV also had an impact on Brighton's development and prosperity:

> Brighton, twenty years ago a small, insignificant fishing village, is striking proof of miracles brought about by fashion. ... His [the Prince Regent's] presence in or absence from Brighton registered the flow of visitors to the spa. When he was absent, the town was empty and desolate; only when he returned did life and pleasure reappear.[1]

As with the king, wherever the Prince of Wales went, a large entourage followed, making him the heart of the social scene. In 1797, Princess Amelia came to Worthing on the recommendation of her doctors, leading to the arrival of other leaders of fashion and prompting a decade of rapid growth, while Princess Charlotte proved popular when she was taken to Southend as a child in 1801.[2]

One of the great royal events in Brighton's history was the return of Queen Victoria in the Royal Yacht to the Chain Pier, following a visit to the French Emperor Louis Philippe in August 1843. The spectacle of this event was captured in a painting by RH Nibbs which is in Brighton Art Gallery.[3] In July 1913, George V visited a gaily decorated Blackpool as part of a tour of Lancashire towns, a visit lasting a mere half an hour during which he was received at the town hall in Talbot Square beside North Pier.[4]

Members of the royal family sometimes attended the unveiling of statues on the seafront or to mark the opening of a new building (Fig 10.2). On 24 July 1907, Princess Louise, Duchess of Argyll, and the sister of Edward VII, visited Herne Bay to open an extension to the Passmore Edwards Railway Men's Convalescent Home.[5] She drove along the seafront with her mounted escort of Dragoon Guards amid a sea of bunting and floral decoration, while local volunteers marched along the seafront to form a guard of honour at the town hall. Princess Louise also visited Blackpool in May 1912 to mark the opening of the Princess Parade; a programme of illuminations at the Metropole Hotel featuring around 10,000 bulbs and an illuminated tram was staged to celebrate her presence.[6] The future Edward VIII visited Hastings on 6 April 1927 for the official opening of the White Rock Pavilion and also took time to visit the nearby gardens where he reviewed a march-past of veterans of the Boer War and World War I.[7] In the Old Town, he met the lifeboat crew and fishermen, and was presented with a Golden Winkle by the Winkle club.[8] Later in the same year, he visited Blackpool to open the Lancashire and Cheshire Miners' Convalescent Home (see Fig 6.34).[9] In December 1935, the future George V came to Bexhill-on-Sea to open the De La Warr Pavilion, royal affirmation for a radical moderne project as well as being an indication of the high regard that the earl enjoyed.[10]

The appearance of national and local dignitaries could also prompt major festive occasions on the seafront. On 3 August 1910,

Fig 10.1
The statue of George III was erected in 1810 on the seafront at Weymouth to mark his Golden Jubilee. Designed by the architect James Hamilton, the king, as well as the lion and unicorn, are said to be the work of Mr Sealy of the firm of Coade and Sealy. [DP058189]

Fig 10.2
The Peace Memorial, dedicated to Edward VII, which straddles the boundary between Brighton and Hove on the seafront, was unveiled in October 1912 by the Duke of Norfolk. [DP054342]

the Lord Mayor of London, Sir John Knill, came to Herne Bay to open the New Pier Pavilion.[11] After arriving by train, his party processed through the town, including along the seafront, passing the clock tower, in 15 carriages in which there were no fewer than seven mayors from Kent. A year later, the renowned circus showman 'Lord' George Sanger was murdered, leading to Margate entering a period of mourning.[12] A huge funeral parade took place through the town as his body was taken to the local cemetery for burial (Fig 10.3).[13]

The seafront is frequently a location for local expressions of national events or purely parochial feasts and pageants. In the past, there were now long-forgotten celebrations of Empire Day and Nelson's Day and at Herne Bay both were celebrated by parades along the seafront in the years before World War I.[14] With the slaughter of World War I, the annual commemoration of the Armistice on 11 November became a key event on seafronts, often where war memorials were located. During both world wars, parades often took place on seafronts to raise funds for the war effort, to welcome returning troops and to serve as morale-boosting occasions. At Blackpool, the town hall is located on Talbot Square beside the North Pier and its proximity to the Tower meant that the two became the centrepieces for military parades during World War II. In July 1942, the commander of Blackpool's adopted ship, HMS Penelope, Captain

A D Nicholl, inspected the town's Sea Cadet Corps outside the town hall. The Tower building was clad in displays of patriotic scenes and slogans for use as the backdrop for events such as 'Dig for Victory Week' and 'Wings for Victory Week'.[15] Talbot Square and the adjacent part of the seafront were the site of Blackpool's VE Day celebrations on 8 May 1945.[16]

The seafront was also a place for celebrations of significant local occasions, as well as being a location for carnivals. After World War I, Blackpool decided to stage an annual carnival in 1923 and 1924. However, the second carnival was marred by drunkenness and hooliganism and so, in 1925, the illuminations returned in an effort to extend the length of the town's visitor season.[17] Weymouth's earliest carnivals were held in November to celebrate Guy Fawkes Night, but poor weather led to their abandonment by 1894. However, in 1890, a number of friendly societies held a parade and an open-air concert in August and this seems to have been the foundation for the summer carnival, designed to raise funds for local hospitals. This event became a permanent fixture around 1910 and, after wartime postponements, resumed again in August 1952.[18] In the 1959 Weymouth Carnival, the floats included one using the Territorial Army's DUKW, which was disguised as the Loch Ness monster, while in 1963 the first prize was won by the 'Sunblest' float decorated by a local baker.[19]

Fig 10.3
The monuments in Margate cemetery commemorate John Sanger and his more famous brother 'Lord' George Sanger. Remarkably, John is commemorated by the mourning horse, while his brother and other members of the family have the larger, but more restrained plot guarded by female figures.
[MF99/0812/12]

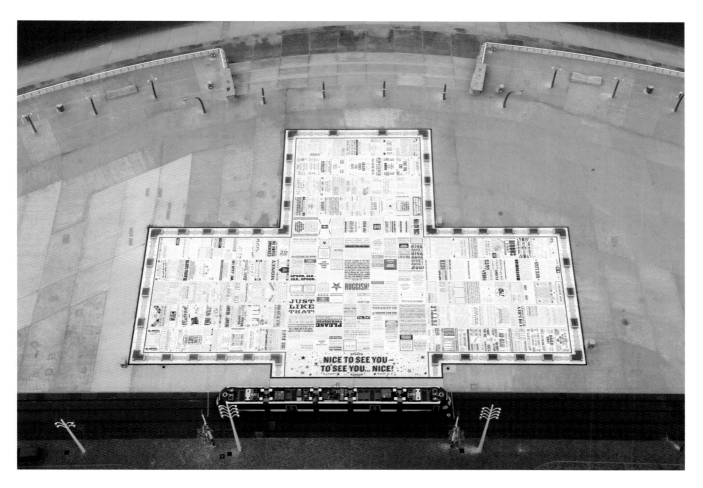

The seafront was a popular location for performances, whether on the sands or in seafront gardens. From the late 19th century onwards, bandstands became important focal points for regular summer concerts and the new seafront in Blackpool has specific areas, particularly the headland in front of the Tower, designed to stage performances (Fig 10.4). Seafronts, bathing pools and pavilions have also been the location for beauty pageants; modern, commercialised versions of the ancient tradition of choosing a May Queen. The oldest pageant in Britain was established in 1945 at Morecambe and in 1956 it became the Miss Great Britain contest, which was held, at least in part, at the seafront Super Swimming Stadium until the mid-1970s.[20] To cater for television, the format of the Grand Final of Miss Great Britain was changed in 1971 and therefore was recorded in three parts, with the Swimwear Parade staged at the Super Swimming Stadium, the Daywear Parade taking place at the Promenade Gardens and the Evening Wear Parade on the stage of a local theatre.

Judging beauty and performance was not limited to people; each year from 1903, Bexhill-on-Sea staged a horse show that originally included a parade of tradesmen's and other horse-drawn carriages.[21] New seafronts with roads that had long, flat, smooth surfaces also proved popular places to stage other forms of wheeled vehicular events. Due to business ties with the Dunlop company, Earl de la Warr constructed a cycle track along the East Parade and built a cycle chalet opposite the Sackville Hotel in 1896.[22] Longer bicycle racing events, such as the Tour of Britain, have also used seafront promenade roads as suitable places to start or finish stages.

The seafront by the beginning of the 20th century also became a magnet for the motor car. In 1895, Harry Lawson (1852–1925) established the Motor Car Club and by 1896 he had successfully campaigned for the Locomotives on Highways Act, which abolished the need for motor vehicles to be preceded by a pedestrian carrying a flag, at the same time raising the speed limit to 12mph.[23] To mark this event, he

Fig 10.4
The site of the Comedy Carpet at Blackpool can be closed off and temporary seating and staging erected for events such as pop concerts and the annual switch-on ceremony of the illuminations. In this view, from the top of the Tower, a modern tram can be seen passing by.
[DP154961]

staged an Emancipation Day Run from London to Brighton on 14 November 1896, probably the maximum distance achievable comfortably by cars of that date, and this became an annual event from 1927.[24]

Racing along seafronts was pioneered by Bexhill-on-Sea. On Whit Monday 1902, trials organised by the Automobile Club in conjunction with Earl de la Warr ran on a circuit of roads including along the seafront. Bexhill ceased to be a venue for motor racing trials with the opening of the famous Brooklands track in 1907.[25] In 1904–6, the newly completed central section of sea defences at Blackpool provided an ideal location for motor speed trials and Brighton's first motor race week was held in July 1905 on the new tarmac surface of Madeira Drive.[26] While high-speed cars are admirably suited to long flat seafront roads, the sands at some resorts have also been used to create exciting motocross circuits for motorbikes, including Weston-super-Mare and British Beach Cross events at Bournemouth and Margate.[27] Briefly, aircraft also used beaches; during the summer of 1913 the Eastbourne Aviation Company Limited ran water plane passenger service flights from the beach, while Worthing's beach on 22 July 1914 saw the crash landing of a naval plane on its way from Portsmouth to Felixstowe.[28]

The seafront and religion

The seafront and beach was sometimes a location for religious events, though the seaside has a long history of struggling to reconcile its naturally carnivalesque character with the needs of the faithful (Fig 10.5). A strong strand of Sabbatarianism tried to restrict access to the seaside to encourage worship on Sundays, but this inevitably proved futile. Therefore, even during the 19th century, a balance was being reached between faith and fun, including the running of trains that allowed both religious worship and the pleasures of the seaside. The Lancashire and Yorkshire Railway offered 'Sea Bathing for the Working Classes' on Sundays and promised that 'Parties availing themselves of these trains will be enabled to bathe and refresh themselves in ample time to attend a Place of Worship.'[29] Religious groups, such as Sunday Schools, had used the railways for excursions from the outset; in 1843 the Stanley Lads of Alderley in Cheshire welcomed almost 3,000 children out from Manchester to enjoy 'seeing such scenery and breathing such pure air'.[30]

Regular churchgoers continued to worship on Sundays, though in the early days of seaside resorts the nearest church might be a mile or two away in the nearby, original village. Mary Figgins' short diary of her holiday in Margate in c 1828 described how on Sundays she went to church, but on the second Sunday she only just got there in time and by the third Sunday, she seems to have become so relaxed that she could not get up in time for the morning service.[31] Churchgoing was a habit and a duty, but at the seaside Miss Figgins could slip from the conventions of her ordinary life without fear of censure by her neighbours at home.

The commercial drive of resort development meant that there was little space for non-profit-making features on the seafront, including churches (see Figs 9.42 and 9.45). In the absence

Fig 10.5 (below right)
This post-war photograph by John Gay shows members of the Salvation Army playing on the beach in the shadow of Blackpool Tower. An attentive crowd has gathered on the promenade to listen to the music.
[AA047906]

Fig 10.6 (far right)
This sign on the beach at Worthing states that this space is reserved for sermons and public speeches. A nearby information board describes how a byelaw still exists, allowing the public to 'Hold Sermons and Public Speeches' as long as their speeches are lawful and not offensive.
[© A Brodie]

Fig 10.7
This post-war photograph shows the Salvation Army on Blackpool beach heroically trying to teach the words to that childhood favourite, 'All Things Bright and Beautiful'. [AA047908]

of many churches, some religious groups took to the beach. At Worthing, there is a pole set into the beach marking an officially sanctioned location for preaching, though in recent years the sign has been removed (Fig 10.6). A photograph taken in September 1907 shows a Children's Special Service Mission taking place on the beach at Splash Point and the Scripture Union still carries out Summer Missions at some seaside resorts.[32] The Salvation Army sometimes made its presence felt at resorts, hosting Beach Missions and classes for children, though the arrival of its brass band at Eastbourne during the 1890s did not prove to be universally popular (Fig 10.7).[33] Weddings on beaches are popular at exotic foreign resorts, though at Bournemouth one company offers couples the chance to marry in a marquee by the British seaside, while the Tunnel Beaches at Ilfracombe offers a 120-seat wedding venue and a thatched gazebo overlooking the sea (Fig 10.8).[34] As well as weddings, some churches stage individual, or mass, baptisms using the sea to welcome new members of the faith.

Fig 10.8
The recently opened Festival House on Blackpool's new promenade includes a first-floor ceremony room with a large window allowing couples to make their vows while admiring the Tower. [DP153147]

Civic memory and commemoration

Public statues and memorials first began to appear regularly on seafronts during the mid-19th century. On the seafront at Lowestoft, Samuel Morton Peto commissioned a pair of sculptures of the Greek God Triton to adorn the Esplanade, which had been built in 1849 (Fig 10.9).[35] At Robertson Terrace in Hastings, 1.8m-high lion and unicorn sculptures attributed to James George Bubb (1782–1853), and inspired by the arms of the United Kingdom, are set above a coat of arms.[36] It has been suggested that the sculptures were made for Buckingham Palace as part of the second phase of work carried out there by Decimus Burton in 1850–1, but were surplus to requirement. They appear in a print of 1872 in their current location.

The seafront was also a location for war memorials from an early date. A monument to Admiral Lord Nelson, the earliest in England, was erected in 1817–19 by another Norfolk man, William Wilkins, a short distance to the south of Great Yarmouth's developing resort (Fig 10.10).[37] Memorials commemorating specific wars or military events begin to appear regularly on seafronts during the third quarter of the 19th century. Their forms drew on a number of traditions. Obelisks can trace their origins back to ancient Egypt and columnar monuments reflect the Roman Empire, while a range of cruciform shapes, including Celtic crosses and variations on the Eleanor Cross, were also employed.[38] By the early 20th century,

figures were also incorporated into the more ambitious memorials, either in the form of statues or depicted in low relief on plaques.

The seafront with the earliest war memorials, and the best collection, is unsurprisingly Southsea, its proximity to the naval dockyard being the reason for its wealth of memorials.[39] In 1857, a Portland stone obelisk commemorating the Crimean war was unveiled.[40] It was 'Erected by the Debating Society of Portsmouth aided by their fellow townsmen' to commemorate 'those brave soldiers and sailors who during the late war with Russia died of their wounds and are buried in this garrison'. In 1860, the Peel or Shannon Naval Brigade Monument was unveiled beside the Crimean Memorial (Fig 10.11).[41] It consists of a four-sided tapering pier, topped by an elaborate bronze finial cast from the metal of a gun captured at Lucknow and it stands on a stepped stone plinth with cannon bollards at the four corners. The Trident Memorial was erected in c 1860 and re-erected in 1877.[42] This four-sided, polished pink granite obelisk is dedicated 'To the memory of forty-four Officers and Men of H.M.S. Trident' who died during a yellow fever epidemic in Sierra Leone in 1859. The nearby Chesapeake Monument of 1862 consists of a polished granite column set on a square sandstone base with a foliated stone capital surmounted by a bronze tripod and naval crown.[43] It commemorates fallen comrades and marks their actions in India 1857–8, Arabia 1858–9, and China 1859–61. The Aboukir Memorial of c 1875 (see Fig 1.3) is a stone, four-sided obelisk on a stepped base that was erected 'In memory of 48 Officers and Men who died during the epidemic of yellow fever on board H.M.S. Aboukir at Jamaica in 1873–74.'[44] To complete this unrivalled set of early war memorials, there is the Trafalgar Monument, which incorporates an anchor from HMS *Victory* set on a battered granite stone plinth.[45]

Southsea enjoys such a rich legacy because of its location close to the naval dockyard and the fact that during the 19th century this was an available, and convenient, place in which to erect memorials. Similar factors explain why the Hoe at Plymouth was chosen as the site for early memorials celebrating Sir Francis Drake and victory over the Armada.[46] The Armada Memorial of 1888, by the architect Herbert A Gribble and the sculptor W Charles May, was created to celebrate the tercentenary of the defeat of the Armada (Fig 10.12).[47]

Fig 10.9
The northernmost Triton at Lowestoft is now part of the modern public realm, embracing the war memorial and incorporating new signage. The Royal Plain Fountains, a modern feature consisting of 74 individual interactive water jets with variable lighting, forms a striking centrepiece to this recently enhanced area. [DP070191]

Fig 10.10 (far left)
At Great Yarmouth, the column is topped by the figure of Britannia standing on a disc supported by six Caryatid figures rather than featuring Admiral Nelson. The figures were originally made of Coade stone but were replaced in concrete in 1896 and then fibreglass during the restoration of 1982–4.
[DP027134]

Fig 10.11 (above)
The Peel or Shannon Naval Brigade Monument was erected by the officers and crew of HMS Shannon in memory of fellow members of their Naval Brigade who died during the Indian mutiny in 1857–8.
[DP219524]

Fig 10.12 (left)
Close to the Armada memorial is the Drake Statue of 1884 by the sculptor J E Boem. Sir Francis is looking out to sea from Plymouth Hoe where he reputedly played bowls before defeating the Spanish.
[MF99/0719/19]

Drake's statue inevitably features a depiction of the famous sailor, but most war memorials during the 19th century simply incorporate obelisks or columns as their central feature. The Boer War was the first conflict to have widespread sculptural monuments in prominent public places.[48] At Worthing and Llandudno, obelisks were the basis of Boer War memorials, while the memorial at White Rock at Hastings, which was unveiled on 6 May 1903, consists of a pink granite column. It is topped with a grenade in gun metal on top of a granite sphere, with bronze trophy flags representing the Union Jack and the colours of the Royal Sussex Regiment at the base of the pillar.[49] This conflict also saw depictions of single soldiers mourning their fallen comrades, standing at ease or standing guard (Fig 10.13).[50]

As well as war memorials to commemorate local people who died in a conflict, some regiments were the subject, and funders, of memorials. The Royal Sussex Regiment seems to have been particularly keen on seafront memorials to mark their losses in South Africa. Their colours appear on the war memorial at Hastings, and the Brighton Memorial not only pays tribute to the fallen of the Boer War but also lists their previous engagements dating back to Québec in 1759.[51] At Eastbourne, the Royal Sussex Memorial on the seafront was unveiled on 7 February 1906 and features a life-size bronze figure of a young officer (Fig 10.14).[52]

Although war memorials commemorating the Boer War were more common than those from any previous conflict, they were few in number due to the relatively small number of participants involved. World War I was exactly the opposite; this was a conflict that was even experienced on the British mainland and involved every family in the country. During the war, a decision was taken not to repatriate the bodies of dead servicemen. The Imperial War Graves Commission (the Commonwealth War Graves Commission since 1960) was

Fig 10.13 (right)
The c 1905 South Africa war memorial to the men of the Royal Sussex Regiment is located at the seafront end of Regency Square in Brighton. Designed by the architect John W Simpson, it features a figure of a regimental trumpeter by Charles Hartwell.
[DP217903]

Fig 10.14 (far right)
The pedestal of the Royal Sussex Memorial on the seafront at Eastbourne, by the sculptor William Goscombe John, has bronze plaques on all sides, two with inscriptions and two with pictorial reliefs of soldiers in action.
[DP217941]

founded in 1917 initially, when possible, to care for the graves of the fallen, but after the war its prime function was to establish proper cemeteries.[53] It was soon realised that many victims had no known grave and, therefore, appropriate means of commemoration needed to be found.[54] In the years immediately after World War I, tributes were established in communities of all sizes, ranging from commemorative cottage hospitals or hospital wings to public baths, libraries, reading rooms, halls, and parks and gardens.[55] However, the most widespread form of commemoration was a memorial and these continued, and developed, the forms pioneered to mark previous conflicts.

To erect a war memorial, as well as funding, a suitable site was required. This needed to be available, dignified, free from too much traffic and large enough not only for the memorial, but also to host any parades to mark Armistice Day. It should also be near the centre of a settlement, but in many places these areas were congested and some of the best sites were already occupied by previous memorials.[56] Therefore, many towns opted to locate the new memorial in the town's park, and in the absence of such an open space at seaside resorts, the seafront proved to be a suitable, if not always an ideal, location. Fortunately, the Armistice, falling in mid-November, drastically reduced the likelihood of any clash between the solemn dignity of remembrance and the carnivalesque play of seaside holidaymakers.

The most spectacular seafront war memorial is adjacent to North Pier at Blackpool. In 1923, a temporary Cenotaph was replaced by an obelisk almost 100ft high, designed by the Lancashire architect Ernest Prestwich, with carved reliefs by Gilbert Ledward (Fig 10.15).[57] The Blackpool memorial has colossal reliefs cast in bronze entitled '1914 the outbreak of War' and '1918 the end of War'.[58] There are four main figures in each corner: two soldiers, an armed sailor and an aviator. The names of the war dead are on two catafalques at the foot of the obelisk's Cenotaph and no ranks, or awards, are mentioned, except for the two Victoria Cross winners.[59]

Seafront obelisks provided both a fitting memorial, and, if large enough like Blackpool, could serve as a navigational aid for ships at sea. Most local seafront memorials were less monumental and reflected the more limited budget available. Teignmouth's War Memorial on the seafront is a simple obelisk of 1921 funded by public subscription (Fig 10.16).[60]

Fig 10.15 (left)
Blackpool's War Memorial cost £17,000 and is reputed to have been funded from the profits of the Tramways Department. These three photographs show it contributing to the annual illuminations. [DP129894, DP129895, DP129896]

Fig 10.16 (below)
Weymouth's World War I memorial on the Esplanade is a cenotaph-type design of Portland stone with inscribed bronze plaques on each face bearing the names of the dead and a stone relief of Christ being borne aloft by angels. [DP176464]

However, even modest memorials might be the work of a leading architect; there was a pause in new building at the start of the 1920s as Britain began to recover from the war and many great architects including Sir Giles Gilbert Scott, Sir Reginald Blomfield and Sir Edwin Lutyens were glad to work on commemorative buildings and war memorials.[61] The war memorial in the seafront Princess Gardens at Torquay of 1920 by Blomfield is a Portland stone three-tiered, square monument with bronze inscription panels, wreaths and inverted torches on each face, as well as an urn on the top.[62] Lutyens created the 1921 war memorial at Hove, a short distance inland up Grand Avenue, the ideal location nearer the seafront already being occupied by a statue of Queen Victoria.[63] At Bexhill-on-Sea, a traditional obelisk form was chosen for the 1920 memorial, but was given a dramatic twist by applying a bronze figure of Victory by the sculptor Louis Frederick Roslyn.[64]

As well as local memorials, some seaside resorts became the site for national memorials. Plymouth Naval Memorial commemorates the action of the Royal Marines who fell during World War I, its location reflecting their close association with the town and its naval base.[65] The Royal Navy, and the navies of the Dominions, lost around 48,000 men, with 25,563 being lost or buried at sea. Their sacrifice was not recorded in any cemetery, or on any battlefield, and so it was decided that three national memorials of the same design should be established near the Royal Navy's home ports at Portsmouth, Plymouth and Chatham.[66] Therefore, memorials were established on the seafront at Southsea and on the Hoe at Plymouth, both locations where previous conflicts had been commemorated (Fig 10.17).[67] The memorial at Plymouth, between the Armada Memorial and the Drake statue, was unveiled in July 1924, while the Southsea one was inaugurated by the Duke of York in October 1924.[68] These, and the Chatham Memorial, were designed by the Scottish architect Sir Robert Lorimer (1864–1929), using but adapting the navy's preferred obelisk design with sculpture provided by Henry Poole.[69] At Chatham, bronze panels were inscribed with 8,541 names, the memorial on Southsea Common commemorates 9,666 sailors, while the Plymouth Memorial initially had 7,256 names.[70]

After World War II, these navy memorials were enlarged and updated by Sir Edward Maufe, principal architect for the Imperial War Graves Commission, with figurative sculpture by Sir Charles Wheeler and William McMillan.[71] Southsea's extension took the form of a sunken garden with statues around it, mostly of naval personnel. On the walls 78 bronze panels are mounted bearing the names of 14,921 sailors from the port who died during the war.

Fig 10.17
The World War I naval memorials, such as this one on the seafront at Southsea, were the largest built at any seaside resorts.
[DP176431]

It was inaugurated by Queen Elizabeth, the Queen Mother on 29 April 1953.[72] Plymouth's extension opened in 1954 and also featured a sunken garden with statues of naval personnel and bronze plaques naming the 15,935 sailors lost from the port.

During World War II, there was a debate about the form that any new commemoration should take. There was a feeling that money should not be spent on stone and marble monuments in a country that needed so much rebuilding. A preference was expressed for practical memorials, in the form of a hospital ward, a social club or a playing field, and there was also an appetite for arts centres, restoring historic buildings and buildings of architectural importance.[73] The scale of the extensions to the naval monuments at Plymouth and Portsmouth are notable exceptions, and in most cases the names of the war dead were simply added to existing memorials by the addition of extra plaques. For instance, at Bexhill-on-Sea, an inscription was added for World War II, and three bronze plaques were added to Weymouth's seafront Cenotaph.[74] At Teignmouth after 1945, the memorial was raised when the second tier of the base was replaced by a larger ashlar stone inscribed with the names of those killed during World War II.[75]

Although general World War II monuments are not particularly common on seafronts, some specific events are commemorated. As Dover is the town closest to the Continent, its seafront boasts a wealth of wartime and peacetime monuments that result from this geographical proximity. A 1975 memorial marks the Dunkirk Evacuation and a 2012 memorial commemorates a daring dash made by a group of Kriegsmarine ships in February 1942 through the Straits of Dover and the RAF's and Fleet Air Arm's response to it in Operation Fuller.[76] There is also a plaque in German noting the date of 84 shells that hit Dover. It was a section of armoured plating removed from one of the long-range guns at Sangatte near Calais.

The D-Day Port Memorial on the Esplanade at Weymouth, unveiled in December 1947, consists of a pillar surmounted by a lamp that is never extinguished. A copper plaque records the contribution of the more than half a million American servicemen who passed through Weymouth and Portland en route to the beaches of Normandy between 6 June 1944 and the end of the war.[77] Among the events commemorated is Exercise or Operation Tiger, a rehearsal exercise

for the D-Day landings off the Devon coast. It was disastrously intercepted by a force of German E boats with the loss of hundreds of lives. As well as being featured on the Weymouth D-Day memorial, a Sherman Tank recovered from a sunken ship has been set up as a memorial to this event on the beach at Slapton Sands.[78]

After World War II, some services, and branches of the services, were commemorated separately on seafronts when there was no suitable existing memorial from a previous conflict, or the service was a new phenomenon (Fig 10.18). A 2008 monument to the men of the Merchant Navy has been erected at Dover, commemorating the 35,000 seamen who died or went missing, as well as the 10,000 who were wounded or taken prisoner of war (Fig 10.19).[79]

Fig 10.18
The memorial to the Merchant Navy by Vivien Mallock consists of a figure of a Merchant Navy Officer standing on a square incised plinth. She was also responsible for figurative war memorials on Southsea's seafront.
[DP217431]

Fig 10.19
Prisoners of war were a
much larger part of World
War II than of World War I
and at Great Yarmouth, a
four-sided clock tower was
constructed in 1958 as a
memorial to people held
prisoner in the Far East.
There is a dedication plaque
on the front face and a
circular brass map of South
East Asia on each face.
[DP217480]

On the seafront at Lee-on-Solent, at the south-east corner of the former Royal Naval Air Station, is the Fleet Air Arm Memorial that was unveiled on 20 May 1953 by the Duchess of Kent.[80] With the threat of invasion diminishing during 1944, major mine-clearing operations began and a memorial to the 26 men of the Royal Engineer Bomb Disposal squadron who lost their lives in Norfolk between 1944 and 1953 was unveiled at Mundesley in May 2004.[81] It takes the form of a 1,000lb (445kg) bomb case with its fins uppermost with attached stainless-steel plaques bearing the names of the dead. At many seaside resorts, old sea mines were similarly set up on seafronts with a slot to allow people to make donations to the Shipwrecked Mariners Society. Civilians of World War II rarely receive separate recognition for what they endured, the names of victims sometimes featuring on a plaque near where they fell or included on a settlement's war memorial. In April 2016, approval was granted to construct a memorial wall within the moat of the seafront Wish Tower at Eastbourne; this will be engraved with the names of 174 people who lost their lives in 112 raids during World War II.[82]

Conflicts after World War II are usually commemorated by additions to existing war memorials. At Teignmouth, three names were added to remember members of the armed forces who died in conflicts in Malaya (1948–60), Kenya (1952–60) and Cyprus (1954).[83]

The most well-known commemoration of a post-World War II conflict is the statue at the entrance to the Royal Marines Museum at Eastney by Philip Jackson of 'The Yomper', depicting a Royal Marine during the Falklands War (Fig 10.20).[84]

Fig 10.20
Looking out over the Solent
and Eastney Beach, 'The
Yomper' is based on a
celebrated photograph of
Corporal Peter Robinson
on the march into Stanley
in the Falkland Islands. It
was unveiled in 1992.
[MF99/0645/06]

Commemorating people

The seafront is also a place to celebrate individuals, whether military, civilian, royalty or celebrity. These may range from personal tributes in the form of a small brass plaque affixed to a bench recording the life of an ordinary person to the 44m-high tribute to Admiral Nelson at Great Yarmouth (*see* Fig 10.10). Sir Francis Drake is commemorated on the Hoe at Plymouth, Captain Cook has a statue of 1912 on the West Cliff at Whitby and Sir John Moore, the hero of Corunna, has a 1909 memorial at Sandgate, close to the site of his home while he commanded the Shorncliffe camp in 1803–4 (Fig 10.21; *see also* Fig 10.12).[85] T E Lawrence is celebrated far from Arabia, in South Cliff Gardens at Bridlington, where a sun dial is dedicated to him under the name of Aircraftsman Shaw, commemorating his service in the RAF between 1929 and 1935.[86] Lawrence spent the final three months of his service life in Bridlington and was discharged from the RAF there on 26 February 1935, shortly before his death.

Less famous, but no less courageous, service personnel are also commemorated on the seafront of some resorts. The Adamson Memorial Drinking Fountain at Cullercoats (Fig 10.22) near Tynemouth was

> Erected by a few friends in memory of Bryan John Huthwaite Adamson Lieut. R.N. Commanding H.M.S. Wasp which sailed from Singapore Sep. 10-1887 and was never heard of after. The site was given for this memorial by His Grace the Duke of Northumberland 1888.[87]

Fig 10.21
Captain Cook is commemorated at Whitby, as he was an apprentice to John Walker, whose ships were based there and were involved in the North Sea coal trade.
[DP175059]

Fig 10.22
The Cullercoats fountain consists of a white marble spire rising from an octagonal trough with bronze lion-head spouts. It is also decorated with dolphins, shells and foliate reliefs.
[DP174962]

Outside the D-Day Museum on the seafront at Southsea, two statues were created by the sculptor Vivien Mallock in 1997. One depicts Field Marshal Montgomery (Fig 10.23) and nearby, in marked contrast to the nationally famed commander, Mallock also produced a statue poignantly depicting a young soldier sitting on a jerry can relaxing, but thinking of home.[88]

Civilian services and their personnel may be honoured on the seafront. In 2013, a memorial honouring Blackpool's emergency services, and specifically three police officers who drowned 30 years before, was unveiled on the clifftop to the north of the town at Jubilee Gardens. The sculptor Matt Titherington won a competition as a student at Blackpool and the Fylde College for a composition of four figures linking hands, symbolising the protection that the emergency services provide.

The most common civilian monument celebrates and commemorates the work of people who have saved lives at sea, particularly the volunteers of the Royal National Lifeboat Institution (RNLI). The German barque *Mexico* was wrecked off Southport on 9 December 1886 and three lifeboats set out to save lives. The Lytham lifeboat rescued the crew, but all 13 members of the St Annes lifeboat were lost, along with 14 members of the Southport boat. A fund raised £31,000 to help the dependents of the men lost and £200 was donated to each community to erect a monument commemorating this heroic action (Fig 10.24). The most famous lifeboatman is probably Henry Blogg, Coxswain of the Cromer boat from 1909 to 1947.[89] His distinguished service, which saved hundreds of lives and included the whole of World War II, led to him receiving the gold medal of the RNLI three times, the silver

Fig 10.23 (right)
Vivien Mallock depicted 'Monty', who had been the Garrison Commander at Portsmouth during the 1930s, as well as being in operational control of the land forces of Operation Overlord.
[DP196961]

Fig 10.24 (far right)
At St Annes, this tribute to the lost boatmen was placed in the gardens on the seafront close to the pier. Designed by William Birnie Rhind of Edinburgh, it depicts a lifeboatman looking out to sea.
[DP175047]

medal four times, as well as the George Cross and the British Empire Medal. His career is commemorated with three busts depicting him in his sou'wester, oilskins and lifejacket, gazing out to sea (Fig 10.25).

The seafront is also a place to remember disasters. A huge storm struck the Devon and Dorset coast on 23 November 1824 leading to a major inundation of Weymouth. Two commemorative stones were incorporated into the wall opposite what used to be Harvey's Assembly Rooms. They are inscribed 'Esplanade destroyed by Tempest Nov. 23 1824' and 'Rebuilt by T. Vining builder April 23 1825'. At Hunstanton, there is a clifftop memorial to members of the United States Air Force who drowned in the floods that devastated the area in 1953.[90] The seafront may also be a location to remember loss of life at sea. One of the capstans on Worthing beach came from the *Ophir*, which sank offshore in a storm in 1896, an event modestly remembered by a small plaque.

The seafront is also a place to remember, commemorate and celebrate family and friends. The most common form of private, personal memorial is the simple plaque attached to the deck timbers of a pier or affixed to a bench where the person enjoyed looking out to sea. A typical example is a plaque on a new seat on the seafront at Dover commemorating the life of Lilian Elizabeth Shirley (1925–99) a 'dearly loved wife, mother and grandmother'.

At the opposite end of the spectrum are memorials to monarchs, the earliest in terms of their reign being the Memorial to Alfred the Great on the seafront at Swanage, erected in 1862 by John Mowlem.[91] It consists of a granite, Tuscan column topped with four cannon balls, brought back from the Crimean War. A 1960 plaque on the seafront at Dover was unveiled to mark the landing there of Charles II, 300 years earlier, and the resultant restoration of the monarchy. Neither of these memorials have any direct link to the seaside holiday, but the monument to George III on the seafront at Weymouth celebrates the resort's link with the king (*see* Fig 10.1).

The monarch most often depicted on the seafront is Queen Victoria, though this is not because of any particular association with a seaside resort, as her family seaside holidays were enjoyed privately at Osborne House on the Isle of Wight. The large number of statues is a result of a long reign, and the fact that her golden and diamond jubilees, as well as her death in 1901,

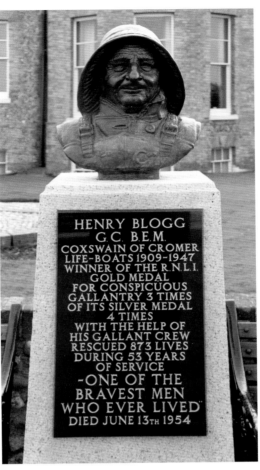

Fig 10.25
The original bust of Henry Blogg is located on the Upper Promenade on the East Cliff at Cromer, while the others are in the RNLI Henry Blogg Museum and at the end of the pier in the rooms above the lifeboat. [MF99/0816/13]

coincided with Britain having the wealth, and appetite, to invest in monumental statuary. At its most modest, such commemorations might be a simple bust, such as the one on a ledge on the facade of the Fairhaven Hotel at Weymouth. It was originally placed there in 1887 to mark her golden jubilee and updated a decade later for her diamond jubilee. The life-size sculpture of the queen on the seafront at Hove by the sculptor Thomas Brock was commissioned to commemorate her diamond jubilee. However, it was not unveiled until February 1901, just days after her death, meaning that it was the first posthumous memorial to the queen.[92] The delay in its completion was due to the diamond jubilee being what the *Art Journal* described as a 'thanksgiving year for sculptors'.[93]

As well as monarchs, some aristocrats were afforded prominent seafront locations for their memorials. Two of the Dukes of Devonshire are commemorated on the seafront of Eastbourne, the town they created. The statue of the seventh Duke of Devonshire, William Cavendish (1808–91) is situated on Devonshire Place.

This 1.5m-high bronze figure on a stone pedestal was unveiled on 17 August 1901 and was funded by voluntary subscriptions from the inhabitants of Eastbourne.[94] The eighth Duke, who died in 1908, is commemorated by a 2.6m-high bronze statue on a granite pedestal on King Edward's Parade. It was unveiled on 24 October 1910 and again was erected by public subscription.[95] As well as aristocrats, some Members of Parliament are commemorated by seafront statues. On the seafront at Weymouth, the statue of Sir Henry Edwards, who was MP for Weymouth and Melcombe Regis for 18 years from 1867 to 1885, is unusual as it was erected during his lifetime as a tribute rather than being a posthumous memorial (Fig 10.26).[96]

Seafronts are often the location to celebrate the achievements of daredevils and adventurers. Captain Cook has a statue on the clifftop overlooking Whitby Harbour because of his association with the town, but others are commemorated because the specific seaside town was where their deed took place (see Fig 10.21). Among the seafront memorials at Dover is a bust of Captain Matthew Webb, the first person to swim the English Channel in 1875 (see Fig 6.17). It was funded by public subscription and was unveiled in 1910. Coincidentally, this was the same year in which Charles Stewart Rolls became the first man to make a double crossing of the Channel by air, an event commemorated by a full-size figure near Webb's bust (Fig 10.27).[97] These achievements were worthy of national recognition, but some seafronts also have poignant reminders of selfless acts by local people. At Torquay, a plaque set into a seafront wall commemorates how Henry Cranmer March-Phillips, a local Justice of the Peace, aged 80 years old, jumped into the sea on 12 April 1873 to rescue a drowning child.

Seafronts also pay tribute to important figures in the arts. At Torquay, a plaque on the side of the seafront Pavilion commemorates Agatha Christie and nearby there is a bust of the author, who was born in the town. Dover's seafront has Portrait Bench, one of a series placed by Sustrans on their cycle routes. This one has outline statues of Jamie Clark who brought the Olympic flame to Dover in July 2012, Dame Vera Lynn and Ian Fleming, a former resident of St Margaret's Bay who included Dover and the surrounding area in his James Bond novels.[98]

Fig 10.26 (right)
Henry Edwards, the local Liberal Member of Parliament, made many generous gifts to the town, including money to pay for the clock in the 1887 jubilee clock tower in the centre of the seafront. See Fig 10.31. [DP219591]

Fig 10.27 (far right)
The statue of Charles Stewart Rolls on the seafront at Dover commemorates his cross-channel flight in June 1910 and his untimely death in a flying accident a month later. He was the first Englishman to be killed flying an aeroplane. [DP217434]

Fig 10.28 (left)
The bronze statue by
Graham Ibbeson of Eric
Morecambe doing his
famous dance occupies
a prominent position on
the central promenade.
It is rare to find it without
a person wanting to have
their photograph taken
beside it.
[DP175072]

Fig 10.29 (below)
The Titanic Memorial
at Eastbourne consists
of a granite plaque with
four bronze panels. The
central feature is a portrait
medallion with a relief of
a violin and a scroll of
music underneath. The
left-hand plaque bears
the inscription while the
plaque on the right-hand
side depicts the sinking
Titanic and lifeboats.
[DP217936]

Nationally famous, popular entertainers are also celebrated at a couple of resorts. Graham Ibbeson created a statue celebrating Les Dawson at Lytham St Anne's, which was unveiled in 2009, but he is more famous for his statue of Eric Morecambe (Fig 10.28).[99]

Entertainers with local connections are also celebrated on seafronts. John Wesley Woodward, formerly a member of the Eastbourne Municipal Orchestra, the Duke of Devonshire's Orchestra and the Grand Hotel Orchestra in Eastbourne, was one of the musicians who perished with the sinking of the *Titanic* on 15 April 1912.[100] The Titanic Memorial set into the bandstand was created by the sculptor Charles Godfrey Garrard and was unveiled on 24 October 1914 by the opera singer Clara Butt (Fig 10.29). At Broadstairs, there is a plaque commemorating Uncle Mack, who had entertained residents and visitors from 1895 to 1948 with his minstrel troupe. The memorial was placed on the promenade opposite Victoria Parade following his death in 1949 at the age of 73 and was paid for by public subscription.[101]

The seafront can also be a site to celebrate ordinary people who meant something to the community. At Aldeburgh, a naturalistic portrait of a dog named 'Snooks' by the sculptor

Gwynneth Holt was unveiled in 1961 on the seafront overlooking the boating pond. The memorial commemorates Dr Robin P M Acheson who practised from 1931 to 1959, while his wife Dr Nora Acheson is remembered in an inscription that was added when she died in 1981.[102]

Fig 10.30
Herne Bay's round clock tower is surrounded on the ground floor by four fluted Doric columns on each side supporting a triglyph frieze and projecting cornice. The middle storey consists of a small cylindrical core surrounded by four Corinthian columns while the top storey is square with Corinthian pilasters at the corners.
[DP076195]

Practical monuments

As well as statuary, other more practical forms of memorial were erected on seafronts. The earliest example is the clock tower that was erected at Herne Bay in 1836–7 by the architect Edwin J Dangerfield (Fig 10.30).[103] An inscription reveals that it was 'The gift of Mrs Ann Thwaites to this town, 11 October, A.D. 1837.' This quirky design, with its mixed use of classical orders, predates other examples of seafront clocks by a generation, and other practical forms of memorial normally belong to the last decades of the 19th century and the early 20th century. At Swanage, a Gothic-style clock tower that was originally built in 1854 at the southern approach to London Bridge as a memorial to the Duke of Wellington was re-erected on its present site in 1867–8 by Mowlem and Burt.[104] A small combined clock tower and weather station was built on the seafront at Ventnor in 1870, but the most common reason for the erection of a clock tower was to celebrate one of Queen Victoria's jubilees (Figs 10.31 and 10.32). Morecambe's red-brick clock tower of 1905 by Cressey and Keighley was 'Presented by John Robert Birkett Esq JP Mayor 1903 to 1906', while the art deco

Fig 10.31 (right)
Weymouth's jubilee clock tower marked Queen Victoria's Golden Jubilee in 1887. The clock was a gift from the town's recently retired MP Sir Henry Edwards, while the cast- and wrought-iron clock tower was paid for by public subscription.
[DP054495]

Fig 10.32 (far right)
Skegness' octagonal red-brick and stone clock tower, which marked the Diamond Jubilee of 1897, occupies a central location on the seafront.
[MF99/0697/13]

clock tower at Seaton Carew once formed a vital part of the seafront bus station.[105] The most entertaining seafront clock is Tim Hunkin's *Mechanical water clock* on Southwold Pier. Commissioned by Thames Water and the Iredale family in 1998 as a temporary feature about water recycling, a new version of the clock is now a permanent feature on the pier that entertains holidaymakers, much as the mechanics of mediaeval clocks intrigue visitors to cathedrals.[106]

Another useful form of memorial on seafronts is the provision of a drinking water fountain, a practical and hygienic necessity at a time when public water supplies could be hazardous to health. At Eastbourne in 1865, a local resident, Elizabeth Curling, paid for the erection of an elaborate cast-iron fountain that originally had a gas lantern on top of it. The sides originally had a tap, a bowl and two small circular shelves (now missing) on which drinking cups could be rested and two of the faces have quotes celebrating drinking water and the words of Jesus.[107] The seafront Canoe Lake Gardens at Southsea has been home to the Emanuel Emanuel Memorial Drinking Fountain of *c* 1870 since 1934. It celebrates the life of Baron Emanuel Emanuel, who was Mayor

of Portsmouth from 1866 to 1877 (Fig 10.33).[108] At Shanklin, a combined clock tower and drinking fountain on the Esplanade, which dates from the late 19th century, probably marked one of Queen Victoria's jubilees (*see* Fig 5.30).[109]

At Ventnor, the drinking fountain was paid for by Ventnor and Bonchurch Temperance Society and at Great Yarmouth the local branch of the Royal Society for the Prevention of Cruelty to Animals paid for a granite horse trough with a drinking fountain in 1912.[110] Like a counterpart at Blackpool, it was placed at a strategic location on the seafront where it could provide water for the horses that took holidaymakers for coach rides along the promenade (*see* Fig 5.32). Other types of commemorative structures found on seafronts include a paddling pool built on the beach at Burnham-on-Sea in 1921 by Mr and Mrs JB Braithwaite in thanks for the safe return of their five sons from World War I.[111]

Other seafront features include items related to location. At Ventnor, there is a combined clock and weather station and Hastings also has a highly informative weather station on its seafront. Ventnor also boasts a marker on its seafront recording the town's latitude and longitude (Fig 10.34). Many seafronts also have

Fig 10.33 (far left) Paid for by his son and daughter, the Emanuel Emanuel Memorial Drinking Fountain at Southsea consists of a bronze angel of peace within an elaborate cast-iron canopy supported on four columns all mounted on a polished granite base. [DP139184]

Fig 10.34 (left) This location marker at Ventnor was presented in 1851 by Sir Thomas Brisbane, a former Governor of New South Wales, who had a passion for astronomy. [MF99/0738/21]

information panels or signs pointing to exotic foreign places that lie over the sea. At Lowestoft, one example has been turned into a work of art entitled *Euroscope*, designed by John Wylson and unveiled in 1998.[112] It consists of a circular concrete form with a central brass roundel and 64 perimeter plates showing the distances to places, such as John O'Groats, Warsaw, and Berlin. The reason for commissioning this work of art is to celebrate Ness Point, which is the most easterly point of England.

Public art

The seafront has long attracted artists to capture the drama of the sea, Britain's two most famous landscape painters John Constable and J M W Turner both having visited Brighton during the 1820s and enjoyed painting the novel Chain Pier. Increasingly during the latter half of the 19th century, the seafront became a place to observe the theatre of the seaside holiday, as it unfolded on beaches around the coast.[113] However, prior to the late 20th century, it was not often recognised as a location for 'public art' in the contemporary sense. Nevertheless, there are examples of buildings on the seafront to which

works of art were applied as part of the design (Fig 10.35). The Gem Cinema at Great Yarmouth of 1908 is decorated with applied faience cartouches, ceramic tiles and swags on the side of piers on the first floor of its facade, while the nearby Hippodrome of 1903 similarly has architectural decoration on its facade.[114] In *c* 1960 four concrete panels signed by Laurence Bradshaw were installed on the west wall of the Denton Lounge on Worthing Pier. The two end panels depict the same dolphin and trident motif, but the two central panels feature Minerva, the Roman goddess of wisdom, mental activities and the arts, while the second one depicts Neptune, the Roman god of the sea.[115]

By the end of the 20th century, works of public art had become an essential element of regeneration and development schemes and their importance to the historic environment was celebrated by English Heritage in 2000, with its publication of *A User's Guide to Sculpture*.[116] In the introduction to this guide, Henry Moore is quoted as believing that 'There is no background better than the sky, because you are contrasting solid form with its opposite – space', while Andrew Saint argued that 'Location is critical to the success and accessibility of public art.'[117] While neither were specifically considering a seaside location, the combination of sea, sand and sky makes a perfect backdrop for works of public art. The seafront is also the busiest part of the seaside town, at least during summer months, and therefore guarantees something else that public art requires, an audience.

Public art may be part of a concerted programme of renewal or a single work of art, even if it consists of dozens of elements. The largest example of a concerted programme is Blackpool's South Promenade, the location for the Great Promenade Show. Since 2001, 10 large-scale, permanent works have been installed at special viewing points along the redesigned 2km-long walkway (Fig 10.36). *Desire* by Chris Knight is a monumental steel work with a central opening surrounded by sharp teeth. The *High Tide Organ*, designed by Liam Curtin and John Goodin, has pipes that are blown by the in-rushing sea and there were three Swivelling Wind Shelters by the architect Ian McChesney. The seafront at Southport also has a range of modern works of art, including *Shoal* designed by Eaton Waygood Associates in 1998. It consists of a shoal of 30 stainless-steel fish covering an area 9.1m in diameter set

Fig 10.35
The White Rock Theatre on the seafront at Hastings, which opened in 1928, has a series of Doulton stoneware roundels, depicting cherubs personifying an aspect of the arts with an accompanying banner proclaiming its title.
[DP217970]

on steel poles around 6.5m high. *Irish Sea to North Sea*, also called the Sea Mark, was also designed by Eaton Waygood Associates in 2002. It marks the western end of the Trans-Pennine Trail, which opened in September 2001. Eaton Waygood also designed seating, lighting, paving, balustrades, five wind sculptures and a 40m-long Conger Eel wall relief.[118] There are also statues celebrating divers who used to entertain holidaymakers, one of whom was Professor Osborne who sometimes used to 'dive' with a bicycle and Professor Gadsby, a one-legged diver.

At Bridlington, the South Promenade Improvement Scheme, which was completed in 1998, includes the *Nautical Mile*, a terrazzo pavement 1.9km long with inset text that refers to the town's history and natural history Fig 10.37).[119]

At most resorts, there has not been an opportunity to undertake an overarching programme, but the desire to entertain visitors, and celebrate a town's coastal location, has led to the creation of a wide variety of public works. As well as figurative statues, some modern works of art are more symbolic and abstract (Fig 10.38).

Fig 10.36
Among the works on view on Blackpool's South Promenade is They Shoot Horses Don't They*, a 6m diameter mirror ball by Michael Trainor covered with 47,000 mirrors.*
[DP154876]

Fig 10.37
At Redcar, some of the seafront railings were designed in 1994–5 by Chris Topp. They celebrate the town and the art of the seaside postcard in steel panels and they are joined by nine 'somewhat bemused' 1m-high steel penguins.
[MF99/0803/34]

Fig 10.38
At Bexhill-on-Sea, the
Serpolet Sculpture designed
by Peter Fairhurst in 2002
is a tubular stainless-steel
sculpture of a racing car
commemorating the
century since the town
became the birthplace
of British motor racing.
It depicts in outline Leon
Serpolet's record-breaking
'Easter Egg' car.
[DP217871]

Fig 10.38
At Bexhill-on-Sea, the
Serpolet Sculpture designed
by Peter Fairhurst in 2002
is a tubular stainless-steel
sculpture of a racing car
commemorating the
century since the town
became the birthplace
of British motor racing.
It depicts in outline Leon
Serpolet's record-breaking
'Easter Egg' car.
[DP217871]

At Aldeburgh, *Scallop, A conversation with the sea* by Maggi Hambling, unveiled on 8 November 2003, is a stainless-steel scallop shell. It includes a quotation from Benjamin Britten's 1945 opera *Peter Grimes* and commemorates a spot on a shingle beach where the composer walked and swam.[120] At Brighton, *Afloat* by the sculptor Hamish Black was installed in 1998 at the end of the groyne beside Brighton's Palace Pier. Affectionately known locally as the doughnut, this patinated 2.5m-diameter bronze torus, which weighs 2.2 tonnes, is based on a speculative form of how a black hole might look. It was commissioned by Brighton Borough Council as part of the Seafront Development Initiative of the late 1990s.[121] Another work in the same scheme was *Passacaglia* by Charles Hadcock, a tile tessellation of 18 cast plates that sits on the beach opposite the Kings Road arches.[122] Such challenging geographical locations for public art requires the chosen medium to be durable and the work to be large-scale, Hadcock's work weighing in at 20 tonnes.

Some single works of art can consist of more than a single figure or form. Juan Munoz's *Conversation Piece*, which was installed in December 1998 on the beach at South Shields, consists of 22 bronze figures, each 1.6m high, set on a 40m-wide paved area (Fig 10.39).[123] Antony Gormley's *oeuvre*, once considered radical because of its elegant simplicity in using depictions of his body, is now celebrated both as important works of art, but also as tourist attractions. The beach at Crosby, where 300 years earlier the Blundell family may have bathed in the sea, is now a destination for local residents and tourists alike. *Another Place* consists of 100 of his figures, which were placed on Crosby beach in 2005. Originally this work was installed on the beach at Cuxhaven in Germany in 1997 and was subsequently re-erected at Stavanger in Norway and De Panne in Belgium (Fig 10.40; *see also* Fig 2.1).[124]

As well as sculptures and solid works of art, the seafront has proved an inviting place to experiment with works of art using light and water. Blackpool, with its illuminations and its elaborate year-round lighting, leads the way, but other resorts have adopted some lower-key, smaller-scale works using light. Weymouth seafront's laser display was launched in May 2012 in anticipation of the 2012 Olympic Games, a welcome addition to the fairy lights that hung between the main street lights. Southend Council installed several lighting structures on the seafront as part of their City Beach revamp in 2011 (Fig 10.41).

Fig 10.39
In Juan Munoz's Conversation Piece, *the lower part of each figure is treated like a filled sack, giving the figures a roly-poly form. Each figure is depicted in a different pose, listening, leaning or talking, hence the title of the piece.* [MF99/0797/08]

Fig 10.40 (far left)
After Crosby, Another Place *was due to be moved to New York in November 2006, but Sefton Council, reacting to public enthusiasm, decided to retain the work permanently. See also Fig 2.1.* [DP034503]

Fig 10.41 (left)
The seafront at Southend-on-Sea now boasts a brightly lit fountain and illuminated lamp posts. [DP219100]

At St Leonards, *Stream* was installed in March 2002 on the Grand Parade promenade opposite Marine Court, and consists of seven steel and blue glass columns extending along the promenade for approximately 40m. They light up in sequence to provide a 'wave' echoing the movement of the sea.[125] As part of the regeneration of the seafront at Worthing, a water feature was created using small jets set into paving and a similar type of feature is part of the renewed promenade at the northern end of the seafront at Lowestoft.[126]

The seafront has become a location for local art galleries and museums, sometimes with a maritime theme. In 1897, the architect John Frederick Fogerty was commissioned by Merton Russell-Cotes, the owner of the Royal Bath Hotel, to build East Cliff Hall as a birthday present for his wife Annie. In 1907, she donated the house and its contents to Bournemouth to serve as a museum while living in part of the house (Fig 10.42).[127] In recent years, art galleries have been recognised as a powerful driver for regeneration programmes at some seaside resorts. The ultimate inspiration may be the De La Warr Pavilion at Bexhill-on-Sea, a conscious attempt by Earl De La Warr to stimulate the cultural and economic life of the town.

The modern inspiration for this trend was the opening of the Tate Gallery at St Ives in 1993, which has proved to be a popular focal point for interest in British art, and particularly the work of the St Ives School.[128]

There was no was similar tradition at Margate, but the town had its close association with J M W Turner to exploit and it identified that the presence of a gallery, and an accompanying strategy to lure artists and 'creatives', could revive the historic Old Town. Margate was quick to realise that in the modern world physical proximity to London and major population centres was becoming less significant as the Internet became more important. The Turner Contemporary was constructed by David Chipperfield Architects and opened to the public in April 2011 (Fig 10.43).[129] The Jerwood Gallery located on the Stade in Hastings opened in March 2012 at a cost of £4 million and was designed for both temporary exhibitions and a permanent collection showcasing the work of a range of 20th- and 21st-century artists (Fig 10.44). While it was highly regarded by architectural critics, there was concern that it had replaced a coach park, which might reduce the number of visitors, and that the presence of an art gallery might lead to the gentrification of the surrounding area.[130]

Fig 10.42
After the deaths of Merton Russell-Cotes and his wife Annie, the Borough of Bournemouth reopened their house as the Russell-Cotes Art Gallery and Museum on 10 March 1922. [DP001245]

Fig 10.43
Measures of the success of the Turner Contemporary gallery at Margate are that the gallery had already welcomed its millionth visitor by August 2013 and there has been a clear revival of the Old Town, which is evident in the restored fabric of its buildings.
[DP139571]

Fig 10.44
The Jerwood Gallery on the seafront Stade at Hastings is clad in more than 8,000 glazed brick tiles. It is designed to echo the nearby net lofts in colour and height.
[DP153081]

These galleries are using art to create a destination, but they are themselves works of art. On a smaller scale, the same is true of the East Beach Café at Littlehampton, which was completed in June 2007 and has since won more than 20 national and international awards for design, architecture, steelwork, craftsmanship and engineering.[131] Rather than simply creating a standard box, Thomas Heatherwick was commissioned to create a work that would make Littlehampton a destination. The exterior consists of four separate pieces of rusted mild steel, welded together in a quasi-natural shape that evokes shells, waves and the sandy beach. A feature in *The Guardian* after it opened imagined that it might have its own 'Guggenheim effect' (*see* Fig 9.44).[132]

The seafronts of some seaside resorts have been used for more occasional arts events, ranging from art exhibitions to pop festivals for thousands.

The leading art festival at a seaside resort is the Folkestone Triennial, the latest having taken place between 2 September and 5 November 2017. Since its inception in 2008, it has established itself as a significant event in the international calendar of recurring art exhibitions.[133] Some of the works of art may be placed on the seafront, though the event always features works throughout the town. From 21 August to 27 September 2015, Banksy opened his Bemusement Park, Dismaland, a 'family theme park unsuitable for children', which was located in the long-closed Tropicana open-air pool at Weston-super-Mare (*see* Figs 6.19 and 6.25). It was a pop-up art project featuring 10 new works by Banksy, as well as 58 other artists.[134] Other popular cultural events have also been held on seafronts. At one time, BBC1 held summer variety shows while Radio 1 between 1973 and 2000 held large-scale roadshows, often at seaside resorts. At Brighton, DJ Fatboy Slim, aka Norman Cook, hosted the Big Beach Boutique concert, which was attended by a quarter of a million fans.[135] As well as one-off events, some resorts have planned for more regular cultural events on the seafront; the Tower Festival Headland in front of Blackpool Tower, home to the Comedy Carpet, is designed for use for performances (*see* Fig 10.4).

Conclusion

The seafront is a special place, with its own history and character. It is this that has made it particularly appealing to artists over the past 200 years. The sight of a giant mirror ball with the sea as a backdrop or a statue of Queen Victoria in front of a grand Regency square has a greater impact than if they had been simply tucked into a gap in a busy town centre.

On seafronts, there is space for works of art to breathe and make a statement. They also have changing light and weather, providing an additional theatrical dimension to works of art, as Claude Monet recognised when repeatedly painting the facade of Rouen Cathedral. Some modern works of art have even broken free of traditional solid materials to exploit water and light as part of enlivening seafronts.

By the sea, time can almost slow down; people on holiday have time to pause and admire works of art that they might otherwise simply pass every day. The seafront also serves the local population by providing a civic space for them to gather, celebrate and commemorate. It is a focal point for community activities and events and despite the hedonism and triviality of much that goes on at the seaside, the power of the sea and nature evokes the spiritual in people, irrespective of their religious faith. During the summer it may be the site for fun and frolics, but on Remembrance Sunday it becomes a suitable place for sombre, silent tribute to people who made the ultimate sacrifice.

Throughout this book, a recurrent theme has been the diversity of the buildings, structures and activities that occur in a small part of seaside towns and how they have been adapted over 300 years of holidaymaking. The final chapter of this book will examine the challenges facing the seafront today. Some of the issues would have been familiar to visitors and residents of seaside towns in the 18th and 19th centuries, but climate change is a new threat to their future prosperity and perhaps even their very existence. It is perhaps ironic that seaside tourism boomed in the 19th century as a result of industrialisation, the very process that now perhaps casts a shadow over its future.

11

Challenges facing the seafront

The seafront is the interface between a seaside town and the sea. It is the transition from the natural to the man-made, a place that was largely ignored, but is now more or less revered. Over three centuries, there has been a shift from the seafront being a place to improve one's health to a playground and a place to relax, a move from sea bathing in the 18th century to sun worshipping in the 20th century. This period has also seen a shift from the seafront being a place of work to a site for leisure. Once an exclusive space only enjoyed by the wealthiest, it has now become a place for a universal audience. During the 18th century, it was populated by handfuls of wealthy 'patients' exploiting the curative value of the sea, but by the 20th century, the need to cater for millions of fun-seeking holidaymakers required a transformation from the simple, natural and small-scale, to the large, man-made and complex.

This book has documented the changing appearance, function, uses and scale of the seafront, as the numbers and character of its users has changed. The growth in visitor numbers, and the resident population, has been met by more investment in larger numbers of houses, better facilities, larger venues and more substantial sea defences. And the area occupied by towns, and the distance that they spread along the coast, has increased, as the seafront has proven to be a premium location for residents and holidaymakers. This has prompted greater local government involvement to defend this investment from the sea and, in recent years, reliance on national and European funds as the size of projects has increased.

Many of the changes that have occurred during the past 300 years have resulted from changing tastes, fashions and scientific beliefs, creating economic opportunities and new challenges for coastal towns. Seaside resorts and their seafronts have also had to respond to issues arising from their coastal location and anthropogenic climate change. In this chapter, these challenges will be reviewed to establish how they have affected the history of seaside resorts and continue today, and in the future, to shape these settlements.

Enduring challenges

The challenges facing seaside resorts today can mostly be classified as enduring. The first and most obvious is the issue of location and the resultant physical challenges. There is a need to resist storms on seafronts, with salty spray and rasping, sand-filled winds frequently causing damage to structures and increasing the maintenance required. Seafront structures may be light, cheap and hence easily replaced or, alternatively, they may be expensive, being constructed of robust materials designed to overcome the challenges of this location. And gardens also have to respond to being on the seafront, a careful choice of plants, especially perennials, being essential to their success.

A related issue on seafronts is the necessity for a continuing programme of maintenance to ensure that buildings and structures do not look neglected. Underinvestment is particularly noticeable and, if prolonged, can prove expensive to remedy. Iron, a popular material since the 19th century because of its affordability, practicality and decorative qualities, is prone to corrosion and without regular maintenance rust can turn to rot, with catastrophic results. Wood, particularly any exposed to sea water, can rot and decay very quickly. The story of piers highlights the vulnerability of structures made from both materials; while England offered holidaymakers around 100 seaside piers a century ago, under half this number survive today.

Therefore, a consequence of a seafront location is greater costs, but also potentially greater rewards. However, a potentially vicious circle can be created where neglected attractions lead to decreasing popularity and consequently less private and public income to invest, which in turn leads to poorer facilities and therefore fewer visitors. This danger has been recognised by local and national government. In recent years, various national government initiatives, such as Sea Change (2008–11) and its successor, the Coastal Communities Fund, have sought to fund a variety of projects designed to keep the seaside, and coastal towns, firmly on the country's tourism agenda.[1] These are recognition that seaside resorts must continue to adapt, as they have done for 300 years, to meet the changing tastes and demands of their customers.

Since the 1960s, a substantial part of the holiday industry has been devoted to supplying its customers with guaranteed sunshine and the highly prized suntan. While British seaside resorts may have more or less impressive records of annual sunshine, this may not necessarily be accompanied by warmth, and while seeking to continue to provide the family beach holiday, resorts around the country are recognising that they have many other attractions to offer. Therefore, as well as a beach and a seafront lined with chip shops and bars, as might be found in some Mediterranean resorts, British seaside resorts can market themselves by promoting their heritage, culture and cuisine. This requires significant investment; at some resorts local and national government money has transformed the public realm, providing new paving, seating and features to amuse and entertain visitors (Fig 11.1).

However, investment in private-sector properties may still be lacking and therefore there may be a significant disparity between the attractiveness of the seafront and the less well-maintained buildings lining it. Blackpool and Morecambe are both examples where major programmes of investment have transformed the seafront, but the state of repair of many of the buildings lining these new seafronts leaves a lot to be desired. These are the buildings in which holidaymakers are fed, watered and entertained, and while there may be a desire to invest in the ground-floor, revenue-generating facility, the upper floors of many seafront buildings are largely unused and unfortunately unloved. A key factor in underinvestment in the private sector is the seasonal nature of the seaside resort, income being plentiful during the middle months of the year, but negligible, or entirely absent, from many businesses for the rest of the year. This inevitably leads to a focus in investing on where income can be maximised, leaving the remainder of the property to hopefully take care of itself (Fig 11.2).

As well as physical and economic challenges, many seafronts face aesthetic problems concerning the quality of their buildings and finishes. The quiet elegance of the Georgian townhouses of Weymouth's seafront, the elaborate detailing of Blackpool's Tower Building and the stream-lined design of the De La Warr Pavilion are all too easily drowned out by apparently necessarily garish fascia and illuminated signs of chip shops and amusement arcades (Figs 11.3 and 11.4).

Fig 11.1
The high quality of the new seafront at Blackpool is obvious to visitors to the Comedy Carpet. Considerable thought and expense has gone into bins, benches and the new lights around the headland, as well as the giant dune grass blowing in the wind. [DP154765]

Seafronts are also the places where new sea defences are having a profound impact on the appearance of the town. To maximise profits, substantial developments of shops and apartments have taken place at some resorts, but these can have a negative effect on the appearance of the seafront. This is of course not something that is new today; in fact, most modern schemes are positively sensitive to the historic environment in comparison to the visual impact of Marine Court at St Leonards in the 1930s, which thundered aesthetically into a Regency seafront terrace (*see* Fig 9.18).

Looking out to sea, there are concerns at some resorts about the visual impact of wind farms (*see* Fig 4.17). On some stretches of coastline, these are within a few kilometres of the beach, but these are predominantly relics

Fig 11.2 (above)
A few yards away from the Comedy Carpet a hint of the difficulties facing seafront businesses is evident. The issue is what to do with the upper floors of buildings when the money is made on the ground floor.
[DP174890]

Fig 11.3 (left)
The restrained elegance of the houses of Brunswick Terrace on the seafront at Hove is a far cry from the vivid fascias of businesses in the central parts of the seafront, but both have been created to attract their part of the market at the time of their creation.
[DP017943]

Fig 11.4
In contrast to the elegance of Georgian housing, Blackpool's Lucky Star arcade typifies one modern approach to design, a simple industrial box with a garish fascia to catch the tourist's eye.
[DP154945]

of a time before the technology permitted the construction of wind turbines on, or over, the horizon. In 2017, Britain could proudly boast the largest offshore wind farm in the world and 10 of the largest 25.[2] New complexes of wind turbines are continuing to be developed at sea; as these are now often beyond the horizon, they are largely out of mind. The construction of turbines has helped to regenerate some coastal shipyards and the vessels needed to service them have contributed to the economies of some ports. However, the impact of connecting offshore wind farms to the National Grid has caused some concern due to potential damage to the archaeology of the seabed where supply cables are laid.[3] As well as heritage concerns, the siting of wind turbines is carefully considered for its impact on the natural environment; the second phase of the London Array was cancelled due to concerns regarding the red-throated diver that overwinters within the wind farm's boundaries.[4]

A new challenge: climate change and coastal defences in the 21st century

In May 1966, a conference held in London hosted by the National Parks Commission was attended by the local authorities and county councils responsible for the care of the Kent and Sussex coastline. In a wide-ranging discussion, they examined the impact of the desire for new leisure facilities, the pressure to provide more retirement properties, the growth of traffic, the threat of caravan sites and the likely impact of marina development.[5] They did not discuss improving sea defences and coastal protection to prevent flooding and to reduce coastal erosion. Fifty years on, England's sea defences have become a central issue. They are in the process of being renewed, due to their age and the growing realisation that they will be in the front line, literally, of protecting seaside resorts from increased storminess and higher sea levels in the coming century.

The fifth report of the Intergovernmental Panel on Climate Change (IPCC), published in 2013, provides clear evidence of climate change during the past century. Between 1880 and 2012, the world warmed by 0.85°C, though the rate of increase has been faster recently, averaging 0.12°C per decade between 1951 and 2012.[6] Global sea level has risen in line with this warming, rising by an average of 0.19m per decade between 1901 and 2010 and there are further concerns due to the Greenland and Antarctic ice sheets losing mass, and glaciers and sea ice shrinking almost worldwide.[7] In the 21st century, it is forecast that global temperatures will continue to rise, perhaps faster than in the recent past, and a further rise in sea level of between 0.5m and 2m is forecast.[8] When combined with more frequent, and more severe, storm events, and greater variations in precipitation and temperature, the vulnerability of coastal towns around the globe is obvious.

The projections published by the United Kingdom Climate Impacts Programme (UKCP09) suggest that mean summer temperatures in parts of southern England may rise by between 2.2°C and 6.8°C, while sea-level rise around Britain has been around 1mm per year during the 20th century, though the rate has increased during the past two decades.[9] Projections suggest that sea level will rise around Britain by between 0.12m and 0.76m between 1990 and 2095 if the medium emissions scenario occurs. Any rise may be disproportionately felt in the more populated South East, where there are a larger number of seaside resorts, as this part of the country is sinking slowly, while Scotland is rising, a long-term consequence of the loss of the ice sheet that once burdened northern parts of the country.[10] Consequently, sea-level rise in England may be as much as between 0.93m and 1.9m by 2100. What is less easy to quantify is the rate of increase in extreme weather events, though there are reasons to expect more frequent, and more severe, storm events, and therefore greater challenges for England's coastal towns and their sea defences.

Rising sea levels will mean that waves and storm surges could cause greater damage and coastal erosion, while changes to currents could lead to alterations in the movement of coastal sediments, affecting both deposition and erosion. It could also lead to new risks from coastal flooding, a greater risk of coastal defences failing, more costly maintenance work on defences and a need for more extensive warning systems and management procedures.[11]

The Environment Agency (EA), a non-departmental public body established in 1996 and sponsored by the Department for Environment, Food and Rural Affairs (DEFRA), is the lead organisation for sea-flooding risk management, while responsibility for coastal erosion lies with Coastal Erosion Risk Management Authorities, comprising representatives of the

EA and local authorities.[12] In March 2010, the *Planning Policy Statement 25 Supplement: Development and Coastal Change* outlined the policy hierarchy that the government had adopted. It begins with a mechanism for appraising the risk to stretches of coastline through the use of Shoreline Management Plans (SMP) and then the means to implement policies to protect the coastline.[13] In 1995, the former Ministry of Agriculture, Fisheries and Food (MAFF) and the Welsh Office published guidance for preparing SMPs.[14] The first generation of 39 assessments were completed in 1999 and a second generation began in the mid-2000s to update the projections. Twenty second-generation SMPs cover the English coastline, including two cross-border ones, with a further two considering the Welsh coast. Within each stretch of coastline, smaller policy units are assessed to identify the processes at work now, and in the future, as well as the nature of coastal assets that need to be protected in the conditions that will exist in 20, 50 and 100 years.[15] Once identified, a broad policy is allocated to each unit. For the coast in general, there are four options that policymakers are directed to implement, though for seaside resorts 'no active intervention' and 'managed retreat' are not options. Therefore, local authorities and the EA have to find ways of protecting properties in resorts by 'Holding the Line' or on occasion by 'Advancing the Line'. The findings of the SMPs therefore allow the EA to decide on which schemes to devote its limited funding.

Having carried out the identification and assessment stage, the responsible bodies have to implement the chosen policy to avoid, manage or mitigate against potential risks.[16] New development in vulnerable locations can be avoided through planning policies, but there may be a need to remove some structures that will be in danger, or may interfere with the installation of new sea defences (Fig 11.5). As was discussed in Chapter 9, historic maps and old images show that in some resorts there were formerly major structures effectively located on the beach, in front of the first complete line of buildings (*see* Fig 9.3). Not all such potentially vulnerable groups of buildings have succumbed to demolition; Aldeburgh's Moot Hall still stands proudly on the beach along with a line of other buildings of various dates and at Bexhill-on-Sea the charming seafront houses of Marina Court Avenue remain some of the most desirable houses in the town (*see* Figs 9.2 and 9.4).[17]

Fig 11.5
At Blackpool, the 1937 lifeboat station beside the Central Pier had to be demolished to allow the new sea defences to be constructed.
[AA053359]

In recent years, there has been a major investment programme to strengthen the natural and man-made defences of seaside resorts. Many figures have been published that reveal the scale of spending, though in recent years it has become more difficult to assess the precise meaning of official figures. Spending on sea defences peaked in 2010–11 at £664 million or £670 million, but was dramatically reduced in the following years, though it rose to around £615 million in 2014–15, in part due to emergency funding in response to the major storms of winter 2013–14. Nevertheless, on average around £600 million has been devoted to flood defences and coastal erosion measures each year since 2007–8.[18] Between April 2015 and March 2021, the government intended to invest £2.3 billion in more than 1,500 projects across England.[19]

Most recent sea-defence schemes involve using hard-engineering solutions, in the form of sea walls, revetments, groynes, headlands and manual, or automated, flood gates sealing off access through defences when sea conditions are menacing. Sea defences have existed at Dymchurch for centuries and, by the early 19th century, had been reinforced with stone. During the 1890s, the wall was given a slope of 1:4, a concrete toe was added and groynes were created to stabilise the beach. In 1961, a concrete wave-reflecting wall was added and during the 1970s, 1.6 miles (2.6km) of defences were raised by 1ft (0.3m), with a further 1.3 miles (2.1km) being rebuilt in the 1990s.[20] Despite this regular investment, there was still a need for new defences to protect the town (Fig 11.6).

Fig 11.6
In June 2011, a new 2.2km-long wall was completed at Dymchurch. It consists of 1,640 tonnes of sheet steel piles and almost 3,000 pieces of precast concrete, weighing 47,200 tonnes, as well as 54,000 tonnes of poured concrete.
[DP217445]

Fig 11.7 (opposite)
This view from the Tower of the new seafront at Blackpool shows the series of curved headlands advancing the line into the sea. The new coastal defences were given a stepped profile to reduce wave energy, and provide great places to sit and look out to sea.
[DP157253]

Most of the modern, hard-engineering schemes seek to hold the line, by reinforcing, raising and replacing old sea defences. However, there are some examples where advancing the line has been the preferred solution, creating new defences projecting into the sea to reduce wave energy and to increase the area of the public realm. The most ambitious and costliest scheme in recent years has been the replacement of the old sea defences in central Blackpool. In two separate and contrasting schemes engineers designed a sea wall to hold the line and a subsequent set of defences that advanced the line of the seafront.

In 1981, a 20-year programme to strengthen Blackpool's coastal defences began, culminating in September 2001 with the opening of the sea defences at the south end of the resort.[21] These were in the form of a sloping revetment made up of Seabees (a precast hexagonal unit) topped with a curved, concrete, wave-reflecting wall (*see* Fig 3.15). These sea defences were designed to hold the line, but only provide restricted access to the sea. The SMP in 1999 indicated that there was also a need for new defences to protect the central area of Blackpool. Significant parts of the town's sea defences had less than five years of useful life remaining and therefore a major scheme had to be undertaken.

In 2005, work began on the reconstruction of 3.2km of sea defences between North Pier and South Pier. Far from simply holding the line as had been advocated in the SMP, a bold scheme of advancing the line was favoured (Fig 11.7). Blackpool has made a virtue out of necessity by turning the five large headlands into areas for public entertainment, sports events and musical performances (*see* Fig 10.4). In contrast to further south, there is no high sea wall that impedes access to the beach; any overtopping of the sea that might occur will be dealt with by the width of the enlarged promenade, landscaped banks and cast-concrete seating. Schemes of advancement of the line are rare, and can be expensive, but they do create potentially useful spaces for the public (Fig 11.8).

At some resorts, some lower-key projects have been undertaken to enhance existing defences. At Weston-super-Mare, the decision was taken in 2008 to reinforce the causeway of the seafront Marine Lake, securing a popular amenity for bathers who, for much of the day, cannot reach the sea, but it also provides a body of water that acts as a sea defence for part of the town.[22] The toe of the town's sea wall has also been reinforced and a new low wall containing some flood gates has been created alongside the seafront main

road (*see* Fig 3.13). A subtle feature perhaps missed by many visitors is that the promenade is at a slight slope, to cause any overtopping water to drain back into the sea. The scheme was completed in 2010 and includes a central wide arch, a decorative embellishment to an otherwise purely pragmatic measure (*see* Fig 3.9).[23]

Soft engineering is an important element of these schemes, critically supplementing the more obvious hard-engineering solutions of sea walls and revetments. In 2013–14, the beach at Deal was replenished and a new 410m-long sea wall established behind it to protect the heart of the town from any overtopping (*see* Fig 3.17). In total, 120,000m[3] of shingle and sand were recharged to the beach from south of Deal Pier northwards as far as Sandown Castle.[24] Photographs taken by the author during a visit to Swanage in 2002 reveal that this was a beach in need of attention and a plaque on the seafront commemorates a recharge that took place between October 2005 and May 2006.[25]

Some schemes take on more than just improving sea defences and coastal protection.

At Lyme Regis, the renewal of sea walls was part of a much larger re-engineering of the seafront of the town. By the 1980s, it was evident that the Victorian sewage system had failed, as sewage was being pumped into the sea via two short outfalls that polluted the beach. The 18th-century sea walls were made of limestone and were failing, and the cliffs above the resort were unstable.[26] Therefore, in 1989 West Dorset DC and SW Water developed a proposal that was commissioned in 1995 to include a storm water tank and a sewer inlet to the pumping station within the renewed sea wall.[27] This was the first of four stages of work, the fourth phase being completed in August 2014 at a cost of £19.5 million.[28] This final phase in central Lyme Regis sought to stabilise the land behind the beach by fixing unstable slipped land to firmer rocks below. Additionally, it involved protecting the foreshore with a new sea wall and an extended offshore barrier, as well as replenishing the two areas of the beach with sand and shingle (Fig 11.9; *see also* Fig 4.5).

Fig 11.8
A broad, stepped sea defence was identified as the way to protect properties on the seafront Parade at Margate. Since its opening it has proved a popular place to enjoy lunches or sunsets.
[© A Brodie]

Fig 11.9
As well as safeguarding the resort in the future, new gardens have also been created at Lyme Regis to increase the amenity value of the seafront. [DP083639]

Fig 11.10
The beach at Weymouth on a perfect summer's day. A moment in time – a lasting memory. [DP054532]

Conclusion

Today, seaside resorts and their seafronts face existential challenges, but they always have. If some sensational media reports are to be believed, the English seaside holiday is dead, meaning that resorts are a relic of the past, an unwelcome legacy requiring substantial investment to keep them alive. However, while Spain, Greece and Mexico may be meeting many Britons' taste for a tan, England's seaside resorts still have a loyal following. This may not necessarily be for a two-week beach holiday, but many are still proving themselves to be popular for shorter breaks and day trips (Fig 11.10).

They are also adapting to meet the demands of customers for more or less niche activities, from surfing and fine dining to 1980s revival weekends and nostalgic fairground rides.

The seaside is alive and well, but changing, much as it has been doing for the past 300 years. The seafront will continue to be in the front line, protecting the homes, hotels, entertainments and infrastructure needed by residents and visitors. It will also remain the shop window, an advert for the joys of the town and the seaside in general. And there is no reason to believe that future generations will not also create life-long memories there, of sunshine and storms, romance and laughter, and fish and chips!

Notes

Chapter 1

1 https://historicengland.org.uk/about/contact-us/national-offices/fort-cumberland/ [accessed 20 April 2018].
2 www.southseacastle.co.uk [accessed 20 April 2018].
3 http://theddaystory.com [accessed 20 April 2018].
4 Emery 2008, 55.
5 www.missgreatbritain.co.uk/history [accessed 20 April 2018]; Freeman 2015, 163–4.

Chapter 2

1 Vicary 1587, 55; Mulcaster 1581, 95.
2 Palmer 1854, 104.
3 Wittie 1660, 36; Wittie 1667, 172.
4 Floyer 1702, 191.
5 Floyer 1702, introduction A3.
6 Walton 1974, 234–5; Walton 1983, 10.
7 Tyrer 1968–72, I, 181.
8 Ibid, 225.
9 Tyrer 1968–72, III, 52.
10 Shaw 1735, 35–6.
11 Brodie 2012 (1), 68–72. On 26 August 1727, Nathanial Buck visited the Blundells' house to try to sell prints 'Nathaniall Buck came to see if I would subscribe to his Proposalls for Publishing the perspective Views of some old Abbies and Castles &c: in Lancashire, Chesshire and Darby-Shire.' Tyrer 1968–72, III, 221.
12 On J Gore's *A Plan of Liverpool* ... 1814 on the site of Prince's Dock a faint rectangular shape labelled Baths is shown as if its future removal was expected.
13 Mr H 1757, I, 25.
14 Temple Patterson 1966, I, 39; Hembry 1990, 242.
15 Temple Patterson 1966, I, 39.
16 Kielmansegge 1902, 270.
17 Freeling 1839, 51.
18 Mr H 1757, I, 16.
19 Cartwright, ii, p 114.
20 Maxwell 1755, 15.
21 Brodie *et al* 2008, 12.
22 Anon 1810, 225–9.
23 Ibid, 261.
24 Gill 1993, 193; Rolf 2011, 51.
25 Miskell 2011.

26 Anon 1734 (1); John Setterington, *View of the antient Town, Castle, Harbour, and Spaw of Scarborough*, British Library Maps K.Top.44.47.b ; Anon 1732, Anon 1733, Anon 1734 (2).
27 Whyman 1985, 160.
28 Evans 1821, 37.
29 Bruyn Andrews 1934–6, I, 87.
30 Brodie and Winter 2007, 94–5.
31 Sympson 1679, 5–6.
32 Anon 1734 (1), 38–9.
33 Lyons 1763, 16; Clarke 1975, 76; Baines 1986, 304–5; Moss 1824, 168.
34 Morley 1966, 12–17.
35 Berry 2002, 105; Hutton 1789, 37–8.
36 Staelens 1989, 31; Lee 1795, 536–7.
37 Troide 1988, I, 275.
38 Anon 1785, 57.
39 Ison 1991, 5–6.
40 Anon 1797 (1), 15.
41 Temple Patterson 1966, 39; Brodie 2012 (1).
42 Berry 2002, 99.
43 Brodie *et al* 2008, 9.
44 Cartwright 1888–9, II, 6; Hutton 1789, 20; Baines 1824, 526.
45 Hutton 1789, 5, 34–7.
46 Bailey 1955, 29, 34; Glazebrook 1826, 59–64; Alsop 1832, 39; Robinson 1848, 25.
47 Pevsner 1989, 619; Robinson 1981, 57; Lackington 1974, 312.
48 Neller 2000, 14; Kime 2005, 21–2; Park nd; Henstock 1980, 71.
49 Smith 1991, 3.
50 Anon 1835, 2; Whitehead 1971, 5; Gough 1983, 2.
51 Anon 1838, 5; Butler 1984, 2; Young 1983, 1–8.
52 Hay 1794, 45.
53 The original hotel was destroyed by fire on 26 June 1826. Anon 1838, 9.
54 Pevsner and Lloyd 1967, 281.
55 Colvin 2008, 47. However according to Colvin 2008, 252 William Barnard Clarke is another name associated with Hayling Island.
56 Anon 1843, 17–8; the library was bought in 1867 by G R Divett who enlarged the building and converted it into a house, named on the 1872 map as 'The Lodge'. Trigg 1892, 37.
57 Anon 1843, 16, 18.
58 Clarke 1836, 33.
59 Brannon 1867, 9.
60 Anon 1825, 478; Sherry 1972, 129.

61 Anon 1837, 37.
62 Ibid, 39.
63 Berry 2009, 132.
64 Antram and Morrice 2008, 113; Ray 1989, 211–3; Berry 2015, 221.
65 Anon 1825; Young 1983, 101.
66 Moss 1824, 146.
67 Morrice 2001, 96–7.
68 Baines 1990, 11; Nathaniels 2012, 151.
69 Baines 1956, 23; Nathaniels 2012, 160.
70 Baines 1956, 37.
71 Herne Bay Pier Company Prospectus 1831, Kent Archives Service, K/Herne Bay.
72 Kidd 1832, 8.
73 Ibid, 7.
74 Kidd 1832, 7; Whitehead 1971, 11.
75 Coulson 1984, 7.
76 Anon 1770 (1), 22; Whyman 1981, 114; Scurrell 1982, 60.
77 Anon 1810, 304; Whyman 1993, 35.
78 Keate 1779, **I** 104–5, **II** 200–1.
79 Cleland 1816, 2, 393–4.
80 Whyman 1985, 25.
81 Ibid, 24.
82 Anon 1806, 22; Wills and Phillips 2014, 173.
83 Kidd 1831, 46; Fischer and Walton 1987, 12.
84 Biddle 1990, 30.
85 Simmons and Biddle 1999, 207.
86 Kellett 1969, 90.
87 Walton 1983, 23.
88 Jordan and Jordan 1991, 41.
89 White 1998, 79; Simmons 1986, 252; Biddle 1990, 131.
90 *Dunfermline Sunday Press* 14 September 1867, 4.
91 Perkin 1976, 184.
92 Anon 1899, 18; *Blackpool Gazette and News* 12 May 1899, 1.
93 Dickens, Charles 1836.
94 Limner, Luke (aka John Leighton) 1847.
95 Act of Parliament 1 & 2 Geo 6, c.70.
96 Anon 1938 (2), 240.
97 This echoes the phases of resort development suggested by Butler 1980.

Chapter 3

1 Reeve, Chadwick and Fleming 2012, 3. According to Rendel, Palmer and Tritton 1996, 230 the total is around 1,600km.
2 Brodie and Whitfield 2014, 9–12.
3 Butt 1995, 98.
4 Anon 1938 (2).

5   White 1998, 79.
6   Historic England Archive BB87/00005.
7   http://ukhumanrightsblog.com/
    2015/02/25/supreme-court-the-
    right-to-be-on-the-beach/ [accessed
    24 April 2018].
8   Lane 1995, 52; Bird 2001, 9.
9   Diplock, W nd (1), *The Hastings Guide*.
    Hastings, 30.
10 HE Archive Buildings File 86314.
11 Wills and Phillips 2014, 246–52.
12 Hooke 1998, 21.
13 Sheppard 1986.
14 Rendel, Palmer and Tritton 1996, 217
15 www.happisburgh.org/ccag/history
    [accessed 24 April 2018].
16 Murphy 2009, 187.
17 Summers 1978, 10; Anon nd (1).
18 Rendel, Palmer and Tritton 1996, 219.
19 Ibid, 216.
20 Rossiter 1954, 383; Everard 1980, 15;
    Allen 1998, 9–10; Ministry of Agriculture,
    Fisheries and Food 1993 (1), 25.
21 Rossiter 1954, 371; Rendel, Palmer and
    Tritton 1996, 216
22 Murphy 2009, 182.
23 Summers 1978, 84–5.
24 Ibid, 60, 84–5.
25 Ibid, 93–5.
26 Ibid, 71–3.
27 Murphy 2009, 128.
28 Rendel, Palmer and Tritton 1996, 218;
    Summers 1978, 38, 60.
29 Summers 1978, 51–2.
30 Ibid, 33–6.
31 Ibid, 39.
32 Ibid, 146–51.
33 Rendel, Palmer and Tritton 1996, 218.
34 Summers 1978, 153–5; https://
    en.wikipedia.org/wiki/Gale_of_
    January_1976 [accessed 24 April 2018].
35 Steers *et al* 1979; http://en.wikipedia.org/
    wiki/1978_North_Sea_storm_surge
    [accessed 24 April 2018]; Wills and
    Phillips 2014.
36 Met Office 2014, *The Recent Storms and
    Floods in the UK* www.metoffice.gov.uk/
    binaries/content/assets/mohippo/pdf/
    1/2/recent_storms_briefing_final_slr_
    20140211.pdf [accessed 24 April 2018].
37 Anon 1797 (1), 15.
38 Rymer 1777, 11.
39 Sussex Archives – *see* http://
    historicengland.org.uk/images-books/
    archive/archive-collections/englands-
    places/card/78694; http://historicengland.
    org.uk/images-books/archive/archive-
    collections/englands-places/card/78696
    [accessed 24 April 2018].
40 Rendel, Palmer and Tritton 1996, 225;
    Ministry of Agriculture, Fisheries and Food
    1993 (1), 4.
41 Rendel, Palmer and Tritton 1996, 217.
42 Herbert and Attwool 2003, 29.
43 Walton 1983, 143, 146.
44 Rendel, Palmer and Tritton 1996, 219;
    Allen 1998, 1.
45 Allen 1998, 28.
46 Latham 1903, 25ff; Rendel, Palmer and
    Tritton 1996, 217.
47 Murphy 2014, 41–3.
48 Lackington 1974, 312; Bennett and
    Bennett 1993, 122.
49 Johnson 1739–41, 804–6; Whittaker
    1984, 51–2.
50 Rendel, Palmer and Tritton 1996, 217,
    254; Johnson 1739–41, 804–6; Whittaker
    1984, 51.
51 Lewis 1736.
52 Young 1983, 62.
53 Eddison 1988, 162–3; Eddison 1995, 164;
    Eddison 2000, 137.
54 Anon 2000, ii.
55 HE Archive BB68/09482a.
56 Kime 2005, 68.
57 NHLE 1390857.
58 Hutchins 1774.
59 Boddy and West 1983, 75.
60 Ellis 1829,131–2.
61 Pigot 1824, 253; Griffiths 2001, 89.
62 Baines 1990, 21.
63 Lane 1995, 52; Bird 2001, 9.
64 Whites Directory of Devon 1850, www.
    genuki.org.uk/big/eng/DEV/Sidmouth
    [accessed 24 April 2018]. The wall and
    promenade were completed in 1838 under
    the supervision of architect G H Julian.
    Anon 1845, 17.
65 Anon 1858, 84; NHLE 1380560.
66 Kent Archives Service, K/Herne Bay,
    Herne Bay Pier Company Prospectus 1831;
    Kidd 1831, 7.
67 Post Office 1874, 198.
68 Kelly 1885, 359; NHLE 1161596.
69 Walton 1998, 20–1.
70 Act of Parliament 16 Vict. c.29.
71 Act of Parliament 62 & 63 Vict. c.184.
72 Brodie and Whitfield 2014, 89–91.
73 Warren 2001.
74 Griffiths and Griffiths 1965, 56.
75 Brown and Loosley 1985, 87.
76 Kelly 1887, 1926.
77 Anon 2000, IV–V.
78 Anon 2000, 23.
79 Latham 1903, 33, 37; Pallett and Young
    1989, 219; Allen 1998, 39.
80 Pallett and Young 1989, 222.
81 Rendel, Palmer and Tritton 1996, 231;
    NHLE 1282542 and NHLE 1096085;
    http://hastingschronicle.net/key-events/
    1850-1899/ [accessed 25 April 2018].
82 Kelly 1885, 359; NHLE 1161596.
83 Jackson 1885, 4.
84 Latham 1903, 38; Allen 1998, 1–2.
85 Walton 1983, 143, 146.
86 Kay and Kay 1998, 24; Kelly 1900–1, 82;
    Clements 1992, 46; NHLE 1096085 and
    NHLE 1282542.
87 Latham 1903, 40.
88 Rendel, Palmer and Tritton 1996, 231.
89 Young 1983, 150; Rendel, Palmer and
    Tritton 1996, 218.
90 Kime 2005, 40.
91 Simm and Cruickshank 1998, 341.
92 www.bbc.co.uk/news/uk-england-york-
    north-yorkshire-25355424 [accessed 25
    April 2018].
93 www.canterbury.gov.uk/leisure-
    countryside/coastal-management/
    coastal-defence-works/herne-bay-coastal-
    defence-scheme/ [accessed 25 April 2018]
94 Hooke 1998, 163.
95 Ministry of Agriculture, Fisheries and Food
    1993 (2), 4.
96 Hoyle and King 1961 (1), 20.
97 Hoyle and King 1961 (2), 2.
98 Allen 1998, 28–9; Rendel, Palmer and
    Tritton 1996, 231, 249.
99 www.snh.org.uk/publications/on-line/
    heritagemanagement/erosion/appendix
    _1.7.shtml [accessed 25 April 2018].
100 Hooke 1998, 163–4; Reeve, Chadwick and
    Fleming 2012, 3.
101 Hayman 2010, 602.
102 Hayman 2010, 606.
103 Latham 1903, 46.
104 Emery 2008, 76.
105 Emery 2008, 78.
106 Rendel, Palmer and Tritton 1996, 255.
107 Rendel, Palmer and Tritton 1996, 256;
    Hooke 1998, 166.
108 Rendel, Palmer and Tritton 1996, 224.
109 www.scillytoday.com/2015/10/30/grant-
    bid-to-improve-scillys-sea-defences
    [accessed 25 April 2018].
110 www.oed.com [accessed 25 April 2018].
111 www.uk-loco.com/dotto_road_trains.html
    [accessed 25 April 2018].
112 Sussex Archives – *see* http://
    historicengland.org.uk/images-books/
    archive/archive-collections/englands-
    places/card/78694; http://historicengland.
    org.uk/images-books/archive/archive-
    collections/englands-places/card/78696
    [accessed 25 April 2018].
113 Anon 2003, 11.
114 Rutter 1829, 14 repeated in Rutter, *c* 1840,
    8.
115 Historic England Archive DP022292,
    AA050895.
116 Anon 1806, 22.
117 Berry 2005, 4, 7, 20–22.
118 Hutton 1789, 31.
119 Aillagon *et al* 2015, 96.
120 Ward Lock and Co 1925–6, 20.
121 Lewis 1840, 288.
122 Kent Archives Service, K/Herne Bay,
    Herne Bay Pier Company Prospectus 1831;
    Kidd 1831, 7.
123 Act of Parliament 59 & 60 Vict. c.36.
124 Morrison and Minnis 2012, 9.
125 Brodie and Whitfield 2014, 89.

126 www.discoverbexhill.com/
bexhillmotorracing.php [accessed
25 April 2018].

127 Minnis 2014, 198–9.

128 Morrison and Minnis 2012, 190.

129 Ibid, 194–5.

130 Ibid, 174.

131 Ibid, 186–7.

132 Ibid, 175.

133 Biddle 1990, 112.

134 Scurrell 1982, 61; Butt 1995, 155.

135 Scurrell 1982, 61.

136 Butt 1995, 125, 161. Minehead's station
closed in 1971 but it reopened in 1976
as the terminus of the West Somerset
Railway, www.west-somerset-railway.co.uk
[accessed 25 April 2018].

137 Ekberg 1986, 60; Butt 1995, 63; Kelly
1885, 359; NHLE 1161596.

138 Butt 1995, 170.

139 Ibid, 194, 72.

140 Pulling 1983; Jackson 1993, 3–7. A few
months after Volk's Railway opened an
electric-powered train service from
Portrush to the Giant's Causeway in
Northern Ireland was inaugurated.

141 Jackson 1993, 16–18.

142 Ibid, 45.

143 Johnson c 1986, 4.

144 www.cliffrailwaylynton.co.uk/history
[accessed 25 April 2018].

145 Gordon 1869, 25.

146 NHLE 1391989; www.fors.vision/areas-
we-watch-over/ramsgate-cliff-lifts
[accessed 25 April 2018]; NHLE 1422305.

147 www.discoveryorkshirecoast.com/Whitby-
Cliff-Lift-Whitby/details/?dms=3&venue=
1710962 [accessed 25 April 2018].

148 https://en.wikipedia.org/wiki/Southend_
Cliff_Railway [accessed 25 April 2018].

149 Gale 2000, 93.

150 www.theheritagetrail.co.uk/cliff_trams/
scarborough_tramways.htm [accessed
13 November 2015].

151 Emery 2008, 80–4.

152 www.theheritagetrail.co.uk/cliff_trams/
cliftonville.htm [accessed 13 November
2015].

Chapter 4

1 Brodie and Whitfield 2014, 61.

2 Walton 1998, 108–9, 129; Toulmin 2012,
13ff.

3 Act of Parliament Ferns 1983, 10–18; 45 &
46 Vict. c.56.

4 NHLE 1381656, 1381697.

5 www.hastingsobserver.co.uk/news/local/
hastings-seafront-lights-up-for-paris-1-
7069646 [accessed 26 April 2018].

6 Walton 1983, 133.

7 Hassan 2003, 31ff.

8 Travis 1993, 219 n45.

9 Walton 1983, 136, 138; Travis 1993, 161.

10 Hassan 2003, 43–4.

11 Hassan 2003, 70.

12 Walton 1998, 27–8, 31–2, 80; Hassan
2003, 128.

13 Travis 1993, 160.

14 Ibid, 163.

15 Ibid, 110.

16 Walton 1983, 143; Gale 2000, plate 4.

17 Binns 2003, 215; Hassan 2003, 54.

18 Cossons 1987, 219; Moore 1988, 62–3;
Gale 2000, 54–5.

19 Hassan 2003, 71.

20 Ibid, 137.

21 Ibid, 152.

22 Gale 2000, 56.

23 Hassan 2003, 228.

24 www.unitedutilities.com/documents/
Blackpool_South_leaflet.pdf [accessed
9 March 2016].

25 Camden 1806, 316.

26 Gale 2000, 100; Binns 2003, 131; Murphy
2009, 92.

27 Anon 1734 (1), 1–3.

28 See Chapter 6 and Brodie et al 2008, 9.

29 Barker et al 2007, 5.

30 Gale 2000, 37.

31 Lucking 1971, 11, 12, 19.

32 NHLE 1009391.

33 Hollebone 2012, 153.

34 Berry 2005, 2-5, 10–11.

35 Garner 2003, 46, 49, 64–5.

36 Farrant 1976, 1.

37 Cartwright 1888–9, **I**, 106–7; **II**, 114, 116;
Cartwright 1888–9, **II**, 116–7, 87, 92;
Matkin 1998, 53–5.

38 Whyman 1980, 191, 197.

39 NHLE 1228784.

40 Binns 2003, 90–1; Anon nd (2), 176.

41 Anon nd (2), 186.

42 Marsden 1947.

43 Hayter 2002; https://en.m.wikipedia.org/
wiki/Earl_of_Abergavenny_(1796_EIC_
ship) [accessed 26 April 2018].

44 Henstock 1980, 116.

45 Rowntree 1931, 194–7.

46 Anon 1926 (1), plates 182–4; https://
en.wikipedia.org/wiki/Blackpool_
shipwrecks [accessed 26 April 2018].

47 Anon 1926 (1), plates 221–4; https://
en.wikipedia.org/wiki/HMS_Foudroyant_
(1798) [accessed 26 April 2018].

48 Walton 1992, 23–5.

49 Hannavy 2009, 43.

50 Brodie and Whitfield 2014, 4; Borsay
2011, 104.

51 https://en.wikipedia.org/wiki/2004_
Morecambe_Bay_cockling_disaster
[accessed 26 April 2018].

52 Murphy 2009, 87; Gale 2000, 38; Miller
1888, 147.

53 Fielding 2006, 17.

54 https://en.wikipedia.org/wiki/
Morecambe_Bay#Natural_gas [accessed
26 April 2018].

55 *Wind Energy and the Historic
Environment* – https://historicengland.
org.uk/images-books/publications/wind-
energy-and-the-historic-environment
[accessed 26 April 2018].

56 www.eonenergy.com/about-eon/our-
company/generation/our-current-
portfolio/wind/offshore/scroby-sands
[accessed 21 May 2018]; https://en.
wikipedia.org/wiki/Scroby_Sands_Wind_
Farm [accessed 26 April 2018].

57 https://en.wikipedia.org/wiki/Teesside_
Wind_Farm [accessed 26 April 2018].

58 http://corporate.vattenfall.co.uk/projects/
operational-wind-farms/kentish-flats
[accessed 26 April 2018].

59 https://en.wikipedia.org/wiki/Walnes-
Wind_Farm [accessed 17 September 2018].

60 Denton and Leach 2007, 77.

61 Jackson 1975, 160–1; Woodman and
Wilson 2002, 13; Denton and Leach
2007, 111–2.

62 NHLE 1043368, 1209999; Hague and
Christie 1975, 150; Pearson 1995, 11;
Denton and Leach 2007, 43, 62.

63 Denton and Leach 2007, 80.

64 Pearson 1995, 11.

65 https://en.wikipedia.org/wiki/Deal_
Timeball [accessed 26 April 2018]; NHLE
1069907; Historic England Research
Report 16/2017 *The Time Ball, The
Guildhall, Kingston-upon-Hull: History,
Context and Significance*, 9–11 http://
research.historicengland.org.uk/Report.
aspx?i=15569&ru=%2fResults.aspx%3fp%
3d1%26n%3d10%26t%3dtime%26ns%
3d1 [accessed 26 April 2018].

66 http://rnli.org/aboutus/
lifeboatsandstations/lifeboats/Pages/
The-fleet.aspx [accessed 26 April 2018].

67 Leach 1999, 8; www.zetlandlifeboat.co.uk
[accessed 26 April 2018].

68 Malster and Stibbons 1979, 1.

69 Rowntree 1931, 199.

70 Leach 1999,8; https://en.wikipedia.org/
wiki/Royal_National_Lifeboat_
Institution [accessed 26 April 2018];
http://rnli.org/aboutus/historyandheritage/
Pages/timeline-flash.aspx [accessed
26 April 2018].

71 https://rnli.org/what-we-do/lifeboats-
and-stations [accessed 26 April 2018].

72 NHLE 1269089.

73 NHLE 1196369.

74 Leach 1999, 152; Brodie and Whitfield
2014, 146.

75 Leach 1999, 84; https://rnli.org/find-my-
nearest/lifeboat-stations/swanage-lifeboat-
station [accessed 26 April 2018].

76 www.mineheadlifeboat.org.uk/history.htm
[accessed 26 April 2018]; https://en.
wikipedia.org/wiki/Minehead_Lifeboat_
Station [accessed 26 April 2018].

77 Leach 1999, 10.

78   Leach 1999, 152; Brodie and Whitfield 2014, 146.
79   Leach 1999, 34.
80   Ibid, 12–13.
81   Ibid, 35.
82   Ibid, 155.
83   Ibid, 153.
84   Ibid, 46–7.
85   Ibid, 60–1, 42.
86   Maritime and Coastguard Agency 2004; https://historicengland.org.uk/images-books/publications/iha-coastguard-stations/ [accessed 26 April 2018]; https://en.wikipedia.org/wiki/Her_Majesty%27s_Coastguard [accessed 26 April 2018].
87   www.gov.uk/government/organisations/maritime-and-coastguard-agency [accessed 26 April 2018].
88   NHLE 1144135.
89   NHLE 1221975.
90   NHLE 1284281; NHLE 1262942; http://kentpoi.co.uk/historic/martello/index.html [accessed 27 August 2017].
91   https://historicengland.org.uk/images-books/publications/iha-coastguard-stations [accessed 26 April 2018]; NHLE 1015519.
92   NHLE 1203551.
93   Leach 1999, 26–7; NHLE 1025344; www.tvlb.org [accessed 26 April 2018].
94   NHLE 1025344.
95   NHLE 102536; https://en.wikipedia.org/wiki/Volunteer_Life_Brigade [accessed 26 April 2018].
96   www.nci.org.uk [accessed 26 April 2018].
97   Hogg 1974, 121–7; Longmate 1993, 60–75; Williams 1999, 210–4; Smith 2001, 30–1.
98   Saunders 1989, 171 ff, 202–3; Saunders 1997, 42, 60ff, 91; Smith 2001, 57–9.
99   Morley 1976, 30.
100 Saunders 1989, 37ff; Harrington 2007, 8, 15; Morley 1976, 10ff, 26; Saunders 1997, 46–9; Pattison 2009, 19–28. Williams 1999, 164–7, 174.
101 Saunders 1966, 134–237, 141–2; Saunders 1989, 50–2; Kenyon 1979, 61–77, 62, 68–9.
102 Hogg 1974, 137–9; Saunders 1998, 20, 39–40; Osborne 2011, 54–7, 89, 110, 119, 152.
103 Brodie 2012 (2), 151.
104 Saunders 1989, 119.
105 'I took a ride to Seaford, where we took a walk by the seaside, and took a view of two forts newly erected there, one of which has 24-pounders mounted, and the other five 12-pounders.' Sunday 1 August 1762, Turner 1979, 55.
106 Berry 2005, 63–4.
107 British Library Cotton Augustus I I 32; Brodie et al 2008, 6.
108 Berry 2005, 68; Oxford Dictionary of National Biography.

109 Middleton 1988, 65.
110 Anon 1850, 71.
111 Goodwin 1988, 83–96.
112 Sutcliffe 1972, 59–61; Saunders 1989, 141; Saunders 1997, 82; Smith 2001, 46–7.
113 Saunders 1989, 142; Hutchinson 1994, 13.
114 Millward 2007.
115 Wilson 1976, 10ff; Longmate 1993, 267–9.
116 Wilson 1976, 22–3.
117 Whyman 1983, 178–83.
118 Grandfield 1989, 73.
119 For instance, Lyon 1813–14; Batcheller 1828; Anon 1851; Anon 1861.
120 Anon 1806, 26.
121 Ibid, 27.
122 Berry 2005, 63.
123 Brodie et al 2008, 9–10.
124 Longmate 1993, 429, 438, 440–2, 446–8.
125 Hegarty and Newsome 2007, 25, 27.
126 East Kent Archives FO/S1/3/1: set of 1917 photos of the damage done by the air raid including a school, the Central Station approach, the top floor of Osborne Hotel in Bouverie Road West, the Bouverie Hotel and a number of shops in Tontine Street.
127 Bridgeman and Drury 1977, 95.
128 Hegarty and Newsome 2007, 25.
129 NHLE 1143384; Saunders 1989, 204; Williams 1999, 224.
130 Saunders 1997, 97–9.
131 Wills 1985, 54; Hegarty and Newsome 2007, 56.
132 Lightbown 1994, plate 140.
133 Hegarty and Newsome 2007, 91.
134 Young 1983, 242; Hardy and Ward 1984, 95.
135 www.doversociety.org.uk/history-scrapbook/world-war-ii [accessed 27 April 2018].
136 Thornton 1987, 270–1.
137 Walton 1998, 137.

Chapter 5

1   Garner 2003, 9; Brodie et al 2008, 34.
2   NHLE 1381647.
3   Garner 2003, 37.
4   Miller 1888, 65.
5   Miller 1888, 16.
6   Design Council 1974/75, 214.
7   www.dezeen.com/2010/08/02/the-longest-bench-by-studio-weave [accessed 21 May 2018].
8   Miller 1888, 27, 50.
9   NHLE 1381648-1381653, 1381756–1381758; Miller 1888, 65.
10 Dobraszczyk 2014, 153.
11 NHLE 1413130, 1413149–1413150.
12 NHLE 1393490.
13 NHLE 1381696.
14 Brodie and Winter 2007, 113–4.
15 NHLE 1084437.
16 Rabbitts 2011, 12; https://en.wikipedia.org/wiki/Bandstand [accessed 30 April 2018].

17 Rabbitts 2011, 25; Rabbitts 2014, 81; Dobraszczyk 2014, 157; NHLE 1381657.
18 NHLE 1061200, 1129709; Rabbitts 2011, 24, 26.
19 Wills and Phillips 2014, 138.
20 Wills and Phillips 2014, 149, 212–3.
21 Hannavy 2009, 67.
22 NHLE 1385904; Rabbitts 2011, 23.
23 Brodie et al 2008 46–8, 76.
24 Wills and Phillips 2014, 65.
25 NHLE 1334383; Neave 2000, 217, 249; Neave and Neave 2000, 68.
26 Rabbitts 2011, 27.
27 Rabbitts 2011, 21. It was built between Ordnance Survey maps of 1922 and 1937, and possibly around 1929. www.newspostleader.co.uk/news/local/bandstand-to-be-brought-back-to-its-former-glory-1-1621042 [accessed 30 April 2018].
28 The scale of the losses can be judged by looking at photographs on Paul Rabbitt's website: www.satiche.org.uk/bandstands/bs-uk.htm [accessed 30 April 2018].
29 www.dlwp.com/about-us/our-story [accessed 21 May 2018].
30 Emery 2008, 78.
31 Ferry 2009, 254.
32 NHLE 1387517.
33 Ferry 2009, 285.
34 Whyman 1990, 39.
35 https://en.wikipedia.org/wiki/Public_toilet [accessed 30 April 2018].
36 Warren 1978, 67; Lambton 1979, 10; Oxford Dictionary of National Biography; https://en.wikipedia.org/wiki/George_Jennings [accessed 30 April 2018]; http://thevictorianist.blogspot.co.uk/2011/02/spending-penny-or-first-public-flushing.html [30 April 2018].
37 Rabbitts 2011, 25; Dobraszczyk 2014, 157; NHLE 1381657.
38 www.chroniclelive.co.uk/news/north-east-news/reaction-proposals-fish-chip-business-9781166 [accessed 30 April 2018]; www.shieldsgazette.com/news/business/batter-future-for-south-shields-seafront-with-gandhi-s-temple-plans-1-7388157 [accessed 30 April 2018].
39 NHLE 1393721.
40 NHLE 1386806.
41 NHLE 1145947.
42 NHLE 1276282.
43 NHLE 1043623.
44 NHLE 1393959.
45 Conway 1991, 71, 228–9; Conway 1996, 27; 38 & 39 Vict. c.55.
46 Anon 1844, 24–9; www.brighton-hove.gov.uk/content/press-release/council-starts-work-preserve-one-longest-green-walls-britain [accessed 30 April 2018].
47 NHLE 1001618.
48 Seddon et al 2014, 178.
49 Dale 1967, 81; Berry 2009, 133.

Chapter 6

1   Corbin 1995, 7, 14–16.
2   Floyer 1702, 191.
3   Russell 1752, 65.
4   Brodie 2012 (2), 131–2; Shaw 1734.
5   Floyer 1706, introduction A4.
6   Awsiter 1768, 15.
7   Reid 1795, 15–17.
8   Cole 1828, 109.
9   Walton 1974, 234–5; Walton 1983, 10.
10 Tyrer 1968–72, **I**, 181.
11 Ibid, **I**, 225.
12 Jones 1718. Neller 2000, 13 citing Lincolnshire Record Office LAO, MASS 13/16.
13 Brodie 2012 (1).
14 Anon 1734 (1), 36.
15 Evans 1821, 37.
16 Moule 1883, 125.
17 Cartwright 1888–9, **II**, 86, 91, 114, 242; Berg and Berg 2001 69, 227–8.
18 Hutton 1789, 42.
19 Anon 1770 (2), 22–3.
20 Brodie and Winter 2007, 106–8.
21 Rymer 1777, 17.
22 Brodie 2012 (1); Brodie 2012 (2).
23 Tyrer 1968–72, **III**, 52, 2 August 1721.
24 Shaw 1735, 35–6.
25 John Setterington, *View of the antient Town, Castle, Harbour, and Spaw of Scarborough*, British Library Maps K. Top.44.47.b.
26 Anderson 1795, 32.
27 Cartwright 1888–9, **II**, 86.
28 Lewis 1736.
29 Dickens 1836.
30 Berg and Berg 2001, 227–8.
31 Binns 2003, 121–2.
32 Lyons 1763, 12; Hall 1790, 9; Cozens 1793, 3.
33 Anon 1765, 67–8; Cozens 1793, 3.
34 Smollett 1995, 166.
35 Barrett 1892, 192.
36 Schofield 1787, 20.
37 La Rochefoucauld 1988, 217.
38 Hart 1981, 70.
39 Boddy 1983, 136; Staelens 1989, 22, 25.
40 Southend-on-Sea Record Office D/F 36/6; *The Times*, Thursday 22 July 1920, 10; For a discussion of the shift from bathing machines to more public bathing *see* Walton 2000, 97ff; Ferry 2009, 25ff.
41 Emery 2008, 55.
42 Pimlott 1976, 182.
43 Parkes 2001, 59–60.
44 Clarke 1975, 30.
45 Hawkins 1991, 55, 57.
46 Kent Archives and Local History Service R/U696/T12/1; R/U696/T12/2.
47 Lyons 1763, 12.
48 Anon 1809, 50; Carey 1799, 5–6; Anon 1810, 310.
49 Anon 1865, 60.
50 Carey 1799, 5.

51 Anon 1797 (2), 61; Anon 1800, 86.
52 Anon 1809, 50; Anon 1822 (1), 38–9.
53 Barker 2007, 41.
54 Reid 1795, 70.
55 British Library Collection Brit King Geo **III** Topographical Collection K. Top **XVII** 7 d.
56 Anon 1797 (2), 104; Anon 1797 (3), 70.
57 Tyrer 1968–72, **III**, 221.
58 Brodie 2012 (1), 68–72.
59 *The Kentish Post*, or Canterbury News Letter 14 July 1736 cited in Whyman 1985, 160.
60 *The Kentish Post*, or Canterbury News Letter 27 April 1737 cited in Whyman 1985, 161.
61 *The Kentish Post*, or Canterbury News Letter May 1740 cited in Whyman 1985, 161.
62 Cartwright 1970, **II**, 114.
63 Awsiter 1768, 17–18.
64 Anon 1780, 27; Farrant 1980, 15, 19, 21; Berry 2002, 103–4; Colvin 1995, 412.
65 Anon 1780, 28.
66 www.mybrightonandhove.org.uk/page_id__7742_path__0p116p1442p.aspx [accessed 1 May 2018]; Betjeman and Gray 1972, image 54.
67 Pigot 1824, 253; Griffiths 2001, 89. These baths had been removed by 1890, possibly once the new baths had been built in Carlton Place in 1883 at a cost of £2500 and including hot and cold baths and a large swimming bath. Unlike the earlier facilities these included a swimming pool, a recognition of the shift from bathing towards swimming as a recreational and health-giving activity. Kelly 1889, 546.
68 Southend Record Office D/DS 229/2.
69 Rymer 1777, 13–14.
70 Ibid, 21.
71 Anon 1817, 21; White 1836, 270.
72 Mahomed 1822, opposite 37; Fisher 1997, 161–2, 165.
73 Diplock nd, 40–1; Baines 1986, 305.
74 Baines 1986, 305.
75 Osborne 1860, 61.
76 Fry 1826–9, 36.
77 Whyman 1985, 170–2.
78 Historic England Archive Buildings File 86314; Brodie, Allan, Roethe, Johanna and Hudson-McAulay, Kate 2019 (forthcoming).
79 Historic England Archive Buildings File 86314.
80 Historic England Archive Buildings File 86314.
81 Mackie 1883, 95–6.
82 Kent Archives and Local History Service F1954/2/B2 in the Folkestone Bathing Establishment Company Limited Minute Book 1878–90.
83 Defoe 2008, 19; Baynard 1731, 29.
84 John Setterington, *View of the antient Town, Castle, Harbour, and Spaw of Scarborough*, British Library Maps K.Top.44.47.b.

85 Smollet 1995, 167; *Oxford Dictionary of National Biography*; Parr 2011, 59.
86 Smith 2005, 11–12; Love 2007 (1), 569–70; Gordon and Inglis 2009, 21–2; Parr 2011, 44.
87 Smith 2005, 13, 176.
88 Gordon and Inglis 2009, 26.
89 Hassan 2003, 40: Smith 2005, 13; Historic England Archive Buildings File 86314.
90 Act of Parliament 9 & 10 Vict. c.74.
91 Act of Parliament Love 2007 (2), 621; 10 & 11 Vict. c.61.
92 Gordon and Inglis 2009, 41, 51.
93 *Oxford Dictionary of National Biography*; Love 2007 (1), 577–8.
94 Act of Parliament 38 & 39 Vict. c.55; 41 & 42 Vict. c.14.
95 Love 2007 (1), 574, 579–81; Gordon and Inglis 2009, 56.
96 Gordon and Inglis 2009, 278.
97 Gordon and Inglis 2009, 45.
98 Miller 1888, 51.
99 Barson 2010; Gordon and Inglis 2009, 76–7.
100 Anon 1977, 20–2.
101 van Leeuwen 1998, 38–9.
102 Gordon and Inglis 2009, 120.
103 Parr 2011, 72–3.
104 Anderson and Swinglehurst 1978, 141.
105 Gordon and Inglis 2009, 279–80.
106 Ibid, 280–1.
107 Information board on seafront beside pool.
108 Smith 2005, 58.
109 Binns 2003, 213.
110 Walton 1998, 127–9; Smith 2005, 45, 62–7.
111 Britain's first open-air swimming facility to have been officially titled 'lido' was the Serpentine Lido, which opened in July 1930. Smith 2005, 22.
112 Hassan 2003, 112; Smith 2005, 72–5.
113 Smith 2005, 86–9, 126–31.
114 Ibid, 108–13.
115 Ibid, 134–7.
116 Ibid, 146–51.
117 Ibid, 70–1.
118 Barker *et al* 2007, 48, 68.
119 Gordon and Inglis 2009, 180. Four weeks after it opened, Wembley's pool opened, boasting the world's largest indoor freshwater pool!
120 Gordon and Inglis 2009, 176.
121 Ibid, 180.
122 http://willparry.net/wp-content/uploads/2012/07/Wolfenden-report-1960.pdf [accessed 1 May 2018].
123 Gordon and Inglis 2009, 244–5.
124 Palmer 1854, 103–4.
125 Relhan 1761, 20–24, 26–38.
126 Clark 1820; Clark 1829.
127 Clark 1830, 29.
128 Sydenham 1840; Barker 1860.
129 Granville 1841.
130 *See* various essays in Balducci 2005 and Bica and Balducci 2007.

131 St Clair Strange 1991, 13, 19, 25, 28, 37; Richardson 1998, 127.
132 Anderson 1795, 9.
133 St Clair Strange 1991, 49.
134 Ibid, 62.
135 St Clair Strange 1991, 66; Richardson 1998, 127.
136 Richardson 1998, 127.
137 Hinderwell 1811, 227–9; Richardson 1998, 127.
138 NHLE 1379734.
139 *The Builder*, 25 September 1869, 769; Richardson 1998, 184.
140 *Shields Daily News*, 15 September 1869; *The Builder*, 25 September 1869, 769–70.
141 NRHE AMIE Monument HOB UID 1065738.
142 NRHE AMIE Monument HOB UID 1065313.
143 Richardson 1998, 188.
144 *The Builder*, 6 July 1928, 9–11; Anon 1929, 43.
145 Anon *c* 1895; www.folkestonehistory.org/index.php?page=sandgate [accessed 1 May 2018].
146 Rollier 1927, 3; Saleeby 1928, 62; Anon 1938–9, 347–52; Heller 1990, 333; Brodie and Winter 2007, 108–9, 118–9.
147 Morris 1935, 5.
148 www.bn.org.uk/news/information/about-naturism/history-of-naturism/a-history-of-naturism-timeline-r28 [accessed 1 May 2018].
149 Norwood 1933, 40, 44.
150 www.bn.org.uk/news/information/about-naturism/history-of-naturism/a-history-of-naturism-timeline-r28 [accessed 1 May 2018].
151 www.bn.org.uk/activities/placestogo [accessed 1 May 2018].

Chapter 7

1 Dickens 1836.
2 Limner 1847, 15.
3 https://en.wikipedia.org/wiki/Campaign_furniture [accessed 2 May 2018].
4 Whyman 1985, 195–7; Whyman 1980, 190 note 12 'I must not omit to notice Ramsgate Sands [where] for the accommodation of visitors, a number of chairs (some hundreds) have been placed on them, to a considerable distance – the charge being only 1d. per day, for each person. Sea Side Reminiscences *c* 1835.
5 Historic England Archive OP32694, OP29135.
6 https://en.wikipedia.org/wiki/Deckchair [accessed 2 May 2018].
7 British Library Letter – Add MS 71125, 1775 transcription – Add 5842, ff 122v–136.
8 https://en.wikipedia.org/wiki/International_Fleet_Review_2005 [accessed 2 May 2018].
9 Barrett 1892, 192.
10 Rothwell 2009, 54, 99; Thompson 2010, 70–2, 90.
11 Corbin 1995, 13, plate 2.
12 Emery 2008, 61–4.
13 www.theguardian.com/environment/2016/jan/25/fifth-whale-reported-washed-up-on-lincolnshire-beach [accessed 2 May 2018]; www.theguardian.com/uk-news/2016/jan/29/sperm-whale-mania-skegness-beach-packed-crowds-locals [accessed 2 May 2018].
14 For instance – Gosse and Gosse 1853, Gosse 1853 and Gosse 1856.
15 Travis 1993, 169; Hassan 2003, 47.
16 Walton 1983, 166.
17 www.dealpier.uk/flog.html [accessed 2 May 2018].
18 Roberts 1834, 179–80; Wanklyn 1927, 239–40.
19 *Oxford Dictionary of National Biography*; Roberts 1823.
20 www.whitbyjet.co.uk/about-jet-read-more [accessed 2 May 2018]; http://whamond.com/pages/what-is-whitby-jet [accessed 2 May 2018].
21 www.bbc.co.uk/news/uk-england-cornwall-34975182 [accessed 2 May 2018]; www.bbc.co.uk/news/uk-england-cornwall-35226958 [accessed 2 May 2018].
22 http://news.bbc.co.uk/1/hi/england/devon/6287457.stm [accessed 2 May 2018].
23 https://en.wikipedia.org/wiki/Torrey_Canyon_oil_spill [accessed 2 May 2018].
24 Dickens 1836; Leighton 1847, 1.
25 Butler 1937, 35.
26 www.dorsetecho.co.uk/news/11092078.Top_10_sand_sculptures_that_have_appeared_on_Weymouth_Beach [accessed 2 May 2018].
27 www.westonsandsculpture.co.uk [accessed 2 May 2018]; http://calendarcustoms.com/articles/sandcastle-competition [accessed 2 May 2018].
28 Troide 1988, **I**, 290.
29 *The Times* 31 August 1793, 3.
30 *The Times* 20 August 1805, Brighton, 2; Anon 1822 (1), 42.
31 Limner 1847, 11, 15.
32 Anon 1822 (2), 16; Anon 1899–1900.
33 Whyman 1985, 220 citing *The Thanet Itinerary* 1819, 42–3.
34 www.blackpool.gov.uk/Business/Licensing-and-permits/Documents/Donkey-Charter.pdf [accessed 2 May 2018].
35 Pertwee 1999, 8.
36 Hern 1967, 77; Walton 1983, 182.
37 Adams and Leach 1978, 4; Speaight 1970, 39; Byrom 1972, 5, 8–9.
38 Samuel Pepys Diary, 9 May 1662: www.gutenberg.org/cache/epub/4200/pg4200.txt [accessed 2 May 2018]; www.vam.ac.uk/content/articles/t/thats-the-way-to-do-it!-a-history-of-punch-and-judy/ [accessed 2 May 2018]; Adams and Leach 1978, 4.
39 Charlton 1779, 333.
40 Adams and Leach 1978, 7, 28; Byrom 1972, 1.
41 www.vam.ac.uk/content/articles/t/thats-the-way-to-do-it!-a-history-of-punch-and-judy/ [accessed 2 May 2018].
42 Pickering 1986, 70; Pickering 2008, 1; Toll 1974, 196.
43 Pickering 1974, 5–7, 13; Limner 1847, 16; Anderson and Swinglehurst 1978, 110.
44 Travis 1993, 184.
45 Walton 1983, 194.
46 Anon (2) 1926, 127.
47 Pickering 2008, 5, 24.
48 Anderson and Swinglehurst 1978, 111; Horn 1999, 137.
49 Anon 1906, 71.
50 Marsden 1947, 38.
51 Pertwee 1999, 10.
52 Ibid, 14.
53 Hern 1967, 147.
54 Pertwee 1999, 13.
55 Freeman 2015, 168–9.
56 Historic England Archive CC76/00466.
57 Travis 1993, 172–3.
58 Rabbitts 2011, 24.
59 Walton 1983, 148–9.
60 Anderson and Swinglehurst 1978, 124.
61 Easdown 2007, 110.
62 Goate 1994, 17–19; http://en.wikipedia.org/wiki/Great_Yarmouth_Pleasure_Beach [accessed 2 May 2018].
63 Rothwell 2009, 85.
64 Walton 1992.
65 Lightbown 1994, plate 38; Thompson 2010, 21; Hannavy 2009, 11.
66 Walton 1983, 201.
67 Walton 1998, 77.
68 Walton 1983, 204.
69 Whyman 1990, 47.
70 Brodie, Sargent and Winter 2005, 53.
71 Ibid, 115.
72 Wood and Lightbown 2010, 95.
73 Hassan 2003, 112.
74 Dunn 2014, 33; Salter 2014, 9, 39.
75 NHLE 1413021; a map of the locations of model villages in Britain can be found at: https://themodelvillager.wordpress.com [accessed 2 May 2018].
76 www.merrivalemodelvillage.co.uk/index.html [accessed 2 May 2018]; Salter 2014, 70–3.
77 Salter 2014, 98–9; https://en.wikipedia.org/wiki/Southport_Model_Railway_Village [accessed 2 May 2018]; www.southportmodelrailwayvillage.co.uk [accessed 2 May 2018].
78 https://en.wikipedia.org/wiki/Eastbourne_Redoubt [accessed 2 May 2018]; Salter 2014, 22–6; www.kentonline.co.uk/kent-business/county-news/visitor-slump-spells-end-for-cas-a9461 [accessed 2 May 2018].
79 The governing body is the Fédération Internationale de Volleyball (FIVB) www.fivb.com [accessed 2 May 2018].

80 www.minigolf.org.uk/joomla [accessed 2 May 2018]; www.minigolf.org.uk/joomla/index.php?view=details&id=115&option=com_eventlist&Itemid=56 [accessed 2 May 2018].

81 www.great-yarmouth.co.uk/Great-Yarmouth-Hollywood-Indoor-Adventure-Golf/details/?dms=3&venue=0116765 [accessed 2 May 2018].

82 Hornby 2015, 53.

83 Brodie 2012 (2), 144.

84 Hornby 2015, 165.

85 Historic England Archive, Aerofilms Collection EPW000102.

86 Hornby 2015, 164.

87 Ibid, 185.

88 www.pottersholidays.com/world-bowls [accessed 2 May 2018].

89 An alternative suggestion is that golf originated from an activity that took place in the Low Countries during the Middle Ages, though the modern game can trace its history to the Scottish ancestry. https://en.wikipedia.org/wiki/History_of_golf [accessed 2 May 2018].

90 Durie 2003, 83, 125.

91 www.historytoday.com/john-lowerson/scottish-croquet-english-golf-boom-1880-1914 [accessed 2 May 2018].

92 Cunningham 1980, 136; Travis 1993, 177; www.royalnorthdevongolfclub.co.uk [accessed 2 May 2018].

93 Physick 2007, 130, 134; Hannavy 2009, 35.

94 https://en.wikipedia.org/wiki/List_of_The_Open_Championship_venues.

Chapter 8

1 Wills and Phillips 2014, 2.

2 'We afterwards walked together for an hour on the Cobb', 14 September 1804, www.pemberley.com/janeinfo/auslet22.html#letter121 [accessed 3 May 2018]; Royal Commission on the Historic Monuments of England 1952, 149–50.

3 Anon 1806, 22.

4 Kidd 1831, 46.

5 Fischer and Walton 1987, 12.

6 Cockney, A 1823, 373.

7 Lewis 1840, 226; Clarke 1975, 25; Easdown 2007, 60.

8 Fry 1826–9, 34.

9 Ibid, 34–5.

10 Oxford Dictionary of National Biography.

11 www.grantonhistory.org/buildings/chain_pier.htm [accessed 3 May 2018].

12 Easdown 2007, 11, 13. A company was formed by a Mr Birch in 1842 to build Greenhithe pier. Adamson 1977, 28.

13 Wills and Phillips 2014, 196; Evans 1821, 251.

14 Fischer and Walton 1987, 35.

15 Easdown 2007, 14; Foote Wood 2008, 69; Wills and Phillips 2014,110.

16 Easdown 2007, 19, 35.

17 Fischer and Walton 1987, 49; Oxford Dictionary of National Biography.

18 Oxford Dictionary of National Biography.

19 Adamson 1977, 47.

20 Easdown 2007, 60–73.

21 Fischer and Walton 1987, 16, 18.

22 Ibid, 16.

23 Ibid, 14.

24 Foote Wood 2008, 76.

25 Easdown 2009,103.

26 Fischer and Walton 1987, 18.

27 Easdown 2007, 76; Wills and Phillips 2014,197; Adamson 1977, 51.

28 Fischer and Walton 1987, 20.

29 Ibid, 26.

30 Wills and Phillips 2014, 128, 197, 207.

31 Ibid, 259–61.

32 Easdown 2007, 98; Wills and Phillips 2014, 96–7, 56–9, 60–3.

33 Wills and Phillips 2014, 214.

34 Cockney, A 1823, 373–5, 375.

35 Easdown 2007, 110.

36 Ordnance Survey maps; Walton 2007, 16

37 www.silcock-leisure.co.uk/gallopers.htm [accessed 3 May 2018].

38 www.marksbarfield.com/#/projects/brighton-i360 [accessed 3 May 2018]; https://en.wikipedia.org/wiki/British_Airways_i360 [accessed 3 May 2018].

39 https://en.wikipedia.org/wiki/Watkin%27s_Tower [accessed 3 May 2018]; https://en.wikipedia.org/wiki/New_Brighton_Tower [accessed 3 May 2018].

40 Randl c 2008, 42–5.

41 Parry 1983, 133–5; Walton 2007, 27.

42 Walton 2007, 21–2.

43 Bennett 1996, 12–4; Walton 2007, 22–4.

44 Bennett 1998, 23; Preedy 1992, 8; Walton 2007, 16ff; Kane 2007, 74–5; Toulmin 2011, 11, 15; Kane 2013, 31–2.

45 https://content.historicengland.org.uk/images-books/publications/iha-historic-amusement-parks-fairground-rides/heag057-historic-amusement-parks-iha.pdf [accessed 3 May 2018].

46 NHLE 1436214; Bennett 1996, 19–21.

47 Walton 2007, 29; Toulmin 2011, 21.

48 www.joylandbooks.com/scenicrailway/images/conceptplan2/concept12.htm [accessed 3 May 2018].

49 Toulmin 2011, 18.

50 Oxford Dictionary of National Biography; Walton 2007, 24.

51 Bennett 1996, 23; Walton 2007, 30.

52 Bennett 1996, 31; Walton 2007, 33; Toulmin 2011, 25. The Roller Coaster has subsequently become the Nickelodeon Streak.

53 Bennett 1996, 35–6; Walton 2007, 33–4; Toulmin 2011, 27, 53.

54 NHLE 1436474; Kane 2007, 172; Walton 2007, 47–9, Kane 2013, 147. Strickler also oversaw the construction of Noah's Arks at Morecambe and Southport in 1930, Toulmin 2011, 33, 36.

55 NHLE 1436080; Bennett 1996, 45; Walton 2007, 47, 50; Toulmin 2011, 33; Kane 2013, 148. See Miller's work in the section on rollercoasters.

56 Kane 2007, 173.

57 Bennett 1996, 63; Walton 2007, 61.

58 NHLE 1436894; NHLE 1436382; Bennett 1996, 65; Bennet 1998, 40; Walton 2007, 64; Toulmin 2011, 43, 127.

59 Oxford Dictionary of National Biography.

60 Bennett 1996, 61–2; Toulmin 2011, 33, 44.

61 Bennett 1996, 77–8; Walton 2007, 48; http://boltonworktown.co.uk/photograph/blackpool-ice-drome [accessed 3 May 2018].

62 Bennett 1996, 81–4; Walton 2007, 70; Toulmin 2011, 55, 57; www.c20society.org.uk/botm/joseph-embertons-blackpool-pleasure-beach [accessed 3 May 2018].

63 Walton 2007, 79–81.

64 Walton 2007, 91–2; Toulmin 2011, 82.

65 Walton 2007, 93, 97. Bennett 1996, 98. Bennett 1996, 97 says the monorail opened in 1967.

66 Bennett 1996, 129ff; Walton 2007, 112–5; Toulmin 2011, 133.

67 Bennett 1996, 122; Walton 2007, 110; Toulmin 2011, 97.

68 Kane 2007, 104; Kane 2012, 59.

69 Crowe 2003, 7.

70 Butt 1995, 155; Clements 1992, 125; Evans 2009, 5. The booking hall was unused due to a legal dispute with a rival railway company.

71 Evans 2009, 6.

72 Clements 1992, 125; Mirams 1984, 4.

73 Morley 1966, 93.

74 Barker et al 2007, 42–3.

75 Evans 2009, 10.

76 Preedy 1996, 2–3.

77 Clements 1992, 126; Bennett 1998, 23; Bennet 1998, 23. Frustratingly the company records were destroyed in 1951. Preedy 1996, 3.

78 Evans 2009, 11–14; Morley 1966, 137; Samuelson 2001, 31–2; the Kursaal at Southend was at one point called Luna Park, a homage to another Coney Island Park; Samuelson 2001, 28–31; Preedy 1992, 42.

79 The World's Fair 1 May 1920, 2; Preedy 1992, 32.

80 Evans 2009, 31.

81 Evans 2009, 31–5.

82 www.veterancarrun.com [accessed 3 May 2018].

83 www.visit-westonsupermare.com/events/weston-beach-race-p1548693 [accessed 3 May 2018]; http://rhlactivities.com/events/rhl-beach-race-2015 [accessed 3 May 2018].

84 Anon 1909.

85 Flight, 28 August 1909, 516.

86 Clarke 1923, 263–6.

87 www.simplonpc.co.uk/AllchornDUKW.html [accessed 3 May 2018].

88 www.visitnewquay.org/activities/newquay-surf-capital-of-the-uk/newquay-surf-beaches [accessed 3 May 2018].

89 https://en.wikipedia.org/wiki/Boscombe_Surf_Reef [accessed 3 May 2018].

Chapter 9

1 Sussex Archaeological Society – *see* http://historicengland.org.uk/images-books/archive/archive-collections/englands-places/card/78694; http://historicengland.org.uk/images-books/archive/archive-collections/englands-places/card/78696 [accessed 4 May 2018].

2 NHLE 1269716.

3 NHLE 1152524.

4 Royal Commission on the Historic Monuments of England 1970, 293–4.

5 Historic England Archive, Aerofilms Collection EPW035342, EPW039366, EPW039367.

6 Sussex Archaeological Society – *see* in http://historicengland.org.uk/images-books/archive/archive-collections/englands-places/card/78694; http://historicengland.org.uk/images-books/archive/archive-collections/englands-places/card/78696 [accessed 4 May 2018].

7 British Library Maps 3230 (4).

8 Blackpool Local History Library uncatalogued photograph.

9 NHLE 1072606.

10 Hall 2001, 95–104; Binns 2003, 83. A lack of archaeological evidence and contemporary documentary references suggests there may not have been much use of thatch in the town. Pearson 2005, 68.

11 Hall 2001, 99–101; Pearson 2005, 124–6.

12 Relhan 1761, 15.

13 Hunter 1998, 135–8.

14 Information from the hotel; Taylor 1998, 8.

15 Anon 1935, 167–73.

16 https://doverhistorian.com/2014/10/04/gateway-flats [accessed 4 May 2018].

17 https://en.wikipedia.org/wiki/Van_Alen_Building [accessed 4 May 2018].

18 www.architectsjournal.co.uk/news/allies-and-morrisons-playful-worthing-seaside-homes-win-planning/10016756.article?blocktitle=News&contentID=16149 [accessed 4 May 2018].

19 Pevsner 1976, 173–4.

20 Scott 1826, 8.

21 Barber and Barber 1993, 6; Bishop 1880, 138.

22 Brodie and Winter 2007, 164–5; Antram and Morrice 2008, 102–3.

23 Brodie and Whitfield 2014, 45–6.

24 https://en.wikipedia.org/wiki/Hotel_de_Paris,_Cromer [accessed 4 May 2018]. Bedford Lemere photographed the Metropole soon after it opened.

25 Carter 1989, 36.

26 Barker *et al* 2007, 38–40.

27 www.norfolkpubs.co.uk/norfolkc/cromer/crombah.htm [accessed 4 May 2018].

28 Gordon and Inglis 2009, 68–9.

29 NHLE 1025280; www.morecambewintergardens.co.uk [accessed 5 May 2018].

30 Humphreys 1857, 19; Blunt 1976, 86; Kisling 2000, 40–1, 70.

31 www.mybrightonandhove.org.uk/page_id__7688_path__0p115p195p898p.aspx [accessed 4 May 2018].

32 Act of Parliament 32 & 33 Vict. c.88.

33 Anon 1871.

34 Walton 1983, 170–1.

35 Anon 1890, 1043.

36 Hix 1974, 114.

37 *The Times* 2 September 1833, 4.

38 Pearson 2002, 25, 27.

39 NHLE 1236532, 1250850.

40 NHLE 1336672.

41 https://spapavilion.uk/history [accessed 6 May 2018].

42 Pycroft 1876; Pearson 1991, 66.

43 Clements 1992, 125; Mirams 1984, 4.

44 Brodie and Whitfield 2014, 70–1.

45 Gray 1996, 18.

46 Braggs and Harris 2000, 86.

47 http://allincolorforaquarter.blogspot.co.uk/2012/10/a-trip-to-penny-arcade-circa-1907.html?m=1 [accessed 6 May 2018].

48 www.joyland.co.uk/interview.htm [accessed 6 May 2018].

49 Ferry 2016, 20; www.manningsamusements.co.uk [accessed 6 May 2018].

50 Griffiths and Griffiths 1965, 47.

51 Bulley 1956, 151.

52 Kent History and Library Centre R/U127/1.

53 Morrison 2003, 93.

54 Anon 1835, 11.

55 https://buildingourpast.com/2016/04/22/remembering-littlewoods-stores/?iframe=true&theme_preview=true [accessed 6 May 2018].

56 Brodie and Whitfield, 2014, 79.

57 Walton 1992, 34.

58 Gray 1997–2000, 139.

59 www.morellisgelato.com/our-story [accessed 6 May 2018].

60 www.makcaris.com/restaurants/herne-bay-on-the-corner [accessed 6 May 2018]; www.rossiicecream.com/about-us [accessed 6 May 2018].

61 www.nardinis.co.uk [accessed 6 May 2018]. Thanks for the childhood memories created by Aunt Ina, who introduced the author to this architectural gem.

62 Moss 1824, 146.

63 Morrice 2001, 102.

64 Baines 1956, 54.

Chapter 10

1 Schopenhauer 1988, 130.

2 Bread 1859, 5; Hern 1967, 57.

3 Elleray 1987 figure 136.

4 Thompson 2010, 62–4; Rothwell 2009, 81.

5 Hawkins 1991, 100–3.

6 Parry 1983, 173; Thompson 2010, 61–2. A tram had first been lit up in 1897 to mark Queen Victoria's Diamond Jubilee.

7 Thornton 1987, 133–7; Haines 1991, 41–9.

8 This club still exists today and among the most famous recipients of the Winkle is Winston Churchill; http://winkleclub.webs.com [accessed 8 May 2018].

9 Rothwell 2009, 81.

10 Guilmant 1982, plate 141; *Oxford Dictionary of National Biography.*

11 Hawkins 1991, 104.

12 Speaight 1981, 52; *Oxford Dictionary of National Biography.*

13 Croft-Cooke and Cotes 1976, 92.

14 Hawkins 1991, 98–9.

15 Anon 2005, 148–9.

16 Ibid, 155.

17 Parry 1983, 173–4; Walton 1998, 129; Thompson 2010, 65–8.

18 Attwooll 2006, 31.

19 Ibid, 113.

20 Smith 2005, 128–9; https://en.wikipedia.org/wiki/Miss_Great_Britain [accessed 8 May 2018].

21 Guilmant 1982, plate 133.

22 Pinney and Green 1989, 54.

23 Morrison and Minnis 2012, 8; Zuelow 2016, 115.

24 Morrison and Minnis 2012, 9; www.veterancarrun.com [accessed 8 May 2018]; https://en.wikipedia.org/wiki/London_to_Brighton_Veteran_Car_Run [accessed 8 May 2018].

25 https://en.wikipedia.org/wiki/Brooklands [accessed 8 May 2018].

26 Walton 1974, 363; Middleton 1988, 83; Musgrave 2011, 340; https://en.wikipedia.org/wiki/Brighton_Speed_Trials [accessed 8 May 2018].

27 http://rhlactivities.com/events/rhl-beach-race-2016 [accessed 8 May 2018]; www.bxuk.co.uk [accessed 8 May 2018].

28 Guilmant 1982, plate 103; White 1991, 109.

29 Jordan and Jordan 1991, 35.

30 Turnock 1998, 261.

31 Kent History and Library Centre R/U127/1.

32 White 1991, 87.

33 Elleray 1995, plate 76.

34 www.beachweddingsbournemouth.co.uk [accessed 8 May 2018]; www.tunnelsbeaches.co.uk/weddings.html [accessed 8 May 2018].

35 NHLE 1207047, 1209835.

36 Seddon *et al* 2014, 68; Gunnis 1968, 66–8.

37 NHLE 1246057; Archer 2013, 66–7; Cocke and Cocke 2013, 101; Nelson's Column in Trafalgar Square was

constructed in 1840–3 but Nelson's Pillar in Dublin dating from 1808 was blown up in 1966, https://en.wikipedia.org/wiki/Nelson%27s_Pillar [accessed 8 May 2018].

38 Borg 1991, 90–5.

39 A detailed website records all the monuments in Portsmouth to ships: www.memorialsinportsmouth.co.uk/ship-index.htm [accessed 8 May 2018].

40 NHLE 1386963.

41 NHLE 1386972.

42 NHLE 1386990.

43 NHLE 1386939.

44 NHLE 1386938.

45 NHLE 1386988.

46 *Oxford Dictionary of National Biography*.

47 NHLE 1386462; 1386461.

48 Archer 2013, 186; Seddon *et al* 2014, 69.

49 www.ukniwm.org.uk/server/show/conMemorial.17072 [accessed 8 May 2018]; Seddon *et al* 2014, 69; NHLE 1393520.

50 NHLE 1263174; Barnes 2004, 115; Archer 2013, 191–2.

51 Seddon *et al* 2014, 24.

52 Seddon *et al* 2014, 50–1.

53 Borg 1991, 72; Quinlan 2005, xv. The Commonwealth War Graves Commission is responsible for all British and Commonwealth war dead from the period for August 1914 to 31 August 1921 and 3 September 1939 to 31 December 1947.

54 Archer 2013, 195.

55 https://historicengland.org.uk/images-books/publications/iha-war-memorial-parks-gardens [accessed 8 May 2018].

56 Whittick 1946, 44.

57 Thompson 2010, 23–4; Archer 2009, 176, 196–7.

58 Archer 2009, 197.

59 McIntyre 1990, 90.

60 NHLE 1425753.

61 McIntyre 1990, 200–1.

62 NHLE 1280038; http://myweb.tiscali.co.uk/terryleaman/Tiscali/Torquay_War_Memorial.html [accessed 8 May 2018].

63 NHLE 1187556.

64 Archer 2009, 210; Seddon *et al* 2014, 7; www.iwm.org.uk/memorials/item/memorial/2095 [accessed 8 May 2018].

65 NHLE 1386216.

66 Boorman 2005, 130.

67 NHLE 1386975; NHLE 1386464.

68 Boorman 2005, 130; Quinlan 2005, 223.

69 Borg 1991, 88; Archer 2013, 217; Tomlinson 2015, 95; NHLE 1386975; NHLE 1386464.

70 Quinlan 2005, 223.

71 Borg 1991, 88; Boorman 2005, 132; Quinlan 2005, 244; Archer 2013, 217; NHLE 1386975; NHLE 1386464.

72 Boorman 2005, 132; Quinlan 2005, 244; NHLE 1386975.

73 Whittick 1946, 1–3. https://historicengland.org.uk/images-books/publications/iha-war-memorial-parks-gardens [accessed 8 May 2018].

74 Seddon *et al* 2014, 7; NHLE 1393111; www.iwm.org.uk/memorials/item/memorial/2095 [accessed 8 May 2018]; www.iwm.org.uk/memorials/item/memorial/970 [accessed 8 May 2018].

75 NHLE 1425753.

76 www.fleetairarmoa.org/fleet-air-arm-remembrance-memorials [accessed 8 May 2018].

77 NHLE 1393112.

78 www.exercisetigermemorial.co.uk [accessed 8 May 2018].

79 www.iwm.org.uk/memorials/item/memorial/57771 [accessed 8 May 2018].

80 Smith 1992, 76; Tomlinson 2015, 111; www.cwgc.org/find-a-cemetery/cemetery/2106300/LEE-ON-SOLENT%20MEMORIAL [accessed 8 May 2018].

81 www.roll-of-honour.com/Norfolk/NorfolkCoastalMineClearance.html [accessed 8 May 2018]; www.racns.co.uk/sculptures.asp?action=getsurvey&id=562 [accessed 8 May 2018]; Quinlan 2005, 178.

82 www.eastbourneherald.co.uk/news/new-war-memorial-for-eastbourne-approved-1-7340308 [accessed 8 May 2018]; www.wishtower.org.uk/history [accessed 8 May 2018].

83 NHLE 1425753.

84 Boorman 2005, 234; Archer 2013, 227; Tomlinson 2015,116–7.

85 NHLE 1281319; NHLE 1344165.

86 www.telsociety.org.uk/places-to-visit/bridlington [accessed 8 May 2018].

87 Warren 1978, 50–1; Davies 1989, 89; Morris *et al* 2000, 58; NHLE 1025403.

88 Archer 2013, 110; www.vivienmallock.co.uk/young-soldier-of-wwii [accessed 8 May 2018].

89 Malster and Stibbons 1979, 7, 17; Cocke and Cocke 2013, 87.

90 Smith 1992, 69.

91 NHLE 1153297.

92 Archer 2013, 53; NHLE 1187555.

93 Seddon *et al* 2014, 74.

94 Ibid, 51–2.

95 Ibid, 53.

96 www.pmsa.org.uk/pmsa-database/12296 [accessed 9 May 2018].

97 Smith 1992, 43.

98 www.sustrans.org.uk/ncn/map/national-cycle-network/art-network/explore-portrait-benches [accessed 9 May 2018].

99 www.grahamibbeson.com/mobile/#page3 [accessed 26 April 2017]; Pearson 2006, 50; Archer 2013, 172.

100 Seddon *et al* 2014, 52–3; www.eastbournebandstand.co.uk/about/titanic [accessed 9 May 2018].

101 Whyman 1990, 53.

102 Cocke and Cocke 2013, 188. The memorial was unveiled again in September 2003, having been stolen in February that year.

103 NHLE 1085006.

104 NHLE 1304394.

105 NHLE 1279837; NHLE 1250676.

106 Cocke and Cocke 2013, 246–7.

107 NHLE 1043623.

108 NHLE 1387189; www.memorialsinportsmouth.co.uk/southsea/emanuel.htm [accessed 9 May 2018].

109 NHLE 1034301.

110 NHLE 1393959.

111 Brodie, Sargent and Winter 2005, 53.

112 Cocke and Cocke 2013, 227.

113 McInnes 2014.

114 Cocke and Cocke 2013, 98.

115 Seddon *et al* 2014, 175.

116 English Heritage 2000.

117 Ibid, 20, 22.

118 Morris and Roberts 2012, 207–8.

119 Pearson 2006, 66.

120 Cocke and Cocke 2013, 188–9.

121 Seddon *et al* 2014, 21.

122 Ibid, 23.

123 Morris *et al* 2000, 172; Pearson 2006, 43.

124 Morris and Roberts 2012, 99–103; Archer 2013, 372–3; https://en.wikipedia.org/wiki/Another_Place_%28sculpture%29 [accessed 9 May 2018].

125 Seddon *et al* 2014, 95.

126 www.landscapeinstitute.org/PDF/Contribute/SplashPointstageonebrief.pdf [accessed 21 May 2018]; http://webarchive.nationalarchives.gov.uk/20110118095356/http://www.cabe.org.uk/sea-change/wave-two [accessed 21 May 2018].

127 https://en.wikipedia.org/wiki/Russell-Cotes_Art_Gallery_%26_Museum [accessed 21 May 2018]; NHLE 1108857.

128 The Gallery closed for 18 months in 2015–17 for a major refurbishment and the creation of new gallery space. www.tate.org.uk/visit/tate-st-ives [accessed 8 May 2018].

129 Barker *et al* 2014, 2–3.

130 https://en.wikipedia.org/wiki/Jerwood_Gallery [accessed 8 May 2018].

131 http://eastbeachcafe.co.uk [accessed 8 May 2018].

132 www.theguardian.com/artanddesign/2007/jun/10/architecture.communities [accessed 8 May 2018].

133 www.folkestonetriennial.org.uk/about-the-folkestone-triennial [accessed 9 May 2018].

134 https://en.wikipedia.org/wiki/Dismaland [accessed 9 May 2018].

135 http://news.bbc.co.uk/1/hi/entertainment/2127259.stm [accessed 9 May 2018]; www.telegraph.co.uk/news/uknews/1401411/Chaos-as-250000-swamp-Fatboy-Slim-beach-party.html [accessed 9 May 2018].

Chapter 11

1   www.wired-gov.net/wg/wg-news-1.nsf/0/
    254006D970EF002D80257421002100F4?
    OpenDocument [accessed 9 May 2018];
    www.gov.uk/government/collections/coastal
    -communities-fund [accessed 9 May 2018].

2   https://en.wikipedia.org/wiki/List_of_
    offshore_wind_farms [accessed 9 May
    2018].

3   https://historicengland.org.uk/advice/
    planning/infrastructure/renewable-energy/
    wind-energy [accessed 9 May 2018].

4   www.londonarray.com/the-project-3/
    phase-2 [accessed 9 May 2018].

5   National Parks Commission 1967.

6   www.ipcc.ch/report/ar5/wg1 [accessed
    9 May 2018] – IPCC Climate Change
    2013, the Physical Science Basis final
    report (policy maker summary), 3.

7   www.ipcc.ch/report/ar5/wg1 [accessed
    9 May 2018] – IPCC Climate Change
    2013, the Physical Science Basis final
    report (policy maker summary), 7, 9.

8   Nicholls *et al* 2011.

9   http://ukclimateprojections.metoffice.gov.
    uk/22530 [accessed 9 May 2018] –
    UK Climate Projections, Briefing report
    December 2010, 5–6.

10 http://ukclimateprojections.metoffice.gov.
    uk/22530 [accessed 9 May 2018] –
    UK Climate Projections, Briefing report
    December 2010, 8, 50.

11 www.gov.uk/government/publications/
    national-flood-and-coastal-erosion-risk-
    management-strategy-for-england
    [accessed 9 May 2018] – *Understanding
    the risks, empowering communities,
    building resilience: the national flood and
    coastal erosion risk management strategy
    for England*. Session: 2010–12, Laid
    before Parliament 23/05/11, 10.

12 www.gov.uk/government/uploads/
    system/uploads/attachment_data/
    file/292931/geho0610bsue-e-e.pdf
    [accessed 9 May 2018] – Environment
    Agency, *The coastal handbook* June 2010,
    18, 30.

13 www.gov.uk/government/uploads/
    system/uploads/attachment_data/
    file/7771/1499049.pdf [accessed 9 May
    2018] – Planning Policy Statement 25
    Supplement: Development and Coastal
    Change March 2010, 10.

14 Ministry of Agriculture, Fisheries and
    Food 1995.

15 Murphy 2009, 185–6; Reeve, Chadwick
    and Fleming 2012, 12.

16 www.gov.uk/government/uploads/
    system/uploads/attachment_data/
    file/69206/pb11726-smpg-vol1-060308.
    pdf 13 [accessed 9 May 2018].

17 NHLE 1269716, 1072606.

18 www.nao.org.uk/wp-content/
    uploads/2011/10/10121521.pdf
    [accessed 9 May 2018], 13.

19 www.gov.uk/government/uploads/
    system/uploads/attachment_data/
    file/389789/fcerm-investment-
    plan-201412.pdf [accessed 9 May 2018]
    – Reducing the risks of flooding and
    coastal erosion – An investment plan.

20 Eddison 1988, 162–3; Eddison 1995, 164;
    Eddison 2000, 137.

21 Information plaque on the sea wall.

22 *Civil Engineer* 29 May 2008.

23 Information plaque on the sea wall.

24 www.dover.gov.uk/Environment/Coast--
    Rivers/Coast-Protection/Deals-Secondary-
    Sea-Defences.aspx [accessed 9 May 2018].

25 http://webcache.googleusercontent.com/
    search?q=cache:DwiXrxiv9tsJ:randd.defra.
    gov.uk/Document.aspx%3FDocument%3D
    CaseStudy10BournemouthPooleSwan_
    BeachRep-FD2635.pdf+&cd=5&hl=en&
    ct=clnk&gl=uk [accessed 9 May 2018].

26 Rendel, Palmer and Tritton 1996, 255.

27 Ibid, 255–6.

28 www.bbc.co.uk/news/uk-england-
    dorset-28898711 [accessed 9 May 2018];
    www.dorsetforyou.com/article/340944/
    Phase-IV---multi-million-coast-work
    [accessed 9 May 2018].

Bibliography

Adams, Anthony and Leach, Robert 1978 *The World of Punch & Judy*. London: Harrap

Adamson, S H 1977 *Seaside Piers*. London: Batsford

Aillagon, Jean-Jacques *et al* 2015 *Promenade des Anglais*. Paris: Lienart

Allen, Richard T L (ed) 1998 'The coastal environment'. *Concrete in Coastal Structures*. London: Thomas Telford

Alsop, W 1832 *A Concise History of Southport, etc*. Southport: William Alsop

Anderson, Janice and Swinglehurst, Edmund 1978 *The Victorian and Edwardian Seaside*. London: Country Life Books

Anderson, John 1795 *A Practical Essay on the Good and Bad Effects of Sea-water and Sea-bathing*. London: C Dilly, etc

Anon nd (1) *Dunwich*. Lowestoft: Powell & Co

Anon nd (2) *Scarborough: The Undercliff Study*. Scarborough: Scarborough House Detectives Group, part 1

Anon 1732 *The Scarborough Miscellany for the Year 1732*. London: J Wilford

Anon 1733 *The Scarborough Miscellany for the Year 1733*. London: J Wilford

Anon 1734 (1) *A Journey from London to Scarborough, in several letters*. London: Caesar Ward and Richard Chandler

Anon 1734 (2) *The Scarborough Miscellany for the Year 1734*. London: J Wilford

Anon 1765 *A Description of the Isle of Thanet, and Particularly of the Town of Margate*. London: J Newbery and W Bristow

Anon 1770 (1) *The Margate Guide. Containing a Particular Account of Margate, ... to which is prefix'd, a short description of the Isle of Thanet ... Illustrated with a map of the Isle of Thanet, etc*. London

Anon 1770 (2) *The New Brighthelmstone Directory: or, Sketches in Miniature of the British Shore*. London: T Durham

Anon 1780 *A Description of Brighthelmston and the Adjacent Country*. London: J Bowen

Anon 1785 *The Weymouth Guide*. Weymouth

Anon 1797 (1) *A New Weymouth Guide, etc*. Dorchester

Anon 1797 (2) *The Margate Guide, a Descriptive Poem, with ... notes. Also a general account of Ramsgate, Broadstairs, &c. By an Inhabitant*. Margate

Anon 1797 (3) *The Hastings Guide ...* Hastings: J Barry

Anon 1800 *A Companion to the Watering and Bathing Places of England ...* London: HD Symonds

Anon 1806 *An Historical Guide to Great Yarmouth, in Norfolk*. Yarmouth

Anon 1809 *Picture of Margate, being a guide to all persons visiting Margate, Ramsgate, and Broadstairs*. London

Anon 1810 *A Guide to all the Watering and Sea Bathing Places, with a Description of the Lakes; a Sketch of a Tour in Wales, and Itineraries ...* London

Anon 1817 *An Historical Guide to Great Yarmouth*. Great Yarmouth

Anon 1822 (1) *The Thanet Itinerary*. Margate

Anon 1822 (2) *A Guide to Weston Super Mare, Somersetshire*. Bristol: J Chilcott

Anon 1825 *Prospectus Bognor New Town Company*. London: Whiting in British Library

Anon 1835 *A Picture of the New Town of Herne Bay, its Beauties, History, and the Curiosities in its Vicinity, including some Particulars of the Roman Town called Reculver*. London: John Macrone

Anon 1837 *Historical and Descriptive Account of the Town and Borough of Christchurch; Comprehending a Guide to the Watering Places of Mudford and Bournemouth, etc*. Christchurch: C Tucker & Son

Anon 1838 *The Bognor Guide, Containing the History of Bognor, and the History and Antiquities of Several Adjoining Parishes, including an Account of Goodwood, Arundel Castle, etc., etc., and the Roman Remains at Bignor*. Petworth: John Phillips

Anon 1843 *The Guide to Hayling Island*. Hayling

Anon 1844 *The Stranger's Guide in Brighton; Being a Complete Companion to that Fashionable Place, and the Rides and Drives in its Vicinity*. Brighton: W Saunders

Anon 1845 *The Tourist's and Visitor's Hand-book to Sidmouth and its Neighbourhood, etc*. London

Anon 1850 *The Visitor's New Guide ... to the Isle of Thanet, etc*. Margate

Anon 1851 *A Day's Ramble about Dover Castle*. Dover: W Brett

Anon 1858 *The Guide to Great Yarmouth*. Great Yarmouth: Louis A Meall

Anon 1861 *A Guide to Dover, Ancient and Modern*. Dover

Anon 1865 *All about Margate and Herne Bay ... With ... Frontispiece, Map of the Isle of Thanet, and Forty Engravings*. London

Anon 1871 Life Beneath the Waves, and a Description of the Brighton Aquarium. London

Anon 1890 *History, Topography, and Directory of North Yorkshire*. Preston: T Bulmer & Co

Anon *c* 1895 *Particulars of Beach Rocks Sea-Side Convalescent Home, Sandgate, Kent*. London: London Samaritan Society and Homerton Mission

Anon 1899 *The Alhambra, Blackpool. Erected 1898–1899*. Blackpool

Anon 1899–1900 *Guide to Margate (1899–1900)*. London: Ward, Lock & Co

Anon 1906 *Official Guide to Morecambe*. Morecambe

Anon 1909 Blackpool Aviation Week. October 18th to 23rd, 1909, *etc*. Official Programme-souvenir. Manchester: John Heywood

Anon 1926 (1) *Blackpool's Progress*. Blackpool: Blackpool Borough Council

Anon 1926 (2) *By Loch, Mountain and Sea. Holiday and Health Resorts Guide (Holidays by L.M.S.), etc*. London: London Midland and Scottish Railway Company

Anon 1929 Miners' Welfare Fund Seventh Report of the Committee Appointed by the Board of Trade to Allocate the Fund, together with the Second Report of the Selection Committee Appointed to Administer the Miners' Welfare National Scholarship Scheme, 1928. London

Anon 1935 'Embassy Court, Brighton'. *The Architectural Review*, **LXXVIII**, November, 167–73

Anon 1938 (1) 'Folkestone and its foreshore'. *The Architectural Review*, **LXXXIII**, January, 15–26

Anon 1938 (2) 'Leisure as an architectural problem'. *The Architectural Review*, **LXXXIV** December, 231–310

Anon 1938–9 'Communal mothercraft'. *Mother and Child*, IX, 347–52

Anon 1977 *Bass, Ratcliff & Gretton Limited Excursion to Scarborough*. Burton upon Trent

Anon 2000 *Filey Sea Wall: A Souvenir 19th June 1894*. Driffield: B Fawcett & Co; Filey: K Clegg

Anon 2003 'Beach house', *The Picturesque*, No 44, Autumn 2003, 11–13

Anon 2005 *Images of Blackpool*. Derby: Breedon Books Publishing Company

Antram, Nicholas and Morrice, Richard 2008 *Brighton and Hove*. New Haven and London: Yale University Press

Archer, Geoff 2009 *The Glorious Dead: Figurative Sculpture of British First World War Memorials*. Kirstead: Frontier Publishing

Archer, Geoff 2013 *Public Sculpture in Britain: A History*. Norwich: Frontier Publishing

Attwooll, Maureen 2006 *The Bumper Book of Weymouth*. Tiverton: Halsgrove

Attwooll, Maureen and Herbert, Graham 2002 *Weymouth More Golden Years: A Companion Volume to Weymouth: The Golden Years*. Tiverton: Dorset Books

Awsiter, John 1768 *Thoughts on Brightelmston. Concerning Sea-bathing, and Drinking Sea-water. With some Directions for their Use. In a Letter to a Friend*. London: J Wilkie

Bailey, F A 1955 *A History of Southport*. Southport: A Downie

Baines, Edward 1824 *History, Directory, and Gazetteer of the County Palatine of Lancaster*, **1–2**. Liverpool: William Wales

Baines, J M 1956 *Burton's St Leonards*. Hastings: Hastings Museum

Baines, J M 1986 *Historic Hastings*. St Leonards-on-Sea: Cinque Port

Baines, J M 1990 *Burton St. Leonards*. Hastings: Hastings Museum

Balducci, Valter 2005 *Architetture per le Colonie di Vacanza*. Florence: Esperienze Europeen

Barber, C and Barber S 1993 *Around & About Teignmouth and Shaldon*. Pinhoe: Obelisk

Barker, Nigel *et al* 2007 *Margate's Seaside Heritage*. Swindon: English Heritage

Barker, William Goodyer 1860 *On the Climate of Worthing: Its Remedial Influence in Disease, Especially of the Lungs*. London: John Churchill

Barnes, Richard 2004 *The Obelisk: A Monumental Feature in Britain*. Kirstead: Frontier Publishing

Barrett, Charlotte (ed) 1892 *Diary and Letters of Madame D'Arblay*, **1–7** (III). London: Henry Colburn Bennett

Barson, Susie 2010 'Hastings Promenade, Hastings, East Sussex'. Unpublished Architectural Investigation Report

Batcheller, W 1828 *New History of Dover Castle, During the Roman, Saxon, and Norman Governments; Compiled from Ancient Records, and Continued to the Present Time*. Dover: W Batcheller

Baynard, Edward 1731 *Health A Poem. Shewing How to Procure, Preserve, and Restore it*. London

Belisario, John C 1959 *Cancer of the Skin*. London: Butterworth & Co

Bennett, David 1998 *Roller Coaster*. London: Book Sales Inc

Bennett, Peter 1996 *A Century of Fun*. Blackpool: Blackpool Pleasure Beach

Bennett, S and Bennett, N (eds) 1993 *An Historical Atlas of Lincolnshire*. Hull: The University of Hull Press

Berg, Torsten and Berg, Peter 2001 *RR Angerstein's Illustrated Travel Diary, 1753–1755: Industry in England and Wales from Swedish Perspective*. London: Science Museum

Berry, Sue 2002 'Myth and reality in the representation of resorts; Brighton and the emergence of the "prince and village" myth 1770–1824'. *Sussex Archaeological Collections* **140**, 97–112

Berry, Sue 2005 *Georgian Brighton*. Chichester: Phillimore & Co Ltd

Berry, Sue 2009 'Thomas Read Kemp and the shaping of regency Brighton c.1818 – 1845'. *The Georgian Group Journal* **XVII**, 125–40

Berry, Sue 2015 'A resort town transformed c.1815–1840'. *The Georgian Group Journal* **XXIII**, 213–30

Betjeman, John and Gray, JS 1972 *Victorian and Edwardian Brighton from Old Photographs*. London: BT Batsford Ltd

Bica, Smaranda Maria and Balducci, Valter (eds) 2007 *Architecture and Society of the Holiday Camps: History and Perspectives*. Timisoara: Editura Orizonturi Universitare

Biddle, G 1990 *The Railway Surveyors: The Story of Railway Property Management 1800–1990*. London: Ian Allan

Binns, Jack 2003 *The History of Scarborough*. Pickering: Blackthorn Press

Bird, Sheila 2001 *Sidmouth, Budleigh Salterton & District Companion*. Falmouth

Bishop, J G 1880 *A Peep into the Past: Brighton in the Olden Time*. Brighton: JG Bishop

Blunt, Wilfred 1976 *The Ark in the Park: The Zoo in the Nineteenth Century*. London: Hamilton, Tryon Gallery

Boddy, M and West, J 1983 *Weymouth An Illustrated History*. Wimborne

Boorman, Derek 2005 *A Century of Remembrance: One Hundred Outstanding British War Memorials*. Barnsley: Pen & Sword Military

Borg, Alan 1991 *War Memorials: From Antiquity to the Present*. London: Leo Cooper

Borsay, Peter 2011 'From port to resort: Tenby and the narratives of transition' *in* P Borsay and J Walton (eds), *Resorts and Ports: European Seaside Towns since 1700*. Bristol: Channel View Publications 86–112

Braggs, Steven and Harris, Diane 2000 *Sun, Fun and Crowds: Seaside Holidays Between the Wars*. Stroud: Tempus

Brannon, Philip 1867 *The Illustrated Historical and Picturesque Guide to Bournemouth and the Surrounding Scenery*. London: Longman & Co

Bread, Owen 1859 *Bread's New Guide and Hand-Book to Worthing and its Vicinity*. Worthing: Owen Bread

Bridgeman, H and Drury, E 1977 *Beside the Seaside: A Picture Postcard Album*. London: Elm Tree Books

Brodie, Allan 2012 (1) 'Liverpool and the origins of the seaside resort'. *The Georgian Group Journal* **XX**, 63–76

Brodie, Allan 2012 (2) 'Scarborough in the 1730s: spa, sea and sex'. *Journal of Tourism History* **4**(2), 125–53

Brodie, Allan, Roethe, Johanna and Hudson-McAulay, Kate 2019 *Weston-super-Mare: the town and its seaside heritage*. Swindon: Historic England

Brodie, Allan, Sargent, Andrew and Winter, Gary 2005 *Seaside Holidays in the Past*. London: English Heritage

Brodie, Allan and Whitfield, Matthew 2014, *Blackpool's Seaside Heritage*. Swindon: English Heritage

Brodie, Allan and Winter, Gary 2007 *England's Seaside Resorts*. Swindon: English Heritage

Brodie, Allan *et al* 2008 *Weymouth's Seaside Heritage*. Swindon: English Heritage

Brown B J H and Loosley, J 1985 *Yesterday's Town: Weston-Super-Mare.* Buckingham: Barracuda

Bruyn Andrews, C (ed) 1934–5 *The Torrington Diaries 1781–1794,* **1–4**. London, Eyre & Spottiswoode

Bulley, J A 1956 'Teignmouth as a seaside resort'. *Reports and Transactions of the Devon Association,* **LXXXVIII**, 143–62

Butler, Charles 1984 *The Bognor Estate of Sir Richard Hotham MP.* Bognor

Butler, H E 1937 *The Autobiography of Giraldus Cambrensis.* London: Jonathan Cape

Butler, R W 1980 'The concept of a tourist area cycle of evolution: implications for management of resources'. *Canadian Geographer* **24** (1), 5–12

Butt, R V J 1995 *The Directory of Railway Stations.* Sparkford: PSL Ltd

Byrom, M 1972 *Punch and Judy: Its Origin and Evolution.* Aberdeen: Shiva Publications

Camden, William 1806 *Britannia.* London: John Stockdale

Carey, George Saville 1799 *The Balnea, or, An Impartial Description of all the Popular Watering Places in England …* London: W West

Carter, O 1989 *An Illustrated History of British Railway Hotels, 1838–1983.* St Michael's: Silver Link

Cartwright, J J, (ed) 1888–9 *The Travels Through England of Dr Richard Pococke,* **1–11**. London: Camden Society

Charlton, L 1779 *The History of Whitby, and of Whitby Abbey, etc.* York: A Ward

Clark, James 1820 *Medical Notes on Climate, Diseases, Hospitals, and Medical Schools, in France, Italy, and Switzerland; comprising an inquiry into the effects of a residence in the South of Europe, in cases of pulmonary consumption, etc.* London: T & G Underwood

Clark, James 1829 *The Influence of Climate in the Prevention and Cure of Chronic Diseases, more particularly of the chest and digestive organs …* London: T & G Underwood

Clark, James 1830 *The Influence of Climate in the Prevention and Cure of Chronic Diseases, more particularly of the chest and digestive organs …* London: T & G Underwood

Clarke, Allen 1923 *The Story of Blackpool.* London: Palatine Books

Clarke, G E 1975 *Historic Margate.* Margate: Margate Public Libraries

Clarke, W B 1836 *The Guide to Hayling.* Hayling

Cleland, James 1816 *Annals of Glasgow.* Glasgow: James Hedderwick

Clements, R 1992 *Margate in Old Photographs.* Stroud: Alan Sutton

Cocke, Richard and Cocke, Sarah 2013 *Public Sculpture of Norfolk and Suffolk.* Liverpool: Liverpool University Press

Cockney, A 1823 'A week's journal at Margate'. *The Mirror* 373–5

Cole, John 1828 *The History and Antiquities of Filey in the County of York.* Scarborough: John Cole

Colvin, H M 1995 *A Biographical Dictionary of British Architects, 1600–1840.* New Haven and London: Yale University Press for the Paul Mellon Centre for Studies in British Art

Colvin, Howard 2008 *A Biographical Dictionary of British Architects, 1600–1840.* New Haven and London: Yale University Press for the Paul Mellon Centre for Studies in British Art

Conway, Hazel 1991 *People's Parks: The Design and Development of Victorian Parks in Britain.* Cambridge: Cambridge University Press

Conway, Hazel 1996 *Public Parks.* Princes Risborough: Shire Publications Ltd

Corbin, Alain 1995 *The Lure of the Sea: The Discovery of the Seaside 1750–1840.* London: Penguin Books

Cossons, Neil 1987 *The BP Book of Industrial Archaeology.* Newton Abbot: David & Charles

Coulson, R L H 1984 *A Chronology of Herne Bay to 1913.* Herne Bay: Kent County Council

Cozens, Z 1793 *A Tour Through the Isle of Thanet, and some other parts of East Kent, etc.* London

Croft-Cooke, Rupert and Cotes, Peter 1976 *Circus: A World History.* London: Elek

Crowe, Ken 2003 *Kursaal Memories: A History of Southend's Amusement Park.* St Albans: Skelter Publishing

Cunningham, Hugh 1980 *Leisure in the Industrial Revolution.* New York: St Martin's Press

Dale, Anthony 1967 *Fashionable Brighton 1820–1860.* Newcastle upon Tyne: Oriel Press

Davies, Philip 1989 *Troughs and Drinking Fountains.* London: Chatto & Windus

Defoe, Daniel 2008 *Robinson Crusoe.* Richmond: Oneworld Classics

Denton, Tony and Leach, Nicholas 2007 *Lighthouses of England and Wales.* Ashbourne: Landmark Publishing

Design Council, 1974/75 *Street Furniture from Design Index.* London: Design Council

Dickens, Charles 1836 'The Tuggses at Ramsgate': Sketches by Boz Illustrative of Every-day Life and Every-day People, Chapter IV. www.gutenberg.org/files/882/882-0.txt [accessed 10 May 2018]

Diplock W nd (1), *Diplock's New Guide to Hastings, St Leonards and the Neighbourhood.* Hastings

Diplock, W nd (2) *The Hastings Guide.* Hastings

Dobraszczyk, Paul 2014 *Iron, Ornament and Architecture in Victorian Britain.* Farnham: Ashgate

Docwra Parry, John 1833 *An Historical and Descriptive Account of the Coasts of Sussex, Brighton, Eastbourn, Hastings, St Leonards, Rye Chichester and Tonbridge Wells, forming also a guide to all the watering places, etc.* Brighton

Dunn, Tim 2014 'Top Models'. *C20 Magazine* **3**, 30–5

Durie, Alastair J 2003 *Scotland for the Holidays: A History of Tourism in Scotland, 1780–1939.* East Linton: Tuckwell Press

Easdown, Martin 2007 *Piers of Kent.* Stroud: Tempus

Easdown, Martin 2009 *Lancashire's Seaside Piers.* Barnsley: Wharncliffe Books

Eddison, Jill 1988 *Romney Marsh Evolution, Occupation, Reclamation.* Oxford University Committee for Archaeology Monograph 24

Eddison, Jill 1995 *Romney Marsh: The Debatable Ground.* Oxford University Committee for Archaeology Monograph 41

Eddison, Jill 2000 *Romney Marsh: Survival on a Frontier.* Stroud: Tempus

Ekberg, C 1986 *The Book of Cleethorpes.* Buckingham: Barracuda

Elleray, D Robert 1987 *Brighton: A Pictorial History.* Chichester: Phillimore

Elleray, D Robert 1995 *Eastbourne: A Pictorial History.* Chichester: Phillimore

Ellis, G A 1829 *The History and Antiquities of the Borough and Town of Weymouth and Melcombe Regis.* Weymouth

Emery, Andrew 2008 *A History of Bournemouth Seafront.* Stroud: Tempus

English Heritage 2000 *A User's Guide to Sculpture.* Swindon: English Heritage

Evans, J 1821 *Recreation for the Young and the Old: An Excursion to Brighton, with an Account of the Royal Pavilion, a Visit to Tunbridge Wells, and Southend in a series of letters, etc.* Chiswick

Evans, Nick 2009 *Dreamland Remembered.* Whitstable: Bygone Publishing

Everard, C 1980 'On sea-level changes' *in* FH Thompson (ed) *Archaeology and Coastal Change.* London: Society of Antiquaries of London occasional papers; new series, **1** (15), 1–23

Farrant, Sue 1980 *Georgian Brighton 1740–1820*. Brighton: Centre for Continuing Education, University of Sussex

Ferns, J L 1983 'Electricity supply and industrial archaeology.' *Journal of Industrial Archaeology*, **17**, 10–18

Ferry, Kathryn 2009 *Beach Huts and Bathing Machines*. Oxford: Shire

Ferry, Kathryn 2016 *The Nation's Host: Butlin's and the Story of the British Seaside*. London: Viking

Fielding, Andrew and Fielding, Annelise 2006 *The Salt Industry*. Princes Risborough: Shire Books

Fischer, Richard and Walton, John K 1987 *British Piers*. London: Thames and Hudson

Fisher, Michael H (ed) 1997 *The Travels of Dean Mahomet: An Eighteenth-Century Journey Through India*. Berkeley and London: University of California Press

Floyer, John 1702 *The Ancient Ψυχρολουσια [Psykhrolysia] Revived: Or, an Essay to Prove Cold Bathing both Safe and Useful*. London: S Smith and B Walford

Foote Wood, C 2008 *Walking over the Waves*. Dunbeath: Whittles Publishing

Freeling, A 1839 *Picturesque Excursions: Containing Upwards of Four Hundred Views, at and near Places of Popular Resort, etc.* London

Freeman, Sarah 2015 *Beside the Sea: Britain's Lost Seaside Heritage*. London: Aurum Press

Fry, William 1826–9 *Excursions*. Leicester University Library MS 149

Gale, Alison 2000 *Britain's Historic Coast*. Stroud: Tempus Publishing Ltd

Garner, Philippe 2003 *A Seaside Album: Photographs and Memory*. London: Philip Wilson

Gill, Crispin 1993 *Plymouth: A New History*. Tiverton: Devon Books

Glazebrook, T K 1826 *A Guide to Southport, North Meols in the County of Lancaster: with an Account of the Places in the Immediate Neighbourhood*. London

Goate, Edward 1994 'The old switchback and the Hotchkiss bicycle railway'. *Yarmouth Archaeology* 17–19

Goodwin, John E 1988 'Fortification against a French invasion of the East Kent coast of England: 1750–1815', *Fort*. **16**, 83–96

Gordon, Ian and Inglis, Simon 2009 *Great Lengths*. Swindon: English Heritage

Gordon, Samuel 1869 *The Watering Places of Cleveland: Being Descriptions of these and Other Attractive Localities in that Interesting District of Yorkshire*. Stockton

Gosse, Philip Henry 1853 *A Naturalist's Rambles on the Devonshire Coast*. London

Gosse, Philip Henry 1856 *Tenby: A Sea-side Holiday*. London: Van Voorst

Gosse, Philip Henry and Gosse, Emily 1853 *Sea-Side Pleasures*. London: SPCK

Gough, Harold 1983 *A Picture Book of Old Herne Bay*. Rainham: Meresborough

Grandfield, Yvette 1989 'The Holiday Diary of Thomas Lott; 12–22 July, 1815' *Archaeologia Cantiana*. **CVII**, 63–82

Granville, Augustus Bozzi 1841 *The Spas of England and Principal Sea-bathing Places*, **1–2**. London: Henry Colburn

Gray, R 1996 *Cinemas in Britain: One Hundred Years of Cinema Architecture*. London: Lund Humphries

Gray, Todd (ed) 1997–2000 *Travels in Georgian Devon: The Illustrated Journals of the Reverend John Swete, 1789–1800*, **1–4**. Exeter: Devon Books

Griffiths, Gordon 2001 *History of Teignmouth*. Bradford on Avon:ELPS

Griffiths, Gordon Douglas and Griffiths, Edith Grace Chalmers 1965 *History of Teignmouth*. Teignmouth: Brunswick Press

Guilmant, Aylwin 1982 *Bexhill-on-Sea: A Pictorial History*. Chichester: Phillimore

Gunnis, Rupert 1968 *Dictionary of British Sculptors 1660–1851*. London: The Abbey Library

H, Mr 1757 *A Journal of Eight Days Journey from Portsmouth to Kingston upon Thames ...* London

Hague, Douglas B and Christie, Rosemary 1975 *Lighthouses: Their Architecture, History and Archaeology*. Llandysul: Gomer Press

Haines, P 1991 *Hastings in Old Photographs: A Second Selection*. Gloucester: Sutton

Hall, Christopher 2001 'Domestic Architecture in Medieval Scarborough' in David Crouch and Trevor Pearson (eds) *Medieval Scarborough: Studies in Trade and Civic Life*. Yorkshire Archaeological Society Occasional Paper, **1**, 95–104

Hall, J 1790 *New Margate and Ramsgate Guide ... : And a General Account of the Isle of Thanet*. Ramsgate

Hannavy, John 2009 *The Victorians and Edwardians at Play*. Oxford: Shire Publications

Hardy, D and Ward, C 1984 *Arcadia for All: The Legacy of a Makeshift Landscape*. London: Mansell

Harrington, Peter 2007 *The Castles of Henry VIII*. Oxford: Osprey

Hart, H W 1981 'A transport curiosity. Walter Fagg's broad-gauge line. Notes concerning a Folkestone innovation'. *The Journal of Transport History*, 3 ser **2** (1), March, 69–74

Hassan, John 2003 *The Seaside, Health and the Environment in England and Wales since 1800*. Aldershot: Ashgate

Hawkins, John 1991 *Herne Bay in Old Photographs*. Stroud: Alan Sutton

Hay, A 1794 *The Chichester Guide: Containing, an Account of the antient and present state of the City of Chichester and its neighbourhood, etc.* Chichester: J Seagrave

Hayman, Steve 2010 'Re-building East Anglia's Beaches', *in* William Allsop (ed), *Coasts, Marine Structures and Breakwaters*. London: Thomas Telford, **1**, 602–13

Hayter, Alicia 2002 *The Wreck of the Abergavenny*. London: Macmillan

Hegarty, Cain and Newsome, Sarah 2007 *Suffolk's Defended Shore: Coastal Fortifications from the Air*. Swindon: English Heritage

Heller, Genevieve 1990 'Leysin et son passé médical'. *Gesnerus* 47, part 3/4, 329–44

Hembry, Phyllis 1990 *The English Spa 1560–1815: A Social History*. London: The Athlone Press

Henstock, A (ed) 1980 *The Diary of Abigail Gawthern of Nottingham 1751–1810*. Nottingham: Thoroton Society

Herbert, Graham and Attwooll, Maureen 2003 *Weymouth More Golden Years: A Companion Volume to Weymouth: The Golden Years*. Exeter: Dorset Books

Hern, A 1967 *The Seaside Holiday: The History of the English Seaside Resort*. London: Cresset Press

Hinderwell, Thomas 1811 *History and Antiquities of Scarborough*. York: Thomas Wilson

Hix, John 1974 *The Glass House*. London: Phaidon

Hogg, Ian V 1974 *Coast Defences of England and Wales 1856–1956*. Newton Abbot: David & Charles

Hollebone, Ashley 2012 *The Hovercraft: A History*. Stroud: The History Press

Hooke, Janet (ed) 1998 *Coastal Defence and Earth Science Conservation*. Bath: The Geological Society

Horn, Pamela 1999 *Pleasures and Pastimes in Victorian Britain*. Stroud: Sutton

Hornby, Hugh 2015 *Bowled Over*. Swindon: Historic England

Hoyle, J W and King, G T 1961 (1) 'Features of the coastline'. *The Surveyor and Municipal and County Engineer* 19–22

Hoyle, J W and King, G T 1961 (2) 'Coast protection – groynes'. *Journal of the Institute of Municipal Engineers* 1–9

Humphreys, H Noel 1857 *Ocean Gardens: The History of the Marine Aquarium, and the Best Methods … for its Establishment and Preservation*. London

Hunter, M 1998 'The First Seaside House?', *The Georgian Group Journal* **VIII**, 135–42

Hutchins, John 1774 *The History and Antiquities of the County of Dorset*. London: W Bowyer and J Nichols

Hutchinson, G 1994 *Martello Towers: A Brief History*. Rye: G Hutchinson

Hutton, William 1789 *A Description of Blackpool in Lancashire: Frequented for Sea Bathing*. Birmingham: Pearson and Rollason

Ison, Walter 1991 *The Georgian Buildings of Bath*. Bath: Kingsmead Press

Jackson, A A 1993 *Volk's Railways, Brighton: An Illustrated History*. Brighton: Plateway Press

Jackson, Derrick 1975 *Lighthouses of England and Wales*. Newton Abbot: David & Charles

Jackson, Eliza 1885 *Jackson's Illustrated Guide to Cleethorpes*. Grimsby: E Jackson

Joad, C E M (ed) 1957 *The English Counties*. London: Odhams Press

Johnson, Maurice 1739–41 'An account of an earthquake at Scarborough, on Dec. 29. 1737'. *Philosophical Transactions*, **41**, 804–6

Johnson, Peter *c* 1986 *The Trams in Blackpool*. Leicester: AB Publishing

Jones, Samuel 1718 *Whitby, A Poem*. York: Tho Hammond Junior

Jordan, Arthur and Jordan, Elisabeth 1991 *Away for the Day: The Railway Excursion in Britain, 1830 to the Present Day*. Kettering: Silver Link

Kane, Josephine 2007 'A whirl of wonder!' British amusement parks and the architecture of pleasure 1900–1939'. Unpublished PhD thesis, Univ of London

Kane, Josephine 2013 *The Architecture of Pleasure: British Amusement Parks and the Architecture of Pleasure 1900–1939*. Farnham: Ashgate

Kay, A and Kay, I 1998 *Margate: Then & Now*. Stroud: Tempus

Keate, George 1779 *Sketches from Nature: Taken, and Coloured, in a Journey to Margate* **I**, **II**. London: J Dodsley

Kellett, J R 1969 *The Impact of Railways on Victorian Cities*. London: Routledge & Kegan Paul

Kelly 1885 *Kelly's Directory of Lincolnshire*. London: Kelly's Directories Ltd

Kelly 1887 *Kelly's Directory of Sussex*. London: Kelly's Directories Ltd

Kelly 1889 *Kelly's Directory of Devonshire, 1889*. London: Kelly & Co

Kelly 1900–1 *Kelly's Directory of the Isle of Thanet, 1900–1*. London: Kelly's Directories Ltd

Kenyon, J R 1979 'An aspect of the 1559 survey of the Isle of Wight: the state of all the quenes maties fortresses and castelles', *Post-Medieval Archaeology* **XIII**, 61–77

Kidd, William 1831 *The Picturesque Pocket Companion to Margate, Ramsgate and Broadstairs …* London: William Kidd

Kidd, William 1832 *Kidd's Picturesque Steam-Boat Companion to Herne Bay …* London

Kielmansegge, Friedrich von 1902 *Diary of a Journey to England in the Years 1761–1762 … Translated by Countess Kielmansegg. With Illustrations*. London: Longmans & Co

Kime, Winston 2005 *The Lincolnshire Seaside*. Stroud: Sutton

Kisling, Vernon N (ed) 2000 *Zoo and Aquarium History: Ancient Animal Collections to Zoological Gardens*. Boca Raton and London: CRC Press

La Rochefoucauld, François, Duc de 1988 *A Frenchman's Year in Suffolk: French Impressions of Suffolk Life in 1784: Including a Preliminary Week in London, Brief Visits to Cambridge, Colchester, Mistley and Harwich and a Fortnight's Tour of Norfolk …* Woodbridge: Boydell

Lackington, J 1974 *Memoirs of the First Forty-Five Years of James Lackington*. New York & London: Garland Publishing

Lambton, Lucinda 1979 *Temples of Convenience*. New York: St Martin's Press

Lane, Reginald 1995 *Old Sidmouth*. Tiverton: Devon Books

Latham, Frank 1903 *The Construction of Roads, Paths, and Sea Defences*. London: The Sanitary Publishing Company

Leach, N 1999 *For Those in Peril: The Lifeboat Service of the United Kingdom and the Republic of Ireland, Station by Station*. Kettering: Silver Link

Lee, William 1795 *Ancient and Modern History of Lewes and Brighthelmston*. Lewes

Lewis, John 1736 *The History and Antiquities, Ecclesiastical and Civil, of the Isle of Tenet*. London: John Lewis and Joseph Ames

Lewis, S 1840 *A Topographical Dictionary of England … and the Islands of Guernsey, Jersey and Man … with Maps … and a Plan of London, etc*. 4th edn. London

Lightbown, Ted 1994 *Blackpool: A Pictorial History*. Chichester: Phillimore

Limner, Luke (aka John Leighton) 1847 *London Out of Town, or, The Adventures of the Browns at the Sea Side*. London

Longmate, Norman 1993 *Island Fortress: The Defence of Great Britain 1603–1945*. London: Grafton

Love, Christopher 2007 (1), 'An overview of the development of swimming in England, c. 1750–1918', *The International Journal of the History of Sport*, **24** (5), May 2007, 568–85

Love, Christopher 2007 (2), 'Local aquatic empires: The municipal provision of swimming pools in England, 1828–1918', *The International Journal of the History of Sport*, **24** (5), May 2007, 620–9

Lucking, J H 1971 *The Great Western at Weymouth: A Railway and Shipping History*. Newton Abbot: David & Charles

Lyon, J 1813–14 *The History of the Town and Port of Dover, and of Dover Castle; with a Short Account of the Cinque Ports*, **1–2**. Dover and London

Lyons, J A 1763 *A Description of the Isle of Thanet, and Particularly of the Town of Margate …* London: Newbury and W Bristow

Mackie, S J 1883 *A Descriptive and Historical Account of Folkestone and its Neighbourhood*. Folkestone: J English

MAFF 1993 (1) *Coastal Defence and the Environment: A guide to Good Practice*. MAFF

MAFF 1993 (2) *Coastal Defence and the Environment: A Strategic Guide for Managers …* MAFF

MAFF 1995 *Shoreline Management Plans: A Guide for Coastal Defence Authorities*. PB 2197

Mahomed, Sake Deen 1822 *Shampooing; or, Benefits Resulting from the Use of the Indian Medicated Vapour Bath, as Introduced into this Country*. Brighton: EH Creasy

Malster, R and Stibbons, PJR 1979 *The Cromer Lifeboats 1804–1979*. Cromer: Poppyland Publishing

Marsden, Christopher 1947 *The English at the Seaside*. London: Collins

Mason, Tim 2003 *Shifting Sands: Design and the Changing Image of English Seaside Towns*. London: English Heritage; CABE

Matkin, Robert B 1998 'The construction of Ramsgate Harbour' in Adrian Jarvis (ed) *Portland Harbour Engineering*. Aldershot: Ashgate

Maxwell, A 1755 *Portsmouth: A Descriptive Poem in Two Books.* Portsmouth

McInnes, Robin 2014 *British Coastal Art, 1770–1930.* Chale, IOW: Cross Publishing

McIntyre, Colin 1990 *Monuments of War: How to Read a War Memorial.* London: Hale

Middleton, Judy 1988 *Brighton and Hove in Old Photographs.* Gloucester: Alan Sutton

Miller, William 1888 *Our English Shores.* Edinburgh: Oliphant, Anderson and Ferrier

Millward, Jonathan 2007 *An Assessment of the East Coast Martello Towers.* English Heritage: Research Department Report Series, 89–2007

Minnis, John 2014 *England's Motoring Heritage from the Air.* Swindon: English Heritage

Mirams, Michael David 1984 *Old Margate.* Rainham: Meresborough

Miskell, Louise 2011 'A town divided? Sea-bathing, dock-building and oyster-fishing in nineteenth-century Swansea' *in* Peter Borsay and John K Walton (eds), *Resorts and Ports: European Seaside Towns since 1700.* Bristol: Channel View Publications 113–25

Moore, Pam 1988 *The Industrial Heritage of Hampshire and Isle of Wight.* Chichester: Phillimore

Morley, BM 1976 *Henry VIII and the Development of Coastal Defence.* London: HMSO

Morley, Malcolm 1966 *Margate and its Theatres, 1730–1965.* London: Museum Press

Morrice, Richard 2001 'Palestrina in Hastings'. *The Georgian Group Journal*, **XI**, 93–116

Morris, Catherine, Usherwood, Paul and Beach, Jeremy 2000 *Public Sculpture of North-east England.* Liverpool: Liverpool University Press

Morris, Edward and Roberts, Emma 2012 *Public Sculpture of Cheshire and Merseyside (excluding Liverpool).* Liverpool: Liverpool University Press

Morris, Hugh 1935 *Facts About Nudism.* New York: Padell Book Co

Morrison, Kathryn A 2003 *English Shops and Shopping: An Architectural History.* New Haven and London: Yale University Press

Morrison, Kathryn A and Minnis, John 2012 *Carscapes.* New Haven and London: Yale University Press

Moss, William George 1824 *The History and Antiquities of the Town and Port of Hastings, Illustrated by a Series of Engravings, etc.* London: WG Moss

Moule, H J 1883 *Descriptive Catalogue of the Charter, Minute Books, and other Documents, of the Borough of Weymouth and Melcombe Regis A.D. 1252 to 1800: With Extracts and Some Notes.* Weymouth: Sherren & Son

Mulcaster, Richard 1581 *Positions wherein those Primitive Circumstances be Examined, which are Necessarie for the Training up of Children, either for Skill in their Booke, or Health in their Bodie, etc.* London: T Vautrollier

Murphy, Peter 2009 *The English Coast: A History and a Prospect.* London: Continuum

Murphy, Peter 2014 *England's Coastal Heritage: A Review of Progress Since 1997.* Swindon: English Heritage

Musgrave, Clifford 2011 *Life in Brighton.* Stroud: The History Press

Nathaniels, Elizabeth 2012 'James and Decimus Burton's Regency New Town, 1827–37'. *The Georgian Group Journal*, **XX**, 151–70

National Heritage List for England (NHLE), https://historicengland.org.uk/listing/the-list/, accessed 9 May 2018

National Parks Commission, 1967 *The Coasts of Kent and Sussex Report of the Regional Coastal Conference Held in London on May 27th 1966.* London: HMSO

National Record of the Historic Environment (NRHE), Historic England Archive

Neave, David 2000 *Port, Resort and Market Town.* Howden: Hull Academic Press

Neave, David and Neave, Susan 2000 *Bridlington: An Introduction to its History, and Buildings.* Otley: Smith Settle Limited

Neller, R M 2000 *The Growth of Mablethorpe as a Seaside Resort 1800–1939.* Mablethorpe: SBK Books

Nicholls, R J *et al* 2011 'Sea-level rise and its possible impacts given a 'beyond 4°C world' in the twenty-first century', *Philosophical Transactions of the Royal Society of London*, **A 369**, January, 161–81.

Norwood, Clarence Edward 1933 *Nudism in England.* London: Noel Douglas

Osborne, Charlotte 1860 *Charlotte Osborne's Stranger's Guide to Hastings and St. Leonards.* Hastings

Osborne, Mike 2011 *Defending, Hampshire: the Military Landscape from Prehistory to the Present.* Stroud: The History Press

Pallett, N and Young, SW 1989 'Coastal structures'. *Coastal Management.* London: Institute of Civil Engineers 211–26

Palmer, Charles John (ed) 1854 *The History of Great Yarmouth by Henry Manship.* Great Yarmouth: LA Meall

Park, S nd *A Brief History of the Vine Hotel.* Typescript

Parkes, WH 2001 *Guide to Thorpeness (Leiston Station, G.E.R.): The Home of Peter Pan.* Aldeburgh: Meare

Parr, Susie 2011 *The Story of Swimming.* Stockport: Dewi Lewis Media

Parry, Keith 1983 *Resorts of the Lancashire Coast.* Newton Abbot: David and Charles

Pattison, Paul 2009 *Pendennis Castle and St Mawes Castle.* London: English Heritage

Paul, C Norman 1918 *The Influence of Sunlight in the Production of Cancer of the Skin.* London: HK Lewis & Co

Pearson, Lynn F 1991 *The People's Palaces: The Story of the Seaside Pleasure Buildings of 1870–1914.* Buckingham: Barracuda

Pearson, Lynn F 1995 *Lighthouses.* Princes Risborough: Shire Publications

Pearson, Lynn F 2002 *Piers and other Seaside Architecture.* Princes Risborough: Shire

Pearson, Lynn F 2006 *Public Art Since 1950.* Princes Risborough: Shire

Pearson, Trevor 2005 *The Archaeology of Medieval Scarborough.* Scarborough: Scarborough Archaeological and Historical Society

Perkin, H J 1976 'The "social tone" of Victorian seaside resorts in the North-West'. *Northern History* **XI**, 180–94

Pertwee, Bill 1999 *Beside the Seaside.* London: Collins and Brown

Pevsner, Nikolaus 1976 *A History of Building Types.* London: Thames and Hudson

Pevsner, Nikolaus *et al* 1989 *Lincolnshire.* Harmondsworth: Penguin

Pevsner, Nikolaus and Lloyd, David 1967 *Hampshire and the Isle of Wight.* Harmondsworth: Penguin

Physick, Ray 2007 *Played in Liverpool.* Swindon: English Heritage

Pickering, Michael 1986 'White Skin, black masks: "Nigger" minstrelsy in Victorian England' *in* J S Bratton (ed), *Music Hall: Performance and Style.* Milton Keynes: Open University Press

Pickering, Michael 2008 *Blackface Minstrelsy in Britain.* Aldershot: Ashgate

Pigot 1824 *Pigot and Co.'s: London and Provincial New Commercial Directory, For 1823–4* [Devonshire]. London: J Pigot

Pimlott, J A R 1976 *The Englishman's Holiday*. Hassocks: The Harvester Press Limited

Pinney, Avia and Green, Helen 1989 *Bexhill-on-Sea in Old Photographs*. Gloucester: Alan Sutton

Post Office 1874 *Directory of Essex*. London

Preedy, Robert E 1992 *Roller Coasters: Their Amazing History*. Leeds: Robert E Preedy

Preedy, Robert E 1996 *Roller Coasters: Shake, Rattle and Roll!* Leeds: R E Preedy

Pulling, J 1983 *Volk's Railway Brighton 1883–1983 Centenary*. Brighton: Brighton Borough Council

Pycroft, James 1876 *On Roller Skating*. Brighton: HH Stewart

Quinlan, Mark 2005 *British War Memorials*. Hereford: Authors on Line

Rabbitts, Paul A 2011 *Bandstands*. Oxford: Shire Publications Ltd

Rabbitts, Paul A 2014 *Bandstands of Britain*. Stroud: The History Press

Randl, Chad c 2008 *Revolving Architecture: A History of Buildings that Rotate, Swivel, and Pivot*. New York: Princeton Architectural

Ray, M 1989 'Who were the Brunswick Town Commissioners? A study of a Victorian urban ruling elite 1830–1873'. *Sussex Archaeological Collections*, **127**, 211–28

RCHME 1952 *Dorset, Volume I – West*. London: HMSO

RCHME 1970 *An Inventory of Historical Monuments in the County of Dorset*. **2**, south-east, part 2

Reeve, Dominic, Chadwick, Andrew and Fleming, Chris 2012 *Coastal Engineering*. London: Spon Press

Reid, Thomas 1795 *Directions for Warm and Cold Seabathing; with Observations on their Application and Effects in Different Diseases*. London: T Cadel & W Davies; Ramsgate: P Burgess

Relhan, Anthony 1761 *A Short History of Brighthelmston, with Remarks on its Air, and an Analysis of its Waters, Particularly of an Uncommon Mineral One, etc*. London: W Johnston

Rendel, Palmer and Tritton Limited 1996 'History of coastal engineering in Great Britain', *in* Nicholas C Kraus (ed) *History and Heritage of Coastal Engineering*. New York: American Society of Civil Engineers, 214–74

Richardson, Harriet (ed) 1998 *English Hospitals 1660–1948*. London: HMSO

Roberts, George 1823 *The History of Lyme Regis, Dorset, from the Earliest Periods to the Present Day*. Sherborne

Roberts, George 1834 *The History and Antiquities of the Borough of Lyme Regis and Charmouth*. London

Robinson, D 1981 *The Book of the Lincolnshire Seaside: The Story of the Coastline from the Humber to the Wash*. Buckingham: Barracuda

Robinson, F 1848 *A Descriptive History of Southport, … on the Western Coast of Lancashire*. London: Hall & Co

Rolf, Vivien 2011 *Bathing Houses and Plunge Pools*. Oxford: Shire

Rollier, H A 1927 *Heliotherapy*. 2 edn. Translated by G de Swietochowski. London: Humphrey Milford

Rossiter, J R 1954 'The North Sea Storm Surge of 31 January & 1 February 1953'. *Philosophical Transactions A*, **246**, issue: 915

Rothwell, Catherine 2009 *Blackpool*. Stroud: The History Press

Rowntree, Arthur 1931 *The History of Scarborough*. London: JM Dent

Russell, Richard 1752 *A Dissertation on the Use of Sea-Water in the Diseases of the Glands*. London

Rutter, J 1829 *The Westonian Guide: Intended as a Visitor's Companion to that Favourite Watering Place (Weston super Mare), and its Vicinity, etc*. Shaftesbury: J Rutter

Rutter, J c 1840 *A New Guide to Weston-super-Mare*. Weston-super-Mare: J Whereat

Rymer, J 1777 *A Sketch of Great Yarmouth, in the County of Norfolk; with some Reflections on Cold Bathing*. London

Saleeby, C W 1928 *Sunlight and Health*. 4 edn. London: Nisbet & Co Ltd

Salter, Brian 2014 *Model Towns and Villages*. East Grinstead: 'In House' Publications

Samuelson, Dale 2001 *The American Amusement Park*. St Paul, Minnesota: MBI Publishing

Saunders, A D 1966 'Hampshire Coastal Defence Since the Introduction of Artillery with a Description of Fort Wallington', *The Archaeological Journal*, **CXXIII**, 134–237

Saunders, Andrew 1989 *Fortress Britain: Artillery Fortification in the British Isles and Ireland*. Liphook: Beaufort

Saunders, Andrew 1997 *Channel Defences*. London: BT Batsford

Saunders, Andrew 1998 *Fortifications of Portsmouth and the Solent*. London: Andrew Saunders (typescript in Historic England Library)

Schofield, J 1787 *An Historical and Descriptive Guide to Scarborough and its Environs*. York: W Blanchard

Schopenhauer, J 1988 *A Lady Travels: Journeys in England and Scotland. From the Diaries of Johanna Schopenhauer*. London: Routledge

Scott, Richard 1826 *A Topographical and Historical Account of Hayling Island, Hants*. Havant: I Skelton

Scurrell, D 1982 *The Book of Margate*. Buckingham: Barracuda

Seddon, Peter, McIntosh, Anthony and Seddon, Jill 2014 *Public Sculpture of Sussex*. Liverpool: Liverpool University Press

Shaw, Peter 1734 *An Enquiry into the Contents, Virtues and Uses of the Scarborough Spaw-Waters*. London: Peter Shaw

Shaw, Peter 1735 *A Dissertation on the Contents, Virtues and Uses, of Cold and Hot Mineral Springs; Particularly, those of Scarborough: in a Letter to Robert Robinson. Esq., Recorder of that Corporation*. London: Ward and Chandler

Sheppard, Thomas 1986 *The Lost Towns of the Yorkshire Coast*. Howden: Mr Pye Books

Sherry, D 1972 'Bournemouth: A study of a holiday town'. *The Local Historian* **10** (3), 126–34

Simm, Jonathan and Cruickshank, Ian (eds) 1998 *Construction Risk in Coastal Engineering*. London: Thomas Telford

Simmons, Jack 1986 *The Railway in Town and Country, 1830–1914*. Newton Abbot: David & Charles

Simmons, Jack and Biddle, Gordon (eds) 1999 *The Oxford Companion to British Railway History, from 1603 to the 1990s*. Oxford: Oxford University Press

Smith, David J 1992 *Britain's Aviation Memorials and Mementoes*. Sparkford: Patrick Stephens

Smith, Janet 2005 *Liquid Assets: The Lidos and Open Air Swimming Pools of Britain*. Swindon: English Heritage

Smith, JR 1991 *The Origins and Failure of New South-End*. Chelmsford: Essex Record Office

Smith, Victor 2001 *Front-Line Kent*. Maidstone: Kent County Council

Smollett, Tobias 1995 *The Expedition of Humphry Clinker*. Ware: Wordsworth Classics

Speaight, George 1970 *Punch and Judy: A History*. rev edn. London: Studio Vista

Speaight, George 1981 *A History of the Circus*. London: Tantivy

St Clair Strange, F G 1991 *The History of the Royal Sea Bathing Hospital, Margate 1791–1991*. Rainham: Meresborough Books

Staelens, Y 1989 *Weymouth Through Old Photographs*. Exeter: Dorset Books

Steers, J A *et al* 1979 'The storm surge of 11 January 1978 on the east coast of England'. *The Geographical Journal*, **145**, (2): 192–205

Summers, Dorothy 1978 *The East Coast Floods*. Newton Abbot: David & Charles

Sutcliffe, S 1972 *Martello Towers*. Newton Abbot: David & Charles

Sydenham, John 1840 *Visitor's Guide to Bournemouth*. Bournemouth: J Sydenham

Sympson, W 1679 *The History of Scarborough-Spaw*. London

Taylor, A F 1998 *Folkestone*. Stroud: Tempus

Temple Patterson, A 1966 *A History of Southampton 1700–1914*. Southampton: Southampton University Press

Thompson, Dave 2010 *Blackpool*. Stroud: The History Press

Thornton, David William 1987 *Hastings: A Living History*. Hastings: The Hastings Publishing Company

Thorold, P 2003 *The Motoring Age: The Automobile and Britain 1896–1939*. London: Profile

Toll, R C 1974 *Blacking Up: The Minstrel Show in Nineteenth-Century America*. New York: Oxford University Press

Tomlinson, Barbara 2015 *Commemorating the Seafarer: Monuments, Memorials and Memory*. Woodbridge: The Boydell Press

Toulmin, Vanessa 2011 *Blackpool Pleasure Beach*. Blackpool: Boco Publishing

Travis, John F 1993 *The Rise of the Devon Seaside Resorts 1750–1900*. Exeter: University of Exeter Press

Trigg, H R 1892 *A Guide to Hayling Island*. London

Troide, Lars E (ed) 1988 *The Early Journals and Letters of Fanny Burney*. Oxford: Clarendon Press

Turner, T 1979 *The Diary of a Georgian Shopkeeper*. Oxford: Oxford University Press

Turnock, David 1998 *An Historical Geography of Railways in Great Britain and Ireland*. Aldershot: Ashgate

Tyrer, Frank 1968–72 *The Great Diurnal of Nicholas Blundell of Little Crosby, Lancashire*, **I–II** (1968, 1970, 1972). Manchester: Record Society of Lancashire & Cheshire

van Leeuwen, Thomas A P 1998 *The Springboard in the Pond*. Cambridge, Massachusetts: Massachusetts Institute of Technology

Vicary, Thomas 1587 *The Englishemans Treasure: With the True Anatomie of Mans Bodie*. London: Iohn Perin

Wainewright, Jeremiah 1722 *A Mechanical Account of the Non-naturals: Being a Brief Explication of the Changes Made in Human Bodies, by Air, Diet, …* London: John Clarke

Walton, John K 1974 *The Social Development of Blackpool, 1788–1914*. PhD: University of Lancaster

Walton, John K 1983 *The English Seaside Resort: A Social History, 1750–1914*. Leicester: Leicester University Press

Walton, John K 1992 *Fish and Chips and the British Working Class, 1870–1940*. Leicester: Leicester University Press

Walton, John K 1998 *Blackpool*. Edinburgh: Edinburgh University Press; Lancaster: Carnegie Publishing

Walton, John K 2000 *The British Seaside: Holidays and Resorts in the Twentieth Century*. Manchester: Manchester University Press

Walton, John K 2007 *Riding on Rainbows*. St Albans: Skelter Publishing

Wanklyn, C 1927 *Lyme Regis: A Retrospect*. London: Hatchards

Ward Lock and Co. 1925–6 *A Pictorial and Descriptive Guide to Folkestone …* London: Ward Lock and Co

Warren, Geoffrey 1978 *Vanishing Street Furniture*. Newton Abbot: David & Charles

Warren, Martin 2001 *Cromer: The Chronicle of a Watering Place*. Cromer: Poppyland Publishing

White, Andrew 1998 'The Victorian Development of Whitby as a Seaside Resort'. *The Local Historian*. May, **28** (2), 78–93

White, Sally 1991 *Around Worthing in Old Photographs*. Stroud: Alan Sutton

White, W 1836 *White's History Gazetteer and Directory of Norfolk*. Sheffield: W White

Whitehead, C J 1971 *Herne Bay 1830–1870*. BA thesis: University of Kent, Canterbury

Whittaker, Meredith 1984 *The Book of Scarborough Spaw*. Buckingham: Barracuda

Whittick, Arnold 1946 *War Memorials*. London: Country Life

Whyman, John 1980 'A three-week holiday in Ramsgate during July and August 1829' *Archaeologia Cantiana*, **XCVI**, 185–225

Whyman, John 1981 *Aspects of Holidaymaking and Resort Development within the Isles of Thanet, with Particular Reference to Margate, circa 1736 to circa 1840*. New York: Arno Press

Whyman, John 1983 'The Kentish Portion of an Anonymous Tour of 1809' in Alec Detsicas and Nigel Yates (ed) *Studies in Modern Kentish History*. Maidstone: Kent Archaeological Society, 139–86

Whyman, John 1985 *Kentish Sources: 8, The Early Kentish Seaside: 1736–1840: Selected Documents*. Gloucester: Sutton for Kent Archives Office

Whyman, John 1990 *Broadstairs and St Peter's in old photographs*. Stroud: Alan Sutton

Whyman, John 1993 'The Significance of the Hoy to Margate's Early Growth as a Seaside Resort'. *Archaeological Cantiana* **CXI**, 17–41

Williams, Geoffrey 1999 *Stronghold Britain: Four Thousand Years of British Fortifications*. Stroud: Sutton Publishing

Wills, Anthony and Phillips, Tim 2014 *British Seaside Piers*. Swindon: English Heritage

Wills, Henry 1985 *Pillboxes: A Study of UK Defences in 1940*. London: Leo Cooper

Wilson, Geoffrey 1976 *The Old Telegraphs*. Chichester: Phillimore

Wittie, Robert 1660 Scarbrough *Spaw; or, a Description of the Nature and Vertues of the Spaw at Scarbrough in Yorkshire*. York: Richard Lambert

Wittie, Robert 1667 *Scarbrough Spaw; or, a Description of the Nature and Vertues of the Spaw at Scarbrough in Yorkshire*. York: Richard Lambert

Wood, Alan and Lightbown, Ted 2010 *Blackpool Through Time*. Stroud: Amberley Books

Woodman, Richard and Wilson, Jane 2002 *The Lighthouses of Trinity House*. Bradford on Avon: Thomas Reed Publications

Young, Gerard 1983 *A History of Bognor Regis*. Chichester: Phillimore

Zuelow, Eric G E 2016 *A History of Modern Tourism*. London: Palgrave

Index

Page numbers in **bold** refer to figures.